THE PRICE OF PROSPERITY

Civilization and the Natural World

View of the Earth as seen by the Apollo 17 crew. These photographs of the whole Earth seen from space helped to drive home the understanding that the resources of our world are precious and limited. Photograph courtesy of the Johnson Space Center, NASA.

THE PRICE OF PROSPERITY

Civilization and the Natural World

Byron E. Wall

Department of Mathematics and Statistics
York University

Wall & Emerson, Inc.
Toronto, Ontario • Dayton, Ohio

The Author

Byron E. Wall is Associate Lecturer in the Department of Mathematics and Statistics at York University in Toronto, Canada, and teaches in the Division of Natural Science of the Faculty of Pure & Applied Science. He has a Ph.D. in the History and Philosophy of Science and Technology from the University of Toronto.

Orders for this book or requests for permission to make copies of any part of this work should be sent to:

Wall & Emerson, Inc.
Six O'Connor Drive
Toronto, Ontario, Canada M4K 2K1

Telephone: (416) 467-8685
Fax: (416) 352-5368
E-mail: wall@wallbooks.com
Web site: www.wallbooks.com

Layout and design of text and cover: Alexander Wall

National Library of Canada Cataloguing in Publication
Wall, Byron Emerson, 1943-
    The price of prosperity : civilization and the natural world / Byron E. Wall.

Includes bibliographical references and index.
ISBN 0-921332-53-X

    1. Nature--Effect of human beings on--History. 2. Human ecology--History. I. Title.

GF75.W36 2004   304.2'09   C2003-904421-1

Printed in Canada.

TABLE OF CONTENTS

Preface xiii

Part One   1
Four Case Studies

1. Easter Island 5
The Mystery of Easter Island 5
The Statues 7
Trees 8
The Collapse of Civilization on Easter Island 8
The Terrible Lesson of Easter Island 9

2. Venice 11
The Formation of Venice 11
The Canals 12
Prosperity and Pollution 13
A Losing Battle 14
Venice and Easter Island 15

3. Tsavo National Park 17
The Creation of Tsavo National Park 17
Too Many Elephants 18
Let Nature Take Care of Itself 19
Environmentalists versus Environmentalists 19

4. Isle Royale 23
The Arrival of the Moose 24
Isle Royale Becomes a National Park 24
The Arrival of the Wolves 25
The Balance of Nature 25
Ecology 26
Mathematical Models in Ecology 27
Does Nature Behave? 29

Part Two   33
Getting to the Starting Point

5. Planet Earth 37
Continental Drift 37
Pangaea 39
The Greenhouse Effect 42
Natural Resources 42
Attacks from Outer Space 43
A Constantly Changing Scene 47

6. Life 49
Ecosystems 50
Apes 54
Homo Erectus 55
Homo sapiens 56

7. Hunting and Gathering 59
The San of South West Africa 60
Migration 61
Population Pressure 62
Getting to Remote Places 64
Did Primitive Cultures Live in Harmony with the Environment? 65
The End of the Hunter-Gatherer Era 70

Part Three   73
Civilization

8. Agriculture 77
The Fertile Crescent 79
The Far East 82
Mesoamerica 83
Explaining the Transition to Agriculture 83

9. The Dawn of Civilization 87
Sumer 89
Egypt 91
The Indus Valley 93
China 94

The Mayans 95
The Common Pattern 96

10. Sustaining Civilizations 99

Agriculture is Destructive 100
Deforestation is Inevitable 103
Too Much Growth Too Fast 107
  108

11. China versus Europe 109

Balancing Population Growth and Food Supply 110
The Chinese Solution 111
Europe's Muddle 114
Were China and Europe in the Same Situation? 118

12. European Colonization of the World 121

Goodbye Forests 122
A Stumble and a Restart 123
Making New Land At Home 124
Europe's Position at the Beginning of the Renaissance 126
Go West, Righteously 127
Design and Order 129

13. The Third World 135

The Madeiras 136
The Pattern of Colonization 138
Slavery 138
Loss of Self-Sufficiency 140
The Creation of the Third World 142
The Place of the Third World in the World Economy 149

Part Four   151
The Industrial Revolution

14. Using the Power of Nature 155

Wind and Water 156
The Cottage Industries 158
Winds of Change 159
Let Nature Do the Work 160

15. The Steam Engine 163
Atmospheric Pressure 163
Wielding Atmospheric Pressure as a Force 164
Thomas Newcomen's Steam Engine 165
James Watt's Steam Engine 167
Power Like Nothing Ever Seen Before 168
Starting Down the Non-Renewable Path 168

16. Making Goods for Sale 171
Mining 171
Iron 171
Textiles 173
The Changed Nature of Work 176

17. Railroads and Steamships 179
High-Pressure Steam 179
The Railroads 180
The Steamship 183
The Pre-Eminence of Fossil Fuels 185

18. The Economic Viewpoint 187
Measuring Progress 187
Gross National Product 189

Part Five   193

The Comfortable Life

19. The Automobile 197
Road Locomotives 197
The Bicycle 199
The Steamer 202
The Electric Car 204
The Internal Combustion Engine 205
The Model T 205
The Car Culture 206
Too Much of a Good Thing? 207

20. The Airplane 211
Lighter-than-Air Ships 211
Heavier-than-Air Ships 213
The Wright Brothers 218

Another Human Triumph 219
The Airplane as Mass Transportation 220
Fossil Fuel Dependence 221

21. The Chemical Industry 223
Gas Lighting 223
Petroleum 225
Rubber 229
Industrial Chemistry 231
Synthetic Dyes 232
Explosives 233
Plastics 235

22. Electricity and Communications 239
Signaling 240
The Telegraph 241
The Telephone 242
Electric Lighting 244
The World of Wireless 246
Radio 247
Television 247
The Computer 248
The Electrical Age 252

23. Energy 255
Thermodynamics 255
Energy Production and Consumption 256
Coal 259
Petroleum 259
Electricity 260
Human Ingenuity 264

Part Six   267

Population

24. Population Growth 271
Exponential Functions 272
Human Beings and the Balance of Nature 274
Differences in Growth Patterns Around the World 275
All Populations Tend to Expand 276
What Happens to a Population without Predators 277

25. Famines, Diseases, and Death 283
  Average Temperature of the Earth 283
  Famines 285
  Diseases 290
  Plague 294

26. Extinction 299
  Affecting Animal Habitats 300
  Extinctions Due to Hunters and Gatherers 300
  Agriculture Destroys Habitats 301
  Ancient and Medieval Extinctions 301
  Animals as Pests 302
  The Grass is Greener Elsewhere 302
  The Passenger Pigeon 304
  Local Extinctions 306

27. World Models 309
  The Essay on Population 309
  Feedback 314
  The Limits to Growth 316
  Mankind at the Turning Point 321
  The Fate of World Models 323

28. The Green Revolution and Appropriate Technology 325
  The Green Revolution 325
  Appropriate Technology 328
  Inappropriate Technology 330
  Success Stories of Appropriate Technology 331
  The Aims of Appropriate Technology 334
  How All This Happened 335

Part Seven   339

Fouling Our Nest

29. Silent Spring 343
  DDT 344
  Pesticide Runoffs 347
  Killing the Soil 348
  Poisons For Sale in the Supermarkets 349
  The Chemical Industry Fights Back 350
  The Start of the Environment Movement 351

30. Abusing the Water 355
Beavers 356
The Forests 358
Farming on the Prairies 359
Dams 362
Effluent 365
Oil Spills 369
Sewage 373
Swimming is Dangerous to Your Health 374

31. Abusing the Earth 377
Not in My Backyard 378
Hazardous Waste 381
Nuclear Waste Disposal 384

32. Abusing the Air 389
London Fog 389
Making Electricity 391
Operating Cars and Trucks 392
Pollution from Industry 393
Chlorofluorocarbons 394
The Ozone Layer 396
Steps Toward Repairing the Damage 399

Part Eight   401
Current Issues

33. Hormone Disruption 407
Troubling Evidence 408
Sexuality 408
DES 410
Plastics 414
Surrounded by Hormone Disruptors 416

34. Biotechnology 425
The Microscope 425
The Gene 427
Recombinant DNA Technology 429
Transgenics 430
Frankenstein Foods 434
Stem Cells 437
Biotechnology and Ethics 438

35. Perils, Present and Future. 441
    Technological Mishaps 442
    Resource Depletion 450

36. The Environmental Movement 463
    Environmentalism before Silent Spring 463
    The Silent Spring Wake-up Call 465
    The Movement Mushrooms 467
    Environmental Activism 468
    The Mainstream of Environmentalism 474
    Global Warming—Apocalypse Soon 476
    The Gamut of Environmentalism 483

PREFACE

The thesis of this book is that human civilization, no matter how it is defined, has arisen at a cost to the environment we live in, and there is really no way to prevent that. The aspects of civilized life that are seen as the highest achievements of humanity are all injurious to the natural environment. It has always been so, and always will be.

On the other hand, a great many stupid or thoughtless actions have been taken by people in the past and continue to be taken at present that senselessly destroy or maim the precious world that we depend on for everything. These are the places where change for the better can have the best chance of succeeding. Wanton waste of limited resources for no particular benefit, pollution that is preventable without shutting down an industry we have come to depend upon, failure to take steps to preserve the diversity of living species, and lack of prudence in making innovations that have unknown effects on the environment—all these are places where we can certainly do better.

Yet, too often, those with the best of intentions set out to save the environment by proposing actions, or even taking unilateral steps, to stop the destruction without examining the consequences of their proposals, which may lead to even worse consequences. Or, as frequently enough happens, proposals are made to institute changes that the entire history of the human race indicates just will not work.

We treasure our achievements; we value our comfortable way of life. They are important to us; they are what make us human. But there is no escaping it; they come at a cost to the natural environment. If we are not careful, our environmental abuse can spin out of control and make our planet uninhabitable, or at least, much less welcoming than it is now. Our best hope is to control civilization's environmental costs sensibly so that we and our descendants can continue to enjoy our wonderful life.

The place to begin is to understand how all human endeavors have affected the environment and what was gained and lost in the process. To that end, this book looks at humans versus their environment from the earliest beginnings to contemporary times. It also raises a few questions about our common assumptions about Mother Nature, for example, whether there is an inherent long-term stability that will serve us well if only we let it, or whether we risk our extinction by doing so.

Acknowledgements

I am grateful to York University for providing me with the means to take the time to write this book, and I am indebted to my students for being a sounding board for its ideas. The Division of Natural Science, the Department of Mathematics and Statistics, and the Faculty of Pure and Applied Science have all been supportive and encouraging.

As with my previous book, *Glimpses of Reality*, this has been a most rewarding family effort. Both books have been written over summers spent mostly at a cottage on a lake. My job has been to write the text; my wife, Martha, would then take my drafts, proofread them, rewrite some of my awkward sentences, and tell me when I had failed to get the point across. My son, Alexander, would then take the much improved, edited version, add illustrations and put it all into an attractive book layout. They both provided sounding boards for ideas and sources of things I hadn't thought of, or hadn't thought through very well. Of course, neither of them can be blamed for anything egregious that remained.

Byron Wall
Toronto
August 14, 2003

THE PRICE OF PROSPERITY

Civilization and the Natural World

PART ONE

Four Case Studies

The hardest thing about studying any highly interactive, complex system is knowing where to begin. It would be difficult to isolate any aspect of the environment of the world and state its characteristics without having to take into account the other elements of the environment that interact with it. Each of those other elements interact with still other elements and with each other, making it very hard to come up with clear statements of what causes what, or, more importantly, what the effects would be of any changes one might propose.

As a first step toward finding some principles that one could reason with, four case studies are presented here as the opening foray into an examination of the environment of the Earth.[1] Each of these case studies presents somewhat different problems and each highlights different effects of human actions. They are all intended to serve both as interesting cases on their own and as microcosms of problems common to all of the Earth. Two of these concern the isolated environments of islands; the other two concern environments that have been separated from their neighbors by deliberate human action.

---

1. Most of the details of these four cases are drawn from Daniel B. Botkin, *Discordant Harmonies: A New Ecology for the Twenty-First Century* (New York: Oxford University Press, 1990) and Clive Ponting, *A Green History of the World: The Environment and the Collapse of Great Civilizations* (New York: Penguin, 1993).

The first is the extraordinary situation of Easter Island, where a primitive human culture in the Pacific Ocean was accidentally found by European explorers in the 18th century. What made Easter Island so remarkable was the existence of remnants of a far more complex and developed society that no longer existed there.

The second case is the beautiful cultural center that is the city of Venice, founded just after the fall of the Roman Empire as a refuge, growing to become one of the main cultural and commercial centers of Europe in the Renaissance, and now hanging on to as much of its history as it can while the environment crumbles around it.

The third case is a deliberate attempt by people to create an environmentally protected area, Tsavo National Park in Kenya, where large wild animals are given space to live in a natural habitat. But as the history of the park shows, creating a natural environment takes more than just drawing a boundary around an area and declaring it off limits to developers and poachers.

The fourth case is Isle Royale in Lake Superior, which was also made into a national park. Being an island it had a natural setting already, so making it a protected area had a better chance of preserving whatever balance of nature might exist without human interference. It became the object of study of environmentalists and ecologists who wanted to study the mechanisms of the balance of nature.

For Further Reading

Botkin, Daniel B. *Discordant Harmonies: A New Ecology for the Twenty-First Century.* New York: Oxford University Press, 1990.

Gause, Georgii Frantsevich. *The Struggle for Existence.* Baltimore: Williams and Wilkins, 1934.

Heyerdahl, Thor. *Aku-Aku: The Secret of Easter Island.* New York: Rand-McNally, 1958.

Jennings, J. D. *The Prehistory of Polynesia.* Cambridge: Harvard University Press, 1979.

Norwich, John Julian. *A History of Venice.* New York: Knopf, 1982.

Ponting, Clive. *A Green History of the World: The Environment and the Collapse of Great Civilizations.* New York: Penguin, 1993.

Sheldrick, Daphne, *The Tsavo Story.* London: Collins and Harvill, 1973.

The Moai of Easter Island. Note how the statues consist of two parts, the body and the topknot. The two pieces of each statue were carved out of different kinds of stone in different quarries, before being fitted together and errected on platforms. Altogether, the statues required the transportation of tonnes of stone over hundreds of kilometers.

Chapter 1

Easter Island

Since the day that it was discovered by accident on Easter Sunday, 1722, and given the name of Easter Island by the Dutch Admiral Roggeveen, this remote Pacific island has been the subject of intense interest and scrutiny by anthropologists. The basic situation can be expressed as follows: Easter Island is so remote that it is difficult to imagine how any humans got there. However, the artifacts that still had remained on the island made it clear that there once existed a complex culture with strange religious practices and even stranger huge statues, seemingly impossible to construct. The whole situation seemed even more improbable because the people then on the island lived in a most primitive state and had no idea how any of the statues were built, how they were moved into place, or what they meant.

The island lies out in the Pacific Ocean about 3000 kilometers west of South America. It is about 400 square kilometers in area. The nearest inhabitable island is Pitcairn Island, about 2000 kilometers away. When Roggeveen discovered the island, he found a population of about 3000 living in squalor in reed huts or caves and resorting to cannibalism to get enough to eat. There were other occasional visits over the next 150 years. The Spanish attempted to annex the island in 1770, but without actually colonizing it. In 1877, Peru enslaved and removed most of the population. Finally, Chile turned the island into a sheep ranch.

The Mystery of Easter Island

The most extraordinary feature of Easter island is the array of over 600 massive stone statues, averaging about 6 meters high. It did not seem possible to the European visitors to the island that the barbaric creatures now living on there could possibly have constructed the statues or moved them into place. Many theories have been put forward to explain the mystery, most notably that of the Norwegian Thor Heyerdahl, who proposed that the island was settled by a chance voyage from South America, where

Statues on Easter Island. These giant statues baffled the European explorers who could not understand how they were carved and moved into place by the people there.

sculpture and stone work were well known. Also proposed, of course, have been theories that the statues were built by aliens from outer space and other equally bizarre ideas.

More recent research, making use of a wide variety of information, including cultural habits, diet, and physical characteristics, have put together the following as the most likely sequence of events:

The migration to Easter Island came from southeast Asia, rather than South America. It was part of the very last phase of human migration to all parts of the world, completed around 500 C.E., about the time of the fall of the Roman Empire. In other words, the very first settlement of what would have been a stone-age civilization at the very beginnings of agriculture occurred at the time when the great ancient civilizations of the rest of the world were coming to an end. China had already endured the fall of the Han dynasty and had not yet regrouped. The Gupta empire in India was almost at its

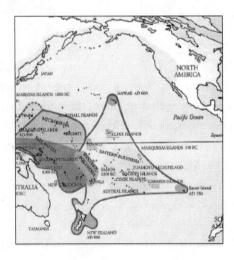

Human migration in the Pacific Ocean. This map shows the spread of people from southeast Asia out into Polynesia and eventually to Easter Island. Easter Island is thought to be one of the last places in the world to be settled by humans, as wind patterns in the Pacific would have made it more difficult for Polynesian settlers to sail east. This is why it is thought that Easter Island was settled later than other isolated islands, such as New Zealand and Hawai.

end. The Mayan civilization in Teotihuacan (Mexico) was in full swing, but even it was nearing its end.

The settlers who ended up on Easter Island were descendants of the original Polynesians, a small group that came from southeast Asia to Tonga and Samoa about 1000 B.C.E. and then moved further east, finally setting sail in what may have been double canoes with a platform between them on which all their belongings, including animals and food, were riding. No more than one or two dozen people may have reached Easter Island. This same ethnic group colonized Hawaii and New Zealand.

Easter Island is actually the remnant of three extinct volcanoes in the middle of the south Pacific. It has all of the problems of land that is essentially a lava field: there is a soil layer, built up over the several centuries that the volcanoes have been extinct, but the drainage is very poor. The only fresh water available is from the lakes that have formed in the volcanic craters. Because of its location, both the ambient temperature and the humidity are high. Since the islands had been thrown up by volcanic eruption out in the middle of the ocean, there were very few indigenous plants and animals. And, although the settlers had brought Polynesian crops with them, most of these were unsuited to the environment.

Life was grim, but marginally viable. The primary diet was sweet potatoes, which would grow where other crops would not, and chicken, eventually supplemented by fishing. One advantage of this extremely monotonous diet was that it took little time, leaving them with a great deal of leisure.

The Statues

As the population grew, it spread around the island in small, extended family groups. Most of the leisure time seems to have been spent in religious activities, which they devoted to the construction of monuments. Large stone platforms were first erected, and then huge statues were placed on them. The statues were made of two kinds of stone, which came from two separate quarries. The body of the statue came from one quarry, and the "topknot" on the head from another quarry. The seemingly impossible feat, as far as the European explorers were concerned, was how the statues were transported the long distances across the island.

Trees

One of the reasons that the European explorers could not fathom how the statues could have been erected and transported is because the landscape in Easter Island was so barren and without any materials that could have been used to make any kind of vehicle or other aid to transporting the stones. However, recent studies of surviving pollen show that at some time in the past a fruit palm tree was native to the island and flourished there for thousands of years. These trees could have been used for many purposes, including making canoes, building shelters, for firewood, and, notably, they could have been used as rollers for dragging the statues across the land to their destination platforms.

Estimates are that the population in Easter Island grew from the few dozen that landed in 500 to about seven thousand in the 16th century. The larger the population became, the more trees were required—for all the purposes they served. Also, since more farmland would have been needed to plant crops, more trees would have been felled just to clear land. The rate at which trees were felled eventually exceeded the replacement rate. Finally, all the trees were gone and the island became completely deforested. It is now completely treeless.

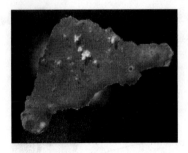

An aerial view of Easter Island reveals how barren the surface of the island is today. Once, much of the land was covered by palm and mulberry trees, but as the human population expanded and the need for lumber increased, all the trees were chopped down.

The Collapse of Civilization on Easter Island

Around 1600, the society on Easter Island went into a sudden and irrevocable decline. The population fell quickly from 7000 to the 3000 found by Admiral Roggeveen in 1722. The island had become incapable of supporting its population.

The absence of trees made life untenable. The construction and erection of statues stopped suddenly. Many statues in various states of completion were abandoned in the quarries, with no way to transport them. Without trees, houses could not be built. People resorted to living in caves and in flimsy reed huts. Canoes could no longer be built, which made it impossible to organize a long voyage to attempt to get off the island. Even fishing was more difficult without trees, because the fishing nets had been made of a fibre from the mulberry tree, which had also been found on the island. Trees also held the loose soil in place. Without them, the arable soil quickly blew away or washed away in rains. Therefore the crops that had sustained the inhabitants failed.

When crops failed, the only remaining sustenance was the chickens. These then became the main source of wealth and had to be guarded against theft. Without wood for a building material, stone was used more. Remains exist of stone chicken coops that would have been built during this period. The different families living in different parts of the island began to fight over the few remaining resources. Warfare became a permanent feature of life. The spoils of battle included captured people, who were enslaved and then in some cases, eaten.

The Terrible Lesson of Easter Island

One thing must have been clear to the residents of Easter Island: they were isolated from the rest of the world. After many generations, they might not even have known that there was any other inhabited part of the world. It would have been clear that their existence depended upon the limited resources available on the island. Despite this, they let their environment become untenable. They cut down the trees, right down to the last one, though they depended on them for so much. It is a classic case of failure of forethought, though the situation was simple enough that it is hard to see how they could have missed the implications of their actions.

A canal in Venice. The Church of Santa Maria della Salute is in the background.

Chapter 2

Venice

As a mark of the glory of human civilization one of the most picturesque and culturally interesting places to visit is the city of Venice. Venice is not an island, totally separated from mainland Europe, but was created out of several small islands in a lagoon and swampland on the edge of northern Italy and is in effect cut off from the rest of the country. That isolation was deliberate.

The Formation of Venice

When the Roman Empire fell around 500 C.E., barbarian tribes from the north – the Goths, Visigoths, Vandals, Jutes, the Lombards, and others – swept over the previous empire and caused considerable grief to the settled populations. Some of the residents around the northwest coast of the Adriatic Sea fled to the swamps and lagoons and offshore islands when a raid was feared. Eventually, they built permanent homes in the area and settled there for good. Since the area was marshy to begin with and even the islands were in danger of submersion by floods, the settlers built their homes on pilings to raise them above the water level. Despite these precautions, the mud shifted so much that all buildings were subject to collapse until the marshland could be stabilized. To do this,

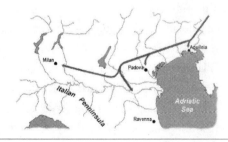 

In 452 C.E., the inhabitants of northern Italy fled before the armies of Attila the Hun (the route of his invasion is shown above), many taking refuge on the islands in the Venetian Lagoon (shown on the right) that eventually became Venice.

the residents felled millions of trees in the area and drove their trunks and larger limbs into the ground, causing a certain amount of deforestation just from that.

The Church of Santa Maria della Salute in Venice.

One of the most extraordinary feats of engineering is the baroque church of Santa Maria della Salute, built upon the shifting and sinking mud by first driving 1,106,657 trunks of alder, oak, and larch trees into the ground to make a secure and immobile foundation. It worked and has lasted hundreds of years, because once the tree trunks were submerged in the mud, they were no longer exposed to air and therefore could not rot.

As the threats from the invaders passed, Venice continued to prosper. Its location, close to major land routes in Europe and convenient by sea from the East via the Mediterranean, made it an ideal trading center. At the same time, its physical separation from the rest of Italy allowed it to fend off being incorporated into the Teutonic Empires and to remain a separate city-state. Under the despotic rule of the doges beginning in 727—elected by a small ruling elite of nobles and merchants—Venice grew into a great commercial, and even later into an artistic, center.

The Canals

The order of the construction of Venice is just the opposite from that of most cities. Venice did not begin on a land site and expand outward, constructing buildings. Instead, the "land" was created by stabilizing the mud and building upon it. The space left between one building and another, or between one area and another, was typically still underwater. Therefore, the natural form of transportation from place to place was by boat. As the city was built up, more land was filled in, but the "roadways" were paths left in the water where buildings had not been erected, which are given the name canals. Unlike canals elsewhere, these were already there, not dug out of the ground. These canals are still the main routes around Venice. Automobile, bus, and railway traffic stops at the edge of the city. There are more than 200 canals in Venice, forming the major "streets" of the city. Over these canals are more than 400 bridges carrying primarily pedestrian traffic. The canals and bridges themselves are among the most popular tourist attractions.

The Bridge of Sighs. This famous bridge (in the center of the photo) spans the canal between the Doge's palace and the prision. Its name comes from the sighs of prisioners being taken into the dungeons; for many, the windows of this bridge provided their last look at freedom.

Prosperity and Pollution

By the time of the Renaissance in Europe, Venice was already a great trading center. It soon became a great cultural center, a natural place from which to rediscover the lost cultural past of Greece and Rome and to integrate it into the structure of Medieval Europe. Great works of art and architecture were built on the stabilized mud platform that is Venice, and more and more people began to live there. The increase in population and in commerce and art brought tremendous prosperity. As Venice became more successful, it became increasingly vulnerable to the perils common to having too many people in too small a place. In the 14th century, Europe was devastated by the Black Death, an epidemic of bubonic plague. The plague, being a communicable disease, hit hardest in the most crowded places, especially in port cities. Between 1347-1349, 60% of the population of Venice perished. And several other epidemics occurred over a 300 year period that were ruinous for the city. Unable to defend itself after the fall of Constantinople in 1453, Venice was subject to frequent raids of its treasures.

Everything about Venice is the result of human alteration of the local environment. The city itself is built in what would otherwise be uninhabitable swampland. The method of stabilizing the ground to make it possible to build upon it involved destroying a huge amount of the natural forest in the area. That forest is what held much of the land in place around Venice. Without it, the watercourses leading into the Venice lagoon where the city is built have undergone considerable alteration.

Venice has naturally attracted industry that locates nearby. In particular, nearby chemical plants dump their effluent into the rivers that make their way into Venetian waters. Greenpeace has organized a "poison tour" for tourists to Venice showing them the effects of industrial pollution to both water and air from nearby industry. Large industries tend to use a lot of water; the chemical and other industries that located on the mainland near Venice have used up so much of the groundwater that the city itself is now sinking. The annual floodwaters that come from winter storms now regularly flood the ground floors of buildings all across Venice.

The canals that form the transportation network throughout the city also serve as the sewage system. Into them is dumped not only all the waste matter from the city's population but, because Venice is located on a lagoon between the mainland and the sea, its canal system also receives the runoff from fertilizers, insecticides, and herbicides used in farmlands nearby. For centuries, the sewage "system" in Venice has relied on the tidewaters taking the waste matter of the city out to sea and flushing the canals and the lagoon itself. However, this action has ceased to be sufficient owing both to the increasing pollution being thrust into the waters and rising sea levels. As a result, the sewage often returns making an intolerable cesspool out of the whole city.

The floodgates at the outer edge of the Venice Lagoon.

In 1998, Venice installed a series of floodgates at the edge of the lagoon that would allow the tidewaters to flow outward, but prevent their return. In 2003, the city began work on a new series of floodgates that can be raised in emergencies to block particularly high tides from entering the lagoon. These measures should provide an element of flood control, but their effectiveness remains to be seen.

A Losing Battle

Venice is a city with a glorious past and remains of immense historical and artistic interest. But its present is a battle to preserve what was, and apparently it is a losing battle. The city is slowly crumbling from air and water pollution, and is slowing sinking into the sea. It was built with technology that was ingenious for its time, but that technology did not anticipate the alteration of the environment that has come with population growth, the rise of modern industry, nor the fatal effect of the alteration of the natural environment that was the original basis on which the city was built. This is a city struggling to preserve its past; it really does not have a future.

Venice and Easter Island

It is interesting to juxtapose the environmental history of Venice next to that of Easter Island, discussed in Chapter 1. The differences are vast, but there are some noteworthy similarities. First, and most surprising, they were originally settled at about the same time. The Easter Island residents arrived by some kind of boat from Polynesia, probably traveling there just because they needed more space to live in and landing at Easter Island by chance, though we will never know the exact reasons. The settlers in Venice were escaping persecution by invading tribes after the fall of the Roman Empire. Second, the area occupied by Venice is roughly the same size as Easter Island. Third, in both cases, the heyday of their respective civilizations was during the period of the European Renaissance. Of course, Venice was a defining feature of that Renaissance, while Easter Island had no contact with it. Nevertheless, the same amount of time elapsed from founding to apex. Now both places survive largely on tourists coming to see the relics of the past. The society of Easter Island collapsed and the people reverted to a primitive state, even to cannibalism. That certainly did not happen in Venice, where the decline was due to the centers of commercial activity moving elsewhere. But now Venice's problems are largely environmental, stemming to a large extent from their considerable overuse of the forests around them. Likewise, Easter Island's demise had much to do with wanton deforestation.

Is there something about human civilizations in finite spaces? Unlike other species, human beings have the skills to alter their environment in dramatic ways. This does not particularly show up when the number of people in an area is small, but as populations grow, if they cannot or will not move elsewhere, they will reach a point where their interventions in the environment make irreversible changes. Easter Island is a stark example where people were essentially trapped on an island with very limited resources. Venice was settled by choice and the people who remained there did so by choice. This made perfect sense when it was the cultural and commercial center of Europe in the Renaissance, and it continues to make sense today because of its great natural beauty, refined culture, and incredible works of art. But in both cases the natural environment has been seriously compromised. Easter Island ceased to be viable hundreds of years ago. Venice is in great danger today. Given human nature and available scientific knowledge and technological know-how, is it reasonable to think it could be otherwise?

Savanah Elephants, like the one pictured here, deforested much of Tsavo National Park in the 1960s. While the results were serious, the elephants were acting normally. To maintain their giant bodies, elephants must eat voraciously, destroying tonnes of plants and ripping up forests. Indeed, were it not for the elephants, much of the savanah in Africa would be covered with trees.

Chapter 3

Tsavo National Park

Another way to create an artificial environment is to take a natural environment and put a fence around it, in effect, declaring that what is within the fence will not be disturbed, will be free of human intervention, and will therefore remain natural. Natural preserves are designated areas within countries that have been set aside and their use restricted in order to attempt to maintain some inherent balance that would otherwise be disrupted. The national park movement of the 20th century was behind the establishment of natural preserves of all sorts all across the world.

An interesting example is one of the largest: Tsavo National Park in Kenya. Tsavo Park is huge. It is divided into two parts, East and West. The East Park alone covers about 13 000 square kilometers. It was meant to preserve a significant piece of Africa for the wildlife that was native to the area and to let it flourish, naturally. But this raises an interesting question, that is, what does "natural" mean in an area cordoned off by human beings, who have only too human ideas about what nature should be?

The Creation of Tsavo National Park

Tsavo Park was created in 1948. Its first warden, David Sheldrick, realized that the viability of the park would depend on its ability to attract tourists to see large animals in the wild. Unfortunately, by the time that the area was designated as a park, much of that wild life had been shot by European settlers in the region. What remained, mostly black rhinoceros and elephants, were in danger of being wiped out by poachers. Sheldrick therefore made it his first priority to carve roads into the park to attract tourists and

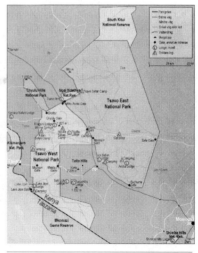

Tsavo National Park in Kenya.

simultaneously to launch a vigilant defence against the poachers. Fifteen hundred kilometers of roads were built into the park for the use of tourists. A river was dammed and wells were dug to provide year-round water for the wildlife. As a result, the elephants, which had been close to extinction in the region, began to build up quickly.

A herd of elephants gathers at a watering hole in Tsavo National Park.

Too Many Elephants

Very quickly, the park went from having hardly any elephants to far too many elephants. What had been human intervention to restore a natural balance had instead produced conditions way beyond what the area could support. The elephants knocked down trees and uprooted shrubs. The area had been so thick in vegetation that tourists would only be able to see an elephant if it crossed the road in front of them. Soon, according to Sheldrick's wife, it began to resemble a "lunar landscape."

Sheldrick became alarmed and in a report wrote:

> ...during the past few years, the destruction of vegetation by elephant has reached serious proportions. If present trends continue, it is doubtful if the Park can continue to support the existing population much longer. What effect this will have on other species remains to be seen, but I think it is important that we should seek scientific advice regarding this problem as soon as possible.[1]

It was actually not entirely clear whether it was the provision of a constant water supply and the vigilance against poachers that had caused the build-up in the elephant population. During the same period a series of droughts may have prevented normal plant growth. In any case, the situation became more desperate, and by 1966 there was broad agreement that the salvation of the park would require reducing the elephant population. But then the weather changed once again bringing rains that helped the vegetation recover. Alas, that only enabled the elephant population to grow even more. The Ford Foundation sponsored a scientific study of the park which came to the

---

1. From Daphne Sheldrick, *The Tsavo Story* (London: Collins and Harvill, 1973), p. 113; quoted in Daniel B. Botkin, *Discordant Harmonies: A New Ecology for the Twenty-First Century* (New York: Oxford University Press, 1990), p. 17.

conclusion that it would be necessary to shoot about 3000 elephants to bring their population in line with the food supply.

Let Nature Take Care of Itself

Sheldrick at first agreed, but then reversed himself on the grounds that the solution was unnatural. Tsavo Park was supposed to be a place where nature achieves its balance without human interference. Sheldrick held out for leaving the elephants alone and limiting human intervention to such actions as keeping out poachers and controlling fires. Sheldrick believed that once the natural ecology reached a "climax" stage, it would maintain itself indefinitely. Therefore, his role should be directed only toward helping that climax stage come about.

Sheldrick took the view that the droughts that had worried them so much were actually nature's way of culling both the elephant population and the vegetation—an example of natural selection at work. This view was soon put to the test. In 1969 and 1970 there was a very severe drought that caused the deaths of about 6000 elephants by starvation as well as destroying the vegetation.

Environmentalists versus Environmentalists

The controversy at Tsavo Park was not one of environmentalists against the advocates of economic progress at all cost, but was firmly within the environmental camp: what was the best way to support and preserve the environment? Was it better to just stand clear and let nature function without human meddling or was it necessary to help keep nature from running off the rails and destroying itself?

The first is the view that nature is basically everything other than humans and it would be just fine if people could be kept away from it. This was ultimately Sheldrick's position. His wife summed up this view in her later book:

> With amazing arrogance we presume omniscience and an understanding of the complexities of Nature, and with amazing impertinence we firmly believe that we can better it. … We have forgotten that we, ourselves, are just a part of nature, an animal which seems to have taken the wrong turning, bent on total destruction.[1]

---

1. *Ibid*, p. 190 in Sheldrick and p. 18 in Botkin.

The second viewpoint is that the stability of nature is not a given. Indeed the history of the Earth is one of many natural disasters that completely destroy habitats over a large area. Nature may be natural, but it isn't always benign. Moreover, if humans have intervened to the extent that they forestall the actions of the poachers, they have already introduced artifice into the forces at play. If the goal is to make some designated area behave as though it is in a state of nature, while all along interfering with natural processes, then maybe it is necessary to make a few more adjustments to natural processes by culling excess populations or altering the environmental conditions.

Or, there is yet another way to look at it. A national park can be large; certainly, Tsavo Park is a very large area, but then elephants are very large animals and their natural habitat may require an even larger area. From an evolutionary viewpoint, elephants evolved thousands of years ago when they could roam all of Africa if necessary to find a suitable home. In the last few hundred years, Africa has become divided into countries with boundaries and borders, and industrialization has introduced barriers such as railroad lines that make migration across the continent much more difficult. Before all this human intervention, elephants facing a drought in one area would have migrated elsewhere. Without those alternatives, a "natural" solution is not possible.

Chapter 4

Isle Royale

Tsavo National Park, discussed in Chapter 3, was carved out of the vast continent of Africa. Its defining perimeter was a matter of human decision. Because of that, it could be argued that it had a necessarily artificial environment, at least to the extent that it was human interference that prevented movement in and out of the area. A more natural setting for a national park refuge is one where the boundaries exist already, for example, an island. Islands are always interesting for ecological studies.

Isle Royale in Lake Superior makes a good case, especially in relation to the others we have considered in the previous chapters. It is an island of about 500 square kilometers in area, located 25 kilometers off the west coast of Lake Superior near the Minnesota-Ontario border. That makes it roughly the size of Easter Island and Venice, but much smaller than Tsavo Park. Its name came from French explorers who found it about 200 years ago. Though these explorers spent a bit of time there and named the island, it was not settled permanently by people, though a few trappers visited the island from time to time.

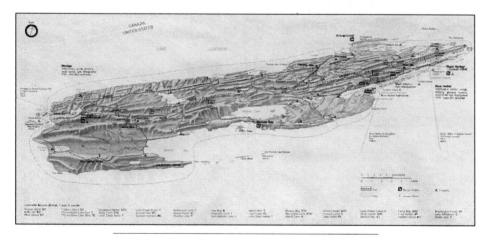

A map of Isle Royale National Park in Lake Superior.

The Arrival of the Moose

Around the year 1900, in the middle of a severe winter when Lake Superior had frozen over near the shore, a small number of moose migrated out over the ice and crossed to the island. The area that the moose had left had been settled by people, but the island presented an undisturbed wilderness. But this was not by any means the "natural" state in which moose normally live because the island was without the chief predator of the moose, the North American timber wolf. The moose quickly began to change the environmental balance on the island. Within 10 years the water lilies, a favourite food of the moose, began to disappear. The dominant ground cover over the island was the yew shrub, which the moose also ate to the point that it nearly became extinct on the island.

Here was a classic case of what happens when the balance of the food chain gets disturbed. Since the moose had the run of the island without having to fear the timber wolf, they began to increase in numbers at an alarming rate. But they depended on the local vegetation for sustenance and were consuming it at a rate considerably higher than it could regenerate. By the early 1930s there were so many moose and so little remaining vegetation that Adolf Murie, a well-known naturalist, predicted that a major die-off would soon occur. In the mid-1930s, the die-off did occur, and Murie estimated that the moose population dropped from 3000 to less than 500.

Soon after, another major environmental event occurred: a forest fire that destroyed more than a third of the island. This burned much of the older forest, but in so doing, it cleared the land for new growth, in particular, the fast-growing white birch, which the moose ate as soon as it began to sprout. Once again, the moose population began to grow at an alarming rate.

Isle Royale Becomes a National Park

In the mid-1940s, Isle Royale was made a national park. One of the first problems that park wardens had to cope with was the fast-growing moose population. It was the same problem that faced Tsavo National Park with their elephant population. Allowing the moose to continue undisturbed would predictably lead to the destruction of the vegetation, followed by mass starvation of the moose.

That was the course of action (or inaction) that represented the natural approach. But here the natural environment had the unnatural feature that there were no predators of the moose on the island. Moreover, the park personnel faced the uncomfortable prospect that if they allowed a massive die-off of moose on the island, it would be ruinous to the tourism that supported the island, since the moose were among its main attractions.

After much soul-searching and trying to find the right approach for a natural refuge, the National Park Service decided that to correct the imbalance, they should import some timber wolves to control the moose population "naturally." In 1946, the park service obtained six timber wolves from various zoos and released them on the island. Unfortunately, the wolves they imported were not typical wild animals, having become accustomed to being fed by zookeepers. Therefore, instead of hunting the moose, they hung about the park headquarters waiting to be fed.

The Arrival of the Wolves

But fortuitously, the Park Service got their wish just a few years later when, in another severe winter, the lake froze over between the shore and Isle Royale and this time, a pack of wolves crossed the ice and took up domicile on the island. These were truly wild wolves and did hunt the moose. The original pack of about 12 wolves in the late 1940s grew to somewhat more than 20 by the 1960s. In consequence, the moose population stabilized at roughly 1000 adult animals. Likewise, the wolf population stabilized. Thus, it appeared that the balance of nature had been achieved and had even occurred through entirely natural causes.

The isolated nature of the island environment, with its relatively simple interactions of organisms, attracted the attention of ecologists eager to study the phenomenon of a balance of nature. In particular, Daniel Botkin of the University of California, Santa Barbara, undertook a study of the environment of Isle Royale over several years beginning in the late 1960s. Botkin's book, *Discordant Harmonies*, is the source for most of the information about Isle Royale in this chapter. This is essentially a précis of his analysis.

Botkin began with the goal of establishing what factors kept the moose population in a steady state. Was it simply the presence of the right number of wolves and a symbiotic relationship between them and the moose, or were there other factors, for example, involving the diet of the moose.

The Balance of Nature

Botkin and his crew fully expected that the populations of moose and wolves would rise and fall within a certain range, but if there was a balance, then their numbers would oscillate around some average figures for each species. Soon after their study began, the moose population began to rise, which naturally provided more prey and easier hunting for the wolves. As expected, the wolf population then began to rise, in fact, doubling in a few years. That made life more dangerous for the moose, and indeed their population began to fall. But while these interactions produced the alternating rise and fall that would be expected between predator and prey, the actual numbers of each species did not conform to any of the predictive models that were in use at the time.

Botkin's team found that other factors also had to be taken into consideration. The sodium content in the moose diet was a critical factor. The amount of sodium available in the vegetation eaten by the moose appeared to establish an upper limit to the population. Botkin studied other variables and tried to find quantitative models that could lead to a more sophisticated predictive model of ecological interactions. Looking back on his work on Isle Royale from the perspective of the late 1980s, Botkin concluded that his fieldwork at Isle Royale was driven by an unwarranted conviction that nature had an inevitable stability and that that stability could be modeled, at least approximately, with mechanistic formulas into a science of nature.

Ecology

Ecology is the study of the relationship between living things and their environment. It is the fundamental science of environmental studies. Ecologists such as Botkin strive to formulate exact principles that have a sound basis in observations. Isle Royale provided an attractive research situation because of its well-defined and relatively simple environment.

Compare this to Tsavo Park (see Chapter 3) where the vast size of the park alone made it difficult to pinpoint cause and effect. David Sheldrick, the warden of Tsavo Park, was prepared to make major decisions on how to deal with crises in the park based upon fixed ideas about the balance of nature. Ecology seeks to replace such articles of faith with precise rules, capable of being expressed in mathematical formulae that can account for environmental interactions with some accuracy—especially so that ecology can be used to good effect in policy decisions.

The word "ecology" was coined in 1866 by the German biologist Ernst Haeckel, an enthusiastic supporter of Charles Darwin. Haeckel was part of the very strong movement in the late 19th century to find an underlying mechanistic explanation for all phenomena, both living and non-living. Ecology developed essentially from three elements: (1) the observational reports of naturalists, which tended to be interpreted in terms of Darwin's concept of natural selection and the survival of the fittest. (2) Pre-ordained beliefs about the existence of order in nature, including the assumption that nature has a natural stability. (3) The mechanist model; that is, the conviction that a scientific explanation of any phenomena in the world had to be expressed in terms that were ultimately nothing other than blind matter in motion. Isaac Newton's *Mathematical Principles of Natural Philosophy* had succeeded in transforming the physical sciences into a mechanist system in the 17th and 18th centuries. In the 19th century, many biologists were striving to carry that mode of explanation into biology by showing that precise laws, describable by mathematics, could be formulated there as well.

Mathematical Models in Ecology

Though the goal of ecology was to achieve a solid scientific foundation, the assumptions built into it from its inception led ecologists to develop mathematical models that gave the appearance of precision, but unfortunately worked better on paper than in reality. These models have been used to calculate quantitative indicators that became tools of public policy. It is worth distinguishing which of these precisely stated measures are based on observational evidence and which flow directly from the assumptions made about the way nature "must" work to fit preconceived ideas.

Carrying Capacity

One of the most used concepts in environmental studies of living populations is that of *carrying capacity*. The term denotes a stable population level for a species in a particular environment. The idea is that a population of any species will increase in size over time provided there are sufficient resources to sustain it (ignoring for the moment the effect of predators). If the sustaining resources are finite, then there will be a point at which the population has just enough food to feed itself and not enough to support greater numbers. This maximum number is the carrying capacity.

The notion was proposed first in 1849. It can be mathematically modeled as an S-shaped logistic curve, and the mathematical model has been verified under controlled conditions of laboratories for small organisms such as bacteria or insects. In the pure case, it is necessary that the environmental conditions and the food supply be constant.

As can be seen from the graph, the growth rate is fastest when the population is at one-half the carrying capacity. This concept has been frequently used to determine the maximum allowable harvest of a population that could be sustained indefinitely. Fishing

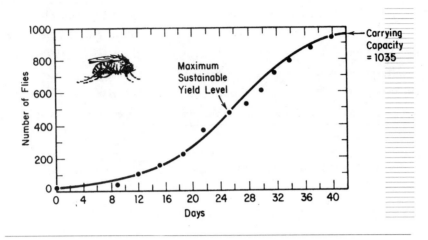

The growth of a population of fruit flies in a laboratory container. From Botkin, *Discordant Harmonies*, p. 21.

for a particular species, for example, would be allowed in an area only to the point where the remaining population was one-half of the carrying capacity.

In practice, while the theory is fine, determining what the carrying capacity is for a species in a particular area may be very difficult. Even if a reasonable number can be calculated, the growth rate may not follow the S-shaped logistic curve closely, because of the presence of predators or changing environmental conditions. Before an allowable harvest target can be set, the present population size must be determined, which may not be feasible. And then, even if all these problems are solved, the whole basis of setting fishing or hunting limits is undone if those doing the fishing or hunting do not all cooperate completely.

Predator-Prey Interactions

As the situation on Isle Royale showed clearly, there is an interaction between predator and prey that tends to produce stability in the two species. On Isle Royale, more wolves led to fewer moose which led to fewer wolves which led to more moose, and on and on. This interactive relationship was studied by several ecologists in the early 20th century. The resulting mathematical formulation is named after two of them, Alfred Lotka and Vito Volterra. The Lotka-Volterra equations are based on an exact theoretical model of predator-prey interactions and therefore describe an ideal condition. In the standard model, the interactions produce a steady oscillation of populations as shown in

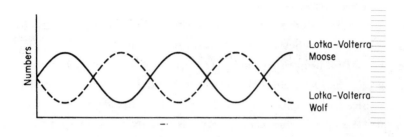

Predator-Prey Relations According to the Lotka-Volterra Equations. From Botkin, *Discordant Harmonies, p. 38.*

the graph below depicting the theoretical interactions between the moose and the timber wolves on Isle Royale.

Does Nature Behave?

The mathematical formulations are ideal abstractions that help to understand ecological processes, but does it work out this way in nature? Have the scientists captured all of the relevant factors in their model and ignored only those which are of minor importance? The only way to know is to test the theoretical predictions with experiments. In 1934, the Russian scientist G. F. Gause decided to test the logistic theory leading to the carrying capacity conception and the Lotka-Volterra equations of predator-prey interactions. He chose an easily controlled experiment that would pit two species of micro-organisms against each other in laboratory flasks.

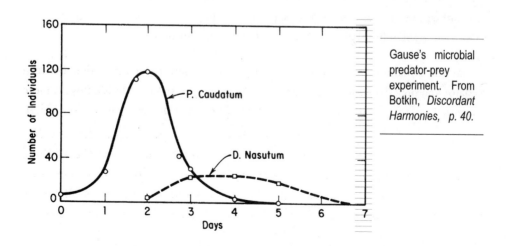

Gause's microbial predator-prey experiment. From Botkin, *Discordant Harmonies, p. 40.*

First he grew *Paramecium caudatum* alone with a constant supply of food and in a uniform environment. Sure enough, he demonstrated that they grew according to the S-shaped logistic curve. When he then went on to test the Lotka-Volterra predator-prey interactions, he got a surprising result. He began by placing five *Paramecia* in each of several test tubes and let them multiply, which they did very rapidly. Two days later, he introduced three *Didinium nasutum*, another microbe, into each test tube. The *Didinium nasutum* preyed on the *Paramecium caudatum*. As expected, no sooner did the *D. nasutum* appear then the *P. caudatum* population began to decline. However, in another two days, the *D. nasutum* population had increased so much and the *P. caudatum* population had declined so much that suddenly all the *P. caudatum* had been eaten and all of the *D. nasutum* starved.

The upshot of Gause's experimental work was that the logistic curve leading to the carrying capacity notion was confirmed, but only under very strict laboratory conditions. The Lotka-Volterra equations describing predator-prey interactions was shown to go wildly out of control even under controlled conditions, not, as had been thought, to achieve a long-term stable relationship. Nevertheless, both concepts have continued to be used extensively in environmental planning.

The wide usage of such mathematical formulae in ecological decision making reflects both a faith in the power of exact science and a faith in the long-term stability of nature. No doubt there are interactions of the sort that these models describe, but their applicability may be much more restricted than their usage would indicate.

The actual history of life on Earth suggests that catastrophe is as much a feature as stability, though over a short term, the interplay that makes an environment stable for a time can look like a permanent feature. The best way to get a sense of how the environment behaves as a whole is to start at the beginning and look at the whole sweep of life, and human history in particular. To that we now turn.

Ice covered mountains tower above this small glacial lake in the Rocky Mountains. Ancient motions of the earth's crust created this mountain range, eventually giving rise to the ecosystem pictured here.

PART TWO

Getting to the Starting Point

The most extraordinary thing about the world environment is that it exists at all. Life on Earth exists because of a whole set of circumstances, each of which is improbable on its own. The Earth must be a proper distance from the Sun so that it is neither scorched nor is it too cold. The Earth must rotate on its axis to provide the necessary changes of day and night that produce variations in the temperature that cause air pressures to change and weather systems to move around. The combination of the tilt of the Earth's axis and the period of revolution around the Sun give us seasonal changes which are necessary for the growth of many different life forms. The Earth must have an atmosphere of the correct thickness and composition to provide the gases necessary for both plant and animal life, to shield us from harmful rays of the sun, and to trap just enough heat of the sun to provide the greenhouse climate that we need for life. The continents must be arranged in such a fashion so as to channel the currents of the seas to circulate away from and back to the equator, bathing the northern land masses that border the Atlantic Ocean with water warm enough to make these lands habitable.

There is a very small range that all of the variables must manage to stay within for terrestrial life to be possible. All of those might be different. All of them *are* different on other planets and elsewhere in the universe. It may be that life, as we know it, exists only on planet Earth. Certainly nothing has been detected elsewhere that resembles anything like our version of life. Moreover, all of these variables have been different on Earth itself. Our planet has not always been as hospitable as it is at present, and there is no reason to think that it will remain so indefinitely. Conditions on Earth suitable for human life have only been in place for a relatively short time compared to the entire existence of the Earth. Our own species has been around for only the tiniest part of that time. And, to continue that line of thought, civilized life has occupied only about the last one percent of human history.

But we are here, in this wonderful and amazing environment that, in cosmic terms, is held together by the flimsiest of ties balanced on the point of a needle for the fraction of a moment that we call all of history.

This book is a brief look at that history from the point of view of those amazing conditions that support life and how our actions affect the balance that holds them together. Part Two is an overview of the formation of the environment, of life in it, and in particular, of human life up to the beginnings of what we call civilization.

For Further Reading

Albritton, Claude C., Jr. *Catastrophic Episodes in Earth History.* London and New York: Chapman and Hall, 1989.

Courtillot, Vincent. *Evolutionary Catastrophes: The Science of Mass Extinction.* Translated by Joe McLinton. Cambridge: Cambridge University Press, 1999.

Dawkins, Richard. *The Blind Watchmaker.* London: Penguin, 1988.

Diamond, Jared. *Guns, Germs, and Steel: The Fate of Human Societies.* New York & London: W. W. Norton & Co., 1999.

Gribbin, John. *The Birth of Time: How We Measured the Age of the Universe.* London: Weidenfeld & Nicolson, 1999.

Gribbin, John and Mary. *Children of the Ice: Climate and Human Origins.* Oxford: Basil Blackwell, 1990.

Gillispie, *Genesis and Geology: A Study in the Relations of Scientific Thought, Natural Theology, and Social Opinion in Great Britain, 1790-1850*. Cambridge, MA: Harvard University Press, 1951, reprinted New York: Harper & Row, 1959.

Grobstein, Clifford. *The Strategy of Life*. San Francisco and London: W. H. Freeman & Co., 1964.

Hallam, Anthony. *Great Geological Controversies*, 2nd ed. Oxford: Oxford University Press, 1989.

Lee, R. B., and I. DeVore. *Man, the Hunter*. Chicago: Aldine Press, 1968.

Lewin, Roger. *Bones of Contention*. New York: Simon & Schuster, 1989.

Lovelock, James. *The Ages of Gaia: A Biography of Our Living Earth*. New York: Norton, 1988.

Millet, Katherine, and Thomson Safaris, "The Hadza Tribe of Tanzania," http://goafrica.about.com/library/weekly/uc150700a.htm

Ponting, Clive. *A Green History of the World: The Environment and the Collapse of Great Civilizations*. New York: Penguin, 1993.

Scotese, Christopher. *Paleomap Project*. www.scotese.com (An interactive website showng the movements of the tectonic plates.)

Stringer, Christopher and Clive Gamble. *In Search of the Neanderthals*. New York: Thames and Hudson, 1993.

Stringer, Christopher and Robin McKie, *African Exodus*. London: Jonathan Cape, 1996.

Walker, Alan, and Pat Shipman. *The Wisdom of Bones: In Search of Human Origins*. London: Weidenfeld and Nicolson, 1996.

Wenke, Robert J. *Patterns in Prehistory: Humankind's First Three Million Years*, 3rd ed. New York & Oxford: Oxford University Press, 1990.

The Earth and its Moon. From pictures taken by the Galileo spacecraft in 1992. Separate images of the Earth and Moon were combined by NASA to generate this view. For more information and other photographs of the Earth, see Great Images in the NASA online library at http://grin.hq.nasa.gov.

Chapter 5

Planet Earth

It is generally accepted by scientists today that the Earth was formed about four and one-half billion years ago out of debris in the solar system pulled together by their mutual gravitational attraction. Over the next several billion years, the surface of the Earth cooled, forming a number of crusts floating on a center of molten rock, or magma. These crusts formed very large landmasses that protruded out of the surrounding surface of water. Today, continents are what we call the part of these landmasses that emerge out of the water, and the water surface is divided up into oceans, defined by the perimeters of the continents.

However, the continents were not always arranged as they are now. The crusts that formed the continents hardened into large plates that slid across the magma, and are still sliding a small amount every year.

Continental Drift

The idea that there has been some major change in the arrangement of the continents over time goes back to the era of world exploration by Europeans in the 15th to the 17th centuries. More particularly, it had its origin, so far as is known, when the first reasonably accurate maps of the continents revealed the remarkable match between the east coast of South America and the west coast of Africa. Were they somehow broken apart from each other?

Alfred Wegener.

The modern idea of drifting continents was first developed by Alfred Wegener around 1912. Wegener, a German lecturer in astronomy and meteorology, had noticed both the remarkable fit of South America and Africa and also correlated similarities in fossil distribution and rock formations in the continents that he believed were once joined. For example, the mountains that run from east to west across South Africa continue in the same pattern in a mountain range near Buenos Aires in Argentina. And the rock strata in South

In 1858, geographer Antonio Snider-Pellegrini made these two maps showing his version of how the American and African continents may once have fit together, then later separated. Left: The formerly joined continents before their separation. Right: The continents after separation.

Africa called the Karoo system are identical with the Santa Catarina system in Brazil. But Wegener's explanation lacked a mechanism for why the continents should have drifted apart and was not widely accepted.[1]

More convincing geological evidence came in the middle of the 20th century with the discovery that the magnetic alignment of the Earth changes over time, and that when magma cools and solidifies it preserves the magnetic orientation of the Earth as it was at the time. A study of rock formations across the world showed that the continents had moved since those rocks were formed. Moreover, in the middle of the Atlantic ocean, there is a ridge which divides the floor of the ocean and which also divides the ocean into two pieces with symmetric alternating patterns of magnetic orientation, which would be consistent with a slow spreading of the sea as the two parts of the ocean move further apart. In other words, it is not so much the continents that drift as it is large rigid plates forming the surface of the Earth that are sliding apart. The continents are those parts of the plates that are above sea level. The plates move apart even now at a rate between 50 mm to 90 mm per year, about the rate at which human fingernails grow.

This slow migration of plates that has continued through the entire existence of the Earth is the greatest factor in the structure and diversity of the environment of this

---

1.   This is despite a considerable amount of evidence that was later produced about the similarities between South America and Africa by the South African geologist Alexander Du Toit, who spent months in South America studying the terrain and finding plant and animal fossils very similar to those in South Africa. The fossils even appeared in the strata of the rock bed in the same complex pattern. It was difficult to account for this in any other way than to consider that South America and Africa were one land mass eons ago. Unfortunately, Du Toit published his findings and his theoretical explanation using a very flamboyant style of exposition that was not in keeping with the academic norms of the day. He was dismissed as a crank. See http://www.hartrao.ac.za/geodesy/tectonics.html.

planet. It is the starting point for understanding how the Earth came to have the physical features that it has, the natural resources that are spread unevenly in different parts of the world, and the seasonal weather patterns that make life more habitable in some parts of the Earth than in others.

Pangaea

The science behind the theory of continental drift, called plate tectonics, is as yet young enough that some of its basic explanatory models are still hotly disputed. The fact of continental drift is well established now by many diverse measurements, both indirect and direct, such as measurements made from satellites orbiting the earth using laser beams. A generally accepted scenario of how the continents have moved over the last half a billion years goes like this:

Several continental plates may have been spread out over a large region of the Earth near the equator, leaving the poles entirely covered by ocean and without ice. The entire environment was warmer, but did not support life on land, as we know it. The continents were barren deserts and bare rock.

By 250 million years ago, whatever plates had been on the Earth before then had pushed together to form one single large mass that scientists call *Pangaea,* meaning "all lands." Pangaea covered the South Pole and extended not quite up to the North Pole. Then, roughly

PERMIAN
225 million years ago

TRIASSIC
200 million years ago

JURASSIC
135 million years ago

in the period 225 to 200 million years ago, Pangaea began to break apart, first into two pieces, usually called *Laurasia* and *Gondwanaland.* Laurasia was in the northern hemisphere and Gondwanaland in the southern, extending down and covering the South Pole. Over the next 150 million years or so, Laurasia broke apart into two major pieces, North America and Europe/Asia, and Gondwanaland broke apart to form South

CRETACEOUS
65 million years ago

PRESENT DAY

America, Africa, Australia, Antarctica, and the sub-continent of India.

It is this breaking apart that has allowed life on Earth to flourish. The Atlantic Ocean, bounded by the Americas on one side and Europe and Africa on the other side, makes a conduit for warm tropical waters, heated year-round by the Sun, to wash up to northern latitudes and keep them ice-free in the winter. The British Isles, for example, is bathed by the Gulf Stream, making it a relatively benign climate in the winter, despite its high latitude. However, the position of Antarctica directly over the South Pole prevents a similar effect in the southern hemisphere. The landmass of Antarctica allows snow and ice to form in permanent layers.

At the edges of the tectonic plates, dramatic and sometimes violent activity takes place. When two plates collide, they jam the surfaces together and form mountain ranges. Or, the plates may slide into each other with one plate being submerged below the other. When that happens, the lower plate begins to melt back into magma, and on the upper plate an arc of volcanoes is formed where the plates have collided. The magma from below rises through the surface of the upper plate and causes a volcanic eruption. Or, the plates may slide against each other and temporarily lock together. The boundary of these plates is called a fault line, and is generally an area with much earthquake activity whenever the plates slip against each other. The San Andreas Fault on the west coast of North America is a well-known example.

Human civilizations that were in the wrong place at the wrong time have been crushed and destroyed forever by earthquakes and volcanic eruptions. Human engineering is no match for the forces of nature when the tectonic plates smash or grind against each other.

People persist in living in geologically dangerous places, even building elaborate cities on the slopes of active volcanoes or in the valleys into which they would erupt or right over fault lines where earthquakes are frequent. Partly this is because these are often dramatically beautiful places with pleasant climates. Some of the more notable natural disasters that caused death and destruction through human history are: the eruption of the volcano Thera, which may have been responsible for the collapse of the great Minoan civilization on Crete around 1200 B.C.E.; the eruption of Mount Vesuvius in Italy in 79 C.E. that destroyed the Roman cities of Herculaneum and Pompeii; in 1556, a series of earthquakes in Shensi province in China that killed an estimated 800 000 people. And of course, many more examples exist throughout history and across the globe.

Many of the wealthiest and most technically advanced communities in North America are positioned close to the San Andreas Fault, where earthquakes are a common occurrence. The famous earthquake in San Francisco in 1906 virtually destroyed the city, but this has not stopped its residents from rebuilding and making it a grander city than ever before, despite several earthquakes since 1906. Silicon Valley, home of much of the most sophisticated computer technology, is located not far from the fault line itself. Even more astounding, the Stanford University Linear Accelerator, used for delicate sub-atomic particle research, actually straddles the San Andreas Fault!

Santa Rosa City Hall after the 1906 San Francisco earthquake.

The Greenhouse Effect

Though we tend to think of the destructive effects of volcanoes and earthquakes, we would not be here at all without them. The atmosphere surrounding the Earth, which we rely upon to sustain life, was created by volcanic activity over millions of years. The atmosphere is itself a protective layer that holds in the warmth of sunlight that would otherwise quickly dissipate into space. It is, in particular, the carbon dioxide in the atmosphere that traps the Earth's heat and keeps the ambient temperature of the air in a range where life is possible. Carbon dioxide is produced in great quantity by volcanic activity. In addition to trapping heat, carbon dioxide is absorbed by plants, enabling them to grow. In general, the plant world strips the carbon out of carbon dioxide and uses it as a structural material while emitting the oxygen back into the atmosphere, where humans and animals breathe it. At the present time, the amount of carbon dioxide in the atmosphere is an environmental concern, since too much CO_2 can trap too much heat and cause undesirable changes that threaten life as we know it. But without the right amount of carbon dioxide we would not exist at all.

Thus, the formation on the surface of the Earth of large solid plates of rock that slide around on the bed of magma at the core of the Earth has been absolutely essential for the miracle of life on Earth. The tectonic plates have formed the continents and done so in a way that fosters a moderate and habitable climate over much of the Earth. The seemingly catastrophic crashes of plates into each other and the sliding of one plate over another have made the volcanoes that produced the atmosphere that we could not live without. Were the arrangement of the continental plates just slightly different or the amount and composition of the gases that make the atmosphere not quite the same as it is due to small changes in the amount of volcanic activity over the past millions of years, life would not be possible. The margin of error is very, very slight. This is one reason that environmental concerns are so very important to our existence.

Natural Resources

Present-day civilization relies very heavily on natural resources that can be used to produce large amounts of power. In particular, coal, petroleum, and natural gas are all indispensable requisites of modern life. These are collectively called fossil fuels because they are the fossilized remains of the decomposition of the tropical forests that existed in the equatorial regions of the continental plates 250 to 300 million years ago. These regions, of course, are not necessarily in tropical regions today. In fact most of the great deposits of fossil fuels are not found in lands that now lie in the tropics. The bulk of them are in what had been the supercontinent of Laurasia, which lay across the equator, while most of Gondwanaland was over the Antarctic and too cold for tropical forest growth. Likewise, the deposits of minerals and metals of all sorts are the result of the churning of the plates that brought magma up to the surface in different places at different times, much of which is found in the former Gondwanaland. Similarly, the size and placement of fresh water resources is due to the cracks and crevasses, and the buckling and stretching of the surfaces of the plates, along with the great scarring effects of retreating icebergs, all occurring millions of years ago, long before human beings appeared on Earth.

Attacks from Outer Space

In the late 18th century and the first half or so of the 19th century, geology as a subject was just getting underway. Rival geological theories had the considerable task of finding an explanation for the many different geological formations: mountains, plains, seas, rivers, gorges, islands, and every other arrangement of land and water on earth. Two basic schools of thought emerged: *uniformitarianism* and *catastrophism.* The uniformitarians held that every different geological shape and situation on Earth was a product of natural processes that we are familiar with today, accumulated over vast amounts of time. These would include the effects of wind and water for slowly producing erosion and wearing away of, for example, a riverbed. Earthquakes and volcanoes are included as sporadic but familiar phenomena. The main point of uniformitarianism is that everything we see in the terrain of the Earth is explainable by applying to the distant past the same principles that govern environmental effects in the present. The uniformitarians were particularly anxious to bring geology into the realm of scientific

Mount Etna. This photograph shows plumes of ash rising from the volcano during its eruption in November 2002. Uniformitarians believed that the occasional eruptions of volcanos like Etna could account for apparently unnatural phenomena in a natural way.

explanation and reason. The leading uniformitarian in the mid-19th century was Charles Lyell, who made an extensive study of the active volcano Mount Etna in Sicily. This prompted him to write his definitive three-volume *Principles of Geology*, which was then carried by Charles Darwin on his five-year voyage of the HMS Beagle and in effect was his geological education. Though Lyell was not himself an evolutionist, his geological theory dovetailed perfectly with Darwin's theory of evolution, and both became the standard of accepted science of the Earth and its inhabitants by the end of the century.

On the other hand, the catastrophists were impressed with the extraordinary aspects of the Earth's surface that seemed to them to be totally beyond what could be explained by the familiar processes. How could huge mountain peaks be created by ordinary processes, even including volcanic activity? And the real inexplicable anomaly: what about those fossilized bones of huge monsters that were turning up in great numbers whenever swamps were drained and canals dug? In particular, those monsters that were called *dinosaurs*. Catastrophists believed that there must have been some extraordinary catastrophic events in the past, totally unlike present-day processes, which caused such major changes on the Earth.

Georges Cuvier. An engraving after an 1831 painting by Pickersgill.

The leading catastrophist was Georges Cuvier, whose greatest contribution was the reconstructing of the skeletons of long-extinct creatures from clues given by a few remaining fossilized bones. Cuvier's work revealed that there had been a vast array of strange creatures that all became extinct long ago. That, he believed, indicated that there had been some extraordinary catastrophes unlike anything known in his day that had caused these mass extinctions. Whether Cuvier intended it or not, catastrophism became aligned with explanations that appealed to supernatural causes, perhaps divine retribution, to account for the inexplicable. This was not in keeping with the scientific spirit of the time which sought only natural explanations. By the end of the 19th century, catastrophism was viewed as a mistake.

But was it? The uniformitarian model attempted to explain all the features of the Earth as the result of processes familiar *on Earth*. The catastrophists viewed these as insufficient to explain many of the most extraordinary aspects. But a catastrophe caused by an unfamiliar process is not necessarily supernatural. It may simply have come from outside the realm of the planet Earth, for example from some large cosmic object that struck the Earth. Many such possible objects exist. Between the orbits of Mars and Jupiter is an entire belt of orbiting rocks, the asteroids, some of them many kilometers across, that from time to time are drawn out of their orbits and spiral into the Sun. They can easily crash into anything in their way, such as the Earth. From farther out, comets are also falling in toward the Sun, some in regular orbits, some in single visits through the solar system, but all capable of hitting a planet that happens to be in their way.

And, plenty of evidence exists that such objects have crashed into the Earth in times past. In Canada alone, where there is much exposed Precambrian rock and little covering vegetation, are some large visible craters, several kilometers across, entirely consistent with what would be produced by an impact with an asteroid or part of a comet. In 1907, a huge explosion occurred in Siberia, doing extensive damage over a large area. Later investigations concluded that the cause was a blast equivalent to several million tonnes of TNT. This was likely caused by a relatively small fragment of ice from the core of a comet entering the atmosphere.[1] It does not take a large object from space to cause a great deal of damage, given the speeds at which they travel.

The Moon is pockmarked all over with craters from such impacts, many of them large enough to be seen clearly from Earth. These are easily preserved in the desolate, airless lunar environment. Space probes have shown similar cratering on Mars. There is every reason to suppose that such extra-terrestrial catastrophes have been a regular feature of the history of the Earth. In fact, one recent theory is that the Moon itself was the result of a giant asteroid or meteor striking the Earth with such force that it broke into two pieces, one of which became the Moon.[2]

Flora and Fauna

The catastrophes that Georges Cuvier imagined would have caused dramatic changes in the weather, such as floods, or sudden eruptions of the land, such as earthquakes. Meteors crashing into the Earth could easily have caused such effects. The magnitude of the asteroid impact necessary to produce some of the craters found must have been large enough to send up a huge cloud of dust into sufficient to make a marked change in the

---

1.   John & Mary Gribbin, *Children of the Ice: Climate and Human Origins* (Oxford: Basil Blackwell Ltd., 1990), p. 18.

2.   This very interesting theory and the evidence that supports it is summarized nicely in the feature story by Karen Wright, "Where Did the Moon Come From?" in *Discover* (February 2003), 61-67.

weather for several years. This is the phenomenon often referred to as "nuclear winter," being one of the predicted effects of a nuclear holocaust. Mass extinctions of both plants and animals could easily occur from such catastrophes.

One mass extinction that is of particular interest is that of the dinosaurs, generally considered to have occurred about 65 million years ago. This is a controversial issue, but a strong case can be made that about that time the Earth was hit by a large comet or meteor of sufficient magnitude to bring on a "nuclear winter" that perhaps the dinosaurs could not adapt to.[1] Likewise, the entire development of life on Earth may well have been shaped inalterably by such catastrophes.

Regular long-term cycles also have had enormous impact on life on Earth. The Earth's orbit itself is not fixed, but varies from nearly circular to more elliptical over a 90-100 thousand year cycle. Now it is becoming more circular. The effect of that is to reduce the difference between when the sun's heat is at a maximum and at a minimum. At this point in the cycle, the Earth is actually closer to the sun in what is winter in the northern hemisphere. The effect of that is to make the winters slightly warmer than they might be otherwise and the summers cooler, with the opposite effect in the southern hemisphere. As the Earth's orbit becomes rounder, the winters will become colder and the summers warmer in the northern hemisphere, and conversely, the difference between the two seasons will be less in the southern hemisphere. This is a regular pattern that has been repeated over and over again during the history of the Earth. It would require only a two percent drop in the heat of the sun during the summer in the northern hemisphere to start the process of glaciation, leading to another ice age. This is due to the closeness of the northern continents to the pole. If ice and snow on land does not melt during the summer, the snow will simply build up year after year and turn to ice, forming glaciers. In the southern hemisphere, Antarctica lies directly over the southern pole and has year-round ice, but its land mass is insufficient to lead to the build up of large glaciers.

Other factors work in the opposite direction or are coordinated on a different cycle. We are concerned now about the possibility of Global Warming because of excess carbon

---

1.   In the 1970s, researchers at the University of California found layers of rock at several places in the world that were about 65 million years old and which contained the element iridium, a heavy metal that is rare on the surface of the Earth (though common in the core), but which is a major component of some meteors. The proposed explanation is that a meteor struck the Earth, perhaps in Mexico, producing a large crater which exists today, and sending up a huge mushroom cloud of dust particles containing iridium into the upper atmosphere, from which it spread around the entire globe. Gribbin, *Children of the Ice*, p. 19.

dioxide in the environment. This is due to human activity in the last 250 years, since the Industrial Revolution, but the Earth has had similar changes in the greenhouse effect before from changes in the output of the sun or from volcanic activity.

Continental drift has also had a dramatic effect on the distribution and evolution of plant and animal life. In periods when the tectonic plates were in contact with each other, plant and animal species evolved and spread across large areas. Later, when the continents drifted apart, species evolved in different directions due to natural selection in their separated environments. Before Gondwanaland broke apart about 130 million years ago, marsupial mammals had evolved and spread across the entire land mass, including what is now Africa, South America, and Australia. When Africa joined up with Eurasia, placental mammals invaded it and drove the marsupials to extinction. However, South America and Australia were then separated. Marsupials continued to populate those continents. In South America, they lived until about 30 million years ago when South America joined with North America, when they were driven to extinction. Now they are native only to the Australian continent. This is but one example of great families of animals (and plants) that thrived for long periods in parts of the world until they came in contact with life forms from elsewhere and then were crowded out. In this case, the contact was caused by the drifting of the continents. In more recent times, it has often been caused by the deliberate or inadvertent introduction of a species into foreign lands by human travelers.

A Constantly Changing Scene

The environment provided by our planet has changed in many ways again and again over a vast period of time. What is remarkable is that life evolved and has been able to sustain itself in this wildly changing environment. Though some form of life has been in existence for about two-thirds of the time that there has been a planet Earth, those forms of life have changed radically and are always at the mercy of the far greater and totally uncontrollable forces of nature itself. At times, the climate changed to become too cold or too hot or too dry or too wet for the species that existed at that time and mass extinctions took place. Sometimes the changes were predictable, and sometimes not. Very small changes in volcanic activity, the tilt and orbit of the Earth, the energy emitted from the Sun, and countless other factors have changed the environment in ways that we certainly would find quite inhospitable. But this is what we have to work with and to live in.

A baby chimpanzee eats a piece of fruit. Chimpanzees are humans' nearest living relatives, their bodies being remarkable similar to ours.

Chapter 6

Life

The origin of life on Earth is an extraordinary and fascinating subject for scientific inquiry, philosophical analysis, and pure speculation. It is, for the most part, beyond the scope of this book. However, some features of that origin seem clear enough. There is a general hierarchy of life forms from simple to complex, and a dependence of the complex upon the simple that suggests that the simpler must have come into existence earlier. Moreover, if the mechanism of the creation of life is an evolutionary process along Darwinian lines, i.e. random processes with natural selection, then it must have taken a very long time for the first steps to have taken place when there was little possible survival value, and progressively shorter time intervals for successive major evolutionary steps. First there is that enormous step from relatively simple inorganic compounds that were already established in the cosmos at the time of the formation of the Earth to the vastly more complicated structure of organic molecules. Only then can those molecules begin to combine in ways that we could deem to be life, and only long after that in anything resembling any sort of life that we are familiar with.

Since all life forms are built up of proteins, and since proteins are essentially chains of amino acids, the amino acids must have evolved from inorganic matter before any more advanced life could have appeared. Over the past several decades several scientists have endeavored to reproduce in the laboratory what they believe must have been the chemical environment of the Earth before the appearance of life, and then subject that environment to intense magnetic and electrical forces and temperature extremes to simulate what may have been natural conditions on Earth. From these experiments, some amino acids have been produced, from strictly inorganic compounds. This is very suggestive. Likewise, similar experiments have yielded some of the base components of DNA and RNA, necessary for the organization and reproduction of life.

Plants must have appeared before animals because animals require oxygen for respiration and metabolic activity. Volcanoes were producing vast quantities of CO_2, but, scientists tell us, there was no free oxygen gas until plants appeared. Plants take in carbon dioxide during photosynthesis and strip off the carbon, emitting the oxygen gas O_2, so necessary for life in the animal world. Plants seem to have appeared about 400 million years ago. Before then there was life in the seas for perhaps three billion years, making the origin of life on Earth about 3½ billion years ago. Invertebrate animal forms, such as insects and mites, developed on land once plants were established, and vertebrate animal forms appeared on land about 360 million years ago, having migrated out of the seas.

By "land," of course, is meant the dry parts of the tectonic plates, which were in motion on the surface of the globe. As the plates came together, life forms that had evolved on one plate could spread into another, possibly coming to dominate and eventually wipe out species that had been viable on the other plate without competition. (Recall the marsupials mentioned in Chapter 5.) As the plates moved apart, populations became isolated from each other and would evolve in different ways. Plants and animals that evolved on a continent after it had separated would not be found on other continents until such time as the plates drifted together or a land bridge was formed or they were carried there by people.

Ecosystems

One of the most remarkable things about life is its complexity and interdependency. Any living organism is an aggregate of thousands, more often millions, of semi-autonomous functioning parts, the presence and health of which are necessary for the life of the large creature in which they reside. Those organisms themselves exist as part of a larger system of life wherein each part helps to maintain the functioning of the whole. The sheer marvelousness of this was seen in the 19th century as a visible proof of divine creation, since it seemed impossible that such a system could have arisen by random processes. It was this "Design Argument" that formed the core of the toughest opposition to Charles Darwin's theory of evolution.

Life exists in a wonderfully organized and stable system. But not just in one system. Instead, life exists in interactive environments, which we can call *ecosystems*. In all ecosystems, there is a characteristic landscape and climate that determines what kinds of species will exist and flourish within it, and there is a characteristic pattern of predator-prey interactions. We can organize these into a handful of major types, which it will be useful to name and classify.

The Food Chain

In all ecosystems, there is a basic food chain that runs something like this: First, the rays of the sun get absorbed and transformed into a material form that provides the chemical energy for life. This is *photosynthesis*, the essential process in plants that turns leaves green, enables plants to grow, and organizes them into viable food for another species. This is, for all practical purposes, the bottom of the food chain. The rest builds up from this base.

A convenient way to analyze the food chain is to classify species by what they eat. At the lowest level, then, are the *photosynthesizers*, the plants, that consume the sun's energy. The photosynthesizers are eaten by the *herbivores*. These are animals that eat only plants; their bodies are suited only for this kind of diet, their jaws and teeth are capable of chewing the tough fibres of plants, and their digestive systems have the requisite caustic chemicals to break down the cell structures of the plants, extract the nutrients, and expel the waste. The herbivores turn the chemical energy available from the photosynthesizers into their own flesh. They then become the diet of choice for the *carnivores*, the meat eaters. The carnivores require much higher concentrations of fats and proteins for their survival. They do not have the physical equipment to live off a mainly plant diet, but their bodies are well suited to hunt and kill herbivores and then eat and digest their flesh. Above the carnivores is another group that can be called *top carnivores*. Top carnivores eat both herbivores and other carnivores. As well as the basic large groupings are all the necessary tiny life forms that make it all work: fungi, bacteria, viruses, and of course insects.

The food chain describes the hierarchical system through which energy reaches all the major large groups, but it accounts for very little of the energy flow. Starting with photosynthesis itself, only about one-fifth of one percent of the energy of the sun that falls on the earth is converted into matter by photosynthesis. Similarly the vast majority, say, 95 percent, of plants are not consumed by animals but die on their own account and rot into the ground – or, to speak more precisely, are consumed by the decomposers in the soil, such as the fungi. Herbivores also die of natural causes, and insects and bacteria and rot attack their carcasses. The proportion of herbivores that become the food of carnivores is relatively small, but much higher now due to human intervention in the form of animal husbandry. Cattle are much more likely to be eaten than wild ruminants on a savannah. Likewise many carnivores and most top carnivores die a natural death and ultimately are returned to the soil. As a consequence, this hierarchy of life has a pronounced pyramid structure, far larger at the bottom than the top. There are vastly more photosynthesizers than herbivores, many more carnivores than herbivores, and fewer top carnivores than any other group. This fact has enormous significance for the stability of an ecosystem.

Types of Ecosystems

The movement of the tectonic plates around the surface of the Earth, their separating from each other and crashing together, and their present positions provide the basic features that determine the bases for life in different places on Earth. Different types of ecosystems depend on the average temperature and the amount of rainfall in a region. These depend heavily on distances from the equator and the poles. Thus, the major different ecosystem types are arranged from north to south in more or less in horizontal bands that go around the globe. These systems remain stable for a very long time – thousands of years – but will respond slowly to changes in climate and other environmental considerations.

Nearest the north and south poles are regions called *tundra*. Tundra is characterized by a lack of moisture, hence low precipitation, low average temperatures, and soil which remains frozen throughout the year (permafrost). The plant life that grows in the tundra is that which can survive in these harsh conditions: low scrub that can hang onto acidic soils with little drainage.

Next in distance from the poles are the *taiga*. These are regions with great coniferous forests. Much of northern Canada, Russia, and Siberia are taiga. In the southern hemisphere, the region that might be taiga is all open sea. Conifers grow well in acidic soil and are less affected by the cold than other trees and many smaller plants. Nevertheless, the conifers dominate the landscape because not many other plants are viable.

Closer to the equator the natural ecosystem is the *temperate forest*, where deciduous plants grow in abundance. Large amounts of leaf droppings provide enrich the soil, which supports many other plants and animals.

...

A rather less rich environment in the slightly warmer but drier next band are the *grasslands*. These are areas that have been much used for farming despite somewhat poorer soils. The land is more easily cleared and the climate is more temperate.

Another type of ecosystem that exists in about the same latitudes is determined very much by the lack of rainfall. These are the *deserts*, large areas where virtually nothing can grow and whatever water is available is conserved in underground cavities.

Closest to the equator are the most productive and complex ecosystems of all, the *tropical rainforests*. As the name suggests, these regions get a lot of moisture. Being close to the equator, the temperature is high year-round. This fosters abundant growth; up to 40 percent of all plant growth is in tropical rainforests. About half of all the plants

and animals on Earth live in these rainforests. However, the tropical forests are more vulnerable than they might seem at first. Plant growth is so abundant that it absorbs nearly all of the chemical energy necessary for life. Only about 8 percent of the nutrients useful for growth make it to the soil. Very little rainwater makes it down to the soil; most of what does not evaporate is absorbed directly into the plants and trees that completely cover the ground.

The soils therefore are actually very poor and not capable of sustaining much life on their own. This is an especially urgent consideration because the rainforests, as rainforests, are so abundant and so vital to life across the planet, but would be very poor contributors if cleared. Yet every year vast tracts of rainforest are cleared to make grazing land for cattle. In fact, the soil does not support grass very well at all. In a very short time, all the topsoil blows away leaving hard clay.

In addition to all these land-based ecosystems, there are corresponding systems in the seas. Most of the seas are relatively barren of life, rather like the deserts. However, certain areas, such as coral reefs and estuaries have a level of abundance of life that is on a plane with that of the tropical rainforests.

The various ecosystems have evolved slowly over millions of years and change at a rate that matches the inexorable changes in the climate and the terrain produced by tectonic shifts and major geological cycles. These ecosystems have great stability – unless they are deliberately changed by forces that operate on a much shorter time-scale than what nature is accustomed to.

Though ecosystems are defined by their plant life, animal life has evolved and become stable in each kind of ecosystem. Because of the rigors of prey and predator, supply and demand, animal life has been maintained on a generally even keel for thousands of years in the ecosystems. But this has changed radically in the past million years or so because of the evolution of a species that is capable of making radical changes in the environment itself. That species is, of course, ourselves. How our species came to be on the planet is the subject of the rest of this chapter. How we have affected the environments of the world is the subject of the rest of the book.

Apes

By the time the dinosaurs died out 65 million years ago, mammals had evolved and found a niche at the edges of the ecosystems in which they lived. When the dinosaurs were gone, mammals developed further and became the dominant large form of animal. Within the class of mammals was a smaller group, the order of primates, which had grasping hands and stereoscopic vision. About 50 million years ago, a new form of primate developed, the monkey.

Monkeys appeared independently, in different parts of the world. South American monkeys have tails that they use to grasp and swing from trees with; African monkeys have tails but can only use them for balance. There are other minor differences, but enough to indicate that they evolved separately.

African monkeys were the ancestors of another evolutionary line, the apes, first appearing about 30 million years ago. The apes are of particular interest to human beings because they are our direct ancestors. In fact, some anthropologists consider human beings *to be* apes, the similarities are so pronounced. The evolutionary steps from apes to humans are the *homonids*. The term hominid really just means human-like, so it is a backward-looking category.

Homo Erectus. On the left: a largely complete skull of *Homo erectus* (the missing pieces have been shaded in to show the probable shape of the whole). On the right: an image of what *Homo erectus* might have looked like. The image was made by analyzing skulls like the one on the left and deducing where and how facial muscles would have attached to the bone.

Homo Erectus

The ancestry of modern humans is unmistakable with the emergence of *homo erectus* sometime between 2 to 1½ million years ago. *Homo erectus*, as the name suggests was a true bi-pedal, walking on two legs, which left the hands free for carrying and for making and wielding tools, leaving the mouth free for communication. It is generally accepted that *homo erectus* evolved in Africa and then slowly migrated to other parts of the world and into every different kind of ecosystem. *Homo erectus* were few in number and lived in small nomadic groups. Their cranial capacity was about ¾ that of modern humans – that being really our only way of measuring their presumed intelligence.

Homo erectus was a tool-making and -using species. Near their fossilized remains have been found a vast number of stone tools, often mere shaped rocks with a sharp edge for cutting or piercing. *Homo erectus* survived until about 100 thousand years ago and in this period of one or two million years they naturally developed their skills considerably so that in their later years their tools were more sophisticated (though still made of shaped stones), and the evidence is that they had a more complex social life.

This was a very big step for humanity. *Homo erectus* is a clear break from the rest of the animal kingdom, showing ingenuity and resourcefulness, very likely developing some kind of language, and in effect taking charge of their environment to the extent possible. They lived, apparently, by hunting in groups, which enabled them to bring down wild animals that would be too ferocious for a single man to hunt, and by gathering wild plants to eat – moving from place to place when necessary to find better prospects.

Homo sapiens

About 100 000 years ago, another step in human evolution took place when *homo erectus* evolved into *homo sapiens* or "wise man." *Homo sapiens* is so called because the evidence suggests another leap in ingenuity and adaptability. *Homo sapiens* appeared to be considerably more inventive in devising and using tools, more adaptable to different environmental conditions, and had rituals and ceremonies and a greater degree of community organization.

In 1856, a skullcap and a few bones were found in a cave in the Neander Valley in Germany. This discovery, three years before Darwin's *Origin of Species*, was the subject of considerable controversy. These remains were later identified as being similar to several other finds that were being made and which collectively came to be called *Neanderthal man*. The characteristics they portrayed were a sharply receding chin, heavy brow ridges, and thick bones. Their skeletons suggested very strong arms and short but sturdy legs. With their remains were found many serviceable, though simple, stone tools, evidence of clothing and other body coverings, and, most remarkable of all, very elaborate burial sites, some with the remains of bouquets of flowers around the deceased. The controversy in the 19th century ranged around whether these creatures were human at all, whether they were or were not ancestors to modern humans, whether they had language skills, and whether they were brutish (as their bodies suggested) or gentle and cultured (as their burial grounds suggested). In the 19th century the term "Neanderthal" became a shorthand for base, stupid, and totally lacking in human virtues. The controversy has continued to the present, but has been further complicated in the 20th century by the discovery that the cranial capacity of Neanderthals was larger than that of modern humans. Were they superior in some way to ourselves? If so, why did they die out? There are many suggestions, including that they did not die out and are indeed part of our ancestry or that they were overspecialized and overadapted to certain climatic conditions (namely the cold) and could not change when the environment changed. Another intriguing suggestion is that their rivals, *Cro Magnon*, who are more directly our ancestors, were more aggressive than Neanderthal and basically wiped them out.

Homo sapiens sapiens, is our own species. It has been on Earth for roughly the last 30 000 years. That's about one one-thousandth of one percent of the time that there has been some form of life on Earth, a fraction so small we can't even imagine it. Taking a long view of the history of the Earth, human beings have had virtually no impact on the general world environment. We just haven't been around long enough, for one thing. The major changes in the environment on the Earth have been caused by physical events from within the core of the Earth, punctuated by the occasional assault from outer space, and the settling in of some sort of balance of nature as different life forms evolved and found their competitive niches in ecosystems. *Cro Magnon*, named after the place in southern France where the  first remains were found, is anatomically the same as ourselves. Having already used the term "wise man" (*homo sapiens*) to refer to a wider group that would include the Neanderthals, a further distinction was called for in the Latin name of the species, so, even more immodestly than before, this strain was named *homo sapiens sapiens,* or "wise wise man."

Nevertheless, having evolved to our present anatomical configuration, we have begun a quite remarkable intervention in the world environment that is extraordinarily out of proportion to other living creatures in terms both of our period of existence and our number of individuals. We have learned to wield power and make changes that go way beyond our natural strengths and our local environments.

Modern Hunters and Gatherers. Clockwise from top left: A Waorani blowdart hunter, southeast Ecuador; a mother and child of the Ningerum tribe, Upper Fly river, Papua New Guinea; an older hunter of the Dani tribe, Irian Jaya, Indonesia; and a San woman, Kgalagadi Province of Botswana.

Chapter 7

Hunting and Gathering

The last chapter ended with the observation that modern humans have been around for an incredibly tiny portion of the time that there has been life on Earth, a mere 30 000 years or so. Now, focusing on just those last 30 000 years, for about two-thirds of that time our ancestors lived in a way that is vastly different from the way of life of almost all people today. They lived in small communities and appeared to have language and social customs, but their means of sustenance was much the same as that of wild animals. They hunted and killed game for meat; they found and gathered nuts, berries, and other edible vegetable matter. They did this in progressively more sophisticated and ingenious ways, but the general life-style this dictated precluded building the foundation for civilization as we know it.

What was this life like? We can try to answer that question by examining several different kinds of evidence. We can look at the fossilized artifacts found with their skeletal remains by paleontologists and anthropologists; we can make some inferences about what the physical environment was like at the time and in the places where they lived; and we can try to understand the cultures of the few remaining hunting and gathering societies that still exist at the margins of present-day society.

One thing seems clear enough: before humans discovered agriculture, the hunter-gatherer societies had spread into every kind of ecosystem and could take the best that each had to offer. Only after the spread of agriculture were the hunter-gatherers pushed out of the most fertile land.

The gathering function would have been relatively easy in an abundant climate. It would only have taken a small part of the day to gather a nutritionally adequate and varied supply of nuts and berries. Hunting parties may have taken longer, perhaps several days, but despite the very primitive weapons that early humans used, the probability of a kill was higher in lands where there were many wild animals.

The San of South West Africa

Since we believe that the modern human species appeared first in Africa and then migrated slowly from there to populate the globe, it is interesting to look at remaining African cultures that still live by hunting and gathering. It is entirely possible that the way of life of these contemporary primitives is not remarkably different from that of their ancestors from tens of thousands of years before.

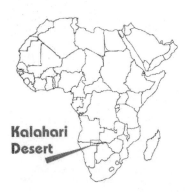

Kalahari Desert

A good subject of study is the group called the San, probably better known as the Bushmen of the Kalahari Desert. The San have a typical hunter-gatherer diet. That diet is perfectly adequate. The men hunt 17 different animals. The women gather 23 different kinds of edible plants. The mainstay of the diet is the mongongo nut, which comes from a drought-resistant tree. The nut contains five times the calories and ten times the protein of the equivalent in cereal crops.

Men and women work about the same amount of time in food production. For women it generally takes about one to three hours every day to gather nuts, berries, and tubers. Men do not work every day, but when they go on a hunt it is continuous activity for several days. Neither the elderly nor children are involved in food production. Altogether the San have a large amount of leisure time, which they value greatly.

Left: San hunters. Above San women gathering mongongo nuts that have fallen to the ground.

Migration

If the diet was good, the living was easy, and the leisure time enjoyed, what caused this to change? What made it possible for people to migrate out of Africa and what made them want to do it?

Much has been written about what made it possible, since that has been seen as synonymous with what made humans become the dominant species and begin to form civilizations. The usual reasons given involve brain size, bipedalism, speech, and tool making. From paleontological evidence we know that there has been a steady growth in the size of the skull throughout the history of the humanoid primates. One may reasonably conclude that the larger skull accommodated a larger brain and that the larger brain was more capable of abstract thought, of making plans, of contemplating the future, of devising technological implements. Bipedalism was a defining feature of *homo erectus* and it was evolving in stages well before then. Full bipedalism makes it possible to use the hands independently; the erect posture enabled humans to see greater distances. With speech, thoughts can be shared and group decisions made, moreover, speech fosters the development of thinking abilities. Tools and weapons enabled humans to overcome their physical limitations, gain control over their environment, and function in new situations.

Tool making and using has set our species apart from the others. The stages of human development can be very well documented with surviving tools that have been found with skeletal remains. The early tools were little more than rocks with a shaped edge, suitable for ripping apart flesh or perhaps as a hammer or an ax. Later on, these tools became more and more developed and refined. Arrows, spears, and harpoons were made, as were implements for more domestic tasks, such as needles for stitching together clothing made of animal skins. Paleontologists distinguish between the early stone age,

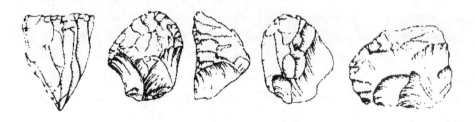

Early Stone Tools. These primitive tools would have been used as choppers or scrapers. While they look simple, they required skill to make.

the *Paleolithic Age*, and the later stone age, the *Neolithic Age*. The distinction is in the complexity of the stone tools made. The time of the onset of the Neolithic age is about 25 000 years ago, by which time *home sapiens sapiens* was well established.

All of the strains of *homo* since *homo erectus* began to migrate out of Africa over one and a half million years ago. Perhaps *homo erectus* got ahead of itself by moving into environments in which it could not cope when the climate changed. Though remains of *homo erectus* have been found widely dispersed in Africa, Europe, and Asia, they did die out. It is *homo sapiens sapiens* that has survived to populate the Earth.

Population Pressure

This still does not answer the question why these people left their homes in Africa to venture forth – unless the expanded brain size is taken to imply a new adventurousness and curiosity about other places in the world. Could there have been more compelling reasons? One proposed answer is population pressure. They *had* to migrate in order to survive because there were too many of them to live off the land where they were.

It would seem to be an ironclad law of the living world that all species reproduce more offspring than live to adulthood. All populations would quickly grow out of control were it not for the predators, diseases, and natural disasters that cull their numbers, as well as the non-availability of the prey that they rely upon for food. For animals in the middle of the food chain, the controls come from both above and below. For those at the top of the food chain, such as human beings, there are fewer checks. The more humans became adept at feeding themselves and staying out of harm's way, the more the natural pressure of population growth would begin to make their numbers increase.

A clue comes from present-day hunter-gatherer groups. All appear to have instituted some measures to control their population size. Common practices include killing or abandoning unwanted children: those born with birth defects, twins, and those of the wrong sex, meaning female. Another way of keeping the population of the young down came from the long period of breast feeding, which reduced female fertility. In some groups, especially nomadic groups where living conditions were harsh, it was expected that everyone contribute fully. So older people who could no longer do the necessary work were sometimes abandoned. These practices may seem inhumane to us today, but they may have been the only alternative for societies living off limited resources.

But did it work? If it did not do the job, the population of any group would continue to grow and would quickly exceed the ability of the local area to support it. Hunting and gathering is a fine way of life provided there is enough readily available food within reach of the population. When there is not, it would make sense that some of the population would set off to find new places to settle. Thus, through stages, the whole expanse of the habitable world became populated.

All the while that the human population was spreading, the world climate was undergoing its usual cyclic changes, which made parts of the world more suitable for human settlement and made other parts that previously had been inviting less so. A case in point is the Ice Age in Europe. Early humans had moved into Europe in considerable numbers during the interglacial period around 40 000 years ago. Then the ice returned and settled in around 25 000 to 20 000 years ago, turning most of Europe into tundra. Since people were already there, they learned to cope. Living off vegetation would no longer be easy, so hunting became more important. Now, however, it was necessary to hunt the large animals that lived and traveled in herds. Thus it was necessary to become nomads, following the herds and killing only what was necessary for survival. This would not support a large number of people.

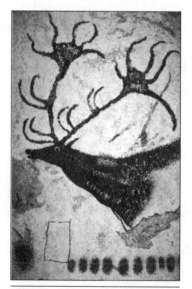

Cave art in Lascaux, France.

An exception during the Ice Age was in south-west France and northern Spain where a large number of animals regularly passed through this confined region, providing the population with an adequate supply of meat. They could also supplement their diet by fishing from the nearby rivers. So a sort of settled community developed. These are the cave dwellers, who have left us some remarkable artwork on the walls of their caves that tell us much about their culture.

It would seem that human beings travel to and settle new territories to find a better life than they left at home. Migration occurred in waves when the climate was benign in the areas being settled. However, once there, the residents learned to cope with adversity as it struck them, in particular becoming more dependent on hunting and less dependent on gathering when the climate no longer supported plant life, and more dependent on fishing when land animals were less available. They also learned to make shelters that would keep out the cold and to use fire for warmth and for cooking. With these fits and starts *homo sapiens sapiens* spread across the world.

Getting to Remote Places

Getting to Europe and to Asia from Africa was a relatively simple matter of overland migration, though it took a long time. Getting to other parts of the world required more than a willingness to walk vast distances. Australia, for example, required some kind of boat. But perhaps not as seaworthy a boat as would be needed today.

Australia was settled by human beings about 40 000 years ago, when the sea levels were at their lowest. It required a voyage of a mere 100 kilometers from the shores of Asia. Once on Australia, getting to Tasmania was easy as there was a land bridge between them until 15 000 years ago. Likewise, New Guinea had been an archipelago of Australia until it became an island about 8000 years ago.

The Australian environment was more benign that that of Europe. The climate was considerably more moderate, and the continent was full of wild animals and plants. It has been estimated that the original group traveling to Australia may have been no more than twenty-five individuals. There was no need here to restrict population growth, so the population grew quickly to about 300 000 people – a lesson in what happens to human populations without any restraints. But perhaps because the living was so easy, these people, the Australian aborigines, did not develop the technological sophistication and the complex social structures that were common elsewhere. When the European explorers first discovered Australia, they found a culture not very much different from what had been in Europe during the stone ages.

The settlement of the American continents by human beings was also facilitated by a land bridge. This one connected Siberia and Alaska across the Bering Strait, which was a land bridge during the Ice Age. The main technological feat that these intrepid migrants had to master was surviving the cold climate in Siberia and Alaska. From Alaska, the settlers migrated south to populate both American continents. That migration might have begun about 30 000 years ago or it might have been much more recent, say, 13 000 years ago. Once they got out of the polar regions, the living became much easier. It was a similar situation to that of the Australian aborigines – a land rich in life forms, but lacking in human beings. As in Australia, the population multiplied rapidly. In just a few thousand years, the continents were populated all the way from the far north to the southern tip of South America.

Finally, the islands in the Pacific Ocean were reached by people. Surely this must have been by boat, but it is controversial whether the voyages were intentional migrations to new places or accidents that washed up ashore. The groups that populated these islands of Oceania appear to have come from Polynesia. They certainly brought with them Polynesian customs and ways of living. The only major region of the world that has escaped being permanently populated by human beings is Antarctica, for obvious reasons.

Did Primitive Cultures Live in Harmony with the Environment?

Since these early populations lived in simple ways and generally did not bring with them the cultural advancements that had taken place back in Europe and Asia, it is an interesting question to consider how well they fit in with their many different environments.

There is certainly evidence that some nomadic hunting and gathering societies had some sense of the limitations of the environment and knew how to live without disturbing its essential balance, thus making it as stable and renewable as they could. The aboriginal people in the American continents are especially interesting since they were relatively late arrivals, bringing a stone-age culture to a virgin land many thousands of years later than happened in the "Old World." Moreover, since their descendants still exist and have preserved some of their customs and ways of life, we can learn much about how, not just them, but perhaps all early hunter-gatherer societies interacted with their environment. Among the Canadian native peoples, there is evidence of rotational hunting – restricting hunting in an area to a specified number of seasons and then moving on to another area, not returning to the original grounds for many years, which would allow for regeneration of the animal populations. Religious practices also were used to ban hunting in special sacred areas or in certain times of the year.

A key point here is that the essential environmentally friendly action taken is to choose another area for exploitation when overusing one area could lead to damage. This was only possible if the population was small relative to the area where they lived. Still there is the issue of whether hunter-gatherer societies really did live in harmony with the environment, or only seemed to since they are few in number. A few more examples from present-day hunter-gatherer communities may help clarify this further.

The Careless Hadza

Consider the Hadza of Tanzania. This is one of the oldest tribes in Tanzania. Despite many attempts by the government of Tanzania to make more modern life available to them, the Hadza people have resisted giving up their ancient ways. It is a typical hunter-gatherer community. The men hunt; the women gather. Both tasks are done when there is a need for food. Otherwise they are content to amuse themselves and participate in social chit-chat. They are few in number, about 400 in total, and they live in small groups of about 18 adults with their children in camps that are easily reconstructed in a couple of hours. They stay in one place only as long as it is convenient, moving when the weather changes, or the local resources are exhausted, or just out of boredom.

Above: a (female) Hadza gatherer digging for roots. Below: a (male) Hadza hunter.

Along with their lack of attachment to any particular place, they also are careless about the resources they live on. The men hunt wild animals, killing whatever is convenient rather than what is needed, often far in excess of what they can use. They also collect a lot of honey, some of which they sell for cash. They get their honey from wild beehives, as they find them. But instead of opening up a honeycomb and removing the honey and resealing it so it will be used again, they destroy the entire hive (getting roundly stung in the process) and then have to find a new one to exploit. Similarly, the women gathering tubers will pull up the entire plant when they find it, leaving nothing to regenerate.

Fire: The Prehistoric Weapon of Mass Destruction

The Hadza's carlessnesses are small acts which may in time damage an environment. But other primitive groups made use of more intense power, such as fire. Until the domestication of animals and the invention of machines giving mechanical advantage, fire was one of the few large forces that could be directed by human beings. Fire can be used to accomplish what a group of hunter-gatherers could not readily accomplish with the primitive tools available to them. Fire can be used not just for warmth and for cooking, but to clear an area by burning off everything on the surface. It would be nearly impossible for primitive peoples to clear a forest area of trees with the stone axes they had, but they *could* set fire to it. Even later cultures with much more capable equipment often found the slash-and-burn method superior for land clearance. A hunter-gatherer group might realize that the plants they relied upon would grow in an open field but not in a heavily wooded one. So even if they were not farming the area, they might clear it to facilitate growth. Or, woodland might be cleared to encourage wild animals to come and forage in an area where they might more easily be hunted. Whether such practices are ultimately harmful or beneficial to the environment, they are certainly interventions, and if carried out repeatedly over a considerable area can make permanent changes. Among the best documented cases of the large-scale use of fire by primitive people is the example of the Australian Aborigines, who regularly used large fires to clear an area to encourage other growth. The effects of these practices are still being debated in Australia today, partly in order to decide whether to encourage the practice to continue or not.[1]

Hunting to Extinction

Despite these strains, the ability of land and plant growth to regenerate is much greater than the ability of animal populations to withstand assaults. This is a simple matter of numbers. In any ecosystem, the quantity of individuals at the bottom of the food chain is far in excess of that at the top. Large animals, on the other hand, regenerate slowly and are easily compromised by over-hunting. Any major diminution of the population of an animal at the top of the food chain will disturb the balance of nature greatly since its prey will immediately begin to increase in numbers and send effects all the way down the line.

We may think of stone-age tools as incapable of doing much damage to the environment, but by the Neolithic period, weaponry had become sophisticated enough that human beings wielded power much greater than the physical capabilities of their bodies that by evolution had given them. Tool making evolved much faster than biological changes, which made the position of human beings in the pecking order of predator-prey change much more rapidly than the rest of nature. By the middle of the Neolithic period, the spears, harpoons, arrows, and other deadly weapons available to

1. See for example, "Burning Issues," *Tropical Savanas CRC,* June 1997 http:// savanna.ntu.edu.au/publications/savanna_links4/burning_issues.html.

hunting nomadic groups gave them the power to bring down almost any other living creature. Changes in the balance of nature that take place that quickly can cause disruptions to the order of life. In particular, such rapid changes are prime conditions for the extinction of species.

It is therefore very suggestive that so many of the large animal species that were healthy and numerous all over the globe went extinct within one or two thousand years of the time that human beings had completed spreading all over the world. To quote Robert Wenke,

> The spread of human hunting and gathering societies over the New World after 12,000 years ago, at the end of the last glacial period, coincides with the extinction of many animal species, and by about 10,000 years ago, all or most of the mammoths, mastodons, long-horned bison, tapirs, horses, giant ground sloths, dire wolves, camels, and many other creatures had disappeared. Extinction is, of course, a natural evolutionary development and can be accounted for by known biological processes. But the number of animal species that became extinct in the New World and their apparently rapid rate of extinction has led some to conclude that human hunters forced many New World animals into extinction shortly after the Pleistocene.[1]

The theory that early humans hunted the large animals to extinction is controversial. In fact, Wenke himself disputes this explanation, but no other explanation is entirely satisfactory either. And, the many examples of humans hunting animals to extinction or near extinction in later years makes this explanation very suggestive. The American bison, or buffalo, at one point reached a population of 50 to 60 million in North America, running wild across the prairies and dominating them. Their numbers were too large for the much smaller number of American native people to endanger them so long as their weapons were arrows and spears—even though there were some dramatically wasteful kills where whole herds were driven off cliffs. But as soon as the natives obtained rifles from the European settlers, the bison was very nearly wiped out.

---

1.   Robert J. Wenke, *Patterns in Prehistory: Humankind's First Three Million Years*, 3rd ed. (New York & Oxford: Oxford University Press, 1990) p218. The Pleistocene is a geological period generally taken to begin 2 million years ago and end about 10 000 years ago. For more coverage of this topic see P. S. Martin and R. Klein, eds. *Quarternary Extinctions: A Prehistoric Revolution*. Tucson: University of Arizona Press, 1984.

It was particularly hard on any species that had evolved in relative isolation and had few natural predators. When human beings migrated into the area, these species suddenly had a powerful predator that they were totally unprepared for. The worst cases of this were on islands that had been separated from contact with the rest of the world for long enough that whole genera had evolved with no defence against a predator such as humans.

Flightless birds were a common form of life on many of the larger islands that had been cut off from the mainland long enough that there were no domestic large mammals that might have preyed upon them. Flightless birds are almost defenseless against a large carnivore—or against armed human beings. There are many examples of flightless birds driven to extinction or near extinction as soon as humans appeared, either due to hunting by the humans themselves or due to the animals that the human beings imported with them.

The Moa

A particularly extraordinary example of the fate of helpless birds is the case of the Moa, a huge flightless bird native to New Zealand.[1] There were several species of Moa in New Zealand before the first humans, the Maoris, arrived around 1250-1300 (C.E.). Their common size was two meters tall, some stood four meters high. They were an imposing bird, and, being flightless, were easy prey for the Maoris. They were quickly hunted to death in perhaps as little as 100 years. One exacerbating feature of all birds is that they give birth by laying eggs, which are then vulnerable to predators. Moa eggs were, of course, huge and provided a lot of food value. Unfortunately, the Moas laid very

The largest moa, *Dinornis giganteus*, was the tallest bird in the world, two meters tall at the top of its back. Paleontologists do not think the giant long-necked moa normally stood erect. As shown above, it would have reached 4 m in height.

---

1. For details see R. N. Holdaway and C. Jacob, "Rapid Extinction of the Moas," *Science* (March 24. 2000), 2250-4.

few eggs to begin with and their nests were easily raided. This is but one example out of many of flightless birds driven to extinction.

The End of the Hunter-Gatherer Era

Taking an inclusive definition of human to include all the humanoid species that get the name *homo* such as *homo habilis*, then we can say that humans have been on Earth for about two million years. For 99 percent of that time, until about 10 000 years ago, their method of subsistence was to live by hunting game and gathering plants. If this was successful for so long, why did it come to an end rather quickly with the transition to agriculture? The usual reason given is that once human beings discovered the wonders of farming, they gave up the uncertain and laborious hunter-gatherer way of life. But recently another explanation has been put forward, namely that human beings couldn't make a go of it any longer by hunting and gathering.[1] Whatever the causes were, the most remarkable change in the way people lived and what they did to their environment began about that time in what we call the Agricultural Revolution.

---

1.   This viewpoint is vigorously pursued in Clive Ponting's *A Green History of the World* (New York: Penguin, 1993).

PART THREE

Civilization

We are able to publish books and read them and act on what we have learned from them because we are literate and cultured. Those are skills that come only with civilization, a certain way of life that devotes time and energy to such skills as reading and writing and finds the time to do that by organizing life in such a way that producing food and making shelters is not all there is to life. The first steps to building this way of life, a different one from the nomadic hunter-gatherers, was to settle in one place, produce food from the land on a regular basis, and have at least a part of the society put its major efforts into making life better.

Ironically, it may be that these first essential steps, what we call the Agricultural Revolution, were taken not to achieve any of these noble goals, but just to feed an otherwise starving population. Moreover, instead of giving the population more free time, farming may have been more arduous, at least at first. Nevertheless, out of this come the settled life, literacy, education, and those things that make us human. The process had fits and starts and began in different ways in different parts of the world.

Growing pains have definitely occurred. The worst aspect of the shift to agriculture is that whenever good times arrive, with benign weather and bumper harvests, the resulting increase in per-capita wealth is short-lived, because soon there are more mouths to feed and the bumper crops become a necessity instead of a boon.

Balancing food and population has been one of the most critical problems for societies to solve throughout their entire histories. How different civilizations across the world approached this problem has greatly determined what their present circumstances are. The present economic pecking order in the world is largely the result of how different parts of the world responded to such crises.

Part Three examines these issues from the beginnings of agriculture up to the formation of the major economic blocs of the day, but for the moment passing over industrialization, which is the subject of Part Four.

For Further Reading

Cipolla, Carlo M., *European Culture and Overseas Expansion.* Harmondsworth: Penguin, 1970.

Diamond, Jared. *Guns, Germs, and Steel: The Fate of Human Societies.* New York & London: W. W. Norton & Co., 1999.

Littlefield, D. C. *Rice and Slaves.* Baton Rouge, LA: Lousiana State University Press, 1981.

Needham, Joseph, Wang Ling, and Lu Gwei-Djen. *Science and Civilization in China,* Volume IV, Part 3, *Civil Engineering and Nautics.* Cambridge: Cambridge University Press, 1971.

Pacey, Arnold. *Technology in World Civilization: A Thousand-Year History.* Cambridge, MA: The MIT Press, 1990.

Ponting, Clive. *A Green History of the World: The Environment and the Collapse of Great Civilizations.* New York: Penguin, 1993.

Wenke, Robert J. *Patterns in Prehistory: Humankind's First Three Million Years,* 3rd ed. New York & Oxford: Oxford University Press, 1990.

White, Lynn, Jr. *Medieval Technololgy and Social Change.* Oxford: Oxford University Press, 1962.

Modern corn, or maize, is a nutritious foodsource. It evolved from plants that have been a staple in the diet of Mesoamerican civilizations for millennia.

Chapter 8

Agriculture

It is traditional to view the transition from hunting and gathering to agriculture as the most fundamental change ever in the way that human life has been lived, as well as the precondition for what we call civilization. For only when people were no longer on the move could they begin to make permanent settlements where there could be cultural institutions on which to build a life that had more to it than self-preservation and idle leisure. The term, Agricultural Revolution, correctly captures the major shift in living that was represented by the advent of farming; it also suggests something relatively quick and full of turmoil. Along with that notion goes the idea that the hunting and gathering life was dropped immediately as soon as the advantages of agriculture were perceived.

In the larger context of prehistoric times, agriculture was adopted very rapidly, but the change still took well over a thousand years, perhaps two or three thousand. It was not an immediate shift by any means. In fact, strong evidence suggests that many traditional hunting and gathering societies knew how to plant and harvest crops and did so in a limited way alongside their hunting and gathering. By modern human standards of change, the process was excruciatingly slow. If farming was so superior to hunting and gathering, why was it not adopted immediately as soon as its benefits were seen? And if farming was not manifestly superior, why was it adopted at all?

From the point of view of nutrition, the hunter-gatherer diet actually may have been superior to that of the settled agrarian peasant. Wild plants are often more nutritious than domestic crops, and certainly offer more variation and balance. Hunting was sporadic and not reliable, but except for obscure places with extreme climates, a greater variety of animals tended to be hunted and eaten than was available through animal husbandry. Yet hunting and gathering was successful only when the community had a fairly large area over which to find their food. The history of the spread of humanity across the globe tracks the migration of people away from their home tribes in order to find better living elsewhere. Except for the cases prompted by climate changes or local disasters, the necessity for moving may have come about because the population at home had grown beyond what the home turf could support. Although hunting and gathering societies may have had various techniques to keep their populations in check, these did not necessarily work effectively. Over those thousands of years that *Homo sapiens* was spreading over the Earth, their total numbers were steadily rising. The human population of the world 10 000 years ago has been estimated at around 4 million people, about the size of one of the world's larger cities today. That may have been the effective limit of population that could be sustained by hunting and gathering.

What is agriculture? It is the deliberate process of clearing tracts of land of all their natural growth, preparing the soil, sowing seeds, usually of a single desired crop, tending that land for a period of months, and then harvesting the crop over a short intensive period of time. It also includes the process of domesticating a very small number of species of animals and caring for their needs, providing pastureland, shepherding them throughout the year, milking, collecting eggs, then butchering and preparing meat for consumption. In short, agriculture involves a lot of work, much more than the typical one to three hours a day needed by hunters and gatherers. Moreover, the work is not spread out evenly over the year. Sowing and harvest times are major commitments. And, if the weather turns bad and a poor harvest results, the community is in trouble. Really, only one reason would impel a hunter-gatherer group to choose to switch over to this lifestyle: to provide the necessities where hunting and gathering failed.

If the population of a tribe or community exceeded the "carrying capacity" of the land, meaning whatever population the local environment could support, and there was no effective place for emigrants to go, a new way had to be found to get more food out of the local area. That is what farming did: it produced a higher yield from a fixed amount of land. It solved the problem of feeding the community. That is, it solved the problem for a certain period of time. Then it made the problem worse. That's because human beings, like all species, will increase their populations to approach what the environment can support.

In a typical predator-prey situation, a symbiotic relationship tends to keep numbers in balance. For example, wolves prey on moose; if the moose population rises, the wolves will have an easier time of it. The result soon will be that there are more wolves born and *their* population will rise. That makes more predators, which will then do a more effective job of culling the prey. So then the moose population will fall. This symbiosis depends on the existence of effective limits of variability of the population of both species and a fairly constant predator-prey relationship. Otherwise, it can fail and spin out of control.

In hunter-gatherer communities, the effective limit on the human population was the amount of food that could be extracted from the land. Ever since human beings learned how to make effective weapons that could take on large animals, they have had no predators to worry about. Farming changed all the rules. Now the land could be made to produce far more than it had before. Crops certainly provided enough food for the expanded hunter-gatherer population, but so much more food was provided that the human population began to rise.

Now there was no turning back. A community could not return to hunting and gathering, because that would not suffice to feed everyone. As the population continued to grow, the only way to keep up was to put more and more land under cultivation. Thus agriculture spread, and spread rapidly. Those few groups that chose to remain hunters and gatherers soon got pushed off the best land and had to retreat to lands that would have made pretty poor farming anyway.

By 10 000 years ago, people had spread all across the globe. Agriculture arose separately in several different areas as each responded to the population problem. Since the terrain was different in various places, agriculture took different forms in different parts of the world. How and when each region responded has had enormous significance for the history of the world. The following is a brief look at the different approaches in three different parts of the world: (1) the Fertile Crescent of South-West Asia and northern Africa, (2) the northern plains of China, and (3) part of what is now Mexico.

The Fertile Crescent

The first area to be transformed to agriculture was near the point where Africa, Europe, and Asia all meet. It is a wide swath of land encompassing what is now Palestine, Syria, south Anatolia (now part of Turkey), Iraq, and a part of Iran. This was a land of rich soils fed by rivers coming out of mountains both to the north and south. The land was extremely productive, and the climate was benign. It was such a special area that it has been given the nickname, the "Fertile Crescent."

The Fertile Crescent region was already thick with naturally occurring wild, edible plants. It was also well populated. Hunters

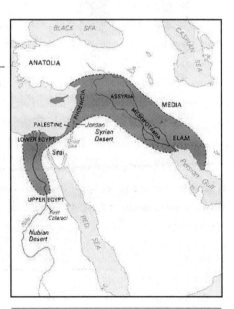

The Fertile Cresent.

and gatherers had lived here for thousands of years, taking advantage of the wild plants and the pleasant climate. What later became the main crop, wheat, existed in a wild form as a grass with seeds that were large enough to be worth separating from the chaff and eating. A fortuitous mutation in one of these grasses resulted in a grain with seeds that were considerably larger than the usual grass. This was emmer, a plant still existing today that grows wild and can be collected for its grain, but also can be cultivated. It seems likely that emmer or another similar plant was first discovered by gatherers to be nutritious and then began to be gathered regularly. At some point it may have been noticed that the seeds of these grasses – the edible part – would also grow into new plants if put back into the ground. Over what was probably a very long time involving many generations, emmer may have come to be planted regularly and harvested.

Emmer and Breadwheat. On the left is a stalk of emmer, on the right a stalk of breadwheat. Note the larger seeds of the breadwheat.

Some many hundreds of years later, after the practice of cultivating emmer had become established, another fortuitous mutation appears to have taken place in which the already nutritious emmer transformed into the even more nutritious "breadwheat," with even larger seeds. Curiously, the seeds of breadwheat are so heavy that they would not easily disperse in the wind as emmer had done. Therefore, it seems clear that the plant would only thrive if deliberately cultivated. As this theory goes, first people learned that emmer was edible and nutritious. Since the plant self-fertilized, a supply would continue to grow nearby. Then, after becoming accustomed to gathering wild emmer and relying on it for food, some person or persons discovered that if they sowed some of the emmer seed in the ground, more would come up in a few months time. Hence, people slowly got in the habit of planting seeds and harvesting crops, despite the fact that emmer, while nutritious, is not really wonderful food. Then, amazingly, right on cue, emmer mutated into breadwheat, which was a much more nutritious grain. But that mutation would not survive were people not already on hand to replant the next crop. Since they were already accustomed to sowing seeds for a new crop, breadwheat survived and agriculture took firm root. But had *emmer evolved/mutated into breadwheat which was able to survive.*

breadwheat appeared before people got the idea of sowing seed instead of merely eating it all, this plant species could have died out.

The only trouble with this explanation is that it is possibly just too convenient. Much evidence exists of plant mutations over long periods of time – it's a very natural process – but the suggestion that agriculture arose *because of* these mutations seems improbable, especially since agriculture rose up independently in several places in the world and was not based on the same crops. A "natural" selection process is also at work here. The early farmers would have favoured the plants with larger seeds and harvested them first. Over time, a natural progression would occur in the genetic pool toward those plants with more favourable characteristics as food. These would be the plants with heavier seeds – those that required cultivation to continue to grow.

Other wild grasses such as barley and einkorn were found and cultivated in different parts of the Fertile Crescent. Over a more limited range, wild legumes, such as lentils, chickpeas, and peas, also came to be cultivated and enriched the diet.

As food production became more efficient, the population grew and permanent settlements were made. These were the first towns. The nature and productivity of early farming, especially in the rich soils of the Fertile Crescent, was best served with a societal organization in which some people did the farming, others distributed the collected crops, still others prepared foods, and some became specialists in making necessary implements and artifacts, such as potters, and all this was overseen by a ruling elite that made the system work. The nature of agriculture itself brought this hierarchy into being.

By about 6000 B.C.E., all the major crops were in place. Dogs, sheep, goats, cattle, and pigs were domesticated. Pottery had been invented, at first to provide containers for harvested grain. As this area filled in and once more population pressures demanded the expansion of farming, this system moved into southern Europe, taking the same selection of crops and domesticated animals, with a few local exceptions. What had been a diet based on a wide variety of plants and animals slowly became specialized upon a few of each. The spread of agriculture into northern and central Europe was very much delayed, because the climate and condition of the soil was so different. A very different approach to farming was required that depended on the technology of heavy ploughs and draft animals to be effective. Except for southern Europe, the rest of the continent's population remained hunters and gatherers for another three millennia.

Slash and Burn

As farming moved into new areas, especially in Europe, the basic technique for clearing land for farming and assuring that the soil would be fertile was what is called the swidden system, or slash and burn. This was the method of choice in a forest, which also provided good farming land. To clear a climax temperate forest, which may have taken a thousand years or more to reach its then stable ecosystem, prospective farmers attacked the smaller growth with their stone axes, then set the forest on fire. The resulting ash-covered soil was rich enough to assure good crops. After several years, however, planting the same crop again and again depleted the soil, which was no longer productive. Then the farmers moved on to a new area, abandoning the first, which was allowed to revert to grasslands and remain untouched for several decades, when it could be cleared once again for crops. Like hunting and gathering, this technique was effective only so long as there remained new areas to move into.

The Far East

The second major area of the world to take up agriculture was the Far East. As with the Fertile Crescent, the original agricultural fields were situated in land already fertile and easily cultivated. In the Far East, these were the alluvial soils on the great Yellow River flood plain in the north. These soils were very fertile and easily tilled, because the atmosphere was so arid that little natural vegetation was there to be cleared. By 4000 B.C.E., the area contained many villages that subsisted on a combination of hunting and gathering and cultivating the land. The main crops were millet, generally considered nutritious and filling, but not very desirable and so the food for the peasants; and rice, which was the food of the elite. But rice in these northern plains was grown as a dry crop and was not nearly as productive as the later rice grown in paddy fields in the south. Throughout the early period of farming, the diet was a monotonous supply of grain crops. Legumes were unknown until about 1600 B.C.E. when soybeans were introduced. Soybeans have the added benefit of re-enriching the soil by fixing nitrogen. An interesting sideline to this is that as soybeans were substituted for milk and meat in the diet, many Asian populations have evolved without the enzymes necessary to digest milk products.

Despite the area's demonstrable need for an adequate food supply for its already burgeoning population and despite the vast amount of land available, agriculture was slow to expand there. Probably the reason was that although suitable areas for cultivation were available, it was a long time before a reliable system of irrigation was developed. This is all the more surprising in the light of China's superiority in agricultural technology in later centuries.

Mesoamerica

The last area to develop agriculture independently was the New World. This took place in the narrow stretches of Central America that connect the two continents. Judging from the scattered remains that are still decipherable, all human cultures in the New World were based on hunting and gathering until around 6000 B.C.E. Then, evidence appears of small plots devoted to growing plants that had previously been wild, as likely happened elsewhere. Unlike the other two major areas, the plants of choice were not grains, but a variety of vegetables.

One of the big differences between New World and Old World agriculture was the lack of domesticated animals in the New World. There were no sheep, goats, or cattle to domesticate. Hunting remained a vital activity for much longer. Ultimately, the major food crop in the Americas became maize, but only after maize was bred into a plant with a much larger edible portion. The original maize was no bigger than a human thumb and was generally chewed whole. Only when later varieties had considerable larger cobs with many kernels did it become a

Maize cob sizes at roughly thousand-year intervals starting in 5000 B.C.E.

major staple. Maize, or as North Americans call it corn, is very nutritious, but it lacks a number of proteins and vitamins, making it unsuitable as a sole source of food. The Mesoamericans compensated for this with considerable reliance on beans and squash. Further south, in the Andes, the potato became the staple of choice.

Explaining the Transition to Agriculture

The shift 10 000 years ago from hunter-gatherer to agricultural life is so extraordinary and so vital for understanding human history that it has quite naturally been and continues to be the subject of a great deal of research and speculation. The account given above is generally agreed upon in most respects, but there is much controversy over the details. Also, some prefer entirely different explanations, and account for the archæological and paleontological evidence in entirely different ways. It is far beyond the scope of this book to explore that controversy further. Before moving on, however, I will cite a brief synopsis of the various theories that have been proposed to explain the Agricultural Revolution. This is a quote from Robert Wenke's *Patterns in Prehistory*:

> To begin with, we can dismiss the idea that people domesticated plants and animals because someone came from outer space and taught them how to do it or because someone in ancient Syria had a brilliant idea and it spread around the world or because people simply got sick of chasing animals and wanted an easier way to live.
>
> The roughly contemporary appearance of a vast variety of domesticates, from palm trees to potatoes, across the same approximate latitudes around the world, and the several millennia it took to domesticate most plant and animal types, make any of the above scenarios improbable. And although there is great variability, hunters and gatherers tend to have more leisure time than primitive agriculturists, and hunters and gatherers rarely spend this time analyzing their economy, designing cathedrals, or improving their standard of living; they spend it either talking or sleeping—skills...they have already thoroughly perfected.
>
> Even so, the idea that people became farmers because it's an easier way of life than hunting-foraging seems so plausible to most Westerners that it is hard to discredit this myth.[1]

In this book, we will assume as a working hypothesis that agriculture arose out of the need to feed a burgeoning population when hunting and gathering no longer sufficed to provide adequate sustenance. As the diagram on the next page illustrates, it takes much more land to support a population of hunters and gathers than of farmers. No doubt the process of change took a great deal of time and was accomplished in small tentative steps, but then so did every change in the life-styles of early humans. Compared to the whole of the hunter-gatherer period, it took hardly any time at all. What it most certainly did was

---

1.   Robert J. Wenke, *Patterns in Prehistory: Humankind's First Three Million Years,* 3rd ed. (New York & Oxford: Oxford University Press, 1990), p. 258.

bring about a vast series of changes that have brought us to the present-day dilemma of a highly advanced, technologically comfortable civilization saddled with a compromised environment due to the very steps that brought us that civilization.

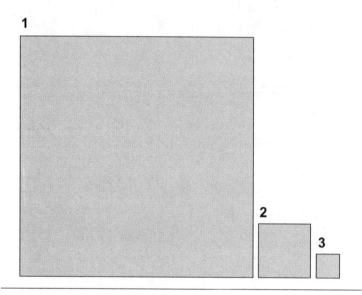

These three squares show the relative amount of land needed to feed individuals obtaining food in different ways. Square 1 represents the land used by a single hunter-gatherer; hunting and gathering requires 10 square kilometers of land to sustain each individual. Square 2 represents the land used by a single dry-farmer. Dry-farming, or farming without irrigation, requires 0.5 square kilometers per person. Square 3 represents the land required to sustain a single individual in a society that employs irrigation-farming; this technique requires only 0.1 square kilometers to support one individual. By changing from hunting and gathering to irrigation farming, a society can feed 100 people with the amount same land as was once needed to feed a single individual.

An Egyptian Obelisk, carved with hieroglyphs.

Chapter 9

The Dawn of Civilization

If human beings switched to agriculture for the purpose of providing enough food to feed their growing populations, it certainly worked. In the pre-agricultural societies, as soon as there was enough food for everyone, hunting and gathering could come to a stop; but with agriculture, a field must be sown, tended, and then later harvested all at once. The harvest will have to last for a whole season, so it must be stored. In a good year, ample grain will be left over. Likewise, domestic animals are maintained as herds of a size more than enough for immediate needs. In both cases, the general result will be the production of a surplus that is not immediately needed and distributed. This is valuable. In a general way, this is what wealth is: a surplus of material or of capability that is not immediately required.

Wealth of all sorts needs management and protection. The Agricultural Revolution marked the beginning of bureaucracies, of standing armies, and of a controlling social elite. For the first time, something tangible and valuable had to be protected that went beyond one's immediate person and one's family. Surplus food was valuable. With it, people could be paid to do work that was something other than food production. Different trades emerged that simplified and organized farming and animal husbandry and made them more efficient. One of the first trades was that of the potter, who made urns to store surplus grain. Tool making had become more and more sophisticated over the entire course of human history, but now such workers as full-time professional toolmakers could be supported. Metal working crafts emerged about this time as well.

Ancient Egyptian surplus grain being collected and stored in large urns. From a tomb mural.

Farming involved more than just sowing seeds and harvesting the crop. It was soon discovered that crop yields could be vastly improved by taking certain steps. First was to get the seeds slightly under the surface of the soil (instead of merely scattering them on top) where they had a better chance to germinate and less chance of being eaten by birds. Here an invention came to the rescue. Some people say this is the most important invention of all time: the plough. The plough was not a single invention, but a whole series of tools that made successive improvements on the original design, and with those improvements came many changes in the social structure of work. The first ploughs were really just digging sticks that could be pulled along to make a rut in the soil. The rut was then filled with seeds and lightly covered over. Those members of the group who had always looked after the plant portion of the diet performed this task: the women. The step from gathering to farming was a natural one. Men looked after the animal side of things; women looked after the plants.

A scratch plough pulled by an ox.

Later plough designs produced sturdier implements with sharp blades held at a fixed angle to the ground and pulled along by a harness attachment. At first, the harnesses were attached to men, later to draft animals. In any case, the task fell to men, who then became farmers. These were the ploughs of ancient times, suitable only for relatively light soils. Much later, elaborate heavy ploughs were introduced to deal with the heavy compacted soil of such places as northern Europe. These had to be pulled by teams of up to eight oxen and required a great deal of cooperation.

A Seed Drill.

Another implement with a similar function was the seed drill, invented and in wide use in China. Instead of cutting a furrow across the ground and throwing seeds into it, the seed drill pushed a small number of seeds directly into the ground in a single place. These are examples of alternate inventions to solve the same problem.

Another innovation of perhaps even greater significance is *irrigation*. Most crops required a considerable amount of water to grow. In some places, rainfall was sufficient to assure a good crop, but generally a better crop was achieved if the amount of water was considerably more than what fell from the skies and was applied more judiciously as required. To get that water to the fields required

Pictured are shadoofs – devices to lift water from a river to an irrigation trench. An early example of infrastructure. From a carving at Nineveh.

irrigation ditches and mechanical devices to transfer water as needed. These are large projects—more than a single farming family can provide for themselves. This required infrastructure, and that required government. Some of the earliest public works projects are irrigation systems; and indeed some of the largest public works projects today concern water management.

Irrigation brought much greater yields than dry farming, so it was quickly adopted wherever the population was reaching the limit of what could be supplied by the dry farming in place. The result was inevitable, and for us, predictable. It was not very long before the population had increased once again, taking advantage of the surplus food being produced. Out of this also came the beginnings of the first really serious environmental problems caused by human civilization: waterlogging of soils, salinisation of farmland, and irreversible damage to precious farmland. That will be discussed in greater detail later.

Sumer

The world's first great civilization arose in the first area to move to an agricultural way of life, the Fertile Crescent. In particular, that part of it that lay in present day Iraq between the Tigris and the Euphrates rivers, an area of particularly rich and easily tilled soil. The ancient Greeks later called this part of the world "Between the Rivers," which in Greek is *Mesopotamia.*

The first civilization of note in Mesopotamia was Sumer. Sumer occupied an area in the southern part of Mesopotamia not far from where the two rivers finally join. Here is where the first known system of writing developed, *cuneiform,* which consists of making

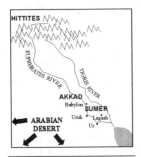

Above: A map of Sumer. Below: A cuneiform tablet, from the later Babylonian Era.

marks with a reed stylus on a piece of wet clay about the size of a human hand and then setting that out to dry. Thousands of cuneiform tablets have survived, due to the arid climate in Mesopotamia. Of these, about 85% deal with economic matters. The first known tablets seem to be some kind of tally of amounts of grain.

There were basically eight main cities that were the centres of society in Sumer. Each of these was dominated by a *Ziggurat*, or temple. The Ziggurat was the religious centre of the region, but it might be better thought of as a sort of city hall, where everything to do with the local government took place. The priest class that lived and worked at the temple were the bureaucrats who kept the society functioning. They were at the top of the social order because everything depended on them. Up close to them in social rank were the military, because the society was at risk if it could not defend itself. Thus in a way, agriculture has been the cause of social stratification.

An interesting feature of the organization of Sumer around eight major cities is that even then the process of urbanization was inexorable. Uruk, for example, in 3500 B.C.E., was a town of several

The ruins of the Ziggurat at Uruk. The Ziggurat, known as the White Temple, stood on a large terrace and housed the sanctuary of Anu, the sky god. The Ziggurat has been excavated since 1912.

thousand people, surrounded by 146 smaller villages. By 3000, the population of Uruk had swelled to a large city of 50 000, but the number of villages had shrunk to 24.

Sumerian society flourished for well over a thousand years until finally invaded and overrun. But not long after, in essentially the same territory, rose the great ancient civilization of Babylonia.

Egypt

Another civilization began soon after Sumer in nearby northeast Africa, Egypt. Egypt had a far longer and more peaceful existence than the empires of Mesopotamia. Partly this was due to the location. Egypt is bounded on the east and south by mountains, on the west by desert, and on the north by the Mediterranean Sea. It is not easy to invade. Mesopotamia, on the other hand lies at what was the crossroads of the entire known world. It has always been hotly contested territory.

Egypt had another enormous advantage that promoted stability, the Nile River. The Nile provided a reliable annual flood, bringing rich black silt washed down by the torrential spring rains from the two main sources of the Nile—the "Blue Nile" on the Ethiopian plateau and the "White Nile" around

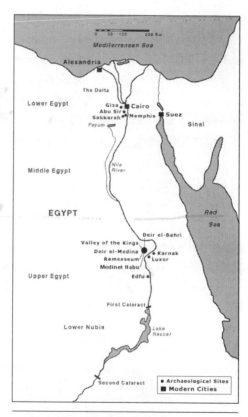

Egypt. This map shows the location of ancient sites and modern cities.

Lake Victoria. The force of the flood overruns the banks of the Nile and deposits this very fertile alluvial soil in a narrow three-kilometer strip running the length of the country. The annual flood of the Nile provided easy solutions to problems that had to be overcome with some effort in other places in the world.

First, of course, was the water itself, which was necessary, especially in an arid desert area like Egypt. But the water had to be neither too much nor too little. Too much would wash away the topsoil and be a danger to the people. Too little would not provide enough for crops to grow. The Nile floods were remarkably reliable. Their occurrence could be predicted with amazing accuracy from the sighting of the star Sirius in the sky just before dawn. People could prepare for the flood, moving out of harm's way, yet be ready to act when necessary. The level of the waters varied from year to year, generally within manageable limits, but periods of drought and periods of too much water did occur. One of the first and most important elements of the infrastructure of Egypt was the building of dams and floodgates to regulate the water to acceptable levels.

Second, the rich silt carried by the floodwaters restored fertility to the soil. Farming tends to degrade soils, especially farming the same crop year after year. In most other farming cultures, the solution to this was to layer the fields with animal manure to restore the missing nutrients. In fact, in Egypt, the mixture of the waters of the Blue Nile and the White Nile provided just the right mix.

Third, the floodwaters loosened the existing soils and made them easy to till. Though ploughing took place in Egypt, it was also effective simply to strew seed on the fields and set cattle and other large animals loose on the land to trample the seeds into the ground. Ploughing, when it was done, was a relatively easy task.

One need only consider what Egypt's prospects would be without the Nile and all it brought to understand why Egypt was called "The Gift of the Nile." If there was any downside to this wonderful arrangement that allowed Egypt to be one of the greatest civilizations of the world for several thousands of years, it was just that perhaps the Nile made life too easy. The Egyptians found what worked, went on to build a rich culture, and then basically remained the same for centuries. Meanwhile, elsewhere in the world where the living was not so easy, people learned how to overcome greater challenges, becoming more resourceful; eventually they became a threat to the relaxed and civilized Egyptians.

The Destruction of the Gift

As a country, Egypt was viable only because of the Nile. It survived as a major power for several thousand years, finally falling to the conquering Greeks under Alexander the Great and then being more or less annexed by other countries and empires for centuries. In the 19th century, when Egypt was under British control, steps were taken that eventually severely compromised the "gift" given by the Nile. Instead of using the rich waters of the Nile to provide the means for a sustainable natural process that could grow food for the entire nation, new goals were sought. The Egyptian economy was agrarian, and its wealth was limited by its lack of participation in the Industrial Revolution. It was not cash rich, so it could not maintain a high standard of living by European standards.

But there was a possible solution: put more land under cultivation—but not to grow more food. Instead, the goal was to produce a cash crop to sell—cotton. This could be accomplished only by diverting more of the waters of the Nile onto land not previously considered arable. Thus, a complex system of artificial irrigation was introduced that, inevitably, caused salinisation sufficient to render the land unproductive.

Another misunderstanding was the judgement that the chief problem to be solved was the amount of water that flowed at different times. Making a dam that allowed the desired amount water to be released when it was wanted, not just when the spring floods came, could control this. The result was the building of the first dam at Aswan in the early 20th century. In the 1950s, a much larger dam was built at Aswan, the so-called "High Dam" that not only controls the water flow for agricultural purposes, but

Looking north from the High Dam at Aswan to the old dam.

also provides a considerable amount of hydroelectric power. Unfortunately, this killed the magic of the Nile for good, because the dam held back the rich silt that had provided natural fertilizers for millennia. Egypt, like so much of the world, is now reliant on artificial fertilizers, which it never needed in the past, to maintain the productivity of its fields.

The Indus Valley

The basis of the great ancient civilization of India was the settlement of the Indus Valley by people moving east from the Fertile Crescent area of southwest Asia and finding a new fertile area for farming. This occurred about 3500 B.C.E. and therefore had a much later beginning than either Mesopotamia or Egypt. The Indian subcontinent is actually not part of Asia at all. It is a piece of Gondwanaland that broke apart 200 million years ago and slowly drifted northwest until it crashed into the Asian mainland. The pressure of the ramming of the subcontinent against Asia pushed up a crust of land to form what are now the Himalayan Mountains. The floods from melting snow in these mountains provided the water for the arable fields below.

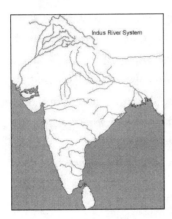

But unlike the Nile, the floodwaters of the Indus River were unpredictable, sometimes coming in huge devastating floods that would wreak havoc to settled communities and wash the useful soil out to sea. Yet the area was so arid that farming was possible only through irrigation from the river. Elaborate waterworks were mandatory from the start. The settlers in this area are believed to have had the most complex municipal water and sewage system in the world.

Relatively little is known about the early days of civilization in the Indus Valley, because the strong floodwaters buried most of the archæological remains far below the surface and well under the water table. For archæologists, this civilization is of particular interest, because its political influence appears to have extended far beyond its geographical area, and, unlike almost all other ancient civilizations, the distribution of wealth appears to have been relatively equitable, yet the society that emerged later was one of the most stratified in the world.

China

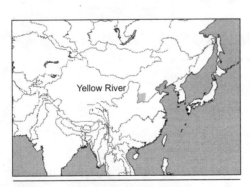

Ancient China. The shaded area on the Yellow River marks the center of the Xia Dynasty, which flourished from 2100 to 1800 B.C.E.

The Chinese civilization began to take shape quite a bit later than the civilizations of Mesopotamia and Egypt and, in the judgement of most archæologists, also several centuries later than the Indian civilization. However, as with the Indus Valley settlements, research into ancient China's beginnings has not yielded sufficient evidence to settle these questions definitively. Archæology as a scientific endeavor is still a relatively new undertaking; in addition, it has had to cope with interruptions of wars and revolutions. Given that China seems to have had a much later start, it is all the more remarkable that it turned into one of the most technologically astute and literarily cultured societies of antiquity.

Modern China stretches across a territory with vastly different environments. Not surprisingly, China's historical development proceeded in different ways in different regions. The productive farming area in the Yellow River valley of North China was the logical place for settlements to begin. In the south was another arable region, near the Yangtze River, where farming got underway a few centuries later. The climate was more benign, but the soils were not of the same superior quality as those in the North. China's amazing rise to dominance around 1000 C.E. has much to do with the shift of their major breadbasket from the north to those fields in the south and the technological problems that had to be overcome to do that. This is discussed further in later chapters.

The Mayans

Settled communities did not emerge until much later in the Americas, around 2000 B.C.E. Migration to the New World occurred much later than to other regions. The naturally occurring grasses that might provide cultivatable crops were not suitable as food. And, there were no animals suitable for domestication, neither for animal husbandry nor as draft animals.

Farming began when a better form of maize was developed. Maize is deficient in several proteins and vitamins. The domestication of beans and squash and some other vegetables greatly improved the diet of the settled communities. In very little time, the population soared to match the food supply and the pattern of civilization began. In central Mesoamerica, now part of Mexico, large ceremonial centres were built, requiring vast amounts of human labour. Social complexity increased further during the "Classic Period" from 300 to 900 C.E., when the length of the corncob doubled.

The centre of the civilization was the city of Teotihuacan, with a population of 100 000. It had enormous pyramids and plazas, indicative of a complex, organized, and structured society capable of marshalling a huge labour force. This was the Mayan civilization, one of the great lost societies that is still mysterious to archæologists. Excavations in the last decades of the 20th century have revealed that the society had considerable knowledge of solar, lunar, and planetary astronomy from which they devised a highly accurate calendar. They also had a form of writing which has not been fully deciphered. A complex system of canals, reservoirs, moats, and terraced fields are evidence of intense agriculture. Given that the lack of domestic animals to produce manure to reinvigorate the fields left the Mayans in a basically unsustainable situation, it is not surprising that at some point a crisis would be reached when there was just not enough to go around. Earthquakes, drought, floods, epidemics, or any other disaster

A Mayan Pyramid; all that remains of the once powerful Mayan civilization are ruins.

could strike at any time. If the society was near the point where it could not sustain itself, it would not take a vast natural disaster to lead to a sudden collapse.

The mystery is, what happened? Why did this society suddenly disappear around 900 C.E., after centuries of building a culture to rival those of the great civilizations of the Old World? The answer might lie in their agricultural system. Unlike some Old World cultures, the Mayans could not rely on the swidden system of slash and burn, moving on to a new field when the land that they had been using lost its productivity. Not enough land was available once the population reached a certain level. The same land had to be used again and again. Unlike other agricultural civilizations in lands with inadequate soil, hunting and fishing could not have provided enough food to make up the shortfalls from crops. And, without suitable animals to domesticate, farming was the only viable alternative.

There are other possible explanations for the sudden failure of the Mayan civilization, including destructive civil wars or invasions. However, these might just have been the ultimate push to a society unable to sustain itself.

The Common Pattern

Human civilizations emerged from hunting and gathering groups all over the world at different times. The general pattern followed was that the population of a hunter-gatherer group would slowly rise to where the land could not support it. Some members of the group would break away and seek other lands to live in. But a time would come when, even with emigrants leaving, the numbers were too great for hunting and gathering to support the population that would not or, in the case of people stranded on islands, could not go elsewhere.

Slowly, over perhaps more than a thousand years, some lands would begin to be cleared for the purpose of growing edible plants that could feed greater numbers. And, as has been seen again and again, when more than enough food is grown to support a population, no matter what population limiting practices are in place, that population grows to meet the food supply. This leads to greater dependence on grown crops and a slow transition to an agricultural state, from which there is no return.

But then, along with that came everything we treasure as the essence of human civilization. The surplus food at any given time freed certain members of society from the duty of providing food and allowed them to become specialists, providing tools and implements, or taking over part food preparation duties, or clothing manufacture, or any other trade. The surplus also had to be managed, leading to a more elaborate organization of society with a bureaucracy to organize and run it, followed by inevitable social stratification. With this organization came the necessity for record keeping, out of which writing emerged.

The surplus represented wealth, since it made all these aspects of civilization possible. Wealth had to be protected, so professional armies were formed to keep external threats at bay and police the local community. With armies came the possibility of significant wars between states; with a local police power came the possibility of coercion, dictatorships, enslavement, and an imposed social structure.

All of this was the basis for civilization. Having achieved a level of political structure and then built upon that a complex and marvelous enterprise, it was natural that human beings focused their attention on those institutions and their interactions instead of on the extraordinary relationship with their environments that had made this possible and which should not have been taken for granted. But taking it for granted was exactly what happened, and all the while the environment was being further and further stretched and more and more was required of it to support human life.

The Ziggurat at Ur. Ur was once the capital of a prosperous empire surrounded by fertile soil; now it stands alone in the center of a vast desert. The very same farming techniques that allowed for the prosperity of the Sumerian civilization soon led to this disastrous decline in the quality of the soil.

Chapter 10

Sustaining Civilizations

The basic situation is easily stated: all forms of life interact with the environment. The environmental balance of any ecosystem depends on all the elements of the environment, both the physical components and the living species. In order for the ecosystem to function smoothly, all species must neither exceed nor fall below a certain ideal number. Too many or too few at any point up or down the food chain will disrupt the conditions of the other elements and potentially damage the ecosystem permanently. Too many of a predator can destroy the prey on which they subsist. Too few predators and the prey population gets out of control. These are the facts of life on Earth everywhere.

Human populations have a somewhat different relationship to the ecosystems of the world, because we have managed to make our way into all of them, and, with our superior technology, turned ecosystems to serve human goals. Our success in doing so has been disruptive. Because of our technology, we have defeated our natural enemies wherever we have met them, be they larger and stronger predators or, the greater threat, microorganisms. The result is that our numbers have continued to grow and grow. The more of us there are, the more demands we make on the rest of the ecosystems in which we live, and the more those systems are thrown out of balance.

And the more successful human beings are at making a more comfortable and prosperous civilization, the more pressure is put on the environment. Fighting starvation and curing disease only adds to our total population. Building great cities and using technology to improve the standard of living is done at the cost of using up finite natural resources and producing much more waste products than the environment can recycle. In short, human civilizations are destructive to environments. There do not seem to be any exceptions to this rule.

Agriculture is Destructive

The greatest and most fundamental step that humans have made in building civilizations is the change from hunting and gathering to farming and animal husbandry. It has been destructive right from the start and continues to become more destructive in each generation.

Planting a field involves clearing the natural growth from an area, which may have taken thousands of years to settle into a stable ecosystem. Almost invariably, what had been a variety of plants growing in an area is replaced by one or two crops that make the same demands on the soil and are all vulnerable to the same blights and diseases. Harvesting a field all at once leaves the loose soil exposed to winds and rain, which can easily blow or wash away the rich topsoil on which crops depend. The normal regeneration process that is provided by the variety of plants natural to the area is disrupted. Farming the same crop season after season in the same plot of land is only possible with the introduction of fertilizers to restore the soil. But any fertilizer, including animal manure, puts a strain on part of the soil system while it restores its short-term ability to grow crops.

Dry farming was bad enough, but early civilizations quickly found that much greater yields were possible on land that was artificially irrigated. Areas that are not accustomed to absorbing so much water may not react well to irrigation. Only so much water is absorbed into the soil. The rest runs off or sinks into the water table. That which runs off can carry away the best part of the soil with it. That which sinks into the water table can cause the table to rise so much that the soil itself becomes waterlogged and no longer suitable for crops.

Water from rivers and streams naturally contains a high mineral content. Depositing the water on the soil deposits those minerals as well, often in concentrations much too high for the health of the soil. The worst in this regard is salt. In hotter and dryer climates much of the irrigated water will evaporate, leaving behind the minerals in greater concentrations. Many important food crops cannot grow, or do so very poorly, in soil with a high salt content.

Another problem is that we tend to clump together into towns and cities, increasing our population density and speeding up the devastation of the area.

Sumer

The earliest human civilization that we have records from was Sumer in Mesopotamia. Naturally, it has been the subject of considerable study by archæologists, who can examine both the physical remains and many written records preserved in cuneiform tablets. Sumer has been a puzzle to archæologists because the records refer to a rich, fertile environment with dense growth, just as one would expect in an area where farming was first found to be viable. Yet the present landscape in the immediate vicinity of the remains of Sumer itself is barren and desolate.

The archæologist Leonard Woolley was one of the excavators of the Sumerian city of Ur. In a book he wrote about his work on Ur, he expressed his amazement at the contrast between the written records and the situation as he found it:

> Only to those who have seen the Mesopotamian desert will the evocation of the ancient world seem well-nigh incredible, so complete is the contrast is between past and present...it is yet more difficult to realize, that the blank waste ever blossomed, bore fruit for the sustenance of a busy world. Why, if Ur was an empire's capital, if Sumer was once a vast granary, has the population dwindled to nothing, the very soil lost its virtue?[1]

What Woolley did not appreciate was that the very nature of the Sumerian society itself destroyed its own environment through a combination of over-cultivation and deforestation.

The source of the water in Sumer that made farming possible was the runoff of the spring meltdown in the mountains to the north that fed the Tigris and the Euphrates rivers. The water level was highest in the spring and lowest in the fall, but the crops grown required water most in the fall. The solution was to store water for later use. This ingenious technological solution is what made possible the abundant yields for which Sumer was known. But only for a time.

The water stored for later use was still subject to natural evaporation, especially in the hot arid climate of Mesopotamia. By the time that stored water was put on the soil, its salt content was much greater than it otherwise would have been. Not only was the soil

---

1. Leonard Wolley, *Ur of the Chaldees*, 1936, quoted in Clive Ponting, *A Green History of the World* (New York: Penguin, 1993), p. 70.

subjected to high doses of salt, it was not able to absorb the water that was directed onto it, leading to waterlogging.

Making the area attractive for farming was one feature of the Tigris and Euphrates Rivers—because the land was so flat these rivers moved quite slowly. This rate of flow allowed the rich silt in the water to be used to fertilize the land instead of being washed out into the Persian Gulf. However, the river drainage was considerably slowed by the human settlements of Sumer as they felled many trees in the highlands to use as construction materials, which allowed more soil erosion, adding to the silt coming downriver and inevitably slowing the runoff even more. The effects of this action were too slow for any one human generation to see, but archæologists can calculate that the extra silt added a depth of nearly 2 meters to the area and extended the delta of the Tigris and the Euphrates by about 25 kilometers every millennium. Waterlogging brought even more salt to the surface. Soon the land could not grow the crops it needed.

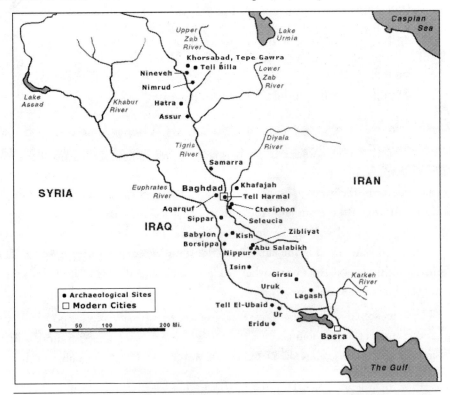

Mesopotamia. This map shows the location of ancient sites and modern cities. Sumer was located in the south at the junction of the Tigris and the Euphrates rivers.

Here are the factors that led inevitably to the destruction of the Sumerian society: Mesopotamia was a restricted area. Only land near enough to the rivers could be used for agriculture. But the land was fertile and the population steadily increased. The more complex the society became, the more people there were who did not do the farming, but needed to be fed, for example, bureaucrats and the military. Moreover, the eight cities of Sumer engaged in a certain amount of competition among themselves for the best level of prosperity and rate of growth. All of this made their requirement for food grow exponentially. There was not time to consider alternate ways of producing food. Intensive agricultural methods with irrigation produced results and were adopted.

We know so much more about Sumer than any earlier human settlements, because of the invention of writing there around 3000 B.C.E. The earliest written records are mostly concerned with the details of the economic system and so are a great help in understanding how people lived and produced their food. For Sumerian farming, the proportion of wheat to barley is telling. Wheat can only grow in soil that is one-half of one percent salt or less. Barley can tolerate up to a full percent of salt. Evidence suggests that around 3500 B.C.E. Sumerians grew about equal amounts of wheat and barley, but by 2500 wheat was down to 15% of the total crop, and by 1700 no wheat was being grown at all.

As everywhere else, when soils became unproductive, fields were abandoned and cultivation was done elsewhere. But this can continue only when there are fresh lands to cultivate and when the population density is below a certain level . When all of the land has ceased to produce the necessary crops, the civilization fails. Sumer itself fell in 2370 B.C.E. to the invading Akkadians. For the next 600 years it was conquered and reconquered until by 1800 B.C.E. it was finally annexed by the growing Babylonian empire.

Deforestation is Inevitable

There is hardly a human civilization anywhere in an area near a forest that has not caused a major change to the size or nature of the forest, unless, perhaps the population of the community is tiny compared to the size of the forest. Wood is a most versatile material. It can be used for construction. It can be burnt for warmth in the winter. It can be used for cooking fires. And so, forests are immensely valuable resources.

At the same time, forests are sometimes viewed as a nuisance, since trees prevent an area from being used for farmland. The rate at which forests near human communities have been cleared since the beginning of permanent settlement has been controlled more by the technology available to the settlers than by any sense of the value of the trees as a resource.

The process is nonetheless a slow one, not particularly noticeable in the lifetime of individuals (except in recent years). But over many generations, the combined effects can be a major disaster: areas that were densely forested become treeless, and with that the soil loosens and blows away, making the land useless.

China

A bend in the Yellow River. The light colour of the water is from eroded soil being washed downstream.

China, for example, lost most of its forests in the northern highlands where the original settlements were located. This included the areas around the Yellow River, land that provided most of the food for the country. As more and more of the grasslands were cleared for millet crops and more of the surrounding hillsides were cleared of trees, the soil became more vulnerable to being washed or blown away. As the banks of the river became more eroded, floods became more of a problem, eventually leading to a series of disasters. Deforestation and erosion were slow processes involving many generations and beginning thousands of years ago. In fact, the "Yellow River" is named for its colour, which is the result of the large amount of eroded soil that it carries from upstream.

Ethiopia and Charcoal

Modern Ethiopia.

China's problems with the Yellow River took millennia to manifest themselves. But rapid changes can also take place when political events alter the usage of a region, and nothing prevents over-exploitation of the local resources. For example, in Ethiopia, when Addis Ababa became the capital in 1883, it was surrounded by dense forest. Within a mere twenty years, a zone stretching for 150 kilometers around the town had been completely stripped of trees by charcoal burners making fuel to be used in the capital.

Charcoal burners have been a particular menace in the last several hundred years. Wood burns at too low a temperature to be useful for many industrial needs involving high temperatures and blast furnaces. However, it is possible to make a product out of wood—charcoal—that does burn at high temperatures. This is done by roasting the wood slowly in a controlled environment with very little oxygen. The remaining "coals" will burn at much higher temperatures, making many industrial processes possible. But it takes a vast amount of wood to make a small amount of charcoal. Still, if the wood in the forests is "free," charcoal burners can make a living by felling huge numbers of trees.

The Mediterranean

Sometimes it is not obvious to us even now that an area we take for granted has actually been devastated by deforestation. Consider the Mediterranean, where the typical fields contain olive trees, vines, low bushes, and herbs. Indeed, much of the cuisine of the Mediterranean has been based on these crops that grow naturally in the fields. Yet the fields themselves are the result of serious deforestation that occurred in this particular landscape. The natural vegetation in the region was forest, both evergreen and deciduous. But as human populations settled the area, that forest was slowly cleared to provide farming land, fuel, and construction materials. Once the trees were removed, the soil began to erode. Silt built up in the rivers and was carried downstream, blocking watercourses and causing large deltas to form. Then, the other side of agriculture took over: animal husbandry. Sheep, goats, and cattle were set to graze on the cleared land, making it impossible for the soil to regenerate. Only about 10% of the original forests from Morocco to Afghanistan that stood in 2000 B.C.E. remain standing today.

In the classical period of antiquity, Phoenician merchants became known for their trade in the cedars of Lebanon. These trees, much prized for their great height and straightness, could be used as building materials for a number of special purposes. The cedars became famous as a landmark of Lebanon. In time, almost all of the cedar forests were destroyed. Today, only four small groves are left in Lebanon, maintained for their symbolic value.

Ancient Greece suffered the same fate. Starting about 650 B.C.E., Greek civilization began to grow and fill in the countryside. The natural terrain of Greece did not have much land suitable for cultivation. Instead, the Greeks used a greater percentage of their land for grazing. But grazing was devastating for marginal land that barely maintained its topsoil at the best of times. The inevitable deforestation was disastrous to the countryside, as has been well documented in several ancient Greek writers, including

Herodotus, Xenophon, and Aristotle. The most famous reference to the devastation is from Plato's dialogue, *Critias:*

> What now remains compared with what then existed is like the skeleton of a sick man, all the fat and soft earth having wasted away, and only the bare framework of the land being left...there are some mountains which now have nothing but food for bees, but they had trees not very long ago...there were many lofty trees of cultivated species and...boundless pasturage for flocks. Moreover, it was enriched by the yearly rains from Zeus, which were not lost to it, as now, by flowing from the bare land into the sea; but the soil it had was deep, and therein it received the water, storing it up in the retentive loamy soil, and...provided all the various districts with abundant supplies of springwaters and streams, whereof the shrines still remain even now, at the spots where the fountains formerly existed.[1]

The Roman Empire

What happened in Greece happened on a considerably larger scale in the Roman Empire, where the consequences may have been critical factors in the fall of the empire. Due to the deforestation that accompanied the rise of the Roman Empire in Italy, its topsoil washed away, its rivers began to silt up, and its fields became less and less productive for crops. The authorities in Rome began to lean on their far-flung provinces to supply food for the capital.

An example is the great north African city of Leptis Magna in what is now Libya. This once rich and productive area became a supplier of food and wood to Rome. But the soils in this area were marginal at best. When the trees were removed, the land quickly became unproductive, and then was used as pastureland until it turned to desert, which it is today. There are similar stories in other provinces of the Roman Empire. Whether these were critical factors in the fall of Rome is too difficult to say, but it certainly is plausible that an empire that ceased to be able to feed itself should weaken and be easily overrun.

---

1.   Plato, *Critias,* 111b-d. The speaker is Critias.

The ruins of Leptis Magna, one of the great centers of the Roman Empire located in present-day Libya. Vast deserts now surround it.

Too Much Growth Too Fast

From the vantage point of the present, we can look back on the ancient empires that spanned centuries or even millennia and see patterns that we cannot see in more recent civilizations. We can see the slow change from one way of life to another, the steady building of a higher standard of living, a more reliable supply of food, and better defences against external enemies. With this prosperity, generally comes population growth—slow at first, but then picking up speed at a rate that soon will use up any accumulated surplus wealth. Inevitably, the population will grow faster than the increases in the food supply necessary to maintain, let alone, increase the standard of living. For those that can expand, migration spreads the culture to new lands, which is how the entire Earth came to have people living in it. Those groups unable to expand into other lands to relieve the demand on the territory that sustains them are pushed closer and closer to an unstable state where they are vulnerable to calamity.

Top: The Forbidden City, center of the Chinese empire.
Below: *The Battle of San Romano: Niccolò da Tolentino at the Head of the Florentines*, by Paolo Uccello.

Chapter 11

China versus Europe

The most powerful and fundamental determinant in the course of human history is the struggle for food. That first major change in human living conditions brought on by the development of agriculture was an answer to the pressing need to get more food out of existing lands. Farming was neither easier nor necessarily more nutritious nor more reliable than hunting and gathering, but did produce more food out of a given area of land. But then the population quickly grew to where farming just barely produced the necessary food for the rising population. In short, for most of human history—up to the last 200 years or so—almost everyone lived on the brink of starvation all the time.

Human life was characterized by high infant mortality, low life expectancy, chronic undernourishment, and the ever-present threat of famine and epidemics. About 95% of the people in the world were peasants—directly dependent on the land.

Very little meat was eaten; almost all food was vegetable in origin. In Asia, the staple was rice; in America, it was maize; in Europe, it was a combination of wheat, oats, and rye. All the practices of agriculture increased the vulnerability of the people. Reliance on a very small number of crops increased the danger of crop failure due to adverse weather or disease. And continuous cultivation lowered the fertility of the soil. The population, of course, was much lower than what it is today, but still it grew to meet the food supply whenever there was a surplus.

It was therefore necessary to put as much land to use as possible. The more land that was devoted to crops, the less there was for pasture. However, without a sufficient supply of domestic animals to produce a supply of manure, the soil deteriorated faster. Even when there was a good crop, its utilization could not be guaranteed. There were limited facilities to store grain, which attracted rodents and was subject to a high rate of spoilage. Getting a harvested crop to where it was to be consumed was difficult without transportation facilities that, to be sure, did not exist until the last 200 years or so. Therefore, food could only be eaten locally. A very limited market existed for exported food, except for some items that had little bulk and stored well, such as spices. But spices cannot prevent starvation. If crops failed in one area but were successful in another, the surplus from one area could not be transported effectively to the other.

Until improvements were made to agricultural technology during the Industrial Revolution in the 18th and 19th centuries, it was difficult to increase the yield of crops significantly. Meanwhile, the population of the world continued to grow.

Balancing Population Growth and Food Supply

Although we are only too familiar with the current problem of runaway world population growth, it is often not realized that this phenomenon has been with us since the dawn of humanity. However, an important difference between the modern problem and the ancient growth pattern is that, in earlier times, the growth was generally checked by the available food supply or knocked down by epidemics and famines. Reliable censuses of the world became available only in the last few hundred years, so all earlier figures are estimates based on indirect information and subject to a large margin of error. Nevertheless, a common pattern seems clear enough: The general world population grew

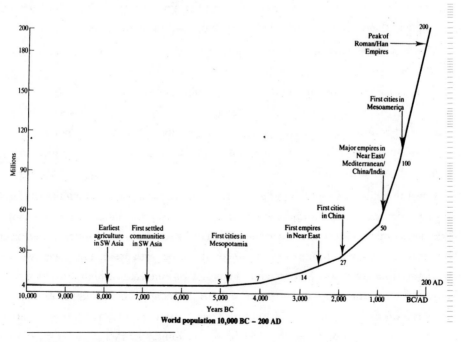

World population from 10,000
B.C.E. to 200 C.E. From Clive Ponting, *A Green History of the World*, p. 90.

slowly, because the food supply grew slowly. Nevertheless, during periods of prosperity, the population shot up, and when disasters occurred, it pulled back suddenly. The result is an exponential growth pattern similar to today's, but at a slower rate and with more deviations.

When agriculture was first adopted, the total human population of the world was about four million people. For comparison, this is the population of the Greater Toronto Area. It then doubled roughly every thousand years to 50 million by 1000 B.C.E. This is the current population of, say, Tokyo and Mexico City combined. Then the rate of population growth picked up a notch and doubled twice more to 200 million by 200 C.E., around the peak of the Roman and Han empires. This is approximately the present population of Pakistan. However, then the great empires declined, more instability occurred, and as a result, the population leveled out until about the year 1000, the traditional end of what is referred to as the Dark Ages in Europe. Though all of the world had to cope with balancing population with food supply, distinctive differences can be seen in different parts of the world as to how this was accomplished, because of both the social structure and the natural environment.

This chapter will contrast the struggles to provide an adequate food supply in two different regions of the world during the period from roughly 500 C.E. to 1500, that is, the Dark Ages and the Middle Ages, to use the reference points in European history. These regions, China and Europe, both changed dramatically during this thousand-year period. How they changed and where their relative economic and political positions stood at the end of that period have led to remarkably different social and economic conditions today.

The Chinese Solution

Chinese society was both highly stratified, with a ruling elite and a large peasant class, and highly centralized. Decisions were made from a central authority and imposed on the whole vast country. Until around 200 C.E., the center of the Chinese state was in the north. Farming was mostly in the Yellow River valley, with millet and rice grown as a dry crop. One of the main tasks of the elite was to assure an adequate supply of food from the peasants to maintain both themselves and the army, which was also stationed mostly in the north.

When the Han empire collapsed in 220 C.E., the center of the empire was pushed further south, toward the Yangtze River, which became the main grain producing area. When China was reunified in 589, it became necessary to transport large amounts of food north to the military and government centers.

The Grand Canal.

To accomplish this, in the 7th century, the Chinese built an extraordinary waterway, the Grand Canal, which extended from the southern farming areas almost 2000 kilometers north to the capital in Beijing. On its waters 400 000 tonnes of grain were shipped north each year. One of the major problems for the Chinese was providing defence against the raiding nomadic tribes in northern Asia; to this end they maintained a very large army, which required a great deal of provisions. By the 11th century, an army of one million soldiers was fed from grain shipped up the Grand Canal—an extraordinary burden on the peasantry, but one that was necessary for the protection of the country.

Wet Rice Production

The farmland in the south was more productive because of a new technique that revolutionized agriculture in China. This was the technique of wet farming in paddy fields. Rice was a successful, if not spectacular, crop when grown on the rich loess plains of the north, but the same methods were unsuccessful in the south, which had poorer soils. That is, until a new method of farming in the tropical soils that kept the cropland continuously under water. The technique actually appeared as early as 500 B.C.E. in southeast Asia, but it spread very slowly into other parts of the continent.

An urban rice paddy.

It was not an easy technique, requiring a great deal of management and resources. Adopted in southern China around the year 400 C.E., it made possible the support of so many from what was marginal soil. The key was to have a large quantity of water moving slowly over the fields. This encouraged the growth of algae, which fixed nitrogen from the atmosphere, thereby restoring one of the chief lacks in the soil. The water cover also allowed a large amount of organic matter, both vegetable waste and manures (animal and human), to rot in the water. Continual tramping through the fields by animals and farmers pushed the nutrients into the soil. Altogether, this method of farming produced huge increases in yields over what would have been available in the same land by other means. But, and this is a key point about the Chinese approach to so many tasks, it required enormous amounts of human labour.

Intensive Farming, Intensive Labour

Between the 4th century and the 13th century, the Chinese solution to feeding its steadily rising population was to adopt a system of farming that made very heavy use of the land, bombarding it with more nutrients. It also made heavy demands on the farmers for backbreaking labour. But it produced results. In addition, the Chinese developed new varieties of quicker growing rice that allowed for two crops per year in both the south and the north. They also developed sophisticated techniques for land management and preservation. For example, they practiced crop rotation, which Europe adopted only much later. They also invented advanced farming tools, such as the seed drill that placed a small amount of seed carefully under the top layer of soil where it had a much higher chance of germinating than seeds that were merely scattered.

China Hits Its Carrying Capacity

By 1200 China was the largest, most literate, and most advanced country in the world. Its population grew from 50 million to 115 million in the early 13th century. The Chinese story is a perfect example of the problem of growth in a finite world, aided by human ingenuity. Every improvement in farming brought a temporary increase in the per capita food supply, but that was quickly used up by increases in the population. The Chinese system of paddy fields had yields that were about as high as possible before the introduction of artificial fertilizers. The population increased so much that most of the areas that were fertile enough to grow crops were already densely populated. In a familiar problem met elsewhere, so much land was needed for

A lion in the Forbidden City.

growing crops that not enough land was left to keep domestic animals, which would provide manure needed for fertilizer. The population was reaching the limit of what the land could support and became vulnerable to unexpected shocks.

These shocks, when they came, took several different forms: There was the Mongol invasion that killed 35 million people, mostly in the north. There were massive epidemics in 1586-89 and 1639-44, each of which killed one-fifth of the population. Then, after 1600, there were no more increases in yields from lands under cultivation. The amount of land cultivated rose, but the amount of food available per person was the same in 1850 as it had been in 1550. The result is that throughout this period, the majority of the population of the country lived on the brink of starvation.

Europe's Muddle

One of the goals of this book is to show how environmental opportunities and challenges have helped to shape living conditions and political and economic affiliations throughout the world today. Why are the western countries rich compared to those in the east? Why did Europe colonize the world instead of China?

Part of the answer to these questions may come, paradoxically enough, from the vastly inferior condition of the farmland in Europe and the chaotic organization of society after the fall of Rome. Unlike China, which was able to find a fertile land, produce enormous amounts of food, and ship it thousands of kilometers to feed large standing armies, Europe had neither the soil nor the political clout to use resources in an organized way.

While the soil in the Mediterranean area was suitable for farming some crops, as soon as one went a distance north, into the body of Central Europe, the soil became very heavy and laden with clay. Nutrients that did exist in the soil were easily washed out in summer rains. The little productive topsoil there was eroded easily. Any arable land that was found that was farmed over and over, eventually using up its fertility without replacing the necessary nutrients. The only practical way to maintain fertility was with animal manure, but unlike warmer climates where grazing was still possible in the winter, in the snow and ice covered lands of northern and central Europe a store of feed had to be laid in for the winter. Because the poor soil also made it difficult to grow suitable fodder, the number of animals that could be maintained was necessarily limited. Many animals had to be slaughtered every fall for lack of food for the winter.

It was a classic vicious circle: fewer animals led to less manure, which led to lower productivity in the fields, which led to less fodder for the animals, which led to even fewer animals next year. Europe also failed to adopt the technological improvements that had become common in the Orient, such as tilling implements and crop rotation. The result was that, compared to China, Europe kept a smaller number of people on the verge of starvation through the period from the onset of the Dark Ages till the 14th century.

The Heavy Plough

The agricultural technology that had worked so well in the Fertile Crescent and then in the Mediterranean area employed a simple plough to turn the soil before sowing seed. The simple plough, or "scratch plough" was essentially a sharpened stick that was drawn across the ground at an angle. Later versions of it had a triangular metal share at the end, was attached to handles that allowed the farmer to guide it, and was pulled by a pair of oxen in harness. This was effective in the loose soils of the south, though the fields generally had to be cross-ploughed at right angles to turn over enough soil and bring the subsoil to the surface. But these ploughs simply wouldn't do the job in the heavier northern soil. Even two oxen were not enough to pull the share through the ground, and even if they could, it would not break up the soil enough to make it fertile.

A major breakthrough came around the 6th century with the introduction of the heavy plough, a much different implement that could lift an entire layer of soil and turn it completely over, breaking it up. The plough had a curved blade that got under the soil and lifted it onto a mouldboard, which flipped it over. It was often mounted on a wheeled chassis for stability. With the heavy plough came a whole transformation of the society. To begin with, the heavy plough required about eight oxen to pull it

The heavy plough, from an illuminated manuscript.

through the tough ground. No simple farmer could afford to keep eight oxen all year. To use such a plough, farmers had to join together into small groups that would pool their resources, jointly owning the plough, sharing their oxen, and making decisions collectively. Thus began small collectives that evolved into the manorial system of feudal Europe. Small, independent groups of people lived in harmony with each other, making a living out of the land, thanks to a piece of technology that bound them together. It took roughly 400 years for the heavy plough to come into general usage across Europe.

Three-Field Crop Rotation

There are other important features of this as well. The earlier system of farming, practiced in southern Europe, used a two-field system of crop rotation. A farmer would sow one field in a season and leave a second one fallow. Then, the next season the fields would be reversed. Only half of the tilled land was in use at any one time. In the 8th century another innovation spread across Europe: three-field rotation. Medieval historian Lynn White describes the difference as follows:

> Under the three-field plan the arable was divided roughly into thirds. One section was planted in the autumn with winter wheat or rye. The following spring the second field was planted with oats, barley, peas, chickpeas, lentils, or broad beans. The third field was left fallow. The next year the first field was planted to summer crops; the second was left fallow; the third field was put into winter grains.[1]

Three-field rotation produced tremendous increases in productivity. This technique combined with the switch to using horses as draft animals instead of oxen, once a proper horse harness had been invented, resulted in a dramatic jump in the amount of available food per capita. It can be compared to the switch to paddy-field rice production in China. And it had a similar effect: a brief, glorious rise in wealth represented by surplus grain that made other ventures possible, followed by a rapid increase in the population.

Europeans Spread Across the Continent

The chief difference between the social structure in China and in Europe during the Middle Ages was that China had a centralized government while Europe was divided into many small, independent political units. China was organized to fend off the great enemy from the north, the Mongols; Europeans squabbled among themselves and had frequent but less serious conflicts. From the point of view of agriculture, China was organized to get much of its food from the most productive area, near the Yangtze River, and ship it well across the country to feed the ruling elite and the military. Europeans consumed most of their food locally and supported small, primarily defensive home guards.

---

1. Lynn White, Jr., *Medieval Technology and Social Change* (Oxford: Oxford University Press, 1962). p. 69.

As the population began to increase beyond what could be sustained by the produce of the local area, Europeans spread farther afield into areas formerly relegated to nomadic tribes and also began to till more marginal land closer to home. Because of the decentralization in Europe, this took many different forms in different places. Much ingenuity was shown in finding solutions to particular environmental challenges and devising contraptions to help solve problems as they arose. By any measure, the Middle Ages in Europe was a time of tremendous innovation and experimentation, and, of course, population increase.

Europe Gets Close to Its Carrying Capacity

Like China, European populations shot up to meet the surplus food. In the year 1000, Europe's population was about 36 million people. By 1300 it had risen to 80 million. Many parts of Europe became overcrowded. The supply of new land was in effect exhausted. Because more demands were put on existing fields, they were not given time to recover and became less productive. More land had to be put under cultivation, meaning that there was even less land for pasture, and hence fewer domestic animals and less manure to restore the fields. The surplus provided by the changes in farming technology let more people pursue lives other than in farming. As seemed to happen everywhere, other occupations carried a higher social status. Those who were not peasants and did not produce food began to consume more and more of it. The newly risen nobility and the clergy consumed about one-half of all of the output of food, leaving the bulk of the population malnourished. Disaster loomed.

As the 14th century began in Europe, the population was already beginning to fall due to chronic malnourishment. Then came a famine in 1316-1317. With little in the way of stored grain, the casualties were high. The population however remained right at the level where almost everyone was hungry.

Nature's Solution: The Black Death

Then came nature's solution to the problem: a devastating epidemic of bubonic plague, called the Black Death. This is discussed at greater length later in this book. For now, it suffices to note that an estimated one-third of the population of Europe died during the period 1347-1349 from the plague.

Prosperity Follows

Anyplace where fewer people share the same total wealth as another place is relatively richer. When the plague abated, it had killed a great many people but had not destroyed crops, nor (as wars sometimes do) did it destroy the infrastructure on which a society depends. From the late 14th century to the mid-15th century, Europe enjoyed a tremendous boom. There was more of everything to go around, including food.

The result was inevitable: soon there were many more people. By 1600 the population of Europe was near 90 million people, and the overpopulation problem was back in an even bigger way. Once again the growth rate slowed because there was not enough food to go around. Europeans spread further into new areas where the soils were even poorer.

Were China and Europe in the Same Situation?

In both of these scenarios, the two regions, China and Europe, experienced a crisis of insufficient food for the population. In both cases, the regions made technological breakthroughs that solved the supply problem—wet rice production in China, the heavy plough and three-field rotation in Europe. In both cases, the population quickly began to rise to meet the increased food supply and per capita food dropped again to dangerous levels. In both cases, disasters struck that knocked the population back to levels where there was plenty of food to feed the diminished population. Finally, in both cases, each region once again had population increases that brought back the risk of severe malnutrition and vulnerability to shocks.

But there the similarity ends. China's centralized policy continued to make great demands on the peasants, who produced as much as they could. But so long as the population continued to rise, the people edged closer to starvation levels. The wet-field rice production was a great boon, but the extra food it produced translated into extra mouths to feed a few generations later. And China had nowhere to expand to. They could make raids and even take over neighboring countries, which they did from time to time, but policy decisions made many years before put a priority on keeping invaders out, not on going out and finding new virgin lands offshore.

Europe on the other hand did not have a uniform domestic and foreign policy. Whatever seemed to work was reinforced and whatever did not was forgotten. The crisis in Europe occurred at just about the time that Europeans learned to build ocean-going ships that could travel off into strange lands and perhaps bring back treasures and indeed crops. This is the process of world colonization by Europeans, which is the subject of the next chapter.

Chapter 12

European Colonization of the World

What we think of as the basic layout of the modern world by countries, political affiliations, and economic ties is largely the result of Europe's rise to a position of dominance across the globe. It is quite extraordinary that such a backward and disorganized place as Europe should have become the dominant world power instead of far more powerful and well-run empires, such as China and Islam, or more ancient and more populous India.

Like so many other major changes in human history, the need to feed a rising population was the chief motivation for Europe's ventures outside its own boundaries. For most of human history, only the southern part of Europe near the Mediterranean was developed. Agriculture itself developed first in other areas, the Fertile Crescent in particular, and only moved into Europe thousands of years later. Even so, the cultivated lands and the high civilizations were all in or around the Mediterranean Sea: Minoan Crete, Mycenæ in the Greek Peloponesus, the Greek city-states, the Etruscans in Italy, Carthage, and even Alexander the Great's empire. Thereafter, the Roman Empire organized the Mediterranean area and ventured settlements in northern and western Europe. Important as this empire and the others that preceded it in the area were for establishing the social and political institutions that form the backbone of western civilization today, it was still small in its time compared to other parts of the world. For example, in about the year 200 C.E., roughly the height of the Roman Empire, the population of Europe was about 28 million people. But both China and India had at least 50 million people each at that time. Then, when the Roman Empire collapsed over the next couple of hundred years, nomadic tribes quickly invaded northern and western Europe. They destroyed most of the infrastructure, effectively knocking Europe back to a pre-agricultural state. The only advanced civilizations remaining were once again clustered around the Mediterranean: Italy, Greece, and Byzantium.

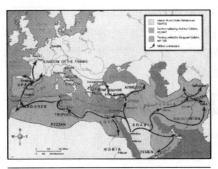

The spread of Islam.

Then, when Islam arose in the Near East in the 7th and 8th centuries, it very quickly became the most sophisticated and advanced civilization west of China. In about 150 years, Islam spread throughout the Middle East, into parts of India, all across the north of Africa, and even into much of Spain. In addition to making a stark comparison with faltering Europe, Islam cut off Europeans from easy travel to Asia and Africa, isolating them even more.

Nevertheless, as discussed in Chapter 11, with the innovations of the heavy plough, three-field rotation, and the manorial system, Europe gained the ability to grow reasonable amounts of food across the continent, form stable societies, and, inevitably, increase its population. The first major increase in population was between the years 1000 and 1300, when the total population of Europe rose from 36 million to 80 million.

Goodbye Forests

Once the most viable land had been put under cultivation, the expanding population had to find other land for crops, so the great forests of Europe began to be cleared. The long-term ecosystem that had been in place in most of northern and western Europe since the Ice Ages was primarily mature temperate forests. At first, the encroachment on forests was by the swidden system of slash and burn, i.e., cut down enough of the forest that a controlled forest fire could finish off the rest within a desired area. The charred remains of the trees and underbrush would provide enough natural fertilizer that crops would grow readily for a number of years in the newly cleared field. Then, when the land became less productive, it would be abandoned and another part of the forest would be cleared. The original land would be allowed to regrow as forest, which would take several decades. On average, the same land would be used only about four times per century. This system was practical only where the population density was low relative to the amount of forest available. In the more densely populated areas, forests were destroyed more quickly and never given the opportunity to recover.

Also, as iron tools became more common, blast furnaces came into greater use for smelting. Charcoal was found to be the ideal fuel to achieve the high temperatures needed in a blast furnace, so vast amounts of climax forestland were cut down to make charcoal. Either way, for the use of the trees or just to clear the land for farming, most of Europe's forests were destroyed during the medieval period. Altogether, this took several centuries, so no one generation would notice much difference. Nonetheless, Europe went from 95% forested land to 20% in no more than 500 years.

By about 1200, most of the productive soils in western Europe had been cleared of forest and put under cultivation. Any new settlements had to make do with heavy clay or sandy soil, neither of which made for good crops.

In Eastern Europe, the process was more that of one people driving another off their land. The Germanic people, who had become farmers, invaded lands that had been occupied by Slavs. The emphasis in the Slav culture was on animal husbandry, so they had been more concerned with grazing land than with cropland. They had used the swidden system successfully because of their lower population density. When the Germans moved in, bringing the heavy plough, huge stretches of forest were cleared.

There was no question in their minds about the advisability of clearing forests. No one saw any particular use for them. Forests just got in the way of agriculture. One of the new German settlements of the 13th century was Fellarich, whose abbot wrote "I believe that the forest which adjoins Fellarich covers the land to no purpose, and hold this to be an unbearable harm."[1]

A Stumble and a Restart

By the beginning of the 14th century, the expansion into new areas slowed to a halt. The weather had changed for the worse; the soils everywhere were being overused. The population was at the limit of what the land could sustain. Some significant famines occurred in the early decades of the century, and then the Black Death hit in mid-century wiping out a third of the population of Europe.

Though Europe saw a tremendous surge of prosperity in the 100 years or so after the Black Death cleared, this took place in a very different environment from what had been the case in 1200, when the population was at about the same level. Much of the soil had been depleted to the point where it was less productive. The weather had turned colder, slowing growth and reducing harvests. And, there were far fewer forests to clear for new land.

---

1.   Quoted in Clive Ponting, *A Green History of the World: The Environment and the Collapse of Great Civilizations.* (New York: Penguin, 1993), p. 123.

Making New Land At Home

Soon, Europe would be looking beyond its borders for new lands to conquer, but before then, there were some remarkable efforts made to bring the environment to heel and provide the sustenance required for the advancing and prospering civilization. The most extraordinary of these were the drainage projects that began in the Netherlands.

The Netherlands are so named because much of the country, about 40 percent, is below sea level. In its natural state, the Netherlands was basically swampland and marshes. But below the water level was fertile soil that could produce abundant crops, if only it could be made dry enough to farm. At first, most of the effort was to reclaim land at the coasts, done by building up islands in river estuaries. In the 16th century, the Dutch began a process of draining their hinterlands. To do this they had to be able to pump tremendous amounts of water out of swampland, and to succeed they required a source of power greater than either human or animal muscle. Their solution, perfectly suited to the windy area that is Holland, was windmills. However, windmills cost a great deal to build and maintain. Think of them as comparable to sizeable generating stations of today.

Raising the money to build these windmills and then using them to drain the marshes was one of the largest capital projects of the 16th and 17th centuries. It became the model for the way to raise money for capital intensive public works projects. One lake, Lake Beemster, was drained in 1612. The project required 43 windmills in order to drain 4 meters of depth over a 63 square kilometer surface. The result was 7,000 hectares of fertile land. Nearly 160,000 hectares were reclaimed in the hundred years between 1550 and 1650, and the process still goes on. Some of the reclamation projects themselves took centuries to complete. From the 13th century to the present, the Dutch created about 1 million hectares of usable land out of marshes and the sea.

The success of the Dutch at making new farmland in their own backyard was followed elsewhere in Europe, often using Dutch expertise. A particularly notorious example of this was the draining of the fens in England. The British, wishing to create new farmland in the southeast of the country, began an extensive project in the 17th

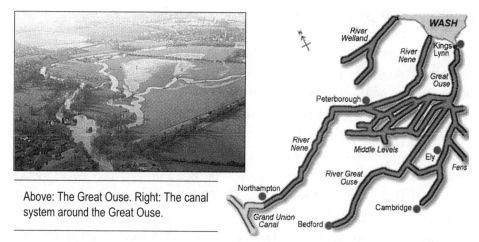

Above: The Great Ouse. Right: The canal system around the Great Ouse.

century, and hired the Dutch engineer, Cornelius Vermuyden, to manage the project. The center of drainage was to be the Great Ouse River, which itself was diverted for 33 kilometers. Many canals were dug to drain into the Great Ouse or one of the other natural rivers that empty into the bay known as the Wash.

At first these projects were viewed as great technological successes, making nature serve human purposes. But the euphoria did not last long. No allowance had been made for what would happen to the land once the water had been drained. Since much of it was peat moss, it began to shrink, with the result that the ground level was now below the level of the rivers, making levees necessary. Also, the drainage canals and the rivers they drained into built up a great amount of silt, which was then dumped into the Wash. The effect of that was that the coastline of the Wash was extended by five kilometers. This was not the only one of Vermuyden's projects to go awry. He was in charge of several others around England, some of which were just abandoned. The Fens project was continued and still exists today, though it requires a great deal of maintenance. In the rest of Europe, the record is spotty. Some projects worked, others failed outright, some provided partial solutions.

Europe's Position at the Beginning of the Renaissance

The term "Renaissance" – rebirth – puts European history in a certain light vis-à-vis its origins and future direction. What was "reborn" in Europe in the early 15th century were the artistic and cultural elements of the ancient Greek and Roman civilizations, that had been lost for about 1000 years. Western Europe suddenly became aware of treasures of a cultural tradition that they had been cut off from after the fall of Rome and the later rise of Islam. Much of the relics of the ancient civilization that was reborn in the minds of Western Europeans had been in the custody of the Byzantine Empire and in the libraries of the Muslim world. Byzantine scholars fearing the imminent fall of their empire to the Ottoman Turks left their country to find refuge in Italy, bringing with them their libraries. Some of the abortive Crusades by European Christians into Muslim-held territory discovered that a vast culture existed there unlike anything they could aspire to—but astoundingly, much of it was originally of Latin or Greek origin. This certainly gave Europeans much to think about and new ideals to aspire to.

It did not do much to feed them, however. The Byzantine Empire collapsed with the fall of Constantinople to the Ottoman Turks in 1453. The Ottoman conquest extended the range of Islam from southeast Europe, through the Middle East and across northern Africa, effectively cutting off Europeans from land and inland sea journeys in both directions. In the 13th century, the Mongol tribes that had worried the Chinese for so long extended their influence westward to the Oder River and nearly extended that into Eastern Europe itself. Soon they were to control more land than any other empire in the world. Even the Chinese were pushing outward with huge ships exploring the coasts of India and Africa.

Although Europe had a new-found identity and much optimism, compared to other political groupings in the world it was a disorganized mess and was effectively blocked off from most of the possibly useful travel in the known world. But Europeans did have one very important technological innovation that proved to make all the difference. They had developed viable ocean-going ships, the Caravel and the Carrack. What made these great innovations was that they could both handle rough seas and navigate well.

Formerly, European countries had built some largish ocean-going vessels that moved along readily enough when the wind was behind them, but were not at all adept at moving against the prevailing wind. This made it very difficult and precarious to use these ships for anything other than very well known and reliable routes, preferably close to shore. Meanwhile, a different kind of sailing vessel had been developed in the Islamic countries where the waters to be navigated were primarily lakes and rivers, where heavy seas were unlikely, but very mild breezes might be all that was available as a motive force,

Left: A carrack. Above. A caravel.

and not necessarily in the desired direction. The European innovation was to take the best of both of these designs and make a totally new ship from them. The large European ships had what were called "square" sails (actually rectangular), which caught the wind well and moved the ship along. The smaller boats from Northern Africa and the Middle East had triangular sails, which had the virtue that they could be maneuvered in such a way as to catch a bit of the wind from any direction and move the boat where it was wanted to go. The European Caravels and Carracks combined these, putting the "square" sails on the front and middle masts and putting triangular sails (called, incongruously, "Lateen" sails, though there was nothing Latin about them) on the rear mast. This, along with a keel and a sternpost rudder, made an ocean-going vessel that could go anywhere.

Go West, Righteously

By the late 15th century, the following factors were all in place. Europeans had the desire to expand their influence and reclaim the glory of classical antiquity that was "rightly" theirs. They had developed the technology to sail ships almost anywhere. They found it extremely difficult to make their way around the known world because they were surrounded by huge empires that were at least perceived to be hostile to them. And, among the treasurers of the old world that became part of the Renaissance were maps by ancient Greeks, in particular by Claudius Ptolemy. These laid out the whole world on paper in a fashion that made sense and fit what was already known; some hardy explorers, Christopher Columbus, for one, were emboldened to trust them to guide him out where no one had gone before. Viewed thusly, it seems almost inevitable that some intrepid explorers representing their home countries and financial backers, would venture across the Atlantic with the goal of reaching the orient by going west.

As we know, before any explorers did manage to get to the east by going west, they ran into another pair of continents that blocked their way around the globe. But that was a greater bonanza for the European explorers, for what they found was rich, virtually untouched land with resources that Europe had not seen for centuries. This "New World" was in its apparently virgin state because not very many people lived in it, and those who did were far behind the Europeans in technological advancement. For example, when the Spanish explorers came to the Caribbean and then on to Central America at the beginning of the 16th century, they encountered the Aztec and the Inca empires, the highest civilizations in the region. But from the point of view of technology, these people were living in a Stone Age, roughly 3000 years behind the Europeans. The Spanish were few in number compared to the residents of the New World, but there was no question that the Spanish would win any conflict.

This raises the question, why should there have been any conflict? Why was it inevitable that the Spanish explorers would arrive in a new land, populated by people who they have never seen before and proceed to slaughter them? An explanation for that also comes out of the Renaissance in Europe. Not only did Europeans gain knowledge of their lost past, they also forged a new image of themselves, from a combination of Judeo-

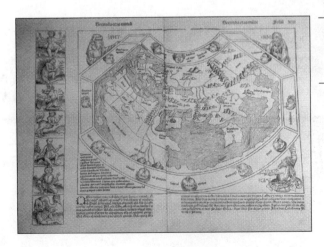

A Ptolemaic world map in the *Liber Chronicarum*, 1493.

Christian theology and Greco-Roman philosophy. This self image led them to a conviction that their civilization was superior to all others and that their mission was to bring the whole world around to their way of thinking where this was possible, and to rule over the rest where it was not possible.

Wherever European explorers landed and found another culture, they crushed it—unless it was one of the long-established cultures, such as India and China that predated European civilization anyway. But even those ultimately had to yield to economic and military pressure. The backward cultures, especially those that were still hunter-gatherers or not far from it, lost their land, their livelihood, their independence, their culture, their health, and in many cases, their lives. The Europeans had no compunctions about this. They were convinced of their own superiority and saw no value in other cultural practices. Indigenous peoples that they came across were used as forced labourers in the same way that domestic animals were used. This all stemmed from firmly held convictions about the divine order of the world, and their place near the top of it.

Design and Order

Whether they could articulate these beliefs or nor, the European explorers, colonizers, and later settlers, who ventured forth from their native lands to encounter a very different kind of life elsewhere, met that life with a common viewpoint that had its origins in the Bible and in the writings of the classical philosophers: the world had a design and a purpose; that purpose was for the benefit of man; the role of man was to aid the divine powers in achieving the ultimate goals of existence. Moreover, only those with the necessary culture and breeding, i.e., Europeans, could assume this role.

The Design Argument

One of the most popular arguments to prove that there is order and purpose in the world is called the *Design Argument*. Its basic structure is very simple: Look at the world. It's amazing how everything works together. It can't be an accident. It must be created that way on purpose. Learned men have been impressed with this awesome order for thousands of years. Often the argument has been used as a proof of the existence of God.

In 44 BCE, the Roman philosopher Cicero wrote:

> Everything in the world is marvelously ordered by divine providence and wisdom for the safety and protection of us all…. Who cannot wonder at this harmony of things, at this symphony of nature which

seems to will the well-being of the world? (From *The Nature of the Gods.*)

In the 19th century, the same argument was often used as a proof of the existence of God. Eminent scientists wrote treatises describing some intricacies of nature as a way of asserting that the world could not have come about except by plan. One written by the prominent physiologist Charles Bell described the perfect adaptability of the hand for all its tasks and concluded:

> It has been shown, that...there is nothing like chance or irregularity in the composition of the system. In proportion indeed as we comprehend the principles of mechanics, or of hydrolics, as applicable to the animal machinery, we shall be satisfied of the perfection of the design. (From *The Hand,* 1933.)

The Pre-Eminence of Man

Another notion, closely related to the idea that the entire world has been designed for some purpose, is the belief that of all creatures human beings are above all others in importance, and perhaps even that the whole of the world exists only to support the life of human beings. This has roots in both the Judeo-Christian tradition and in Greek philosophy.

A bust of Aristotle.

The philosopher Aristotle, who is very likely the most important thinker that the Western world has ever known and whose thought had overwhelming influence in Europe, after arguing that plants are made for the sake of animals went on

> Now, if Nature makes nothing incomplete, and nothing in vain, the inference must be that she has made all animals for the sake of man. (From *The Politics.*)

In the Bible, of course, this idea is manifest in the creation story in Genesis:

> Be fruitful and multiply, and fill the earth and subdue it; and have dominion over the fish of the sea and over the birds of the air and over every living thing that moves upon the earth.... Be fruitful and multiply and replenish the earth and subdue it.

Or, in the story of Noah and the Flood, God's directions to Noah about what to do when the ark puts down on dry land:

> Every moving thing that lives shall be food for you; and as I gave you the green plants, I give you everything.... The fear of you and the dread of you shall be upon every beast of the earth, and upon every fowl of the air, upon all that moveth upon the earth, and upon all the fishes of the sea; into your hand are they delivered.

In the period of European exploration and colonization of the world, the idea that man was the appointed caretaker of nature was especially prominent and frequently expressed. Sir Matthew Hale wrote:

> This was the one End of the Creation of Man, namely To be Vice-Regent of Almighty God, in the subordinate Regiment especially of the Animal and Vegetable Provinces. (From *The Primitive Origination of Mankind*, 1677.)

And the great spokesman for the "new philosophy" of confident optimism that had taken hold in Europe in the 17th century, Sir Francis Bacon, saw man as the whole point of everything:

> The world is made for man, not man for the world.... Man, if we look to final causes, may be regarded as the centre of the world, insomuch that if man were taken away from the world, the rest would seem to be all astray without aim or purpose. (From *Novum Organum*, 1620.)

In the following century, the 18th, when European colonization of the world was at a high point and Europeans were enjoying the wealth and privilege that was made possible by all the goods shipped to them from abroad, the idea of inevitable progress took hold. Everything seemed to be getting better and better. There was a direction to life and it was upward. Europeans and other high civilizations were farther along down the road of progress, but there was hope for the rest of the world, if and when they would follow the same path:

> Three-fourths of the habitable globe, are now uncultivated. The improvements to be made in cultivation, and the augmentations the earth is capable of receiving in the article of productiveness, cannot as yet, be reduced to any limits of calculation. Myriads of centuries of still increasing population may pass away, and the earth be yet found sufficient for the support of its inhabitants. (William Goodwin, *Political Justice*, 1793.)

> The perfectibility of man is truly indefinite; and that the progress of this perfectibility, from now onwards independent of any power that might wish to halt it, has no limit than the duration of the globe upon which nature has cast us...this progress...will never be reversed as long as the earth occupies its present place in the system of the universe. (Marquis de Condorcet, *Sketches for a Historical Picture of the Progress of the Human Mind*, 1793.)

And so, the European colonizers went forth to conquer new lands around the world with the conviction that (1) they had every right to do so, since it was all created for them anyway—primitive people being put on a par with useful animals; (2) they had the responsibility to make sure everything was operating to the proper ends, being God's representatives; (3) their civilization back home was just farther ahead on the road to perfection and the rest of the world would follow in good time; and finally, (4) not just their civilization, but everything to do with human existence was getting better and better. With these beliefs there was no reason to be ashamed of any of their exploits.

"We must find new lands from which we can easily obtain raw materials and at the same time exploit the cheap slave labour that is available from the natives of the colonies. The colonies would also provide a dumping ground for the surplus goods produced in our factories."

Cecil Rhodes, Founder of Rhodesia, now Zimbabwe

Chapter 13

The Third World

Once Europeans began exploring and colonizing the world about 500 years ago, they made steady progress toward a position of dominance. This position was held both by the European countries themselves and by those colonized countries where the local citizenry was largely of European extraction, mostly North America.

One-sidedness had not been the way of the world before then. Before the 16th century, the world consisted of separate regions with little mutual contact. In the old world cultures, Europe, India, China, and the Near East, all had separate civilizations with different customs and values. Whatever contact existed, tended to be trade on a small scale. The rest of the world was even more isolated.

As soon as the explorers arrived in new lands, they found an immense expanse of resources—unlike anything back home, since that had all been used up long before they were born. They quickly saw that here was an opportunity for exploitation, first for their own good of course, but also for the good of the natives they encountered, because they would be bringing them into modernity, that is, if they thought about the natives at all.

To stake their claims, the explorers made their new discoveries into colonies of their home countries. At the outset, the main purpose of these colonies was to provide a source of inexpensive materials, such as furs, timber, and metals, to the European market or give access to desirable goods not available elsewhere. Sometimes these were crops that just did not grow in European climates; harvesting them and sending them home certainly improved the diet of Europeans who had access to them. Or they might be crops that conceivably could grow in Europe, but no one had tried raising them there because they required too much labour. The colonies could fill the bill with rich soils and a vast labour force that would (or had to) work for almost nothing. Many of the discovered lands were particularly rich in natural resources much desired in Europe. These might be mineral deposits that simply were not available in the European terrain, but because of the geological history of the Earth were to be found in these remote places. Or they might be that most useful renewable resource, timber, which at one point covered Europe but had long since been decimated by deliberate forest clearance and wanton wasteful over-usage of timber to make charcoal.

Supplying the rich resources that Europe and, later, other developed regions like North America, needed to cover their own deficiencies became the chief economic role of those parts of the world that had existed outside of the main developed world. This role still remains theirs today. These places, once independent and untouched by European/ North American influence, first became colonies, then, mostly in the 20th century, regained their political independence. But by the time of independence, the former colonies had grown dependent on the economic trade with the developed nations; therefore, their only practical way to proceed was to continue in the role of supplier of resources.

The Madeiras

One of the earliest examples of a European colony set up in untouched land was in the Madeiras Islands off the coast of North Africa. In 1420, Portuguese explorers discovered the islands on one of their ventures down the coast of Africa. At that time they were totally unoccupied by human beings. The terrain was mountainous and forested, but, being close to the equator, the climate was ideal for certain kinds of farming.

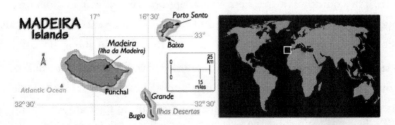

The Portuguese settled the main island of Madeira and quickly transformed it from its original natural state into agricultural land. Fires were set across the island to clear out the forests. The settlers brought in pigs and cattle, doing further irreparable damage to the existing ecosystem. Then in the 1450s, the Portuguese began to cultivate sugar cane on the island. Sugar had not long before then been introduced into Europe and was a much sought after luxury. Before that time, Europeans relied on honey collected from beehives for whatever

Madeira today.

slash
burn

sweeteners they had. But once the taste of pure sugar had been experienced, all those who could afford it wanted it and were willing to pay premium prices for it. The problem was, making sugar was a laborious and intensive project requiring vast tracts of land and a huge supply of willing labour.

The Plantation System

The Madeira settlers solved the vast management problem of how to grow sugar in considerable quantities by copying an organizational system already in use in Cyprus and on some other Mediterranean islands. Terraces had to be built across the mountainous land to prevent erosion of the necessarily loose topsoil. That soil needed regular irrigation, even at higher elevations, so complex artificial water courses had to be built. That was for the initial setup, all of which would need regular maintenance. The greatest demand for labour would come from the cultivation and harvesting of the crop.

Here the Portuguese adopted the labour practice that has always been associated with plantations. They brought in slaves, thousands of them, from North Africa and the Canary Islands. From 1450 and 1500, Madeira was transformed from a self-sufficient community of about 500 Portuguese farmers to a colony of around 20 000 people. Instead of farming a variety of crops that the original settlers had done, a single crop, sugar, was raised on huge plantations, all for export to Portugal.

The Cash Crop Model

The plantations on Madeira were a great economic success. They soon became the model for other colonizing ventures by the Portuguese and the Spanish in islands off the coast of Africa. The pattern was always the same: First the local ecosystem was destroyed by clearing forest growth, burning off local vegetation, and re-landscaping to suit the requirements of the plantation. Then, to provide the necessary labour force, any local population still around was enslaved. Since this was usually insufficient, slaves were brought in from other nearby locations, mostly mainland Africa, making the population density far greater than the local ecosystem could ever have supported.

If the territory colonized was an island, it would be converted in its entirety to a single cash crop, generally sugar, or later on, possibly cotton, but in either case requiring vast amounts of labour.

The Pattern of Colonization

As the European explorers went out and returned to their home countries with reports of vast resources waiting to be tapped, venturesome settlers followed and set up colonies. Economically, they were attractive propositions, offering undeveloped land and other natural resources—and a ready supply of human labour that could be used much the same way that domesticated animals were.

Though many European and a few other countries set up colonies all over the world, there was a surprising similarity to the process. The newly conquered territories were developed not for their own benefit, but for the benefit of the home country of the colonizers, though sometimes the colonizers claimed that the greater benefit was to the colony that was being modernized. The colonies were used to supply some kind of commodity in demand at home. This usually was a crop, such as sugar, that was too expensive to be grown at home, or a resource like timber, that had all been used up at home, or mineral deposits that were important in industry and that were available only abroad. In any case, the costs of cultivation or extraction, basically labour, were low since people were either pressed into slavery or paid trivial amounts.

In the usual case of cultivation of a single large crop, the best land was invariably chosen, leaving only the poorest ground for the cultivation of the subsistence crops that would provide food for the local residents. The division of labour on the plantation was starkly defined: white Europeans were the managers, while the usually non-white locals or imported slaves provided the backbreaking labour. The settlers were a very small proportion of the total population and did very little of the manual work.

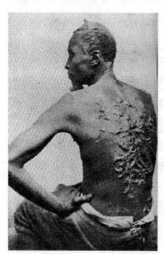

Slavery

Slavery was not an institution devised by the European colonizers in the 15th century, but had been a common feature of human society since its very beginnings. Most of the great city-states and empires of the ancient world made considerable use of slaves for building and other manual work. Often, these slaves were obtained as captives, the spoils of war. Indeed many wars were fought just to obtain slaves. People who ended up as slaves were members of groups too weak to defend themselves from raids. Some of the strongest ties that bound early communities together were those that provided the strength in numbers to fend off slave-raiding sorties from other groups.

The colonizers generally hoped to be able to enslave the local population that was already in place in the land they had taken over, and so they usually did. But more happened than this when two formerly separated peoples were suddenly brought together. They also communicated microorganisms. Diseases that one population had become accustomed to ran through another group and wreaked havoc. European colonists were inadvertent carriers of bacteria or viruses that did them no harm, but with which the indigenous populations had no experience and no defences. Often the colonists did not realize this until after the local population had been virtually wiped out.

But, not to worry. Slaves could be imported, and were. For the Spanish and Portuguese, in particular, there was no difficulty getting slaves for their colonies. They merely tapped into the well-established and well-run slave trade already existent in Africa, where one group of Africans sold other Africans to anyone with the required payment. The Spanish and Portuguese were the first to make use of this market, because their home countries and their original colonies were nearby. Soon, this ready trade came to the attention of the other European colonists, especially the Dutch and British, who began making extensive use of it as well.

Quasi-slaves

Slavery became socially unacceptable to Europeans and others of European descent (e.g., Americans) in the 19th century and was abolished within a few decades in virtually all of the colonies and former colonies. But the plantations were well established by then. Another source of labour needed to be found. Two that served just as well as slavery were indentured servants and convicts.

When economic conditions turned for the worse in Europe, as happened frequently enough, those without any other resources had few options at their disposal. In former ages, these would have been the people who migrated elsewhere and found new lands to settle in. By the 19th century, so much of the world was already populated that it was well nigh impossible to find an area that a penniless person could set off for, by foot or otherwise, that would offer better prospects. It was really necessary to get off the continent and go to one of the colonies that still had more resources than people. There was a way to do this. You could get passage on a ship paid for and guaranteed employment at the destination by signing a contract known as an *indenture* that committed you to work for a fixed number of years for the employer who paid for your voyage and provided you with food and shelter.

On paper this sounded like a fair enough bargain and in fact was the only way out for these people. For many, it gave them a new start in life. But the system was often abused. Many of those who sponsored indentured servants viewed them as slaves by another name and treated them just as badly. The life expectancy of the typical indentured servant was low. Often those who indentured themselves for a fixed number of years died before their indenture contract ran out.[1]

In addition to indentured servants from Europe, many otherwise desperate and destitute people from India, China, and the Pacific Islands also signed on to become plantation workers in the West Indies and other places. Life was especially grim for these people, as it had been for the slaves themselves.

And then there were the convicts. Persons who had been convicted of serious crimes and sentenced to long terms in prison or even execution needed to be kept off the streets at home, but they still could be a source of labour. In Britain, in particular, a scheme that seemed to win approval all around was to ship them abroad. So long as the destination was one from which they could not return, it was just as good as keeping them in prison, and certainly a lot cheaper for the state. Crossing the ocean was sufficient distance, so originally many were sent to the American colonies. However, after the Americans declared independence, this destination was closed off, and the British instead found the perfect place, the British colony on the opposite side of the world, Australia. The majority of settlers in Australia, until some time in the 19th century, were convicts.

Loss of Self-Sufficiency

By European standards, the new lands they discovered and then colonized were indeed backward, with the inhabitants living in a manner much like Europeans did hundreds if not thousands of years earlier. Their way of life may have been primitive, even laughable, to the culturally advanced explorers and settlers who found them or who moved there to exploit the land. But these people had managed to get along without European help for all these thousands of years and had found some way of living in

---

1. According to Clive Ponting, only a fifth of the white indentured servants who went to North America before 1783 survived to the end of their period of indenture. Clive Ponting, *A Green History of the World* (New York: Penguin, 1993), p. 198.

enough harmony with their environments that there was a viable, if unspectacular, means of existence in place. If the society had adopted agriculture, the people had found both a way of working with the land and crops that grew well in the climate and soil. In most cases, the methods in these places involved only minimal disturbance to the land, great reliance on natural irrigation, and all cultivation done by hand. The result was little erosion of the soil and little deterioration of its fertility. Likewise, a diversity of crops grew, which both provided a varied and healthier diet and prevented depletion of the soil.

All this changed with the colonial approach. Agriculture was turned into a specialization where far fewer crops, indeed usually only one, was produced in order to achieve the maximum efficiency of management and output. The crops chosen were those that fetched the highest price when exported. Feeding the local population was not a consideration. A single crop, planted in the same fields year after year would almost invariably cause the soil to become less fertile. Also, the lack of variety tended to leave the fields vulnerable to erosion from wind and water, especially after the harvest or after ploughing when everything that held the soil in place had been removed or loosened. Also, the same crop planted side by side in a large field was especially vulnerable to the spread of disease. A blight affecting one and only one species could not spread quickly if fields were planted with a variety of crops intermixed with each other, but if they were all arranged next to each other in neat rows, the disease could spread rapidly. A drought or a frost or heavy rains might be devastating for one crop, but not particularly injurious to another. If a field was planted with one and only one crop, then it was all or nothing.

The worst of this was its permanence. Once the land was compromised by being turned into a plantation for growing one crop, it was nearly impossible for it to return to its previous natural state. The ecosystem that had provided the balance was disrupted and all the links within it broken. It took a vast amount of time for nature just to generate the topsoil on which everything else depended. If this had been allowed to erode or lose its vitality, regenerating that was a very long process. Likewise, many of the other natural facets of a mature ecosystem did not just revert once the plantation was abandoned. Water courses, forest cover, naturally occurring silt in irrigation all took much longer than human lifetimes to recover, if they ever could.

To take the most charitable view, the colonists may have truly believed they were bringing an improved life to the wretched creatures living in these places when they arrived, and in a certain sense, they may have done so. But at the same time, they took away the self-sufficiency of the land to provide for the people and therefore took away the possibility of independence from those they colonized.

The Creation of the Third World

By the early 20th century, Europe and the United States had brought about a major transformation of the economies and the societies of the less developed parts of the world. In so doing, the standard of living of the most developed nations has risen, while that of the less developed nations has become alarmingly dependent. The resulting differences in living conditions in different parts of the world have become so stark that commentators have classified them into separate groups and given them names that convey in a phrase much about the way of life. Europe, the United States, and other free market economies that have a highly developed infrastructure and a high standard of living comprise the *First World*. These categories were established during the mid-20th century Cold War period, when another bloc of countries could be identified that had a rather different lifestyle. These were the communist countries, the Soviet Union and its allied countries in Europe. These were industrialized nations, but not free market economies. They produced their own goods and traded with each other, but all was done centrally with the goal of providing what was deemed at some high level to be a suitable standard of living. The result was that the level of consumption—and of production—in those countries was significantly below that of the First World, but it was self-contained. These were dubbed the *Second World,* a term which went out of use well before the collapse of the Soviet bloc.

The third group were those countries that had been colonized and then turned into subservient providers to the First World countries. It included the ancient high civilizations that had not jumped on the industrialization bandwagon and became vulnerable to economic pressures from the First World and even fell under the political control of Europe for a time. These would include India, China, and Egypt, the pinnacles of early civilization. All of these collectively were known as the Third World.

In the parlance of a few writers, there was also a *Fourth World*, namely those parts of the world that had been touched by none of this. These would be the few remaining pockets of the world where hunting and gathering or simple farming remained a way of life—places with no interest in the industrialized world and places that were not of much interest to the colonizers and resource extractors.

Of all of these terms, only the Third World has remained in current usage as a standalone term describing these places in the world that have an economic dependence on the rich countries. It is worth reviewing how these countries came to be in their present situation and why they remain there.

Making a Third World Country

A Third World country did not just evolve into that category on its own. Its position was the result of direct intervention by outside powers. The making of a Third World country followed a predictable sequence that has been repeated over and over again.

To begin, a country or region of the world existed, as it probably had for centuries, in a relatively stable—though perhaps by European standards—very backward state. Whatever the organization of the community, system of government, and way of life were, they were home-grown and hence fitted to the local environment. If there was agriculture, the crops grown were those that suited the soils and the climate, generally produced a varied diet, and did not cause radical harm to the fertility or stability of the land.

Then, the colonizers would arrive and see the local natural resources as an opportunity that was not being exploited. Here, negotiations may have been friendly or hostile, but the result was the same: land that had either been dormant or used for local agriculture was taken over in a massive way to grow crops for export back to the home country or another developed nation. The crops would be those that would fetch a high price back home—typically inessential luxuries, such as sugar or tea, or components for industry, such as cotton or rubber. These crops would be grown on large plantations managed by the colonizers and worked by slaves or ill-paid labourers living under conditions of extreme poverty. The workers may either have been local people or brought in from elsewhere to work on the plantations. There were plantations for many different crops at locations all over the world. The most common plantation crops were sugar cane, tobacco, cotton, tea, rice, rubber, coffee, cocoa, palm oil, and bananas. On this list, the only staple food is rice, which could have fed the local population were it not exported. The banana was a late entry on the list of plantation crops, not being practical until the invention of refrigerated ships.

The countries receiving the plantation produce enjoyed a diversification of products at their disposal and a richer life therefrom. The producing countries were crippled by their plantations, because all or most of their best land was used for export crops, leaving only marginal land to support the local population. Moreover, growing the same crop again and again in the same field depleted the soils and left the land more vulnerable to plant diseases. The Third World countries generally were the homes of a huge variety of plant species that grew there and there alone. Clearing the land for plantations growing only the export crop drove many of these species to extinction. And, of course, there was tremendous loss of prime forest land.

The Third World countries soon had to begin importing food for their own sustenance since they no longer had the land available to feed themselves. Cash crops for export generally took a majority of the available farmland—certainly the best farmland— and sometimes up to 80 percent of the total arable land.

When the political climate shifted in the 20th century and it was no longer popular, advisable, or even feasible for the First World countries to continue holding colonies, a process was set in place through which most of the colonies and protectorates achieved independence and could once again determine their own destinies. But those colonial patterns of farming, trading, and land-ownership in the hands of a few were not easy to change. It was difficult to revert to a more general approach to farming and to a more diverse economy. These countries had become tied to the money economy. The only way to raise cash was to produce more of the export crop and sell it abroad. Even in cases where the plantations and other foreign-owned projects were simply nationalized, it was difficult to alter the pattern of operation, because making these projects profitable depended on interaction with foreign buyers, which was not within the control of the Third World country. By and large, these countries attempted to dig themselves out of their poverty by finding even more products that they could export for cash.

Meat

Since the beginning of the Agricultural Revolution 10 000 years ago right up to the present, human beings have lived almost exclusively on vegetable matter. Very few cultures relied on animal flesh for part of their regular diet, usually only those in regions with such poor soils that there was no alternative. On the other hand, meat has always been prized as a treat and has been enjoyed by the wealthy whenever possible. In Europe in particular, the great feasts sometimes held were marked by the slaughter of many animals and the conspicuous consumption of great amounts of meat and drink. But these events were (1) not that frequent, and (2) reserved for a tiny minority of the population.

Prosperity changed that pattern for part of the world. In the First World countries, meat has become more and more a staple of the diet. Since the Industrial Revolution, when the standard of living rose in all industrialized nations, meat has come to be considered essential. Apart from wild game, most meat comes from slaughtered domestic animals raised for the purpose. The number of species that have been raised for this purpose is extremely small compared to the number of species of wild animals. The animals chosen have not changed dramatically since the beginnings of animal husbandry: sheep, goats, pigs, cattle, chickens, later turkeys and rabbits, and a few others. A single trip to the local supermarket's butcher counter will confirm that of this list, cattle and chicken count for the vast majority of meats sold, with pigs and sheep (lamb) accounting for most of the rest.

For most North Americans and many Europeans, a main meal without some kind of meat served is incomplete. (Not counting confirmed vegetarians and immigrants from other parts of the world.) Where does all this meat come from?

Originally domestic animals were just part of the agriculturalist's operation. A few cows and chicken were maintained, primarily for milk, cheese, and eggs, and then slaughtered and eaten rarely. When the Americas were settled by the Europeans, there were huge wild herds of bison roaming the plains, which were subsequently nearly slaughtered to extinction. The great North American plains were clearly excellent grazing lands. While the bison were too wild to domesticate, cattle were perfect. They were much more docile and easily managed. The great ranches of the American West began raising huge herds to be fattened and then slaughtered. With more meat available to the American consumer, meat became a regular part of the diet. This popular practice spread quickly to the other relatively wealthy countries. Land that had before been used for other purposes or not used at all was turned into ranches for cattle.

The taste for red meat continued to grow and the demand soon exceeded the supply. The consumption of beef has more than doubled in the last half of the 20th century. It was almost inevitable that the Third World would be called upon to take over the raising of cattle to satisfy this demand in Europe and North America. Thus, in many Third World countries, notably in South America, huge tracts of forest and jungle have been cleared in order to provide pastureland for cattle, almost all of it for export to the First World countries. As with the plantation crops, the production is in one place, the consumption in another. It has been said that a cat in the United States eats more beef than an inhabitant of Costa Rica.

Timber

The very earliest records of human civilizations show that people cannot resist cutting down trees and using them in all their versatility as construction materials, rollers, and fuel for cooking and heating. This itself has led to deforestation in any area settled by large groups of people. To make matters worse, clearing forests to make agricultural land and harvesting huge numbers of trees to make charcoal for industry have produced the inevitable: almost every settled place in the world with a certain population density no longer has its native forests. But the demand for timber has not abated. Meanwhile, the Third World has many virgin forests, still untouched by their local populations. If trends are indicative, most of that will soon be gone.

It does not take long to strip an area of its woodland, or more particularly its most valuable hardwoods, those that take the longest time to grow. Here are two horrific examples:

Teak has always been a prized wood. By the early 19th century, British merchants had nearly exhausted the teak forests on part of India's coast and sought a new supply. They moved on to Burma (conquering it in 1826) and within 20 years had stripped all the teak from the first area opened up.

In British-controlled India in the 19th century, rail lines were built all over the country to bring goods to market more efficiently. Railways require wooden ties every meter or so. The number of trees felled for this purpose alone is phenomenal. In the 1870s, well after the most reachable areas had been depleted, half a million trees each year were being felled just for railway ties.

Example after example could be cited. But the pattern is predictable: the Third World countries viewed their forests as another cash crop and valued cash in hand above the long-term survival of their woodlands. And, also typical of Third-World economics, the timber was sold as raw logs to the developed nations and then processed wood products, such as paper and board, had to be imported back for Third World people's use.

Minerals

Unlike timber, which existed widely across the globe and then was wantonly used up in the developed countries, driving them to the Third World to find further supplies, minerals of all sorts were never evenly distributed. The process of the formation of the

Earth's crust millions of years ago, long before the first humans appeared, determined what minerals would lie where on which continents. Some parts of the world are just naturally rich in certain deposits while others are not. These do not necessarily correspond to the distribution of human civilizations. One need only think of the distribution of petroleum reserves on the Earth to realize that their configuration is not related to the history of human civilization.

Petroleum is a commodity that has come into demand only since uses were found for it in the mid-19th century, but minerals of all sorts have been used since the beginnings of civilization. Some, those we call precious metals, were so valued both for their beauty and for their physical properties that finding and extracting them was a sure road to riches. One of the astounding discoveries of the Spanish explorers who landed in Mexico and Peru was the quantity of gold and silver just waiting to be taken. Likewise, much of Africa has been of especial interest to the European countries that colonized it, because of the large deposits of mineral resources, such as copper, gold, and diamonds. As with cash crops, mining became a central part of the economy of the African colonies, and that role did not change after they gained their independence. Almost all mining is done for export, to raise cash. The local economies are totally dependent on it.

Fertilizers

The trade in natural fertilizers is particularly poignant as it underscores the inherent problems of intensive agriculture in the First World and the extent to which the solutions found were destructive to the Third World.

Intensive farming is any way of growing crops that does not rely upon the natural fertility of the soil and the naturally occurring rainfall for the growth cycle. Artificial irrigation provides water and the soil is restored by adding a layer of fertilizer each season. Intensive farming would not work without fertilizer. It takes very little time for any overworked soil to lose its fertility, a fact discovered very early on in the history of agriculture. The solution was to spread animal manure over the fields, a practice still in wide use today. However, if not enough animals are available—especially if pastureland had to be converted to farmland to produce more crops—then another fertilizer had to be found.

One of the bonanza discoveries for the Europeans was that there was another sort of "manure" that would do the trick just as well, and it was available in huge supply in great deposits elsewhere in the world. This was *guano*—bird droppings. Anywhere that birds gather soon gets covered in guano, which hardens and forms a layer on any surface. There is a long coastline in Chile where seabirds congregated. Over centuries, the coastline built up a very deep layer of guano. This made a very valuable export product for Chile and was much welcomed in Europe. Imported Chinese labourers worked the guano in appalling conditions. But it was a bonanza for Chile. The tax that the Chilean government levied on the sale of the guano amounted to 80 percent of the revenue of the government.

Nauru and Banaba

There are other ways to revitalize soil with natural products other than animal excrement. Phosphates work very well also, and, like guano, there are large phosphate deposits at various spots around the world. The discovery in the early 20th century of some very large deposits on islands in the Pacific Ocean was of immense interest to the British, who then were totally dependent on imported fertilizers. The British envisaged obtaining large amounts of phosphates for Britain itself and for Australia and New Zealand.

The islands were Nauru and Banaba, called by the British "Ocean Island," in Micronesia, to the northeast of Australia. How Britain came to extract phosphates from these islands and what happened to the local residents is a tale of abuse of both people and the environment.

Each island had an area of about 20 square kilometers. Nauru had a population of about 1,400 people, Banaba had about 2,000 residents. The residents of these islands lived in a very simple, very primitive way, relying on fishing and the very lush vegetation that grew naturally in all the wonderful phosphate. In 1901, Britain annexed Banaba and changed its name to Ocean Island. Nauru was already a possession of Germany. Virtually the entire surface of both islands was solid phosphate. Even before the annexation of Banaba, the British had moved to obtain the phosphates by purchasing all the mineral rights on the island from the local chief in a dubious treaty for a

Below: A Banaba village before phosphate extraction began.

payment of £50 per year. Another contract was drawn up with the German government for Nauru. Extraction began, with an imported labour force.

By the early 1920s, 600 000 tonnes of phosphates were being extracted from the islands each year. The extraction process involved removing the top 15 meters of the land, leaving an uninhabitable wasteland behind. The islands were headed for permanent ruin. Nevertheless, despite protests the mining continued. During the Second World War, the residents of both islands were evacuated. When the war was over, the British resettled the Banabans on one of the Fiji islands, which has a very different climate from Banaba and where they were very unhappy. The Naurus returned and in 1968 finally regained their independence.

The Naurus first significant action as an independent state was to recommence the phosphate mining, but now the royalties would come to them. There is very little left of the island, so they live on a tiny fringe around the coast that is all that has not been mined. But they do not live in destitute poverty, not at all. Despite the total loss of their traditional way of life and their lack of most marketable skills, they have an extremely high standard of living, all funded by the phosphate sales.

The ring road on Nauru. Note the modern houses and electrical cables.

There is one and only one road in Nauru. It runs for 19 kilometers, ringing the island. And it is full of cars, expensive ones. Nauru has one of the highest rates of car ownership in the world. The population of Nauru import all their food from the West. They have begun to develop health problems typical of the industrialized nations.

The Place of the Third World in the World Economy

The Third World has fulfilled the role envisaged for it by Cecil Rhodes, quoted at the beginning of this chapter. It is a source of resources and cheap labour for the First World. Whatever development has happened in the Third World countries is very much dependent upon selling off their resources rather than building viable industries. Efforts are made in many Third World countries to break off this ultimately ruinous way of life. Unfortunately, the only actions that seem to have a chance of rescuing them from poverty are to sell off their resources even faster, which just continues to degrade the environment in which they live.

PART FOUR

The Industrial Revolution

Those who try to assess the whole scope and range of human existence usually identify a few major turning points where the whole character of human life made a permanent and irreversible change in a relatively short time, then built a vastly different way of life from a new beginning. The most critical of these was provided by the Agricultural Revolution, about 10 000 years ago, where the change in the way that people fed themselves ushered in settled life, permanent institutions, written language, and in general, civilization. It would be hard for any changes to human living to equal that.

But there certainly was another huge change that occurred much more recently: the *Industrial Revolution*, that changed the character of life for a large segment of the world and subsequently changed the economic balance of the entire globe.

Neither of these revolutions happened overnight and neither affected all people across the Earth in a comparable fashion. The Agricultural Revolution was a transition over perhaps two or three thousand years. It only looks like a short time when compared to the length of the hunting and gathering era and the slow pace of changes within that. The Agricultural Revolution did not bring everyone along with it, but very few regions of the world that had any contact with agriculture failed to adapt to it. For the most part, those that did not were places unsuitable for farming or which had such a small population relative to their living space that there was no pressing need to switch.

In contrast, the Industrial Revolution was a much quicker affair, spanning at most 250 years, or, to take a narrower definition, just 100 years. And, also in contrast with the Agricultural Revolution, the Industrial Revolution—at least, to the present day—has transformed life in only a portion of the world, perhaps less than half.

Nevertheless, the changes wrought in that affected portion were profound. Food production ceased to be the predominant occupation of the population. Local communities ceased to be the focus of social and economic activity. Well-being came to be measured as monetary wealth instead of food, shelter, clothing, and community.

For those countries that did become industrialized, the monetary wealth did bring with it more and better food, grander homes, more adequate and even stylish clothing, and community life changed from the simple interactions with neighbors in small towns and villages to choices from the dazzling array of possibilities offered by the great metropolises. A common comparison of the state of material wealth before and after the Industrial Revolution is that after industrialization ordinary people lived as only royalty had done before.

There are indeed few among us in the industrialized countries who would wish to return to the lifestyle of the common man as it existed before the Industrial Revolution. We would like to stay here, please, or get even better.

But there is a sense in which all this has been achieved on borrowed time and at other people's expense, and because of that does not have a stable future.

For Further Reading

Ashton, T. S. *The Industrial Revolution 1760-1830*. Oxford: Oxford University Press, 1968.

Basalla, George. *The Evolution of Technology*. Cambridge: Cambridge University Press, 1988.

Bury, J. B. *The Idea of Progress*. New York: Dover, 1955.

Cardwell, Donald. *The Norton History of Technology*. New York: W. W. Norton & Co., 1995.

Cotgrove, Stephen, *Catastrophe or Cornucopia: The Environment, Politics and the Future*. New York: John Wiley & Sons, 1982.

Dickinson, H. W. *A Short History of the Steam Engine*. Cambridge: Cambridge University Press, 1938.

Dijksterhuis, E. J. *The Mechanization of the World Picture*, trans. by C. Dikshoorn. Oxford: Oxford University Press, 1961.

Ellul, Jacques. *The Technological Society*, trans. by John Wilkinson. New York: Jonathan Cape, 1965.

Gordon, Anita and David Suzuki. *It's a Matter of Survival*. Toronto: Stoddart, 1990.

Jevons, W. Stanley. *The Coal Question: An Inquiry Concerning the Progress of the Nation, and the Probable Exhaustion of Our Coal-Mines* London, 1865.

Landes, D. S. *The Unbound Prometheus: Technological Change and Industrial Development in Western Europe form 1750*. Cambridge: Cambridge University Press, 1969.

MacLachlan, James. *Children of Prometheus: A History of Science and Technology*, 2nd ed. Toronto: Wall & Emerson, 2002.

Marx, Leo. *The Machine in the Garden: Technology and the Pastoral Ideal in America*. New York: Oxford University Press, 1964.

Morison, Elting E. *Men, Machines and Modern Times*. Cambridge, MA: The MIT Press, 1966.

Mumford, Lewis, *Technics and Civilization*. London: Routledge, 1946.

Pacey, Arnold. *The Culture of Technology*. Cambridge, MA: The MIT Press, 1983.

_____. *The Maze of Ingenuity: Ideas and Idealism in the Development of Technology*. Cambridge, MA: The MIT Press, 1976.

_____. *Technology in World Civilization: A Thousand-Year History*. Cambridge, MA: The MIT Press, 1990.

Smith, Adam. *An Inquiry into the Nature and Causes of the Wealth of Nations*. London, 1776.

A medieval conception of how to use the power of running water to turn a waterwheel to pump keep water out of a mine. From Agricola, *De Re Metallica.*, 1556.

Chapter 14

Using the Power of Nature

What makes human beings different from other animals? The traditional answer of anthropologists and others concerned with this issue is that human beings make and use tools. That is, we do not simply use the resources of our own bodies to accomplish tasks, we fashion some implement or device that gives us an advantage. If we did not do so, the chances are that we would be extinct by now, since our physical endowments are poor for survival purposes: we are slow runners compared to many predators; we have a poor sense of smell and only so-so sight and hearing that might alert us of danger; we lack fur for protection from the cold; we can climb trees only with difficulty, etc. Our physical bodies have little survival value.

But of course, we don't rely on our physical bodies. Those anthropologists who cite the making and using of tools use the archæological records of prehistoric tools as a measure of how advanced our forebears had become at various stages. The earliest tools had much to do with improving the hunt or keeping warm or making food more palatable. When agriculture began, the important new tools were those that made farming better—ploughs, harnesses and yokes for draught animals, contraptions for irrigating crops—or that protected the new wealth of surplus grain—urns for storage, weapons for defence, and a writing system to keep track of what belonged to whom.

At every stage, human invention has sought some way to improve the status quo and extend human power and influence beyond what came to us naturally. The domestication of the draft animal to pull the plough and transport heavy burdens was another way that human beings had found of extending the power at their command. The progress of civilization is measurable by the ways in which human ingenuity has found ways of leaning on the rest of nature for the power to do what otherwise would be impossible.

Wind and Water

In the Middle Ages, an incredible number of mechanical devices were invented to perform all sorts of tasks that previously had been done by hand. Looms, spinning wheels, drop hammers, grinding mills, and water pumps were among many other inventions. Some of them were totally new, others were refinements of ancient devices, but all had the noteworthy feature of having moving parts. Some like the loom and the spinning wheel were operated by human power pushing on pedals or turning cranks. These achieved an advantage either from leverage or by converting a tiring back and forth motion into a smooth continuous one. Others used a power of nature that was readily available if only it could be tapped. These often delivered power far in excess of what human beings could provide from their own strength.

The waterwheel and the windmill are the classic examples. It is hard for us to imagine how common these machines were in medieval Europe. The most reliable figures come from the beginning of that period in William the Conqueror's *Domesday Book* of 1086 that catalogued what was found across England after his conquest. The book lists 5600 working waterwheels in central, southern, and eastern England. That works out to one mill for every 50 households or one mill in every 10 square kilometers.

A waterwheel operating a set of bellows.

Waterwheels were standard all across Europe. All they required was reasonably fast or reasonably strong running water, and there were many rivers and streams that fit the bill. Using a waterwheel for the laborious task of grinding grain was a tremendous saving of effort over hand mills that had been used for centuries before. Somewhat later waterwheels were adapted to running any sort of repetitive task: pumping a bellows for a blast furnace or fulling cloth (a pounding process), even sawing wood.

In arid countries, such as in the Middle East, another kind of waterwheel was common, the *noria*, which was a water-raising device for irrigation. A waterwheel similar to those used in Europe was turned by the force of the stream of water flowing under it; at the same time, the wheel had containers attached to it, urns or buckets, which filled with water as they passed below the water level and then emptied this water out at the top of the cycle into a trough that carried the water away for irrigation of a nearby field.

A post-windmill, such as the one above, can be turned to face into the wind by an operator; later windmills had a sail that made this process automatic.

The windmill was similar to the waterwheel in design and adaptation, except that it was practical only in lands where there were regular strong winds. For that reason, windmills were not as evenly spread across the continent, but where they were in use, they were plentiful—for example, in the Netherlands where windmills were used to pump water out of the marshes to reclaim the land, as discussed in Chapter 12. Where there was a prevailing direction of wind, the windmill could be made facing in one direction. Otherwise it was practical to have a way to turn the windmill into the wind. An early solution to this problem was the *post-windmill*, where the windmill keeper could rotate the entire windmill structure as necessary.

In their heyday, waterwheels and windmills produced a greater force than any other that human beings had found. Unlike draft animals, these machines did not need to be fed constantly. What they did was take an existing force of nature and channel it to human uses. Moreover, the forces tapped were entirely renewable. The winds were not used up by the windmills, and more water came down the mountain streams and along the rivers to replace what had pushed the waterwheels around—though the waterwheels did slow down the current and interfere with the transport of silt.

The Cottage Industries

The Middle Ages in Europe was a time of immense innovation and enterprise. Highly skilled crafts were practiced by specialists who devoted their working lives to their particular art, often having gone through long training periods or apprenticeships and certifications, all protected by coveted membership in guilds, which had high and exacting standards. Frequently, the trade of the father was passed on to the sons, producing generations of millers, bakers, weavers, toolmakers, fullers, smiths, and indeed candlestick makers, to name some of them. Generally these craftsmen would work in a shop that was attached to or part of their homes; hence, these are commonly called *cottage industries.*

A stocking-maker.

The medieval cottage industry fit into the economy of the small European communities in a stable equilibrium that might have gone on forever, in the same way that a species fit into a self-contained ecosystem. The number of bakers or millers or cabinetmakers tended to be just the number that was appropriate for the community. Too many millers, and there was not enough grinding to support all of them; not enough and there was strong motivation for someone to choose milling as a vocation. These "market economy" forces worked well because the communities were essentially isolated from each other. The local craftsmen worked with local materials. Likewise, they sold their products within the local community. Most goods were produced to order. There was no point in producing surplus finished products, because there would be nowhere to sell them. Roads were rare, and when they existed at all, they were not suitable for haulage. Any prospect of expanding an operation by obtaining financial backing was hopeless since there were no banks or other possible ways of raising public money. This produced a natural limit to the amount of work done by an individual and also a limit to the amount of wealth that any craftsman could accumulate.

Winds of Change

The stability of the medieval economy with its local suppliers, local craftsmen, and local markets began to be threatened in the period of world exploration. The great European voyages of discovery of the 15th and 16th centuries found vast untapped resources elsewhere in the world and began to bring some of that back home. Usually what was brought back were items that were highly prized, like gold or spices, or of special value because of their scarcity at home, such as timber and beaver pelts. Unlike the cottage craftsmen who worked to a fixed market, the explorers who returned to Europe from afar, and those who followed them to colonize, were able to amass great wealth by providing a supply of materials for which there appeared to be an unlimited market.

The lure of great wealth spawned new institutions that began to break down the isolation of the communities. Crossing the Atlantic in ships was expensive, but if great profits could be made from such trips, it would be worthwhile finding a way to raise money for these ventures. The institutions of finance as we know them today originated in efforts to meet these needs. Banks, joint stock companies, and insurance companies all arose in order to raise money from those who could afford to venture some of their wealth, and at the same time to protect them from the worst of the risks that would be encountered. What made these new financial institutions different is that they existed only for the purpose of making money from investment. Unlike the work of a craftsman in his own shop making his own products, there was no natural upper limit to how much wealth could be accumulated by those who participated in these ventures.

Once the financial institutions existed and the raw materials began coming in from abroad, the balance of the economy began to change. Much larger projects began to be undertaken. Manufacturing of finished goods was done on a grander scale. New markets were reached by building roads and canals that made it possible to transport finished goods deep into the hinterlands, where they were welcomed, having previously been either unavailable or much more expensive.

These operations were usually powered by waterwheels, just as the smaller mills for grinding grain had been. But much attention was paid to the design of waterwheels, making them far more efficient and practical than the medieval ones. Improvements to waterwheel design were some of the first examples of engineering applied in a precise way to large machines.

A characteristic sight of the early industrial period: a barge hauling freight through canals built specially for barge traffic. The barge is pulled by a horse walking on a towpath beside the canal. This canal was built as a bridge over another body of water at a lower elevation.

More people were employed. They were no longer cottage industries. In England, a business run by a waterwheel had generally been a grain mill. Despite the changed size and function, the name stuck and the term *mill* is often used to refer to these sizeable facilities that have nothing to do with grinding. Even after the power source was no longer provided by water turning a wheel, they were called mills, and frequently still are in Britain. The name we are more familiar with is *factory*.[1]

Let Nature Do the Work

What started all these changes? Human civilization had shown enormous ingenuity in finding better ways to provide for the necessities of life and had reached a stage in the Middle Ages—at least in Europe—where there was a workable balance. Like any mature ecosystem, such a system can remain stable for a long time. Of course, there was the problem of running out of food, which motivated some of the voyages of discovery. But that would not have been able to transform society were it not for an essential discovery

---

1.   This is another borrowed term, taken out of its original context. The East India Company in India operated trading posts that they called "factories" because that is where their agents, known as "factors" operated. A factory in this context generally had a warehouse for storing goods, but rarely had anything to do with manufacturing. But close enough, so the term was applied to the new grand-scale manufacturing plants.

made early in the Middle Ages: There are natural forces in the world that are much more powerful than people or even draft animals. These forces can be directed to human goals, enabling people to do things that would be totally beyond their abilities.

Wind made some tasks far easier and faster and made others possible for the first time. The waterwheel and the windmill had many variable designs and were put to use for many different purposes all over the civilized world. Wind is also what made transatlantic voyages possible. In antiquity, ships were generally moved by rowing—i.e., human muscle. That would not work for long voyages, but if a ship could be designed with sails that could capture the winds and move in the desired direction, travel anywhere was possible.

Letting nature provide the power opened a whole new chapter of human civilization. In the new one, the power harnessed was so great that the central organizing principle of human life for the past 10 000 years shifted away from the provision of food to the production and consumption of previously unimaginable goods. This, at least, is what happened in the industrialized nations because of what we call the Industrial Revolution.

Chapter 15

The Steam Engine

Wind and water could provide a lot of power that could be used by people for all sorts of tasks that they could not have done before. But before long, another much greater natural force was discovered and put to use. That force was a vacuum, or, more properly speaking, it was the weight of the atmosphere.

Atmospheric Pressure

Our concept of the atmosphere is a consequence of the mechanist viewpoint that became current in the 17th century. In the ancient view, air floated above the ground because it was inherently light. It partook of the quality of "lightness," as did fire, while water and earth partook of the quality of "heaviness," which is why they fell down if released in the air. This view was replaced by the explanation of Sir Isaac Newton: all matter, including air, has mass, and all mass is attracted to other masses by the gravitational force. For Newton, the mystery to be explained was not why air floats above water and earth, but why it does not dissipate into the heavens. The answer is that all particles of air are pulled toward the surface of the Earth by their mutual gravitational attraction, which is another way of saying that the atmosphere has weight. That would explain a certain well-known observation that had puzzled some of the best minds in science: why is it that a suction pump can only lift water a distance of about 10 meters? The explanation is that a height of a column of water 10 meters high must have the same weight as a column of the atmosphere with the same cross-sectional area.[1] A suction pump works by removing the pressure of the atmosphere from above the water within the pump. Air pushes down on the exposed surface of the water, driving it up the pump, until

---

1. This was tested with a liquid of a very different density, mercury, and it was found that the comparable height of a column of mercury was about 75 centimeters, exactly proportional to the differences in their respective densities. This is the principle of the barometer, which measures the pressure of the air by the height of the column of mercury. .

equilibrium is reached. But a few people realized that this put another, much more powerful piece of nature at their disposal.

Wielding Atmospheric Pressure as a Force

The point was driven home by a German by the name of Otto von Guericke, from Magdeburg. Von Guericke had a flair for the dramatic; he found a way to demonstrate the power of the atmosphere in ways that the general public could understand. He cnstructed two nearly identical bronze hemispheres with perfectly smooth edges. Placing the hemispheres against each other, he attached an air pump to a valve on one of the hemispheres and to suck out the air, which left a bronze spherical shell surrounding a vacuum. The atmosphere pressed inward on it from all directions, but that was all that held the hemispheres together. The hemispheres were fitted with rings. At a public demonstration that became famous all over Europe he attached a team of eight horses to the rings on each side and set them off in opposite directions, trying to pull the hemispheres apart. They failed, indicating that the power of the atmosphere was greater than the most powerful force his audience could imagine, a team of 16 horses.

Thomas Newcomen's Steam Engine

It did not take long for practical applications of the principle to be devised. The first usage of the force of the atmosphere on an industrial scale came from Thomas Newcomen, an ironmonger from Devon in England, a mining area. One of the most serious problems that always plagues mining is keeping the mine from filling up with water and drowning the miners. Efforts had been made by some of the best practical minds for centuries on how to overcome this problem. A suction pump could work for only the first 10 meters down. Thereafter it was a laborious process of hauling the water up and getting it out of the mineshaft.

Newcomen devised an effective pump for a coal mine. The driving force was actually atmospheric pressure against piston that had a vacuum on its other side. The means used to create the necessary vacuum was steam. One of the very useful features of water is that when it is boiled, it expands to a gas that fills a vastly larger volume than the liquid water did. Conversely, when a large amount of steam is allowed to condense back to water, its

A Newcomen steam engine powering a pump in a mine. Note the size of the engine compared to the man in the engraving.

volume will suddenly reduce to a very small volume of water. This is the trick that Newcomen used for his pump. He built a large brass cylinder, closed on the bottom and open at the top. At the top he fitted a piston that could ride up and down. The piston was attached by chain to a pivot beam arm. The other side of the pivot beam was a lift pump that could be lowered any distance desired into a mine. He filled the cylinder with steam, driving out any air that might have been there. When the cylinder was full, he introduced a spray of cold water to condense the steam into a small amount of water. This left a vacuum inside the cylinder, and the weight of the atmosphere pushed the piston down with great force. This caused the lift pump on the other side of the beam to rise and bring up water.

An Incredible Waste

There are a number of things one could say about the Newcomen engine: First, it solved the problem that had made deep mining next to impossible. It did so by cleverly using a force of nature—atmospheric pressure—to do the work while the human design merely channeled it in the desired direction. Second, because the engine was a success, the mining of coal and of metal ores could proceed much more expeditiously and much more of both were soon available to satisfy the demand of expanding industry. But third, the waste, the squandering of resources to accomplish its task was just horrific.

What made the Newcomen engine viable at all was that its first use was to pump water out of a coal mine. Thus it was placed right at the source of coal and could use what it needed of it without the cost being a burden. The Newcomen engine was remarkably inefficient. First, a rather large amount of coal was placed in a furnace to produce a high constant heat. That heat was used to boil water. The resulting steam filled a chamber that it first had to heat up, otherwise the steam would condense too soon. Then, when the chamber was full, the entire process was reversed by cooling it down. Moreover, the piston that rode up and down was very ill fitting and much steam escaped. Modern calculations show that the Newcomen Engine had a theoretical efficiency of one percent, meaning that of the potential energy available in the coal used as fuel, only one percent of it was made into useful work in the lifting of water. Everything else was lost to inefficiencies.Of course, the Newcomen engine's inefficiency was only a problem if the cost of the coal was factored in. So long as it was not, the engine was a miracle. Later, the Newcomen engine began to be used for metal mines, far away from coal fields so that the coal fuel had to be purchased and transported. Then it began to seem like a pretty high price to pay.

James Watt.

James Watt's Steam Engine

James Watt was an instrument repairman working for the University of Glasgow when he was asked to repair a working model of a Newcomen engine that was used for teaching purposes. Watt quickly became aware of the inherent inefficiencies of the engine and gave some thought to how it could be made better. He succeeded in improving the Newcomen design so much that it is now James Watt that is popularly considered the inventor of the steam engine.

Watt's improvements were many, enough to make his steam engine four times as efficient as Newcomen's, which was enough to assure that it would quickly replace them for mine pumping duties. But much more important was that Watt introduced refinements that smoothed the motion of the piston and he connected the reciprocating beam to a gear mechanism that turned it into rotary motion. With a smooth turning rotary motion, the steam engine could power any factory operation, not just pumping.

The Watt-Boulton engine.

Watt went into partnership with an entrepreneur named Matthew Boulton. Together they set up a manufacturing operation in Birmingham to sell steam engines "for the whole world," as Boulton said once. The Watt-Boulton engine so transformed the face of industry in the world that many historians use the date of the registration of Watt's patent in 1769 as the start of the Industrial Revolution.

Power Like Nothing Ever Seen Before

The smoothly working steam engine was a marvel of technology. It could provide power that was unimaginable to the people of the 18th century. Now it was possible to conceive projects far larger than anything humans had attempted before. And it was so versatile. Factories could be located anywhere, not just where there was a strong current of water to turn a waterwheel. All that was needed was a certain amount of water to turn into steam, most of which was reusable, and a lot of coal to fire the boiler.

Unlike other sources of power that people had tapped into, the Watt-Boulton steam engine used energy in two very different ways: the power stroke of the engine came from atmospheric pressure, which can is an inexhaustible resource since it is an effect of gravity. But to make that usable, a sizeable vacuum has to be made in a fairly large chamber to give the atmosphere something to push against. To make that vacuum, water is boiled, turned to steam filling the chamber, and then condensed back to water, which has a much smaller volume, leaving a vacuum in the rest of the chamber. All these are reversible processes with little waste. There the free ride ends.

Starting Down the Non-Renewable Path

The trouble comes with the boiling of the water. That requires a heat source, and the only readily available heat source for the 18th century that was strong enough to do the job was coal. Burning coal produces an exothermic reaction as the carbon in the coal combines with oxygen from the air, releasing quite a bit of heat. Three things happen here: (1) the coal is used up; (2) a great deal of carbon dioxide is produced; and (3) the desired heat is produced. Only the last is what is wanted, the others are just necessary costs.

The carbon dioxide produced did not seem a problem in the early years of the steam engine. It did reduce the amount of free oxygen in the atmosphere, but this was of little consequence. The fact that CO_2 is a greenhouse gas and having too much of it might cause global warming was certainly not on anyone's mind. There *was* an aspect of the burning that was quite disturbing. Raw coal is full of impurities. Burning it in quantity in a furnace produces a terrific amount of foul sulphurous gas, leading to what we now call smog. In the early years of the Industrial Revolution, the gases produced from steam engines, blast furnaces, and homes that used coal for heating produced dangerous amounts of toxic fumes making the cities dangerous places for anyone with respiratory problems. Some of these problems have been addressed, but even today, coal burning remains one of the largest sources of atmospheric pollution.

Coal

Troublesome as the pollutant problems were and still are, the really momentous change that the steam engine brought to human civilization was the reliance upon a totally non-renewable resource—a fossil fuel. Coal is the fossilized residue of tropical forests that all died over 280 million years ago, *before* Pangaea was even formed. The trees and other vegetable matter in the tropical forests died, fell into the swampy land and decomposed into peat. Then with the advances and receding of the seas in long cycles, heavy layers of rock formed on top of the peat. As the rock layers increased, the pressure on the peat increased until it began to change into coal, which now exists in various forms, having to do with just how much pressure was put on the forming coal bed. The hardest coal, anthracite, lies under mountain ranges, formed when the tectonic plates pushed together.

By any measure of time relevant to the human race, coal is totally non-renewable. What there is was all formed so long ago that we cannot possibly imagine that there will ever be any more than what there already is. This is not to say that people have found all the coal in the world, but only that if they ever do, there won't be any more after that.

Coal is but the first of the non-renewable resources that we have come to depend upon. Petroleum and natural gas are others, both carrying the same caveat that what there is now is all there ever will be.

It is the steam engine that started humanity down this path, from which there does not seem to be any return.

The machine section at one of the great industrial expositions in the 19th century. The products shown were the state-of-the-art technology of the time.

Chapter 16

Making Goods for Sale

The Watt-Boulton steam engine is often credited with starting the revolutionary industrialization that was so noticeable in Britain in the mid-18th century. But the Industrial Revolution did not begin from a dead stop in 1769 when Watt lodged his patent. If a significant industry had not already been in place, one that required a large reliable power source, then there would have been no customers for Watt & Boulton's new machine.

Mining

There were such industries already flourishing. The first customers for the Watt-Boulton engines were the mines, where they were used as a superior pump, as discussed in the previous chapter. Even the Newcomen engine was a success as a pump for the mines, especially coal mines, where the fuel necessary was cheap. The Watt-Boulton engine was superior to the Newcomen engine as a pump in all respects, because of its greater efficiency, especially for other sorts of mines—iron ore mines, for example. There was one hitch, however. Watt's superior design cost a lot more to build. These large steam engines were very expensive to begin with; it would not have been easy to convince mine owners that they would be better off with a much more expensive model when their Newcomen engine did the job. Boulton had the stroke of genius *not* to try to sell their steam engines, but instead to lease them. The cost of the lease would be one-third of the savings in fuel costs that the mine operators would gain by switching to the Watt-Boulton engine. Since the engines were four times as efficient, Watt and Boulton made a lot of money and placed a lot of engines.

Iron

Another closely related industry that was a prime target for the new steam engine was metal fabrication, or, more specifically, the iron business. Iron quickly became one of the most recognizable features of the Industrial Revolution. Just as wood had been the chief building material of the Middle Ages, iron was the medium of choice for almost any kind of construction as soon as it became practical to make it in large quantities. It was much stronger than wood, did not wear away from repeated usage, could be made into any shape desired, and was fireproof. Iron had been smelted since ancient times and used for special purposes, but until the 18th century it proved too expensive to manufacture in quantity for general use. The high heat required to melt iron, 1500° C, could only be achieved in a blast furnace. This required a continuous blast of fresh air to be forced over the fire to make it burn at a higher temperature. In antiquity, bellows were worked by hand. Starting in the 15th century, bellows were attached to waterwheels to provide a steady, untiring supply of air.

With the invention of the iron cannon, as well as other uses, demand for iron was on a constant increase. Iron foundries expanded and began operating continuously. The blast furnaces needed not just air, but a fuel that would burn at a very high temperature. Ordinary wood fires were insufficient, but charcoal, made from wood, was excellent. Unfortunately, it takes a lot of trees to make even a medium amount of charcoal, so with increasing demand for iron the pressure on the forests was palpable. An alternative to charcoal was much needed.

The obvious alternative was coal—especially in the British Isles that had so much coal in the ground. But coal had a number of faults. Ordinary coal contains many impurities, notably sulphur, which is part of the reason that it is such a pollutant. Those impurities are fatal for making iron, because they find their way into the molten iron and make it brittle. The situation can be improved by heating the coal in a closed container without air, which drives off some of the impurities. This is very much the same process as that by which charcoal is made from timber. The resultant reduced coal is called *coke*. Coke had many advantages over raw coal and found many uses. However, for iron smelting, there was still the problem of the remaining impurities, which damaged the iron too much.

In 1709, an ironmonger named Abraham Darby worked out a process to make a higher grade of coke that would suit an iron foundry. This removed one of the obstacles to increased iron production. There followed one of those interactive patterns that economists call a virtuous circle: an increase in one industry causes an increase in a second industry, which causes an increase in a third, which then makes the first industry even more successful, and so on. In this case the cycle looked something like this: (1) the improved coke helped the iron industry achieve a higher output; (2) this increased the demand for coal from which to make the coke; (3) the added activity in the coal mines required more steam engines to pump them dry; (4) steam engines are made out of iron, as much as 10 tonnes of it in each one.

With the Watt-Boulton engine came a further input to this cycle. Their engines made excellent bellows operators. The new use for the steam engine just added to the cycle: more iron mongering, more coal mining, more steam engine manufacturing.

Textiles

If the steam engine was the single piece of technology that characterized the Industrial Revolution, the single industry that filled the same role was the textile industry. Clothing has been made all over the world for as long as there has been any kind of human civilization at all. Every step of the process could be done in the home, within the family of the ultimate wearers of the garments, or the parts of the process could be separated and made into viable and respected crafts that readily found a place in society. The thread maker, the weaver, and the tailor were all mainstream cottage industries from the Middle Ages onward.

As with other cottage industries, there was a natural limit to what any individual craftsman could produce, and until there was considerably better freight transportation, there was a limited market for the finished product. All this changed in the Industrial Revolution. As it was with the development of the steam engine, the critical steps in textile manufacturing occurred first in Britain.

The British Isles are home to a great many sheep. Their wool was the traditional material of British clothing since it was readily available locally and could be worked with fairly easily. By the 17th century, British wool was much in demand, not just for domestic consumption, but also as a major export product to Europe. But export worked both ways. Soon Britain was importing cotton fabric from India, which was eating into the domestic wool market.

The British textile manufacturers tried to compete with cotton goods of their own, importing raw cotton and fabricating it themselves. However, wool and cotton have very different properties that make working with them different. Cotton is much more delicate and requires very careful handling at every stage, especially the spinning of thread. Some of the most ingenious inventions of the early Industrial Revolution were machines that could automate some of these tasks which otherwise were very labour intensive. The first such inventions were still operated by human muscle turning a crank. Then some of the machines were adapted to being turned by conveyor belts driven by waterwheels, or even draft animals. After the Watt-Boulton engine became available, it became the engine that ran the textile industry.

What happened to textile manufacture in Britain provides the classic case study to illustrate First World/Third World economic relations and how the Industrial Revolution changed the context of supply and demand. Britain, as mentioned before, had a lot of sheep. The woolen industry fit naturally into the local economy. Cotton was another matter. The British climate suited sheep; it did not suit growing cotton. What's more, growing cotton is very hard work.

Here's where the Third World came in. Britain could obtain an unlimited supply of cotton by producing it in the colonies on large plantations and then shipping it to the textile industry at home. The efficiency of the mechanized textile industry meant that the British could manufacture inexpensive cotton fabric and cotton clothing for export. Local supply and demand was completely subverted. The raw goods came in; the finished goods went out; the profit

Cotton plants, ready to be picked.

remained. Since there was no natural local balance between supply and demand, the only limit to how much profit could be made was how fast the goods could be produced. Therefore, there was every incentive to keep the factories open longer, preferably 24 hours a day, and to build more and larger factories. All the other factors were offshore and mostly in areas where there was essentially unlimited room for expansion. If the manufacturers needed more raw cotton, they opened another plantation or expanded an existing one. If they had more goods to sell, they simply sent them farther afield where their affordability assured a sale. There was no particular incentive to make superior fabrics if more money could be made by producing a higher volume of shoddy ones. Somewhere in the world there would be a market for whatever had the lowest price, even if not at home.

There is another "virtuous circle"—though "vicious" seems the more appropriate term—that worked in the British textile industry: (1) more raw cotton was sent to the factories in Britain; (2) therefore, more finished fabric was made available for sale; (3)

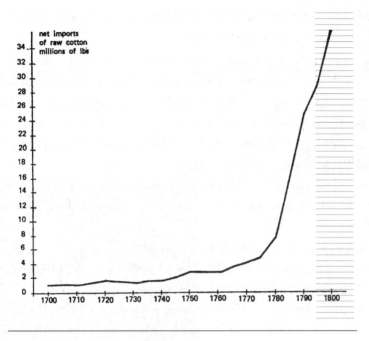

Raw cotton used in the British textile industry in the 18th century.

these products were sent abroad to poor people who could afford nothing else, in particular they were often sold in Africa; (4) the Africans, having no money with which to pay for the fabric instead paid in slaves which they captured from other tribes; (5) those slaves were sent to the colonies to work on the plantations, where they produced more raw cotton. This sort of cycle can escalate very quickly. What happened in this particular industry can be illustrated by a graph of the quantity of raw cotton that was used in the British textile industry in the 18th century.

The other aspect of the changes wrought by the Industrial Revolution that is illustrated so well by the British textile industry is the inevitability of uniformity. Machines are very good at repetitive tasks. They can perform them quickly and accurately, and they don't get bored doing so. If the chief goal of a manufacturing operation is to get goods made and out the door to be sold, there is no better way to do it than to make the same thing over and over again. If the potential market is virtually limitless, there is no reason to vary the product. This leads to the standardization of goods for sale that is so familiar to us now. Instead of every item being different, with its own character, each is the same as the next one, we expect it to be so and otherwise wonder if it is faulty. This is the realm of mass producing, which the large factory operations perfected.

The Changed Nature of Work

The Industrial Revolution changed the nature of work from largely home-based, serving a local market, to factory-based, producing goods for export to anywhere at all. The worker no longer had any control over the product, and the pace of work was determined by the machine, usually a steam engine, that ran a conveyor belt or other moving parts of the factory. More was better generally, because more output meant more profit. So long as markets could be found, there were no inherent limits to what could be produced.

The road to happiness was through more work and more goods, both produced and consumed. These trumped almost everything else, leading to a society that valued growth above all. The poster "By Industry We Thrive" that is reproduced at the beginning of Chapter 18 (page 186) captures this sentiment, widely shared throughout the Industrial Revolution. Industry is progress. Progress is the greatest goal. Notice that in the poster, the factory in the background is proudly shown emitting a huge plume of smoke into the atmosphere. Smoke meant work and work meant progress.

George Stephenson driving "Locomotion No. 1" at opening of the Stockton and Darlington Railway, September 27, 1825. This was the first passenger-carrying railway open to the public. Note that the passengers are riding in open freight cars, which must have been extremely uncomfortable, especially with the smoke from the locomotive blowing in their faces.

Chapter 17

Railroads and Steamships

The Watt-Boulton steam engine provided the power to industry to be able to manufacture on a large scale. That in itself proved to be a problem. Not only was the power produced large, so was the size of the engine. The Newcomen engine and the Watt-Boulton engine were what are now called *atmospheric steam engines*. They worked by using steam to fill a chamber, then condensing it to produce a vacuum, with the power stroke coming from the pressure of the atmosphere. From 1769 when Watt filed his patent until 1800 when it finally expired, he and Boulton had control of almost every aspect of steam engine production in Britain, where most of the industrial activity was.

They used their monopoly not just for their own profit but also to keep certain standards which they believed were necessary for safety. One of their concerns was the state of metallurgy in the 18th century. Both the boiler that produced the steam and the chamber that would be evacuated had to withstand pressure on their walls. Some of the iron of the day was brittle and would suddenly fail. There had been a number of dramatic accidents with cannon that burst when fired, killing the soldiers doing the shooting instead of those aimed at. This was only a minor risk with the Watt-Boulton engine, because the steam produced remained at standard atmospheric pressure, which the metal walls could bear.

High-Pressure Steam

However, there is another way to make a steam engine, using steam at much higher pressures. Water, when boiled, turns to steam, occupying a much larger volume. But it does not stop there. If the steam is heated further, it expands more and more—or would if it were not contained. Instead, it builds up greater and greater pressure, which all pushes against the walls of whatever contains it. For that reason, Watt and Boulton did not allow its use in steam engines so long as they could prevent it.

But if the metallurgical problem could be overcome, there were great advantages to using high-pressure steam. In the time between Watt's 1769 patent and its expiry in

1800, great strides were made in manufacturing iron of higher tensile strength. Perhaps Watt and Boulton were over cautious or perhaps they were just riding their patent. In any case, other engineers were ready and waiting with new designs for steam engines when the 19th century began.

A high-pressure steam engine works differently. Instead of filling a chamber with steam and then condensing it to produce a vacuum, the pressure of the steam itself is what moves the piston in the steam chamber. In a low-pressure engine, it is the atmospheric pressure pushing the piston inward that is the power stroke. In high-pressure engines, the power stroke is in the opposite direction and is caused by the much higher pressure of the steam compared to the atmosphere.

The advantage of high-pressure steam is that it can deliver much more power from a much smaller machine. The Newcomen and the Watt-Boulton engines were of a category sometimes called *stationary engines*. They were so called because it was really unthinkable that these huge contraptions could be mounted on any moving platform.[1] But a high-pressure steam engine could be made compactly enough that it could be used onboard vehicles and vessels. There was tremendous potential here for new means of transporting all those goods that were being produced in the industrial centers.

The Railroads

Several of the best engineering minds of the late 18th and early 19th centuries put their talents to devising a self-contained steam engine that would turn the wheels under the platform on which it was mounted and cause it to move by itself. In the same way that a draft animal is hitched to a load, these *locomotives* would then be attached to carts laden with freight that needed to be moved. If the carts were attached to each other in a line, the result was a *train*.

Such a locomotive could be used to pull carts around in the work area of a factory or a colliery, for example, as in the picture at the beginning of Part IV. This was useful, but it would not do for transporting finished goods to faraway markets. There just were not adequate roads to travel on that could accommodate a heavy mobile machine pulling a cart or carts of freight. An earlier solution to getting bulk goods to market was the canal

---

1. There were exceptions. The Watt-Boulton engine was used to power some ships and even a land vehicle. The water transport worked but the land vehicle was impractically heavy.

system. Britain, in particular, crisscrossed their country with canals for barges that could transport a heavy load long distances.

The solution found was to build a special road just for them, consisting of two parallel bands of iron at a distance from each other equal to that of the wheel base of the locomotive. In other words, what we call a *railroad*, or *railway*. Tracks actually came into use before the invention of the railroad locomotive. The smooth path they provided was such an improvement over bumpy roads that they were used for moving loaded carts drawn by horses or even people.

As with so many steps in the Industrial Revolution, the leadership in locomotive design came from Britain. When it became clear to the leaders of industry that the railroads were the ideal solution to their problem of getting raw materials to their factories and finished goods to market, great efforts were made to get the best equipment that the engineers could deliver. Hence competitions were held to entice the engineers to outdo each other in creating the ideal locomotive.

The Rainhill Competition

A famous case was the newly authorized line between Liverpool and Manchester—one a port and the other a major manufacturing center. Demand was high for a better way to transport goods back and forth other than over land. The demand came from the rapidly growing cotton industry. Raw cotton was delivered through Liverpool, transported to Manchester, where it was processed and then shipped back out via Liverpool to markets abroad.

It was decided that a competition to decide the best locomotive for the line should be held in October, 1829. The site chosen was an area near Liverpool called Rainhill. The task put to the participating engineers was to design a locomotive that would be able to pull three times its own weight at 10 miles per hour over a 1½ mile track for 10 round trips. The winning engine was designed by the father and son team of George and Robert Stephenson. They called it the *Rocket*. It weighed 4¼ tonnes, pulled the required 12¾ tonnes at an average of 13.8 miles per hour for the 10 required laps. It even achieved a maximum speed of 24.1 miles per hour, which was totally unheard of in its day.

George and Robert Stephenson's *Rocket*, winner of the Rainhill competition.

Railroads Take Off

When the Liverpool-Manchester line did open, it was expected to be used primarily for freight haulage. What surprised all the planners was that as soon as the opportunity presented itself, people wanted to travel by train too. What had begun as a desperately needed solution to moving freight quickly turned into a people mover. Not only did the railroad soon displace the stage coach as the conveyance of choice, much more travel was undertaken than ever before. Given the opportunity, people did not choose to live all their lives in the same community, but rather wanted to visit other parts of the world, even if it was only a few hours' journey away.

In the mid-19th century, railroads began to spread out all over the world at a phenomenal rate. As in Britain, they generally were intended as a more reliable and faster way of transporting freight, but quickly began to accommodate passengers as well. Railroads had the effect of intensifying rather than changing the character of the economy of the countries where they were introduced. In Britain, mainland Europe, and North America, the railroads brought the countries together. Physical travel and commerce extended from one end of a country to another. For adjacent countries, such as in Europe, the railroads facilitated both commercial and political relations. In Canada and the United States, the distances across the countries were so vast that the relatively quick travel provided by transcontinental rail service served as much as anything else to solidify the countries' political identities.

The ceremony of driving the last spike in the completion of the Canadian Pacific Railway line providing rail service across Canada from "sea to sea," i.e., from Montreal to Vancouver, 1886.

In the Third World, railroads served a different purpose. They were set up to facilitate the export of raw materials from these countries back to the First World countries. This increased commercial activity coupled with the lower costs of transportation produced higher profits. But the profits accrued to the foreign investors, not the local industry, so little was spent on building an indigenous industrial base, nor on improving social services. Thus, the countries gained no diversification in their economies; to the contrary, they became more dependent on the sale of their resources.

The Steamship

Transporting goods by water has always been the least expensive method wherever possible. The ancient trading civilizations were always located near navigable bodies of water so that traders could load their boats with goods and sail off to markets, rather than trek over the rugged, irregular, and often dangerous terrain. When industrialization got underway, canals were seen as superior to roads for moving freight.

The steam engine seemed like a natural extension of existing water transportation. One could imagine a steam engine that somehow propelled a barge in a canal or a steam engine that took the place of (or supplemented) sails or even oars on a ship or boat. All these were tried. Some worked better than others.

The earliest vessels to function with steam power actually used the Watt-Boulton engine. The first technological problem to be solved was how to turn the up-and-down motion of the piston in the engine into something that propelled the boat. There were three different solutions: (1) Connect the reciprocating motion of the piston directly to a set of oars and pull the boat along like any rowboat. This actually worked and a passenger service was operated in the Delaware River starting in 1787 that could carry 30 passengers 30 kilometers up or down the river in just over 3 hours. (2) Use the piston motion to operate a pump that will push water out of the back of the boat to propel it forward. Nice idea, but it was not made to work in any practical way. (3) Turn the reciprocal motion to rotary motion with a crank attachment and use it to turn paddlewheels that will push the boat forward. This, of course, became the standard model for steamboats.

Robert Fulton's boat, *The Clermont*, sailed up and down the Hudson River in New York, on a regular commercial run beginning in 1807, making it clear that steam power could successfully replace sails on a large vessel. The boat still had masts as though sails were used, but it was entirely

The Clermont Steamship, operating on the Hudson River.

powered by the steam engine. Fulton also had other boats built with the same design to cross the Atlantic. The paddlewheel was amidships. Later designs, particularly the famed Mississippi River Steamboats, had the paddlewheel at the stern.

With the viability of sea travel by steam-powered vessels established early in the 19th century, larger steamships were soon constructed to compete with the clipper sailing ships for the transatlantic trade routes. The early steamships could not keep pace with the well-designed clipper ships, but they were more reliable in adverse winds. In 1840, the screw propeller was developed and found to be superior to the paddlewheel for the large ships. By 1887, steamships were carrying greater tonnage than sailing vessels, and the age of sail was coming to an end.

The Pre-Eminence of Fossil Fuels

With the exception of a few factories that succeeded in running on power from waterwheels and even fewer that needed no external power source at all, manufacturing became totally dependent on the steam engine to drive its conveyor belts and other moving parts. Likewise, with the transition to railroads and steamships, the steam engine also accounted for most of the transportation that was essential to the economy of the industrialized nations.

In short, to be industrialized, it was necessary to get energy from something formed millions of years ago and in finite supply. Later on, both railroads and steamships switched to Diesel fuel, which is another fossil fuel. No matter how it was done, power came from the past.

The resources of the Industrial Revolution were to a large extent imported from elsewhere, mostly the Third World. The nations that did industrialize first were those that had already overused their own resources and were then beginning to consume those from other parts of the world.

The Industrial Revolution brought a much higher standard of living to the First World countries. Because of it those of us who live in the industrialized nations enjoy a quality of life that we view as unthinkable to part with.

"By Industry We Thrive: 'Progress' Our Motto." An inspiring engraved poster extolling the virtues of industry. Smithsonian Institution.

Chapter 18

The Economic Viewpoint

In the period following the Scientific Revolution of the 16th and 17th centuries, science was seen to give those who understood it a power over nature. If the forces of nature could be understood and put into formulae, then surely every other mystery of life would yield to similar analysis. This produced the Enlightenment, a period in which the leading thinkers of Europe believed that true understanding was within human reach. With understanding would come power. The result would be that there would be a steady improvement in the fate of humanity as it learned to take control of the world around it.

Measuring Progress

This is the idea of *progress*, which became the dominant sentiment later in the 18th century and through the 19th century, basically the same period as the Industrial Revolution. Progress meant that the future was surely going to be better than the present, just as the present is better than the past.

If things are getting better and better, how would you measure that? As the self-appointed custodians of nature, those at the top of the ladder of progress had some responsibilities toward all of nature to help it along in its "inevitable" perfecting process. It would be nice to know how to find the best way of doing things. Commerce, for example.

Adam Smith.

The 18th century was replete with thinkers pondering just such questions. One of the most influential then, and still, was Adam Smith, the founder of classical economics. In his seminal work, *Wealth of Nations*, published first in 1776, Smith argued that when individuals act in their own self interest in the pursuit of greater wealth, whether as producers or consumers, buying and selling, so long as there is fair competition on both sides, the resulting trades would take place at the prices that would produce the greatest benefit for all of society. Thus the best way to run any complex society was to allow the maximum amount of competition over the same goods and services.

This is the basis of the market economy. When it comes to regulating trade in common commodities with many buyers and many sellers, it works pretty well. But Smith probably intended it to have wider and greater applicability. In any case, an economic viewpoint built up around Smith's thought that had implications that went well beyond his theory of ideal pricing.

When classical economics is applied to trade in natural resources, the resources are treated in the same way as a commodity that was produced from start to finish by the seller. The seller's price is closely related to the value they put on their labour and the direct costs of their materials. An entrepreneur who obtains some resource from a Third World country for very little cost drives down the price that could be fetched for the same resource obtained at home where it may be in short supply.

The tidy supply-demand graphs of classical economics take into account the current costs of providing a resource; they do not have any way of taking into consideration that these resources are finite. Indeed the entire economic system that supports the market economy and has underlying it a faith in the inevitable progress of the human enterprise is based upon the assumption that necessary resources *will* always be available, and growth can and will continue forever. This is what provides the justification for the continual increase in the amount of natural resources that are consumed and the damage to the environment that follows from it. Economic activity is considered a virtue and it trumps all other considerations.

Anita Gordon and David Suzuki, in their book *It's a Matter of Survival*, recount a telling incident recalled by a U.N. executive from his youth:

> Mostafa Tolba, the head of the U.N. Environment Program, remembers that as a schoolboy growing up in Egypt he was shown pictures of factories in Cairo belching out thick smoke over the countryside, and proudly told by his teacher, "This is a sign of progress." Indeed it was such an important sign that in the 1960s Egyptian banknotes carried a picture of smokestacks. "This was a symbol of development for us…. Industrialization meant smokestacks, and smokestacks meant progress."[1]

---

1. Anita Gordon and David Suzuki, *It's a Matter of Survival* (Toronto: Stoddart, 1990), p. 133.

It seems crazy to us, but throughout the Industrial Revolution, smokestacks, foul air, and pollution of all sorts *were* seen as tangible evidence of progress, of life getting better and better. Out of that smoke and stench would come better things. The pollution would be cleaned up later, or if it couldn't, that was just the price paid for prosperity.

It is the economic viewpoint that supports this illusion. Economic measures are, by and large, of short-term effects: inputs and outputs. The underlying assumption is that the short-term effects accumulate and over time will tell the whole story. The long-term effects that are invariably left out of consideration—because they are too difficult to assess accurately, for one thing—do not appear relevant at all. So, natural resources continue to be valued by the costs of extraction with no consideration taken of the limit to their supply. Pollution is considered a temporary *dis*-commodity, one to be minimized, perhaps, if not just ignored, but the possibility of long-term accumulation of pollutants that is not reversible is not considered.

Gross National Product

John   Maynard
Keynes.

A telling measure of economic health used by governments and industry in all the advanced countries was proposed in the 1930s by the economist John Maynard Keynes. Keynes was looking for a general index that would be easy to calculate and that would give a quick measure of the pulse of the economy in a country. His measure was the Gross National Product, or GNP for short. The GNP is a measure of all production, consumption, and investment in an economy. Using this tool, a country is an economic success, i.e., it is "progressing," if its GNP is rising.

Because of the ease with which this figure can be calculated and its close correlation with other economic measures, it has been adopted by economic planners all over the world as a key indicator to watch and a guide to government policy. (In recent years, the related measure, GDP, or Gross Domestic Product, has been favoured. The difference between the two is that the GDP omits income from foreign investment by domestic companies.)

The GNP (or GDP) assigns a positive value to spending of all sorts. That may include purchases of consumable or durable goods, which would indicate a higher economic standard of living, but it also would include money spent on fixing things that are seriously wrong, such as cleaning up an oil spill. Or, even more insidiously, the GNP can give a higher value to shoddy workmanship than to an excellent product. For example, poorly made automobiles that need constant repair will add more to GNP or GDP than a well-engineered product that needs little maintenance.

This is all part of the intellectual baggage of the Industrial Revolution. The shift from a primary concern with food, shelter, and the necessities of life to a focus on creating wealth, and from that to buying what was needed or desired, meant that the measure of value became an abstraction, money. It had the appealing simplicity of being a single variable to assess and to strive to increase, but it had the fatal flaw of omitting much that then was no longer considered in any serious policy decisions. The Industrial Revolution gave us tremendous wealth—at least in the countries that became industrialized—and also brought with it tremendous waste.

PART FIVE

The Comfortable Life

I am writing this book at a cottage overlooking a beautiful lake. I can hear the water lapping the shore, birds singing in the trees. There is a pleasant breeze of fresh air flowing through the cabin. I have a feeling of tranquility, security, and well-being. But I am not cut off from the rest of the world by any means.

The cottage is several hundred kilometers from downtown Toronto, where I live, but I can be there in three hours by car, driving on limited access expressways at over 100 kilometers an hour. But I don't need to be there to be in contact. I can be reached by telephone and by email and can access the Internet from my notebook computer. For most purposes, I am just as accessible here as I am in my office in the city. I have difficulty imagining a more comfortable and satisfying life.

In the introduction to Part Four, I made reference to the adage that after industrialization people lived as only royalty had done before. But actually what kings could possibly have had the comfort and convenience and the opportunities that we have at our fingertips? We are the recipients of the products of human ingenuity and enterprise that has given us civilization as we know it. It has not come without cost, in some cases a very high cost, but it is hard to imagine that we would be better off without the technological advances that give us life as we know it.

The Industrial Revolution initiated the radical changes in our way of life that made all this possible. It changed the nature of work and vastly increased the material productivity of the workforce. Mechanized transportation improved the level of nutrition by making it possible to import varied fresh food from far away and widened the vistas of ordinary people, who began to travel away from their homes for the first time. There was time and money to support education, public health projects, cultural activities, and more comfortable living quarters.

The Industrial Revolution also kicked off a spate of inventiveness bringing us a steady stream of new products that have continued to offer more and more convenience and capability to the rich store already available. We adjust to these new opportunities so quickly that each generation now views its elders as quaintly old fashioned and far behind the times.

In Part Five, we look at some of the major inventions and developments that have followed the Industrial Revolution and once again changed our lives beyond recognition: the automobile and the airplane, the world of chemistry, electricity and communications, and what is necessary for all of this to work, our sources of energy.

For Further Reading

Adams, Henry. *The Education of Henry Adams.* Boston: Houghton Mifflin, 1974.

An Age of Innovation: The World of Electronics 1930-2000. By the editors of Electronics magazine. New York: McGraw-Hill, 1981.

Allan, Roy A. *A History of the Personal Computer: The People and the Technology.* London, ON: Allan Pub., 2001.

Arbib, Michael A. *Computers and the Cybernetic Society,* 2nd ed. Orlando, FL: Academic Press, 1984.

Arora, Ashish, Ralph Landau, and Nathan Rosenberg. *Chemicals and Long Term Growth: Insights from the Chemical Industry.* New York: Wiley, 1998.

Atherton, W. A. *From Compass to Computer: A History of Electrical and Electronics Engineering.* London: Macmillan, 1984.

Bowers, Brian. *Lengthening the Day: A History of Lighting Technology.* Oxford: Oxford University Press, 1998.

Cardwell, Donald. *The Norton History of Technology.* New York: W.W. Norton, 1995.

Cohn, Steve Mark. *Too Cheap to Meter: An Economic and Philosophical Analysis of the Nuclear Dream.* Albany: State University of New York Press, 1997.

Davis, Martin. *The Universal Computer: The Road from Leibniz to Turing.* New York: Norton, 2000.

Ellul, Jacques. *The Technological Society,* trans. by John Wilkinson. New York: Knopf, 1967.

————. *The Technological System.* New York: Continuum, 1980.

Flink, James J. *The Car Culture.* Cambridge: MIT Press, 1975.

Florman, Samuel C. *Blaming Technology: The Irrational Search for Scapegoats.* New York: St. Martin's Press, 1981

————. *The Existential Pleasures of Engineering.* New York: St. Martin's Press, 1976.

Freund. Peter E. S., and George Martin. *The Ecology of the Automobile.* Montreal: Black Rose Books, 1993.

Galbraith, John K. *The Affluent Society.* New York: Houghton, 1958.

Charles C. Gillispie. *The Montgolfier Brothers and the Invention of Aviation.* Princeton: Princeton University Press, 1983.

Glasstone, Samuel, and Walter H. Jordan. *Nuclear Power and Its Environmental Effects.* La Grange Park, IL: American Nuclear Society, 1981.

Gordon, Anita, and David Suzuki. *It's a Matter of Survival.* Toronto: Stoddart, 1990.

Henry, J T. *The Early and Later History of Petroleum: With Authentic Facts in Regard to Its Development in Western Pennsylvania.* New York: Burt Franklin, 1964. Originally published: Philadelphia, J.B. Rodgers, 1873.

Ifrah, Georges. *The Universal History of Computing: From the Abacus to the Quantum Computer,* trans. by E.F. Harding. New York: John Wiley, 2001.

MacLachlan, James. *Children of Prometheus: A History of Science and Technology,* 2nd ed. Toronto: Wall & Emerson, 2002.

Meikle, Jeffrey L. *American Plastic: A Cultural History.* New Brunswick, NJ: Rutgers University Press, 1995.

Mossman, Susan, ed. *Early Plastics: Perspectives, 1850-1950.* London: Leicester University Press, 1997.

Mumford, Lewis, *The City in History: Its Origins, Its Transformations, and Its Prospects.* New York: Harcourt, Brace & World, 1961.

————. *The Culture of Cities.* New York : Harcourt, Brace, Jovanovich, 1970.

————. *Myth of the Machine.* 2 vols. New York: Harcourt, Brace & World, 1967-70.

————. *Technics and Civilization.* New York: Harcourt, Brace & World, 1963.

Nelson, Joyce. *The Perfect Machine: Television and the Bomb.* Philadelphia, PA: New Society, 1992.

Silverberg, Robert. *Light for the World: Edison and the Power Industry.* Princeton, NJ: Van Nostrand, 1967.

Smith, Merritt Roe, and Leo Marx. *Does Technology Drive History?: The Dilemma of Technological Determinism.* Cambridge, MA: The MIT Press, 1995.

Tammemagi, H. Y. *Unlocking the Atom: The Canadian Book on Nuclear Technology.* Hamilton, ON: McMaster University Press, 2002.

Wurster, Christian. *Computers: An Illustrated History,* trans. by Hugh Casement. New York: Taschen, 2002.

Zygmont, Jeffrey. *Microchip: An Idea, Its Genesis, and the Revolution It Created.* Cambridge, MA: Perseus, 2003.

Clockwise from the upper left: the 1803 Trevithick steam carriage; the Columbia electric car, made by the Pope Manufacturing Company of Connecticut in 1897; the Ford Motor Works production line, circa 1930; traffic as seen across North America today.

Chapter 19

The Automobile

It was the railroad that gave the public the taste for travel. You could hop on a train, take a ride through unfamiliar scenery, and arrive at a destination you might never have reached otherwise. Sure, there were stage coaches before the trains came in, and you could also travel by horseback or even walk, but such trips were taken rarely and only by a small segment of society. The railroad made travel affordable and easy.

The railroad locomotive was a steam engine on wheels. That is, it was a machine that ran on power produced from materials that it carried with it, and was capable of pulling along a string of other carriages or freight cars. It ran on rails for two reasons: (1) it was much easier to pull a load on smooth tracks than on bumpy roads, and (2) there weren't suitable roads anyway. A steam locomotive was a heavy machine on its own. Add to that the boiler, the water supply, and the coal fuel, and there was quite a load to move around. Anything as heavy as a locomotive would sink right into the ground if metal rails did not hold it up.

The rails had one severe drawback, however; they could only take you where the tracks went. So long as the destinations remained the same and were required again and again, the trains were hard to beat. But wouldn't it be nice if the power of a steam engine could be attached to a land vehicle that could go anywhere?

Road Locomotives

Steam locomotives without rails actually were in use before they were made to run on tracks, but they were useful only to move heavy equipment around an industrial site, such as a colliery. Heading out on roads or on open fields was not successful.

One failed attempt was a French invention, Cugnot's Steam Dray, which was intended to pull heavy loads, such as artillery for the military. It had a large boiler, slung off the front end, to keep the heat away from the operator, and an atmospheric steam engine to turn a drive wheel. It was all mounted on a large platform with heavy, wide wheels. As soon as it left a surfaced road, it was so heavy that it sank into the ground. The French decided that pulling their artillery with horses was a much better idea.

The Cugnot Steam Dray.

The Cugnot machine used a low-pressure engine, which was bulky and not very powerful. Once high-pressure steam engines came into use, there were other attempts to adapt them to road vehicles. Richard Trevithick, one of the pioneers of the railroad locomotive, adapted a small high-pressure steam engine to a carriage. He was able to achieve speeds of up to 19 kilometers an hour, but there were few roads good enough to drive on. Another idea was a stagecoach run by steam that would be loaded with passengers and luggage both inside and outside. Like the Cugnot machine, it tended to get stuck in the mud.

The Red Flag Act

Britain was where the Industrial Revolution got started and for a time it was head-and-shoulders above other countries in industrialization. At the beginning of the 19th century it was the acknowledged leader in precision machines, quality tools, large stationary engines, and in mechanized transportation. Sometime during the 19th century it lost its edge; by the end of the century both the United States and the rest of Europe had caught up and in many ways surpassed the British in technological leadership. How and why this happened is a subject of great interest to historians of the Industrial Revolution, who have written much on the subject. It is a subject beyond the scope of this book, but nonetheless, a few events that are very suggestive will be mentioned.

The first is what came to be called the *Red Flag Act*. This was an act of Parliament passed in 1865 at the instigation of the owners of the British railroads, ostensibly to protect the citizenry from dangerous accidents involving road locomotives. Its greater effect, and the real motive behind it, was to prevent the development of a mechanized road vehicle industry in Britain so as to forestall competition with the railroads. It killed the development of the automobile in Britain.

The "Red Flag Act"—its official name was the Locomotive Act—specified that the maximum speed of "road locomotives" was to be two miles per hour in towns and four miles per hour on the open highways. Where the red flag came in was that the act also specified that an attendant must walk 60 yards ahead of the vehicle carrying a red flag to warn of the impending danger from the speeding vehicle behind him. At night, a red lantern was to be substituted. The act was finally repealed in 1896 at the urging of wealthy automotive pioneers, but by then Britain had lost the leadership in the industry, which it never regained.

Poor Roads

Prior to the Industrial Revolution, overland routes were very poor everywhere. Whatever roads did exist were either horse trails, no wider than necessary for one or two horses and with no attention paid to the evenness of the surface. Or, another possibility was that they were remaining Roman roads, built for carts and chariots back in the Roman Empire and mostly allowed to fall into disrepair since then. It was a testament to the quality of Roman engineering that well over a thousand years after its collapse, the best roads in Europe were often those built for the governance of the Roman Empire.

The Industrial Revolution produced a demand for land routes that could be used for commercial traffic. By the beginning of the 19th century, a program of road construction had begun in all the industrialized countries, and especially in Britain. However, the success of the railroads in the first half of the 19th century was so great that the perceived need for roads diminished, and road building basically ceased.

Road building was not revived until the last two decades of the 19th century. The reason for the renewed interest in roadways was not impetus from the fledgling automobile industry, which was having a very hard time getting going, but instead was the result of another invention to ride on the roads, the bicycle.

The Draisienne, or "hobby horse." It was a fad in England in 1819 among the leisure class.

The Bicycle

The bicycle is now a major form of personal transportation in certain countries, in China in particular. Although China has an industrial base, automobiles remain a luxury that only the relatively wealthy can afford. In the main industrialized nations, the bicycle is a vehicle for sport and for the young, but only rarely as the main form of transportation. It was for sport that the bicycle was originally conceived.

The first two-wheeled contraption for riding was a French invention called the *draisienne*. Though a French invention, it caught on in England in the first decades of the 19th century where it was a fad among the British upper classes. They called it the "hobby horse." It had two fixed wheels and could not really be steered, though there was a handlebar to grip onto. There were no pedals. The rider sat on a saddle between the wheels and pushed the whole thing along with his feet. It was rather ridiculous and also dangerous.

The first two-wheeled vehicle with pedals was also a French invention, introduced in the 1860s. As with the draisienne, it was more popular in Britain than in France. This vehicle had one large wheel in front to which the pedals were directly attached, and a small wheel in the back for balance. The rider sat on a seat atop the large wheel and had handlebars for turning and for stability. There was also a women's version, which had an awkward sidesaddle so the woman, dressed, of course, in a long skirt, would not have to straddle the large wheel, much as the also awkward sidesaddle for horseback riding.

The Penny Farthing. Men's and women's version.

The British also had a nickname for this vehicle. They called it the *Penny Farthing*, which referred to the relative sizes of two of their coins, the large penny and the tiny farthing. Like the earlier Hobby Horse, the Penny Farthing was only for the athletically inclined and the foolhardy.

Then there were direct attempts to provide stability with another wheel. Various tricycles designs were invented and trotted out, but none of them caught on, partly because the third wheel required a wider clear space on the roads and partly because they were that much harder to pedal.

The breakthrough came in 1885 in Coventry, England, with the invention of what was called the *Safety Bicycle*. It is the basic design familiar to us today: front and back wheels of the same size, a saddle in the middle, between the wheels, and pedals that operated a chain drive connected to the back wheel. This was an immediate success and was in much demand. It was mass-produced in the Coventry shop and sold for $30.

Better Roads

Now there was a real reason to have better roads. Horses could cope with ruts, but riding a bicycle over heavily gouged mud paths was not much fun, and fun was what bicycle riding was about. The best roads in Europe were in France—which did not have the disincentive of the Red Flag Act—but French roads were generally gravel surfaced, not ideal for bicycles.

Bicycle owners formed clubs and published magazines and newsletters. Together, they pressured their governments for better roads. Their success was related to their pecking order in the social hierarchies in their respective countries. Right from the beginning, the British enthusiasts for the bicycle tended to come from the upper classes, those who had leisure, money, and influence with the government. In France and the rest of mainland Europe, cycling had caught on more with the lower social classes who were more easily ignored. What's more, in Britain there was a growing perception that power had been abused by the railroad barons and this needed correcting. The result was that British roads began to be significantly improved in the 1880s and 1890s. The cyclists had less effect in the rest of Europe.

For different reasons, there was a push for better roads in the United States. This came from the farmers who needed to get their produce to market. Agricultural techniques and technology had significantly improved the output of the farms, but this would be of little use if farmers could not get their harvest to the markets before it spoiled. There was also a backlash in the United States against the railroads, which were perceived to have wrongfully stifled competition from road travel.

The Bicycle Industry

It is hard to imagine how the modern automobile industry might have developed had it not been preceded by the bicycle industry. All the basic components of the early automobiles were adapted from what had been worked out by the bicycle manufacturers. For example, the steel tube frame, that was discovered to be just as strong as solid steel, but, of course, much lighter; the concept of ball bearings to make a wheel turn freely around an axle without wear and tear and without massive friction; the important innovation of the chain drive to allow the driving force—in the case of bicycles, the pedals—to be placed in a more convenient location and thence to adjust the ratio of revolutions of the power source to revolutions of the drive wheel. (The Penny Farthing front wheel was as huge as it was because one revolution of the pedals made one revolution of the "penny" wheel. A smaller front wheel would have forced the cyclist to pedal madly to get up any speed.) Later on, the ratio of power source to drive wheel was given further flexibility with the invention of differential gears, a device that was also essential in automobiles.

The pneumatic tire was invented by John Dunlop in Ireland in 1888 and quickly replaced the uncomfortable solid rubber tires that had been in use on the earlier bicycles. This too, made a huge difference to the ride quality in automobiles and was adopted from the start. And then there were all the trappings of mass production worked out in detail for bicycles and easily adapted to automobiles, such as specialized machine tools to perform delicate tasks again and again with great precision and sheet metal stamping and electric welding. Bicycles attracted the best mechanical engineering talent of the late 19th century, and they honed their skills on making this relatively new invention as good a machine as they could. But also, they pioneered the process of making it in quantity to satisfy a growing demand.

The Steamer

With bicycle technology, the self-powered road vehicle had a useful model for building a light-weight, yet strong, body that could be propelled by an engine that weighed less than the sort of steam engines that were used to propel the railroad locomotives. But there were still unsolved problems that made such an application less than ideal.

Consider the old steam locomotives with the coal car behind. The fireman busies himself shoveling coal into the furnace and the engineer has an elaborate array of levers and signals to coordinate so as to get the right amount of steam into the pressure chambers and then to ease the linkage to the drive wheels into place. The engine also takes a considerable amount of time to build up a head of steam sufficient to start the locomotive moving.

The entire operation is cumbersome and complicated. For a self-powered road vehicle to be practical, it had to be made as easy to handle as driving a team of horses. All of these problems were solved in the last decades of the 19th century when the steam engine became a practical motor for a road vehicle.

First, the matter of weight was solved. New engines were made that were considerably lighter and worked at higher pressures. Automatic controls were perfected so that human intervention could be minimized. There was still the problem of the long wait for the water to boil. This was solved in 1889 with the invention by Léon Serpollet in France of the flash boiler, which produces a small amount of steam within seconds, enough to get started.

Then the issue of fuel was solved. Earlier steam engines all ran on coal. This was not practical for a relatively small road vehicle. Another fossil fuel came to the rescue, petroleum. The steam engines did not use gasoline, but instead used kerosene, a petroleum distillate that had been developed for lighting in the middle of the 19th century. (More on this in Chapter 21.)

One of the first companies to latch onto the new technology was the French bicycle manufacturer, Peugeot. Peugeot used the Serpollet engine to build a motorized tricycle, and Serpollet himself demonstrated it by driving it 480 kilometers from Paris to Lyons in January 1890 over a period of two weeks.

The Red Flag Act had effectively stopped development of the steam car in Britain, but in the United States, several practical steam cars were built in the thirty years from 1860 to 1890. Ransom Olds, another bicycle manufacture, built steamers in 1887-1897—the first Oldsmobiles. And then the company of Whitney and Stanley in Boston mass-produced the best selling steam car ever, the *Locomobile Steamer*. It was the top selling car of any kind in the United States in the years 1900 to 1901.

Whitney and Stanley's 1900 Locomobile Steamer.

The Stanley Steamer was an extremely well built car, and very efficient. In 1906 a Stanley Steamer set a speed record of an incredible 207 km/hr. The Stanley was the luxury vehicle of the turn of the century. It was made in many different models, from a single passenger "Locomobile" to large models with several rows of seats and luggage room.

Despite everything that the steamer had in its favour, around 1910, all manufacturers switched to gasoline engines. The steamer had some inherent drawbacks and one flaw brought on by its own success. The inherent flaws were that it had a lower thermal efficiency than an internal combustion engine, and it actually used just as much petroleum fuel to boil water as the gasoline engine did in its combustion chambers.

Driving a steam car left a trail of steam blowing all around—evidence of the large quantities of water the car required.

The flaw that it brought on itself had to do with water. Since it was a steam engine, it had to be frequently refilled with soft water, from which to make the steam. In the early days of the steam car, there was plenty of water around wherever horse-drawn transportation was to be found, in troughs for the horses to slake their thirst. The steamer could pull up and fill its tank any time it needed. However, as mechanized vehicles became more common and horses less common, the troughs disappeared.

The Electric Car

Environmentalists have a particular affinity for the electric car. It is quiet; it does not pollute; and it is easy to drive. It has been around as long as any other kind of automobile, but still has not caught on. That's because it has had and continues to have some serious drawbacks.

The electric car operates on stored electrical power. The storage is done in a battery. The electric storage batters was first invented in 1859 and then was made practical in 1880 in France. But the French did not take much interest in the possibility of an electric car. It was in the United States that the idea was pursued. A company in New York City actually ran a fleet of twelve taxicabs in 1897 that all ran on electricity.

The leading American bicycle maker, the Pope Manufacturing Company, became the leading electric car builder in the United States. An important consideration used in the advertising of the day was that these cars were more suitable for women drivers than the gasoline engines. (The early gasoline engines had a manual crank that was used to start the engine. The crank could be quite stiff and could recoil, causing injury.) But despite this consideration and the other virtues of being silent and clean, the car was not a commercial success. It was considerably more expensive to manufacture than a gasoline engine and three times as expensive to operate. In 1910, the maximum range was 80 to 125 kilometers, after which it needed a recharge. And, because of the very heavy weight of the storage batteries, it had very poor hill climbing and acceleration capability. It could not compete with gasoline.

The batteries have improved enormously and the structural design is much better, but still electric cars have not found much of a place on the roads of the world, though they are in common use for golf carts and utility vehicles in factories and warehouses.

The Internal Combustion Engine

Cars and trucks as we know them now generally run on engines that have a different principle of action from either the steam engine or the electric motor. Today's vehicles use engines that operate by a rapid series of controlled explosions inside chambers that cause them to expand, producing the motions that drive the engine of the vehicle. There are two basic designs of the internal combustion engine, both of which remain in use today. The first developed was the familiar gasoline engine that works by igniting a mixture of gasoline and air with a spark in a combustion chamber with a movable piston. This was first developed by the German, Nikolaus Otto, in 1876, and then made practical with the invention of the carburetor by another German, Gottlieb Daimler. The second type also involves the combustion of a petroleum distillate with air, but instead of being ignited by a spark, it is ignited by pressure alone that raises the temperature of the mixture above its ignition point. This engine was patented by Rudolf Diesel in 1893 and still bears his name. The Diesel engine uses a heaver petroleum product, "Diesel" fuel, and works best in rather larger engines. The Diesel engine is found most often in large trucks, buses, and railroad locomotives, once they gave up on steam.

It was German technology that made the internal combustion engine and that first made practical automobiles using it. However, the transformation of the industrialized world by the automobile is a quintessential American story.

The Model T

The man who turned the automobile from a plaything of the wealthy to an essential item among an ordinary family's possessions was Henry Ford. He was born in Dearborn, Michigan, in 1863 and grew up on a farm. He was fascinated with machinery of all sorts. At the age of 16 he apprenticed himself to a mechanic in Detroit to learn all he could about machines. In 1896, he built his own first car and drove it around

Henry Ford.

in Detroit. In 1903, he organized the Ford Motor Company with the goal of making automobiles that anyone could afford.

The Model T.

He achieved the cost savings he needed by adopting the principle of the assembly line in mass production. Every worker in his factory had one and only one job, which was performed over and over again. Conveyor belts brought the parts needing assembling to the workers rather than have the workers have to go to them. Efficiency was an obsession with Ford.

In 1908, he introduced the *Model T* car. This was a car that he hoped to put in reach of every family in America. In 1908, the first models sold for $850; by 1927, the price had fallen to $290. This car held the record for numbers sold until the Volkswagen Beetle appeared in the 1950s.

The Car Culture

When the family car became affordable, it quickly became a perceived necessity. For Americans in particular, but to a large degree in all of the industrialized nations, the car was the symbol of success and convenience. The early automobiles were status symbols for the rich or mechanical marvels that required special skills to operate. That all changed with the introduction of the Model T and other cars for the general public. A car became an essential part of the good life. Car ownership grew in the United States from 70 thousand in 1905 to ten million by 1921. By 1930, there were 26 million cars in the U.S., and the rate continued to double every twenty years, reaching 120 million by the mid-1970s. The American rate of car growth was duplicated somewhat later in the rest of the world. European car ownership took off after the Second World War, quadrupling between 1950 and 1970. Across the world, car ownership went from 50 million in 1950 to 532 million by 2000. This is a rate of growth considerably faster than that of the human population.

In the United States, the automobile was such a fad that every conceivable activity was turned into something you could do, or even had to do, in your automobile. An annual vacation from work was to be spent driving your car across the country to visit new places. (On American television in the 1950s, one of the most popular programs starred Dinah Shore, who, on behalf of her sponsor, always sang her theme song, "See the

U.S.A. in your Chevrolet.") When driving to new places in your automobile, you didn't ever want to lose sight of it. Hence a new kind of accommodation was created. Instead of staying in hotels, travelers would stay in the new *Motels* (i.e., motor hotels), where they could park their car just outside their rooms and keep an eye on it all the time.

There were Drive-in versions of everything. Drive-in movies, Drive-in restaurants, Drive-in banks, Drive-in churches. You could take your car everywhere.

Too Much of a Good Thing?

The invention and development of the automobile produced a great transformation of the character of life in the industrialized world. It is traditional to view the steam engine and/or the railroads as making the primary impact of the Industrial Revolution on human life. People began to leave the farms and gravitate toward the industrial centers. Occupations turned from being vocations into a means of earning a paycheque. People began to travel outside their homes on the railroad and had access to products from far away that were brought in to them. All this is true.

But now consider the effect that the automobile has had on the local community. There are so many cars in most North American and European cities that just finding a place to put them is one of the major technical problems. Cars have become essential equipment in most households. Where people used to walk to work or to local shops, now a car is used for everything. Many people live so far from where they work or attend school that it takes them an hour or more to come in each day and another to get home. The farther people live away from the metropolitan centers where they work, the more cars are needed in the family. Only a few cities have really adequate public transportation because everyone wants the freedom to drive their own vehicle where they want and when they want. The big cities that do have viable public transportation are those where the streets are so choked with cars that driving is less attractive.

Some statistics:

> Parking a car at home, the office, and the shopping mall requires on average 372 square meters of asphalt. More than 155 thousand square kilometers of land in the United States have been paved over; that works out to about two percent of the total surface area, and to ten percent of all arable land. Worldwide, at least one-third of an average city's land is devoted to roads, parking lots, and other automobile-related elements. In American cities, close to half of all

the urban space goes to accommodate the automobile; in Los Angeles, the figure reaches two-thirds.[1]

The drawbacks of the automobile are becoming more and more apparent as more of them are on the road. They are noisy; they pollute; they take up a lot of space; they use an incredible amount of fossil fuel. As a result, more and more steps are being taken to curb automobile usage or to make it less attractive: restrictive parking regulations, high parking fees, very high fines for traffic violations, gasoline taxes, road taxes, high registration fees, traffic calming devices to slow traffic through residential areas or a maze of one-way and dead-end streets.

But cars appeal to something that is valued higher than the inconveniences put in their way, and more than substituted conveniences that might be provided. To quote Anita Gordon and David Suzuki,

> Let's face it: in North America we're used to getting where we want to go, when we want to go, and how we want to go. We like the privacy of our own vehicle. It's hard to give up that freedom. In fact, a study done for the Toronto Transit Commission (TTC) revealed that even if public transit were easy to use, cheap, and efficient, people wouldn't give up their cars. The survey found that most of those who didn't use public transit were men aged 25 to 54 with an annual income of $50 000 or more. Over half of them said they loved their cars so much that even if fares were free they still wouldn't ride the TTC.[2]

Given the present layout of modern cities and suburbs and the network of roadways in place, it is difficult to imagine that a few regulations or incentives could effectively reverse the trend.

The car culture transformed North America first, then Europe. Now it is spreading everywhere. It is the ultimate export: the American dream: freedom, power, convenience, affluence. Third World countries are scrambling to raise their standards of living to catch up with the industrialized world. One of the symbols of that higher standard is the automobile. More than that, automobiles are seen as essential to economic development.

---

1.   From Michael Renner, "Transportation Tomorrow," *The Futurist*, March-April, 1989, pp. 14-20, quoted in Anita Gordon and David Suzuki, *It's a Matter of Survival* (Toronto: Stoddart, 1990), p. 201.

2.   Gordon and Suzuki, *It's a Matter of Survival*, p. 200.

Consider the two largest Third World countries, the ancient great empires that missed out on the Industrial Revolution: China and India. Together these account for 38 percent of the human population of the Earth, but, as of 1990, they owned a total of one-half of one percent of the world's automobiles. But that is changing fast. Starting in the late 1970s, both countries have adopted policies for economic growth that will encourage car and truck ownership. In this period, the number of cars in China has already risen by a factor of ten to half a million cars. That number is still very small, but the growth rate is very fast.

As Henry Ford foresaw, the automobile was the key to a different kind of life and would be dearly wanted by all those who had any opportunity to own and drive one. Ford made the automobile affordable for the average American family of the early twentieth century and sold them by the millions. That same process that he began has spread and continues to spread across the world. Wherever it is feasible, it takes root and transforms the local society. It's a bit like the way that agriculture spread around the world ten thousand years ago. The switch to agriculture has proven to be irreversible wherever it was introduced. There is a strong similarity here as well with the automobile industry. Once cars become commonplace, the entire social infrastructure changes in ways that are very difficult to undo. Those who advocate giving up automobiles and returning to some pre-motorized state are fighting against a very strong tide.

Chapter 20

The Airplane

For as long as human beings have had the courage and imagination to try to do something that seemed beyond their abilities, they have been trying to find a way to fly. In the Renaissance, when systematic study of the advantages of machines was beginning, there were many schemes to make human flight possible. The best known of these were the detailed plans left by Leonardo da Vinci, both for contraptions with flapping wings like a bird, and for an ingenious design for a helicopter that would lift off the ground with a screw-like action churning through the air.

Of course, none of these worked. The materials that were contemplated (wood and iron) were much too heavy, and the power available was nowhere nearly adequate. But that was before both the Scientific Revolution and the Industrial Revolution. The Scientific Revolution gave people a much better understanding of details of the problems that had to be overcome—e.g., the weight of the atmosphere versus the weight of the flying object and the conception of air as a fluid with buoyancy and resistance that could be used to advantage. The Industrial Revolution showed that much more powerful machines could be built and perhaps would be equal to the task of getting aloft.

Those who analyzed the problem in the light of their new knowledge and new hopes realized that there were basically two alternatives: (1) produce a craft that in total was actually lighter than the surrounding atmosphere, so that it would float above the heavier air; or (2) make a craft that probably would be heavier than air but that would have the power to push against the air firmly enough that the pressure of the air would drive the craft upward. Both of these were explored.

Lighter-than-Air Ships

Prior to the discovery of atmospheric pressure and the realization that the air around has a considerable weight, it would not have easily occurred to inventors that a craft that might carry people could actually be made that was lighter than the air itself. But with that realization, it was but a matter of time before someone would find a workable method.

The hot-air balloon of the Montgolfier brothers on the first successful manned flight, November 21, 1783.

The credit for the first manned flight has to go to two French paper makers, the brothers Joseph and Etienne Montgolfier. In June 1783, they experimented with a large paper bag that they filled with hot air and found that it rose well up into the sky. Hot air is considerably less dense than unheated air, so the bag altogether was lighter than its surroundings. But this was an unmanned flight. They then set out to repeat the experiment with an even bigger bag sitting above a platform capable of carrying passengers. This they did, and demonstrated it to the extremely surprised residents of Paris on November 21, 1783.

Their device had the familiar balloon shape, though rather more elaborately designed and made entirely of paper. They wished to make it as light as possible, so they did not carry with them, as later balloons did, a means of making hot air. Instead, the entire apparatus sat over an open fire of burning straw, which soon filled the balloon with smoke and hot air. (There is some evidence that they thought the smoke was what gave it the lift.) Around the edge of the air bag was a platform on which two passengers rode. When the device was released from its moorings, it took off and floated across the countryside for about eight kilometers before coming down. It established that lighter-than-air travel was possible. In France, what we call a hot-air balloon is still named after the brothers; it is called a *montgolfière*.

The Montgolfier brothers were able to get up in the air and float about for a considerable time, but they were not able to solve the problem which has always been a challenge for lighter-than-air flight: making the balloon go where you want it to go. It was only solved much later in the late 19th century by the retired German military officer, Graf Ferdinand von Zeppelin. The Germans perfected a design, named *Zeppelin* in honour of its inventor, that combined a long cigar-shaped tube containing a lighter-than-air gas (originally hydrogen) to keep it aloft and a propeller drive motor to push the craft in the desired direction. The Zeppelins were very successful; they could carry large numbers of passengers on long distances. They also made successful warplanes, being used in the First World War to bomb London. After the war, a transatlantic commercial air service was operated with Zeppelins capable of carrying about 100 passengers and traveling at 130 km/hr.

It was an accident with the largest of the Zeppelins, the *Hindenburg*, which put an end to commercial lighter-than-air travel. After ten successful round trips across the Atlantic, the Hindenburg had a freak accident trying to dock at the Naval Air Station at Lakehurst, New Jersey, on May 6, 1937. The cause of the disaster was never satisfactorily determined—perhaps a spark from the engines or static electricity or some property of the covering of the outer layer of the ship that made it vulnerable. The hydrogen gas caught fire and the ship exploded in less than one minute. Since then, lighter-than-air ships have been used primarily for scientific purposes or for advertising, and they have mostly been filled with the less efficient, but less dangerous, gas, helium.[1]

The crash of the Zeppelin *Hindenburg* on May 6, 1937, at Lakehurst, New Jersey.

Heavier-than-Air Ships

Lighter-than-air ships succeeded in overcoming the problem of getting aloft, and even eventually succeeded in getting the ships to go in the right direction. But they were cumbersome. They certainly did not have the grace and speed of birds, which the ambitious inventors always wanted to emulate. They made no use of riding the air currents or of pushing against the air to achieve lift and direction. Though many would-be aviators tried attaching wing-like appendages to themselves to imitate bird flight, this was a dead end, and so was the idea of making a machine with flapping wings.

The theoretical approach that proved sound was a fixed-wing aircraft with a powerful engine. In 1809, a Yorkshire landowner, Sir George Cayley, stated that the solution to flight would be "to make a surface support a given weight by the application of power to

---

1. The proper name in English for lighter-than-air ships is *dirigible*, but the common name mostly used is *blimp*. The word blimp in fact refers to a First World War British military airship that was officially classed as Type B-limp, which referred to its flexible gas envelope that would bend in storms or when making sharp turns. The Zeppelins and subsequent designs had rigid structures to hold the gas bags.

the resistance of air." He proposed to use a propeller and an "explosion" engine. However, the "explosion" engine of the day was the steam engine. The only way a steam engine could provide enough power would have required it to be so heavy that it was impractical. Heavier-than-air flight was at a standstill.

The Failed Attempts

As Donald Cardwell remarked,

> ...for the remainder of that richly creative era [the 19th century], the 'conquest of flight' was a happy hunting ground for conmen, lunatics, enthusiastic amateurs and the occasional devotee: that is, one who would try to view the problems objectively and resolve them systematically or scientifically.[1]

Among those lunatics or devotees, depending on one's point of view, were several who came close to succeeding with different designs.

Sir Hiram Maxim.

Before the steam engine was abandoned as impractical, one more serious attempt was made to fashion a steam-powered aircraft. This was the work of an extraordinarily creative mind, Hiram Maxim. Maxim had several careers, one of which was a position as chief engineer at the Pope Manufacturing Company of Connecticut, the leading U.S. bicycle maker. He is also credited with being the inventor of the machine gun, which in an improved form did so much damage in the First World War. Maxim had emigrated to England, became a British subject, and was knighted for his inventive work. While there he undertook to devise a steam-powered flying machine.

1.   Donald Cardwell, *The Norton History of Technology* (New York: W.W. Norton, 1995), p. 385.

Maxim built a very powerful and compact steam engine that he thought would be both light enough and powerful enough to lift a structure into the air. Following the reasoning of the railroad pioneers who found that locomotives ran more smoothly on rails than on the ground, Maxim built a long track for his flying machine to use for takeoff. The machine weighed 3½ tonnes. On a test in 1894, it sped down the runway, actually made it

Hiram Maxim's flying machine on its runway.

into the air for a few centimeters above the tracks, and then crashed into a guardrail.

If takeoff was the problem, then another idea was to use a catapult to throw the machine into the air. This was the idea of Samuel Pierpont Langley, the Director of the Smithsonian Institution in Washington. Langley did a lot of experimentation with model planes, and even had one flying with a steam engine. But when he tried a full-sized plane, he found that the engine required would be too heavy. He then turned to a recently invented engine with more promise, the internal

Langley's 1903 Aerodrome, ready to be launched from a houseboat in the Potomac River.

combustion gasoline engine. After many attempts, he got an engine built that weighed 50 kilograms and generated 50 horsepower. He had it taken out to a houseboat in the Potomac River and mounted on a catapult built on top. In 1903, his "Aerodrome" was ready to be launched. The catapult was released, the plane flew into the air, only to get caught in the catapult wires and promptly sank.

Flying Machines Are a Scientific Impossibility

One of the reasons that Donald Cardwell (quoted above) said that the conquest of flight was "a happy hunting ground for conmen, lunatics, enthusiastic amateurs and the occasional devotee" was that the best scientific minds of the day held that it was physically impossible. Lighter-than-air flight was grudgingly admitted to work, but the hope of getting a heavy machine into the air like a bird was viewed as regrettable folly. An instance of this scientific nay-saying was an article by the respected American scientist, Professor Simon Newcomb, which appeared just after Langley's disaster with the Aerodrome catapult. This is such a good example of the futility of predicting the future, especially one claiming the authoritative voice of science, that it is quoted here at length.

> Mr. Secretary Langley's trial of his flying machine, which seems to have come to an abortive issue last week, strikes a sympathetic chord in the constitution of our race. Are we not the lords of creation? Have we not girdled the earth with wires through which we speak to our antipodes? Do we not journey from continent to continent over oceans that no animal can cross, and with a speed of which our ancestors would never have dreamed? Is not all the rest of the animal creation so far inferior to us in every point that the best thing it can do is to become completely subservient to our needs, dying, if need be, that its flesh may become a toothsome dish on our tables? And yet here is an insignificant little bird, from whose mind, if mind it has, all conceptions of natural law are excluded, applying the rules of aerodynamics in an application of mechanical force to an end we have never been able to reach, and this with entire ease and absence of consciousness that it is doing an extraordinary thing. Surely our knowledge of natural laws, and that inventive genius which has enabled us to subordinate all nature to our needs, ought also to enable us to do anything that the bird can do. Therefore we must fly. If we cannot yet do it, it is only because we have not got to the bottom of the subject. Our successors of the not distant future will surely succeed....
>
> We may look on the bird as a sort of flying machine complete in itself, of which a brain and nervous system are fundamentally necessary parts. No such machine can navigate the air unless guided by something having life. Apart from this, it could be of little use to us unless it carried human beings on its wings. We thus meet with a difficulty at the first step...we cannot give a brain and nervous system to our machine. These necessary adjuncts must be supplied by a man, who is no part of the machine, but something carried by it. The bird is a complete machine in itself. Our aerial machine must be ship plus man.... The hundred and fifty pounds of dead weight which the manager of the machine must add to it over and above that necessary in the bird may well prove an insurmountable obstacle to success....

Another point to be considered is that the bird operates by the application of a kind of force which is peculiar to the animal creation, and no approach to which has ever been made in any mechanism. This force is that which gives rise to muscular action, of which the necessary condition is the direct action of a nervous system. We cannot have muscles or nerves for our flying machine. We have to replace them by such crude and clumsy adjuncts as steam engines and electric batteries. It may certainly seem singular if man is never to discover any combination of substances which, under the influence of some such agency as an electric current, shall expand and contract like a muscle. But, if he is ever to do so, the time is still in the future. We do not see the dawn of the age in which such a result will be brought forth.... The mathematician of to-day admits that he can neither square the circle, duplicate the cube, nor trisect the angle. May not our mechanicians, in like manner, be ultimately forced to admit that aerial flight is one of that great class of problems with which man can never cope, and give up all attempts to grapple with it?

I do not claim that this is a necessary conclusion from any past experience.... But when we inquire whether aerial flight is possible in the present state of our knowledge; whether, with such materials as we possess, a combination of steel, cloth and wire can be made which, moved by the power of electricity or steam, shall form a successful flying machine, the outlook may be altogether different. To judge it sanely, let us bear in mind the difficulties which are encountered in any flying machine.

There followed here a lengthy technical discussion of the dynamics of what Professor Newcomb called an "aeroplane," which meant a horizontal flat surface that is fixed so that its forward end is slightly higher than its rear. Such an "aeroplane" will have an upward lift as it moves forward, explained Newcomb, and if it is moving fast enough, the front end need only be very slightly higher than the back. This, he said, is the principle on which all those trying to invent a flying machine pin their hopes. What he was describing are the fixed wings on an aircraft. He continued with a remark about Hiram Maxim's failed experiment, and then asks how one would ever land such a machine without crashing.

And, granting complete success, imagine the proud possessor of the aeroplane darting through the air at a speed of several hundred feet per second! It is the speed alone that sustains him. How is he ever going to stop? Once he slackens his speed, down he begins to fall.... Once he stops he falls a dead mass. How shall he reach the ground without destroying his delicate machinery? I do not think the most imaginative inventor has yet even put upon paper a demonstrative, successful way of meeting this difficulty. The only ray of hope is afforded by the bird. The latter does succeed in stopping and reaching the ground safely after its flight. But we have already mentioned the great advantages which the bird possesses in the power of applying force to its wings, which, in its case, form the aeroplanes. But we have already seen that there is no mechanical combination, and no way of applying force, which will give to the aeroplanes the flexibility and rapidity of movement belonging to the wings of a bird. That this difficulty is insurmountable would seem to be a very fair deduction....[1]

If there is any general lesson to be learned from the history of invention, it is that predicting what will or will not be invented in the future is nearly impossible. Nonetheless, people continue to do it, even people who should know better. Looking back at past prognostications, it is hard to resist a chuckle at some of the more pompous pronouncements of what *can't* be done. Professor Newcomb explained with convincing scientific certainty why airplanes were a virtual impossibility, at least, an impossibility, he asserted, given the technology of the times. The timing of his assessment has perfect irony. The article appeared on October 22, 1903, in other words, two months before the Wright brothers' first successful powered flight.

The Wright Brothers

Wilbur and Orville Wright were two brothers with a common fascination and interest in all kinds of machines, and especially in the idea of mechanical flight. At the outset of their careers, they probably qualified as what Donald Cardwell called "enthusiastic amateurs," but before they were finished they definitely had moved to the category of "devotee." They lived in Dayton, Ohio, where as young men they worked together in the hi-tech mechanical environment of the day. That is, they operated a bicycle shop. They studied and built gliders and then set out to put an engine on one of their successful glider designs. They had to manufacture their own 12 horsepower gasoline engine.

---

1.   Simon Newcomb, ìThe Outlook for the Flying Machine,î *The Independent* 55 (1903): Part 2; Oct. 22, 1903.

Looking for a place where they had a combination of hills, flat lands, and steady winds, they chose the beach at Kitty Hawk, North Carolina. They had used this location for testing their glider designs. They shipped their flying machine there and began tests. On December 17, 1903, they succeeded. With Orville at the controls, their plane flew about 37 meters in 12 seconds. It was a modest start, but it was what Professor Newcomb had said was scientifically not possible.

The Wright brothers steadily improved their design over the next several years, demonstrating it to government officials and European royalty, as well as a huge interested public. At the time it seemed as though the last limitation on human power had been breached. As Professor Newcomb had so well put it just two months before, humanity's justified pride in its conquest of nature was compromised by "an insignificant little bird, applying the

The Wright brothers demonstrate an improved airplane at Kitty Hawk in 1911.

rules of aerodynamics with entire ease and absence of consciousness that it is doing an extraordinary thing." For the sake of human dignity, then, it was mandatory that powered flight be conquered.

Another Human Triumph

The successful flight of a powered aircraft was perceived as the "final frontier" of human ingenuity. What the Wright brothers had done was soon copied and then improved by others. The next several years were marked by one record after another being set by some daredevil in an airplane of a new design. It captured the imagination of the public and showed once again what a wonderful thing the human spirit was.

In the First World War that followed soon after, airplanes were used for the first time as part of a fighting arsenal, dropping bombs, doing reconnaissance, and direct combat. The romance that had attached to the original aviators was transferred during the war to the flying aces who engaged in plane-to-plane jousts. When the war was over, the airplane was established as part of the technology of all advanced nations.

The Airplane as Mass Transportation

The automobile and the airplane share a past and a sequence of development. Both had their origin around the turn of the 20th century. Both had a debt to the bicycle industry that preceded them and out of which came their first designers and mechanics. Both depended on the development of the internal combustion engine for a practical power-delivery system. And, both captured the excitement and imagination of the population that saw the new inventions as another triumphal mark of human supremacy.

With respect to the excitement and imagination, they have gone their separate ways in the latter part of the twentieth century. The reason is not hard to find: anyone can aspire to drive a car, and most people in the industrialized nations sooner or later will have the use of one. But few people become pilots. The car is still a personal technology, an extension of the self, and therefore it carries with it some of the thrill of achievement and power just to drive one. Doubtless the airplane has this quality to a much greater extent, but only for those in the cockpits. For the vast majority, the airplane is convenient and rapid mass transportation.

The airplane industry that arose during the war primarily existed to supply the military with warplanes. After the war, demand sagged until a commercial use was conceived: carrying the mail. It was the only way to make airplanes economically viable. The German Zeppelin airships had succeeded as commercial people movers, but the small and uncomfortable airplanes of the 1920s were still technological triumphs, not transportation.

That changed in the 1930s, when three aircraft manufacturers, all still leaders in the industry today, brought out much larger airplanes that could accommodate regular passenger service. The planes were the Boeing 247, the Lockheed Electra, and the Douglas DC-2, followed by the DC-3. With these, regular passenger service came to be established between all the major cities in the world. The remarkably successful DC-3 has been the most widely used plane ever made.

The impact of the airplane has been more akin to that of the railroads than that of the automobile. When commercial air travel became accepted and commonplace, it had an effect similar to the original passenger trains. People began to travel to places they never would have reached before. For the vacationer, the airlines offered reasonably inexpensive transportation to exotic locations. After the Second World War, when the economies of the industrialized nations had enormous growth and the disposable income in the hands of ordinary citizens swelled, tourist flights became a major part of the airline business and catering to tourists became a major part of the economies of many of their destinations. In 1950, there were 25 million international tourists; by 1989, there were 400 million. Over 80 percent of all tourists came from the industrialized world, and over a quarter of them were from Germany alone. Major destinations included the Old World cultural centers, such as Venice, which now relies very heavily on its tourist trade, and Third World locations in benign climates where tourists can take in the sun and swim in tropical waters, spending more money in a few days than most of the indigenous population earns in a year.

For business, the ability to cross the country or even the ocean in a few hours has encouraged the development of commerce on a large scale. Companies can now do business in several countries, manufacturing component parts of a product in one country, assembling it in another, perhaps selling it in still other locations.

Along with the rapid transportation of people and goods around the globe, other components of the world environments are also transported, often inadvertently. It is very easy for a person to contract a communicable disease in one country and travel to the other side of the globe before even showing any signs of infection. In the age of travel by land and sea, attempts were made to prevent the introduction of one disease into another land by the use of quarantines. Suspect ships would be required to drop anchor and remain off shore for a period of time, sometimes over a month, before anyone on board could come ashore, lest a feared disease be let loose in the host country. This is totally impractical in the age of flight. As a result, the world is much more vulnerable to the spread of dangerous infectious diseases. The recent outbreak of Sudden Acute Respiratory Syndrome (SARS) in Canada from a single infected person arriving from the Orient is but one example.

Fossil Fuel Dependence

Both the automobile and the airplane achieve their enormous power from the use of petroleum—fossilized remains from hundreds of millions of years ago. The rate at which this resource is being used for these two technologies alone is staggering. Since these resources are inevitably limited, the automobile and the airplane industries cannot continue to grow indefinitely unless some alternative power sources become available. For some people, this argues strongly for a sharp reduction in the uses, especially the frivolous uses, of both automobiles and airplanes in order to conserve the remaining resources. For others, it is merely a challenge to work harder to find an alternative technological solution.

Clockwise from top left: plastic containers; an oil well; a chemical processing plant; a close-up view of the structure of plastic.

Chapter 21

The Chemical Industry

Some of the technological developments that led to major changes in the way people lived and related to their world in the industrialized countries are so obvious that they can't be missed. The factory, the railroads, the automobile, and the airplane are all good examples. But some equally important developments have had a more subtle effect, not changing what people did so much as how they did it. Some of these are so pervasive that we can hardly imagine modern life without them. Many of these are outgrowths of the industrial applications of chemistry.

The chemical industry arose mid-way through the Industrial Revolution. It began to provide a series of previously unheard of products that increased productivity, led to revolutionary new products, and transformed the economies of some nations. Some of the new products are never seen by the ordinary citizen, but form part of a process that makes other well-known products possible. These are what might be called industrial chemicals. Others are manifestly part of everyday life in modern society. These are the familiar consumer products. This chapter is a brief overview of the origin and development of some of the most important from each group: coal gas, petroleum, rubber, industrial chemicals, synthetic dyes, explosives, and plastics.

Gas Lighting

At the end of the 16th century, a Dutch scientist named Johann Baptista van Helmont made a major study of different kinds of "airs." To distinguish these "airs," he coined a new word, "gas", which was derived from the Ancient Greek word, χαος, from which we also get the English word "chaos." Some investigations showed that an inflammable air obtained from coal burned like the flames of coal itself. The industry nearly got started twice early on in the Industrial Revolution, but each time circumstances worked against it. As early as 1760, an attempt was made to light a room by the gas from coal. But it did not work very well and was not followed up. About 40 years later, a French engineer named Phillipe Lebon produced a gas from heating wood and showed how it could be used for warmth and light. It produced a soft light, which he contained in a glass globe. He conceived of a distribution system involving concealed pipes running throughout a house. This promising idea also did not go very far because Lebon was attacked and killed by muggers in 1804.

Watt and Boulton

Gas lighting finally got underway under the sponsorship of the firm that symbolized the Industrial Revolution itself, the steam engine makers, James Watt and Matthew Boulton. It began when James Watt's son, Gregory Watt, went to Paris to investigate and learn about of Lebon's work. While young Watt was in Paris, one of the company employees in Cornwall, William Murdoch, Watt and Bolton's chief engineer, was working on a way to make a tar from coal for coating ships' bottoms. Accidentally, he produced a gas from coal that could be used for lighting. Because of Gregory Watt's visit to Paris, Watt and Boulton realized the significance of Murdoch's discovery and recalled him to their Birmingham factory.

The famous foundry in Birmingham's Soho district where Watt and Boulton made steam engines became the first factory illuminated 24 hours a day by coal gas. Watt and Boulton went into gas lighting as a side business and outfitted many British factories with gas lights, for example, the Salford cotton mill, which in 1806-1807 was fitted with 900 gas lights. But there was a problem with coal gas. The gas used was not purified nor washed, and it burned imperfectly. The result was a foul odor. The Soho Foundry became nicknamed the "Soho Stinks." Eventually Boulton and Watt decided there were too many problems with gas lighting, and they abandoned the business in 1814.

The Gas Age

Gas lighting had begun, however, and it only needed entrepreneurs to get it better established. A German by the name of F. A. Winzer moved to London, anglicized his name to Winsor, and set up a joint stock company in 1812 to finance street lighting in London, the Gas Light and Coke Company. By 1816, there were 26 miles of gas mains in London. By 1823, there were three rival companies in London north of the Thames. Their goal was to replace the other alternative for night lighting, burning oils from animal fats. Gas lighting cost only about one-third to one-fourth as much as, say, whale oil.

But pollution was a major problem, since the gas was not purified. One suggestion for providing illumination indoors without bringing in the foul air was to place the light outside a window and let it shine through the glass to light the room. It took a few years before the solutions to this problem were found.

In 1840, the atmospheric burner was introduced. It mixed gas and air together before combustion, therefore providing a more complete combustion and less pollution. Much later, in 1895, the gas mantle was introduced whereby a glass sheath enclosed the burning flame, dissipated the light across the mantle and provided a safer and more usable light. With this innovation, most of the difficulties of gas lighting had been overcome and the process was practical for general usage. However, just at that time, electric lighting began to be introduced and the age of gas lighting came to an end.

Social Consequences of Gas Lighting

The British philosopher and spokesman for the industrial age, Andrew Ure, proclaimed that gas lighting was a great liberator. For example, it meant that children could safely work 12-hour shifts in factories! Streets became safer at night because they were better lit. Also the level of literacy and education in general went up because people could more easily read at night. In Britain, night schools were set up all over the country where factory workers could go after work and hear a lecture or study some subject. This pattern, though originating in Britain, spread very quickly throughout the industrialized world.

Gas was used primarily for lighting and only occasionally for warmth. It was only with the introduction of the gas ring in the 1860s that temperatures could be controlled enough to make gas practical for cooking.

Petroleum

Petroleum seepages have been known for millennia. In the Middle East, for example, there are at least 30 places where petroleum seeps up to the surface of the Earth naturally. There are references to petroleum in various forms in even the earliest written records. In the 9th century B.C.E., Assyrians marked the sites of escaping gases as "where the voice of the gods issued forth from the rocks." Ancient Babylonians named the inflammable oil that seeped up "naphtha"—i.e., "the thing that blazes." Naphtha was later used in the Byzantine Empire in the making of a weapon, "Greek Fire," a mixture of crude oil, pitch,

Greek Fire. This drawing from a Byzantine manuscript shows the ancient use of petroleum products in battle. While this weapon was extremely effective, it did not become widely used, mainly because the Byzantines kept its composition secret.

sulphur, phosphorus, and various other chemicals. When mixed with water, it caught fire, so it was used in naval battles. The Byzantines (the "Greeks") would allow an enemy boat to approach until just out of boarding range and then fling the Greek fire mixture at the water in front of the boat, which would then set the boat on fire. It was very effective.

About the only natural form of petroleum that was originally considered useful was solid rock (asphalt) or thicker seepages that could be used to make bitumen (tar) for caulking ships' bottoms and waterproofing.

Lighting

The modern petroleum industry arose as a means to satisfy the existing demand for lighting that had been created by gas lighting. In 1848, James Young, an assistant to the eminent British scientist Michael Faraday, developed a lubricant from a petroleum product—a form of naphtha. He found that when he refined this substance further, it made excellent lighting. He set up a company to manufacture and sell this product in Europe and America to compete with gas lighting and animal oils. The product was developed from residues of coal deposits, hence it was popularly named *"coal oil,"* a name still used by some in Britain, but Young himself called it *paraffin illuminating oil*. In Canada, a very similar process was discovered by Abraham Gesner, who named his product *kerosene*, from the Greek words for oil and wax. "Kerosene" has stuck as the name in North America. Kerosene (or "coal oil" or paraffin oil) was less expensive than whale oil and did make effective lighting, but it smoked and had an unpleasant odor until 1857, when a new process was discovered that made a cleaner burning product. Kerosene then quickly became a highly desired commodity for lighting purposes.

Drilling for Oil

Kerosene was made from oil that rose to the ground from natural seepages or from the residues that adhered to coal deposits (hence "coal oil"). Deliberately digging in the ground looking for oil did not begin until halfway through the 19th century. Impediments to doing so were the lack of hard drills that could cut through rock, the lack of mechanical power to drive the drills, and the small chance of success since there was no body of theoretical knowledge that would direct where to drill.

Several developments preceded any concerted effort to find oil deposits. First, in 1830, the derrick was introduced—but not for oil exploration. In 1850, the steam engine was adapted to power drills. The drills and the derricks were for drilling wells, but what was sought was either water or salt deposits. If any drilling efforts hit petroleum, it was an accident and not necessarily a welcome one. Between 1840 and 1860, more than 15 borings looking for salt hit petroleum.

G. H. Bissell, an American industrialist, considered deliberately searching for oil. He sent a sample of oil from a Pennsylvania seepage to Benjamin Silliman, Jr., who was the son of the famous Yale chemistry professor Benjamin Silliman, Sr., and who eventually succeeded his father in the post. Silliman, Jr., reported back that he thought that several new products could be obtained from the crude oil. Bissell also got some advice on likely places to drill for oil.

Edwin Drake and his first oil well.

He went ahead. He funded exploration led by his contractor, Edwin L. Drake. On August 27, 1859, after drilling 21 meters through bedrock, Drake struck oil. The Pennsylvania Oil Field began. Drake's first well produced 20 barrels of oil per day. This was the turning point in the history of petroleum. Within 15 years, the annual output of oil in the U.S. (mostly all in Pennsylvania) reached 10 million barrels of 160 kilograms each.

The Oil Well Industry

The first big product of the petroleum industry was kerosene. The U.S. exported it in tins worldwide to satisfy a demand for lighting. In Europe, the petroleum industry developed mostly in Russia. By 1901, Russia was the largest oil producer in the world. In the U.S., John D. Rockefeller founded the Standard Oil Company in the 1870s. Standard Oil owned not just the oil drilling rights and the oil wells, but also the pipelines between the wells, the ports, and even the ships. Ultimately, the monopoly of Standard Oil was deemed unfair to the spirit of competition, and Congress broke up the company into smaller companies. This was the first major Anti-Trust suit, solved by breaking apart the dominating company. More recently, the telephone monopoly of AT&T was broken apart into smaller companies, and now Microsoft and other leading companies in the cutting edge technology of the day have been threatened with the same action.

Gasoline was the first distillate obtained in refining, but as it was regarded as both useless and dangerous, it tended to be just burnt off. Until 1900, the main product remained kerosene. Then, gasoline engines began to replace steam in the fledgling automobile industry, and Diesel engines were used in locomotives instead of coal. The growth of the airplane industry in the 20th century also provided more demand for gasoline, especially in its more highly refined version as jet fuel. Also, toward the end of the 19th century, the electric light bulb came into more general use. The result was that demand for kerosene sank to very low levels, but demand for gasoline, Diesel fuel and engine lubricating oils took off.

Gasoline is particularly desirable in an internal combustion engine because it easily vaporizes at ordinary temperatures. When burned, it releases a great amount of energy in the form of expansion, to drive a piston. Gasoline itself is a very complex mixture of hundreds of different hydrocarbons. It can be refined to different levels of effectiveness, and additives can be added to it for a number of purposes—for example, cleaning or lubricating the engine, or facilitating ignition at very low temperatures. Additives can also improve the combustion and add to the energy released. One additive that has been particularly effective at aiding combustion is tetraethyl lead. Gasoline with this additive is commonly called ethyl gasoline. Ethyl gasoline burns much more smoothly without unpredictable explosions that cause what mechanics call knocking in an engine. It therefore considerably increased the efficiency of the fuel. Unfortunately, the lead in the gasoline produces a poisonous lead oxide in the exhaust.

In the late 20th century, a substitute fuel was developed to replace ethyl gasoline, "unleaded" gasoline, which had much of the same efficiency as ethyl gasoline, but required an additional device, a catalytic converter, to be attached to the engine. New cars began to be made with catalytic converters and could accept unleaded gasoline. Gasoline stations installed new pumps for the unleaded gas and sold it alongside the regular ethyl gasoline. Eventually, all new cars came equipped with the converters and leaded gasoline was phased out completely.

Rubber

Rubber is essentially a tropical crop. Its characteristic property is that of recovering its shape after being deformed, and also its impermeability to water. As far back as the 13th century, the inhabitants of Central and South America were noted to have collected latex and coagulated it over a fire to make rubber balls. The Spanish explorers were aware of the native techniques and uses. By 1615, Spanish explorers used rubber to weatherproof the cloaks of soldiers.

In 1751, a French scientist, Charles de la Condamine, brought a sample of rubber back to France from an expedition to Peru. He lectured on its properties in 1751 to the French Academy. In 1770, the British amateur scientist Joseph Priestly, the discoverer of oxygen, gave rubber its English name when he noted that rubbing with it was a good way to erase pencil marks.

When rubber began to be imported into Europe, it came in already coagulated form in "bottles" or in balls, and then was cut into strips. It could be dissolved with turpentine and used as a thinned liquid. Unfortunately, using solvents produced a weak solution of rubber that dried unpredictably.

The Rubber Industry

A British entrepreneur, Thomas Hancock, began using rubber commercially by incorporating strips of rubber into garments and bandages etc. However, he found it was difficult to get the right sizes and shapes of strips because he was dependent on the shape of the bottles in which the rubber was imported. In any case, there was too much waste. He experimented with a process whereby he would take the imported rubber and put it through a shredding machine with revolving spikes. To his surprise, instead of getting small bits of rubber, he produced a solid mass. He redesigned his shredder as a masticator and made from it large cylinders of rubber which could then be cut into whatever shapes he needed. He made rubber sheets by shaving slices off his cylindrical blocks. The sheets could be joined end to end while still warm and thereby made into any size desired.

Charles Macintosh, a Glasgow chemical manufacturer, used coal tar naphtha as a solvent for rubber. He dissolved rubber and made a sort of varnish that could be brushed onto cloth, making an impermeable layer. He then took two pieces of treated cloth and sewed the rubber-treated sides together on the inside, making a surface all around with no "tacky" side to the touch. With this layered cloth, he could make many waterproof

A large masticator for producing cylinders of rubber. These could later be cut into large blocks or thin sheets, making rubber much easier to work with.

products. He set up a factory in 1824 to produce his "macintoshes." In Britain, raincoats are still called macintoshes.

Rubber Tires

A remaining problem was that rubber loses its elasticity in the cold and becomes soft and tacky in the heat. This was especially a problem in America with its great extremes of temperatures. Charles Goodyear, a Philadelphia hardware merchant, experimenting with treating rubber, accidentally overheated a mixture of rubber, sulphur, and white lead. The result was a substance that remained elastic in all weather and did not become soft and tacky. What he had discovered was *vulcanization,* which he patented in the U.S. in 1841. Goodyear tried to sell the process to Macintosh, but before he could do so, Hancock figured it out himself and patented it in Britain.

The demand for rubber goods escalated in Britain. In 1846, Hancock introduced rubber tires. They were made of solid rubber, four centimeters wide and three centimeters thick. In 1888, John Dunlop introduced the pneumatic tire for bicycles. By the end of the 19th century, tires were the biggest use of rubber. Next was insulation for electrical wire.

Plantations

Rubber was still being collected from naturally growing trees in South America, but when demand took off, this supply was inadequate. The rubber plantation came into existence around 1895, whereby whole farms were given over to producing nothing but rubber. The largest of these were located in Ceylon and Singapore and various other places with the right climate.

Industrial Chemistry

The Industrial Revolution increased the demand for alkali for textiles, glass making, and soap manufacture. Originally alkalis were made from natural sources. But with increased demand, synthesis became necessary. Nicholas Leblanc, a French physician, found a method to make *soda* from salt in the late 18th century. This became the first large-scale industrial chemical process. It dominated the chemical industry for over a century.

Potash, potassium hydroxide, is a compound very useful for making soaps, detergents, glass, ceramics, dyes, and as a cleaner. It occurs naturally in deposits and can be mined, but it could also be obtained by leaching wood ashes. Producing potash and selling it abroad was a way for Canadian settlers in forested regions to produce ready money. In fact, Canada supplied Britain with three-fourths of its potash by 1831. This required burning 4 million tons of hardwood annually in Canada—just for the ashes! The deforestation engendered just to supply this one chemical compound was incredible, but it also was an indication of how useful potash was to industry.

Bleaching fabric with buttermilk.

The manufacture of soda produced an unwanted byproduct, *hydrochloric acid*, which was regarded as a foul pollutant. Eventually, it was found to be useful in making bleach, and became a boon to the textile industry. The previous way of bleaching fabric was to lay out strips of fabric in the sun, spread with buttermilk—a slow and unreliable process. Bleaching also was used in papermaking.

The production of chemical dyes became one of the biggest parts of the chemical industry. It arose out of investigations in the newly founded field of organic chemistry in the 19th century. Organic chemistry became a sub-discipline of chemistry near the beginning of the 19th century when it was realized that the chemical compounds found largely only in living matter were of a very different character from the compounds that existed in inorganic matter. In particular, organic chemicals were much, much more complex, and were often themselves assemblies of molecules that could have an existence on their own. Now, organic chemistry is virtually synonymous with the chemistry of compounds involving carbon.

Synthetic Dyes

For most of history, science and technology have gone their separate ways. Science concerned itself only with understanding the natural world; technology sought to control it and make use of the powers of nature. Even into the Industrial Revolution, the two had little to do with each other.[1] Generally, the scientific understanding of technology came after the inventions were made. The chemical industry may have been the first important exception to this rule, one that showed the virtue of trying to work from scientific principles to their application, instead of the reverse. The development of synthetic dyes provided a model of how this could be done.

One of the distinguishing features of British higher education up to the mid-19th century was that it paid very little attention to the useful applications of knowledge and very little attention to the systematic creation of new knowledge, what we would call research. The model of the research institution was in Germany, which for many years had focused both theoretical and applied studies on research. The familiar Ph.D. degree that is considered an essential part of the training of academics in most of the world today is modeled on the German research degree.

In 1845, in an effort to catch up with the successes of German-style research, the Royal College of Chemistry was established in London. A German chemist, A. W. Hoffmann, was hired to head up the college. He instituted a curriculum based upon the investigation of particular problems. One of his students in 1856 was an eighteen-year-old named William Perkin. Hoffmann had set Perkin the task of attempting to make quinine synthetically from aniline, a product that Hoffmann had found a way to make, but could think of no use for. Quinine was a natural product obtained from the bark of the cinchona tree and was the only known effective remedy for malaria. Malaria is primarily a tropical disease, but with the expansion of the British Empire into all parts of

---

1. The steam engine, for example, was invented by mechanics and instrument makers who knew little of the emerging science of gases, though James Watt may have been helped to some of his more important insights by being aware of the work of Joseph Black at the University of Glasgow, where Watt was working.

the world, many high-level British civil servants were contracting the disease. Quinine was in great demand. To have an artificial supply would be a great boon.

An older William H. Perkin.

Perkin did not succeed in synthesizing quinine, but in his researches he discovered that a residue obtained from the aniline he was working with turned solutions a bright purple. Perkin had discovered the dye *mauve*. Though Perkin was only an eighteen-year-old student, he saw an opportunity in the fabric dyeing industry. With the backing of his father and his brother, Perkin set up a factory in Britain to make aniline dye. It was a tremendous success. Perkin made a fortune and retired to a life of research at the age of 38. Dye making began in Britain, the centre of the textile industry, and then was taken up with vigour in France, where a fashion industry existed. However, by the end of the 19th century, German industry completely dominated dye making. Germany had the raw materials, the technical education necessary, and also financial support from the state.

Synthetic dyes, like so many products in the chemical industry, are made from byproducts of petroleum or coal. Synthetic dyes have a straightforward manufacturing process and produce a reliable product. Compared to natural dyes, the supply of raw materials is not limited by the availability of a plant that may only grow in special climates and may require immense amounts of labour to process. It is nearly inevitable that the vast majority of dyes in use in industry today are synthetic, all reliant on the supply of fossil fuels.

Explosives

Until the middle of the 19th century, the only important explosive was gunpowder. Nitro-celluose, or "gun cotton," and nitroglycerin were developed in the middle of the century, but they were considered so dangerous that little practical use could be found for them. The key to making explosives useful was, paradoxically, to make them safe—so that they will only explode when an explosion is wanted.

Alfred Nobel.

The person who discovered how to do this was Alfred Nobel, the son of a Swedish inventor. As a young man, Nobel studied chemistry for a time in Paris and worked with a shipbuilder in the United States. At the age of twenty-one, he returned to St. Petersburg, Russia, where his family had moved, to join his father in his business. His father had done some work with making and using nitroglycerin, but abandoned it when it was more trouble than it was worth. Alfred decided to revive that part of the business and returned to Sweden in 1863 to set up a factory to make nitroglycerin.

An explosion in the factory that killed five people, including Nobel's youngest brother, prompted the Swedish government to ban the rebuilding of the factory. However Nobel was convinced that he could overcome the inherent dangers and moved the entire factory onto a barge in a nearby lake. Though the barge-factory had no further mishaps, there were a series of explosions around the world in ports from ship carrying nitroglycerin. Many nations moved to ban all ships carrying nitroglycerin as a cargo.

Nobel did find a solution to this problem. He mixed the nitroglycerin with a porous clay mixture of clay. This remained inert and could be transported safely unless it was detonated by a blasting cap. This was *dynamite*. It became a very important product for the chemical industry and led to the development of other explosives.

Dynamite is a double-edged product. It and all other explosives can be used to clear away areas for construction and for mining, but it can also be used for purely destructive purposes. In fact, the very first public use of dynamite was in a bomb thrown into a crowd at a labour rally in Chicago in 1886, killing seven policemen. Explosives of all sorts have increased the potential for damage in warfare and have upped the seriousness of armed conflict for the whole world.

Nobel saw the many peaceful uses of dynamite and became very wealthy selling it to industry, enabling them to undertake huge projects which would have been prohibitively expensive without a manageable explosive. Nobel was also aware of the destructive uses and later in life became very concerned about them. As is well known, he left nine million dollars of his fortune to fund prizes to be given to those who had most helped humankind, including a prize for those who have helped the cause of peace.

Plastics

Of all the products brought to the modern world by the chemical industry, those that have made the most obvious impact on our daily lives are plastics. There are so many kinds of plastics and so many different uses of plastics that a person living in a modern industrial setting is probably never in a situation where something made of plastic is not immediately at hand or in view.

The plastic industry has a history that goes back to the early to mid-19th century—much the same as the synthetic dye industry—but most of the development has taken place in the 20th century. It, like the synthetic dye industry, is an offshoot of applied organic chemistry.

The key product is a resin made from petroleum that can be made into any desired shape, hence the name "plastic." Vinyl resins were discovered as early as 1838, but were not made into commercial products until nearly a century later as polyvinyl chloride, which could be readily moulded into any desired shape. Another resin was acrylic, first marketed under the trade name *Plexiglas*, to be used as a safe alternative to glass as it would not shatter.

In 1935, a new plastic product called *nylon* was discovered and soon brought to market, to be used both as a plastic sheeting and, in threads, as a fabric. *Polyurethanes* were introduced in 1954. Another, accidental, discovery was a white powder with the chemical name polytetrafluoroethylene, which was marketed by the Du Pont company under the brand name *Teflon*, used as a coating on cookware to prevent sticking, but also in many other uses where non-adherence is important.

The list goes on. There are so many different products that have been developed out of various combinations of the original resins and other chemical components, all of which have special physical properties that make them ideal for certain applications. To name a few: polystyrene, fluorocarbons, expoxy, silicone preparations, polypropylene, liquid crystal polymers. Many plastics have primarily industrial uses and are not familiar to the ordinary citizen but are essential in the construction industry, in machine parts, in airplanes and space ships, in computers and electronics, and at least somewhere in virtually all manufactured products.

Plastics and the Environment

From an environmental viewpoint, one of the most disturbing features of plastics is one of the features that make them so valuable: durability. They do not rot, rust, or readily come apart from normal uses. Or, to put that another way, they are not biodegradable. They will not break down into simpler substances that nature can then further disintegrate and regroup. There are some efforts to make plastics that *are* biodegradable, but this is almost counterproductive. The difficulty is to make a plastic that will degrade from, say, sunlight, but won't do so before it has served its purpose.

What, then, is to be done with all the tonnes of plastic waste from products that have outlived their usefulness? There are ways of recycling plastics by grinding them up and reprocessing them, but to do so, the plastic products must be separated from the rest of the garbage that is produced in volume by modern society. Even so, the reprocessed plastic no longer has the same physical features as the original, so it cannot be used for the same purpose. Polyethylene milk jugs, for example, can be reprocessed into filler insulation or for plastic building materials, but cannot be made again into a beverage container.

Plastics also make considerable use of chemical agents which release polluting gases; the chlorofluorocarbons (CFCs) that were used to make in Styrofoam containers could damage the ozone layer when released into the atmosphere if the styrofoam ignited. Some of these are perhaps solvable problems that newer products will take care of, but meanwhile, many of the most useful products of the chemical industry are also the most threatening to the environment.

The wonders of chemistry have produced marvels that have changed so much of what we are able to do easily and inexpensively. But the industry is built upon natural resources, in particular, petroleum, that are not replaceable and turns them into products that produce waste that is difficult to dispose of.

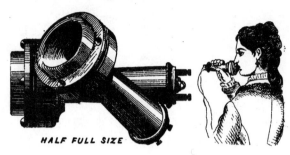

HALF FULL SIZE

THE TELEPHONE.

The Articulating or Speaking Telephone of Professor Alexander Graham Bell has now reached a point of simplicity, perfection, and reliability such as give it undoubted pre-eminence over all other means for telegraphic communication. Its employment necessitates no skilled labour, no technical education, and no special attention on the part of any one individual. Persons using it can converse miles apart, in precisely the same manner as though they were in the same room. It needs but a wire between the two points of communication, though ten or twenty miles apart, with a Telephone or a pair of Telephones—one to receive, the other to transmit, the sound of the voice—to hold communication in any language. It conveys the quality of the voice so that the person speaking can be recognised at the other end of the line. It can be used for any purpose and in any position—for mines, marine exploration, military evolutions, and numerous other purposes other than the hitherto recognised field for Telegraphy; between the manufacturer's office and his factory; between all large commercial houses and their branches; between central and branch banks; in ship-building yards, and factories of every description; in fact wherever conversation is required between the principal and

[1]   P.T.O.

Chapter 22

Electricity and Communications

The modern world is inconceivable without electricity. We live in a world of electric and electronic appliances and gadgets that we would have a difficult time doing without, and we light our homes, offices, and even our streets with electric lighting. Our communication system is based upon electrical energy; anything else is unthinkable. We rely on electricity as the means to provide energy anytime, anywhere, no matter how it was originally generated, because electricity gives us the means to transport that energy anywhere we want and turn it into any other form of energy that we require. A major failure in the electrical system—a blackout—is a very serious setback for any industrialized community.

Electricity entered the industrialized world near the beginning of the Industrial Revolution. Its usefulness has continued to grow throughout that time. It, along with magnetism, was known about and remarked upon for centuries before the Industrial Revolution. Electricity and magnetism were often viewed as magical forces that had curious effects, such as making a compass needle turn north, or attracting bits of metal or chaff. However, not much effort was made to get to the bottom of these phenomena until the 18th century, when all of nature was undergoing scientific investigation.

Benjamin Franklin's famous experiment with lightning.

Benjamin Franklin determined that there were positive charges and negative charges of static electricity, and when you brought them in contact with each other, they both were neutralized. He also is famous for showing that the familiar phenomenon of lightning was indeed the same as electricity by flying a kite in a thunderstorm and causing a charge to travel down his kite string, fortunately not electrocuting him. Still, not much could be done with electricity until some way had been found to store it and then make it flow at will. This was done in 1800 by Alessandro Volta, who made a pile of alternating copper and zinc plates separated by cardboard soaked in acid, thus inventing the electric battery.

The beginnings of a useful role for electricity came in the early 19th century with the discovery that electricity and magnetism were closely related to each other. A changing electric current produces a magnetic attraction, and a moving magnet produces an electric current. These two interrelations, plus the other represented by the battery—that chemical energy can be converted to electricity—are all that is needed to explain why electricity is so incredibly useful to modern society: Electricity can be produced at will from other kinds of energy. The energy tied up in the chemical composition of some compounds can be used to make electricity, and motion itself can also make electricity. Having made the electricity, it can be turned back into other forms of useful energy. For example, it can be used to make magnetism and then the magnetism used to cause motion.

Much of the development of electricity, electrical engineering, and electronics has been simply finding out how to do those things better and more usefully.

Signaling

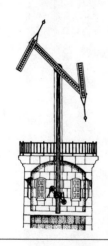

A semaphore station.

The first important application of electricity was for long-distance communication. One of the most characteristic limitations of early human societies was that they were effectively isolated from each other, only able to communicate by sending people back and forth with messages and news. Some of the most ingenious inventions of the early Industrial Revolution were aimed at overcoming the drawbacks of this separation.

For years, the military had adopted its own method of relaying information across a battlefield. There were, of course, all the elaborate bugle calls that had to be recognized by soldiers in battle, but also there was the silent transmission of messages as far as the eye could see by a system of signals using flags: semaphores.

In 1792, the flag-semaphore idea was extended in France to provide a form of telegraphy. A series of high towers were erected on hills at 25-kilometer intervals. On each tower was a long post with movable arms that could be placed in different positions to indicate different letters of the alphabet—the same principle as the flag-semaphores, but for much longer distances. A series of these could relay a message across France in a matter of minutes.

But before these semaphore stations had been erected, inventors were busy trying to harness the attractive properties of electrostatic charges to send signals. The first such device was created in the 1750s. It had a cable containing 26 separate wires, one for each letter of the alphabet. On one end of the cable, a person took a charged rod and brought it near the wire designated for the next letter of the alphabet in a message being sent. On the other end, the wires were arranged over individual pith balls that would rise to the wire if it were electrified. The receiver would write down the sequence of pith balls rising to form the message. Another version of the same idea had bubbles rising in vials when a charge was sent.

The Telegraph

In the 1830s, a forerunner of the modern telegraph system was introduced, the Cooke and Wheatstone five-needle telegraph. Here, positive or negative charges were sent through five separate wires that produced magnetic fields at the receiving end. This made use of the principle that a changing electric current produces a magnetic disturbance. The receiving magnets rotated according to the charge and pointed in one of two directions. Two wires at a time were used. The two magnets each pointed toward a row of letters. The letter that was at the point of intersection was the letter indicated by the charge. It was a slow process, but it got the number of wires needed down to 5.

The Cooke and Wheatstone five-needle telegraph.

In the 1840s, Samuel Morse invented a code for characterizing every letter of the alphabet as a combination of two signals, a long signal and a short signal (dash and dot), which code is still used today. This made it possible for a single wire to be used to transmit signals, which were then merely an alteration of the current going down the line. This revolutionized the telegraph industry and made it commercially practical. By the 1850s, every state east of the Mississippi in the U.S. belonged to the telegraph network. The chief users of the telegraph originally were the railroads. It was easy for them to set up telegraph lines along the railroad right of way, and important for them to be able to signal information about rail traffic to stations down the line. The Morse code key was the high tech communications device of the day. It made it possible for a skilled operator

A Morse telegraph key.

to send reliable signals in Morse code very quickly. At the receiving end, another device made audible clicks when the current was sent and caused a magnet to move. Skilled operators could recognize these as letters and write down the message from the sound of the clicks. Originally, it had been thought that it would be necessary to have a device to record the incoming signals on paper for later translation into ordinary language, but the operators learned to work more efficiently from the sound alone.

With the telegraph, essentially instantaneous communication over vast distances became possible. In 1861, a telegram could be sent across the North American continent, from New York to San Francisco. By 1866, there were two undersea cables that crossed the Atlantic Ocean. To celebrate, the Mayor of Vancouver sent a telegram all 13,000 kilometers to the Lord Mayor of London. By the end of the 19th century, telegraph wires crisscrossed the entire globe, and information of sufficient importance could be sent around the world in minutes.

Alexander Graham Bell inaugurating the first New York to Chicago telephone line.

The Telephone

Alexander Graham Bell, who pursued a career in teaching speech to deaf children while also pursuing a hobby in electrical gadgets, sought to find a device that would send an audible signal of multiple frequencies on a telegraph line. He spent his winters in Boston, working with the deaf and his summers in Brantford, Ontario, where his family had settled. He did some of his work on converting sound to electricity in both places. Predictably, both cities lay claim to being the birthplace of the telephone.

Ultimately, the system he developed converted sound waves into electrical impulses, and the receiver converted those electrical impulses into magnetic fields which vibrated a diaphragm to reconstitute the original sound. The telephone industry expanded quickly once the usefulness of the apparatus became known. At first, the telephone was marketed to businesses that had a demonstrable need to communicate with workers in different locations, e.g., down in mines, out in warehouses, in factories, etc. These were point-to-point connections: single telephones at either end of single wires. Soon the idea arose of using telephones connected in a network, so that it was possible to speak to people at many different locations from a single telephone, so long as each location had its own phone and was connected to the network. Thus began the switchboard, the exchange, and the public telephone service. The picture shown is of a switchboard from the 19th century, probably used in a large commercial operation to connect different departments. Such switchboards (PBX systems) remained in use, looking much the same, until the 1970s.

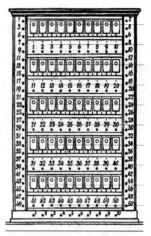

A telephone switchboard.

The telephone took some time to become universally adopted. Its first successes were in the United States and Canada, naturally. In both places the telegraph was well established, partly due to the prominence of the railroads and the long distances between cities. Telegraph lines could easily be adapted to telephone lines, so part of the infrastructure was already there. This is a little like the way that the bicycle made the adoption of the automobile easier. But, partly the headstart in North America was due to the open competition of private enterprise. In the United States, the number of telephones doubled every four years between 1880 and 1900, from 48 000 to 1 350 000. In Europe, the telephone industry tended to be folded into the post office and therefore was government run. By 1911, the number of telephones in the United States was equal to five percent of the population, while in Britain and Germany it was equal to one percent. The rest of Europe was much farther behind.

However, the telephone *has* become universally adopted, at least in the entire industrialized world. Virtually everyone has daily access to a telephone. For many urban sophisticates, a telephone is never more than a few meters away, and with the advent of cellular telephones, those who have them are never out of reach. It would be hard to overestimate the importance of the telephone to the industrialized world and equally hard to imagine anything like the present day society without the telephone. To quote from a biography of Alexander Graham Bell,

> Without the telephone as its nervous system, the twentieth-century metropolis would have been stunted by congestion and slowed to

the primordial pace of messengers and postmen. And the modern industrial age would have been born with cerebral palsy.[1]

Electric Lighting

Already in the 19th century, the industrialized nations had become accustomed to artificial light at night. First, light came from lamps run on animal oils, especially whale oil, produced by a robust whaling industry that nearly drove the whales to extinction, then by a gas made from coal, and then from a petroleum product, coal oil or kerosene. The demand for lighting had been established, and the practical advantages had been shown. It was therefore relatively easy for electric lighting to find a ready market, once the technical details of the product had been worked out.

Thomas Alva Edison.

Though some experimenters before him had limited success, electric lighting is really the invention of Thomas Alva Edison, one of the world's first professional inventors. Edison was extraordinarily productive, lodging a total of 1093 patents for inventions in his lifetime. The electric light bulb may be what gave him the greatest fame, but many others also came to be widely used in homes and in industry—the phonograph, the motion-picture camera, the stock ticker, and the repeating telegraph are among the best known, but there are many more that were incorporated as improvements in existing technology and added to their effectiveness. Several of his improvements were to telephone technology, and he is credited with being the person who started the habit of answering a telephone with the expression "hello."

Most of his best-known inventions used the power of electricity in one way or another. Edison was in the prime of his life when the usefulness of electricity was first being discovered. As mentioned above, the great versatility of electricity is that it can be

---

1. Robert V. Bruce, quoted in James MacLachlan, *Children of Prometheus: A History of Science and Technology*, 2nd ed. (Toronto: Wall & Emerson, 2002), p. 356.

easily produced from other sources of energy, and it can then be transmitted a distance and once again converted into some other form of energy that is useful. The telephone uses the ability of an electric current to affect a magnetic field to make audible sound waves by vibrating the air. Another form of energy that can be produced from electricity is light. If electricity is forced through a medium that does not conduct a current readily, that medium will quickly heat up and begin to glow. This was noticed early on by scientists doing research on electricity and its properties. Usually, a medium that has been made to glow brightly from electricity will quickly catch fire and burn up. However, a fire requires oxygen, so if electricity can be forced through a medium in a vacuum, the fire is prevented and the glow prolonged.

Edison obtained a vacuum pump and evacuated the air from a small container in which he placed an object that he then connected to an electric current. At first all his objects crumbled quickly under the electrical force, but eventually he found some materials that glowed for an extended period. This gave him his first workable light bulb. Curiously, the first filaments for light bulbs that were deemed practical were made of charred bamboo, which Edison had sent to him from jungles all over the world. The familiar tungsten filament used today was a later improvement; likewise the bulbs were later filled with an inert gas instead of leaving them as a vacuum, which improved the luminosity and extended the filament life.

On December 31, 1879, Edison was ready to show the world what his invention could do. He organized a special event in Menlo Park, New Jersey, where his home and laboratory were located, to be attended by dignitaries from government and business, brought in by a special train to witness the first electric street lighting. After this, it did not take long for electric lighting to displace oil and gas lighting on the streets of major cities, in businesses, and then in homes across the industrialized world.

Edison also had to sell his customers a supply of electricity to run his lights. Therefore, along with the electric light, Edison also developed the electric power generating station. Once an electrical supply was readily available, a flood of other inventions that ran on electric power soon came to the market—machinery of all sorts and electric streetcars that soon became the standard means of public transportation in cities. Large manufacturing companies devoted to electrical products came into existence, such as Westinghouse and the company that is now the world's largest corporation, General Electric. These began making electrical products for every conceivable use. The versatility of electricity made all this possible, since electricity can be made to run almost anything.

The World of Wireless

The telegraph had proven to be a most valuable adjunct to the railroad industry, helping it to track schedules and notify stations ahead of impending changes. It quickly also proved itself to be of immense value to business by its ability to transmit important information quickly. But the telegraph only worked over land and through undersea cables. There was still no way to communicate with ships at sea, short of getting within visual range and flashing some kind of signal. A telegraph that worked without wires would be a most useful invention.

Guglielmo Marconi.

Another inventor who saw how the new discoveries in science could be put to practical use was Guglielmo Marconi, son of a wealthy Italian merchant and a British mother from a well-connected family of whisky distillers. As a young man, Marconi read about Heinrich Hertz's work on what we now call radio waves and wondered if they could somehow be used for sending a signal electromagnetically through space. He developed a set of devices that sent a coded message (Morse code) and received it up to three kilometers away. He tried to get the Italian government interested in his invention, but with no success. Hence, he, and his mother, emigrated back to her home country where he believed he could sell his idea. Britain was then, as it always has been, an important center both for the navy and for the merchant marines. Marconi patented his process, and with his family's financial support, formed the Wireless Telegraph and Signal Company in July 1897. The main business of the Marconi company was originally in ship-to-shore communication. Ships that neared the British coast could be contacted by wireless telegraph and exchange information with the shore. By 1903, there were 25 shore stations and 70 ships equipped to send and receive signals.

Wireless telegraphy greatly increased the scope of telegraphed signals. Originally, the purpose of the invention was to send and receive signals from point to point. However, the receiver of a signal did not have to be in a specific place to get a message. When this was first realized, messages of general interest to ships at sea close enough to a transmitter could be sent to all at once. This was the beginning of broadcasting.

Radio

Marconi produced the disturbance in the electromagnetic waves that he used for wireless telegraphy by causing a spark to make a signal. A combination of slow and fast sparks distinguished dot from dash and made sending Morse code possible. In principle, a radio wave could carry much more information by varying the disturbance in much more subtle ways, but the means to do that had not been invented. In the early years of the 20th century, several key devices were developed for working with electric power and with electromagnetic waves, most notably, the vacuum tube, that allowed a continuous wave transmission. The person who put these together was a Canadian named Reginald Fessenden, who discovered how to add a modulation of the continuous wave that could carry the complexities of ordinary sounds, such as speech.

To inaugurate his discovery, Fessenden sent out a message, via Morse code wireless telegraphy to ships at sea off the coast of Massachusetts on December 24, 1906, telling the wireless operators to be tuned in at a specified time for an important message about to be transmitted. Then he switched to his modulating equipment and broadcast a program of vocal Christmas and New Year's greetings and recorded music from phonograph records. His audience was, of course, dumbfounded.

It was another case of one technology paving the way for another. Since wireless sets already existed to receive telegraphy, and since one way or another, they could receive and decipher radio signals carrying voices and music, there was the beginning of a network that a radio industry could build upon. In the 1920s, radio broadcasting began on a regular basis. Marconi set up broadcasts in Britain—at first listened to by existing telegraph operators—and the Westinghouse company set up a radio station in the United States. It did not take long for the public to want to own "radio sets" of their own to listen to these broadcasts, and not long after that for the broadcasting industry to expand to meet demand and create more of it.

Television

Technologically speaking, television is merely an extension of radio. Radio was the technique of broadcasting modulated electromagnetic waves that anyone with the proper equipment could receive and decipher. To transmit pictures along with sound, the same general scientific principles are at work, but the technological problems are much greater. In addition to transmitting sounds the way a radio station would do, a potential television broadcast would have to find a way to translate an entire picture into a series of

An early television set.

pulses that could be reconstructed into a picture at the receiving end. The television receiver would aim each bit of the pulse at a screen that would light up or not depending on the pulse; this would all happen so fast that the eyes watching the screen would see all of the pieces of the screen—the pixels we now call them—as one whole picture. Many essential components had to be invented and then improved to the point where they could be used together, in particular the cathode ray tube on which the picture is projected and the iconoscope that divides the picture into individual pixels of data.

Television broadcasts began in the 1930s, but it was not until after the Second World War that television broadcasting expanded greatly and the general public began to obtain television sets to complement their radio sets and began to expect regular broadcasts. The broadcasting companies were, of course, the radio corporations that simply widened their scope.

The Computer

An account of the development of uses for electricity would be incomplete without at least a mention of the development of that machine that dominates the high-technology world today, the computer. The electronic computer of today is in a direct line of evolution from the first electronic computing machine built during the Second World War by the U.S. Army as a rapid way of calculating how artillery should be aimed. The general conception of mechanical computation that went into the making of that computer has a long history that goes back to mechanical calculators from as early as the 17th century and a full-scale idea developed by Charles Babbage in the mid-19th century for a general purpose calculating engine to be run on steam power. Though the basic mathematical theory of computation existed for some time, the technology to make it practical did not exist until around the middle of the 20th century. It was the same electronic technology that went into radios and televisions. The earliest successful machines required a huge number of vacuum tubes to produce electric currents at the right time and intensity. Later, with the development of the transistor and other aspects of solid-state technology, computers became much more reliable, much faster, and much smaller.

The first electronic computer actually to be built and operated was the U.S. Army's Electronic Numerical Integrator and Computer, or ENIAC for short. It was developed by two electrical engineers at the University of Pennsylvania, John W. Mauchly and John P. Eckert. During the war, the University of Pennsylvania was the site of a major project by the Army to calculate what were called firing tables for their anti-aircraft artillery. A firing table was the result of a complex calculation of the range of a gun, the altitude it needed to reach, the air temperature at the time, and the speed of any wind. Each different kind of gun in the army arsenal would require between two thousand and four thousand trajectory calculations. It was a horrendous task then being performed by rooms full of "human computers," that is, people doing hand calculations. One human computer could calculate a single trajectory in about three days.

Mauchly and Eckert convinced the army that they could replace these banks of human beings by making an electronic machine that could calculate a trajectory in perhaps one hundred seconds. They finally got their project underway, but in fact the war was over before the computer was built. The ENIAC was finally finished in November 1945, three months after the Japanese surrender.

The ENIAC

The machine they built used decimal, not binary mathematics as present day machines do. It was programmable, and could solve any sort of calculation problem, but did not store programs at all, so all was lost when the machine was turned off. It was huge and cumbersome. It had 17 468 vacuum tubes, 70 000 resistors, 10 000 capacitors, 1500 relays, and 6000 manual switches. It was two and a half meters high, 25 meters long, weighed 30 tonnes, and used 174 000 watts of power. It took two days to set up and to solve a problem.

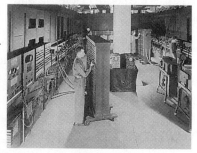

The ENIAC computer.

Nevertheless, the ENIAC kicked off the computer industry. Its first use was to calculate the feasibility for a proposed design for the hydrogen bomb.

Stored Program Computers

The worst drawback of the ENIAC was that it had to be reprogrammed for every different task. There was no storage memory at all that could reset the computer to do something different. After the war, Mauchly and Eckert left the University of Pennsylvania to establish a company to build computers; they received an order from the army to build a computer that could store programs for later use. They sold their company to Remington Rand, which became the first manufacturer of commercially available computers.

Remington Rand built the Universal Automatic Computer, the UNIVAC, first built in 1951. It could store programs and data, be started and stopped at any time and reprogrammed; it was the first generally available computer adopted for use by the major corporations of the world.

As a publicity stunt for the computer, the U.S. television network, CBS, used a UNIVAC to predict the U.S. presidential election on election night in November 1952. At 9 p.m. Eastern Standard Time, with only seven percent of the votes in, the UNIVAC computer awarded 43 states and 438 electoral votes to Dwight Eisenhower and five states with 93 electoral votes to Adlai Stevenson. The computer, of course, was right, but pollsters had predicted a close election. The programmers thought that *they* had surely made a mistake, so they did not release their prediction. Instead, they reprogrammed the computer and had it predict a toss-up at 10 p.m. By midnight, they realized they had been right the first time. The actual result was 442 electoral votes for Eisenhower, 89 for Stevenson. The CBS commentator Edward R. Murrow remarked: "The trouble with machines ... is people."

The Personal Computer

After the UNIVAC, computers got larger, faster, and developed vast capabilities unimaginable to the originators of the first machines. A significant invention of the 1960s, the *semiconductor*, allowed many components to be placed on a single chip, which would run faster and take up much less room. From then on, the trend in computers has been to get smaller and smaller, while getting faster and more powerful. In the 1970s, the *minicomputer* was introduced, a machine that was small enough for moderate-sized businesses to afford to own their own. Many businesses that had previously either maintained their records by hand or farmed out their bookkeeping to large companies with mainframe computers obtained their own computer and their own computer staff.

The computer terminal began to appear on desktops in offices across the industrialized world.

In 1981, International Business Machines brought out the first computer that was really intended for the personal use of the general public in homes, offices and schools— the "personal computer," or PC. The PC was the "Model T" of the computer industry. Almost immediately, IBM clones, less expensive than the name brand, made the price even more affordable. Personal computers in use went from two million in 1981 to 5.5 million in 1982. Ten years later there were 65 million in use.

The trend toward miniaturization has continued with the laptop and notebook computers and all the other devices that have complex computer technology built into them in ways we don't even notice.

Networks

The phenomenon that is overwhelming the present day is a combination of all of the technologies that have been discussed so far in this chapter. The power of individual computers is now linked through communication channels to other computers around the world, producing a new revolution in the way of life in the advanced countries.

The Internet

This linking began with simple connections between a number of smaller computers in, perhaps, an office, that could be linked together, or networked, to share memory space, software, and information, and to communicate with each other. These Local Area Networks, or LANs, had computers directly wired to each other. In addition to direct wiring of computers in a single building, computers from another location could be connected to the network using telephone lines and modulator-demodulators, or modems, for short.

One of the LANs that was expanded to include many computers at many locations was run by the U.S. Defense Department. It was called the Advanced Research Projects Agency Network, or ARPANET. In the 1980s, this network was expanded to connect universities, research institutions, and government agencies around the world. Toward the end of the 1990s, personal computers became widely owned in households all across the industrialized world, and a very high percentage of them had some connection to an even broader version of this network, popularly called the *Internet*.

Every year, the Internet expands its potential for information transfer and its usage as a general reference and communication tool, and is also increasingly abused by hackers, pornographers, and conmen. Although too new to assess, it is hard to see how society could turn back the page and do without it.

The Electrical Age

Even if we could contemplate a world without the Internet, or even without computers, if that were possible, it is just about impossible to imagine life in the industrialized part of the world without any of the products that run on electricity. To quote one of the early founders of electronics, J. A. Fleming said in 1921(!), that if the products of electricity were suddenly no longer available,

> In a month all large cities would be in a state of starvation and the traffic and movement on which our commercial life depends would be destroyed.... Politicians are apt to think that their labours are essential to the prosperity of the community.... They are, in truth, not nearly so valuable as the work of the electrical engineer.[1]

Fleming wrote those words over 80 years ago. Probably 90 percent of all of the electrical devices we use today were not even thought of at that time, and the rest have changed so much that they remain the same only in name and general function.

Present day society in the industrialized countries and, to a lesser extent, even in the Third World is inextricably entwined with the technology that has made it possible. Most of that technology is either conveyed by or powered by or made possible by some application of electricity and electronics. Electrical engineers may be expected to see the whole world as totally dependent on their area of expertise, as J.A. Fleming apparently did, but it is a view difficult to refute. Modern society as we now know it is completely entwined with its technology. As W. A. Atherton expressed it,

> It has become common to talk of technology and society as if the two are quite separate entities, somewhat like strawberries and cream, that are brought together one to enhance the other; or for those who believe the cream has turned sour, one to ruin the other.... Technology and society are not two separate entities coexisting, harmoniously or otherwise. We live in a technological society, not in a society with technology. Technology is part of the

---

1.   J. A. Fleming, *Fifty Years of Electricity* (London: Wireless Press, 1921).

very fabric of our society. As in strawberry-flavoured ice cream, the flavour runs right through the very substance itself. Whether it be the bus, train, or car we take to work, the television that entertains us, the cutlery with which we eat, or the telephone on our desk, technology is a part of our life, not an adjunct to it.[1]

The age we live in is dependent on electricity. That and the other forms of energy that we use so much of has to be produced and made into a form that we can access, otherwise all our marvelous appliances would not work. How we have done that is the subject of the next chapter.

---

1. W. A. Atherton, *From Compass to Computer: A History of Electrical and Electronics Engineering* (London: Macmillan, 1984), p. 311.

Chapter 23

Energy

The very concept of energy was formulated and made precise because of the Industrial Revolution. In particular, scientists wanted to understand exactly what was happening when, for example, a pile of coal or wood was burned, producing heat, which then heated water, which turned into steam, which filled a chamber holding up a piston until the steam condensed, and then finally the power of the atmosphere caused the piston to move with great force, doing work. How could this whole process be understood and given a precise accounting in the mathematical terms of a scientific theory?

Thermodynamics

The Newtonian model of the world had sought to explain everything as the interactions of matter and motion. But while that could account for the motions of the planets and the behaviour of projectiles, it did not seem sufficient to explain what was happening when burning a lump of coal ultimately caused a piston to move and a flywheel to turn. Something running throughout all of these was being passed on. The coal was, in some way, the cause of the work. Nineteenth century scientists in many different disciplines—physics, chemistry, biology, and medicine—reached similar conclusions: that there was another, more general, attribute of things in nature that could be quantified and studied. This was given the name *energy*.

Energy was somehow trapped in the coal—as what we might call chemical energy—that was released when the coal was set on fire. That energy passed into heat—another form of energy—that then raised the temperature of the water until it turned to steam. The steam expanded and produced a pressure—energy in the form of a force that pushed against the atmosphere, or in later steam engines, pushed the piston itself. Similar processes went on in the biological world. An animal consumes food of some sort. Its digestive system breaks that food down into simpler chemical components and in so doing releases heat. This is the process we call metabolism. It is just the transformation of energy from food into another form that can be used differently.

One of the great discoveries of science in the 19th century is the principle of *conservation of energy*, which, simply stated, asserts that there is a fixed amount of energy in any closed system, though that energy can get transformed any number of ways. In other words, there really is no such thing as energy creation, only energy transformation. Much of what we call energy creation or energy production is merely the taking of energy from one form, which we cannot use readily, and converting it into another form, which is useful to us—such as heat or motion. The conservation of energy became the first principle of *thermodynamics*, a new branch of physical science devoted to understanding these transformations of energy from one form to another.

Another scientific discovery about energy is that it is never transferred perfectly from one body to another. There is always some amount of energy that is lost to usefulness. For example, some heat escapes from burning coal into the atmosphere instead of going into heating the water, or friction occurs in moving parts that does not serve the purposes of a machine. This became the second law of thermodynamics. It is the basis of the assertion by scientists that perpetual motion machines are impossible, because they could only work if there were perfect transfers of energy back and forth between two (or more) media. For human civilization, the relevant fact here is that once energy has been converted from one form to another, less of it remains in a useful form. Even if there is theoretically just as much energy in the world later on, the amount available for use is less. In this sense, we can think of ourselves as consumers of energy.

The laws of thermodynamics apply to closed systems—those that are isolated from outside influences. The universe is, presumably, a closed system, but the Earth is not. We are always the recipients of a new supply of energy from the Sun. In fact, nearly all of the usable energy on the Earth may be thought to have come from the Sun. But much of the energy we are using daily in great amounts was laid down by the actions of sunlight millions of years ago. Because of that, we would be well advised to view the energy on the Earth as finite.

Energy Production and Consumption

Interest in thermodynamics arose during the Industrial Revolution, because that was the first time that human beings had begun to command huge amounts of power, far in excess of the visible forces of nature. The power generated by windmills and waterwheels that had been in use for centuries was nevertheless produced by forces that could readily be perceived. In the Industrial Revolution, the power came from things dug out of the ground. To make the engines of industry work, it was necessary to find and extract the materials that would release the energy needed. This was not making new energy so much as finding stores of it in the ground, but as far as industry was concerned, it was producing it. One way to look at the record of civilization through history is to note the energy sources that have been used from the beginning onward. Viewed this way, every step in the advance of civilization has been a step up in the rate of energy being consumed.

Hunter-Gatherers

Hunter-gatherer societies expended the energy of their own bodies in all their daily affairs, including the hunting and gathering of the food which provided them with the energy they needed. Theirs was a very cyclic exchange of energy. The ecosystems in which they lived could be sustained for a very long time. They consumed food, they excreted waste, some of which acted as fertilizer, they culled herds and thinned plant growth so that both of them could regenerate without exceeding their niche in their particular environment. When they died, their bodies decomposed and ultimately added to the richness of the soil. In a sense, this was a nearly perfect exchange of energy, and it was sustainable for a long time. It was not, to be sure, a *perfect* exchange. That would be a perpetual motion machine, but the extra input of energy that kept it going came from the sun and was taken up by plants as photosynthesis.

Hunter-gatherers began to tax their environment when their population grew to the extent that their traditional way of life was incapable of feeding the whole population. Then began the slow process of tinkering with the environment to make it more productive than it might otherwise have been. This tinkering took the form of clearing land of thick growth in order to allow more edible plants to flourish. Then came the move from that to deliberately planting crops in the cleared land to assure a supply of food. Along with that came the change from hunting animals that happened to be around to following herds and periodically killing what they needed to eat. Each step of this process was a departure from what might be called the natural ecological balance of the environments in which they lived.

Agriculture

At some point around 10 000 years ago, hunter-gatherers shifted over permanently to an agricultural way of life. Right from the start, this meant placing more demands on the environment than was indefinitely sustainable with only the added input of sunlight. Crops grown in the same field year after year placed a strain on the soil, which could not regenerate indefinitely. Irrigation added unnatural amounts of silt along with the water, often leaving the land both waterlogged and too salt-laden for crops to grow as they had before. The raising of domestic animals upset the normal life-cycle of the species raised. Generally, more animals were kept in a restricted area than would normally occur in the wild. The waste matter of the animals was used as a fertilizer for the soil to push it to regenerate, but the high concentrations of manure from a few kinds of animals in a given field slowly changed the chemical composition of the soil and put it under stress. And living in one place led to building more permanent dwellings, often of wood, and using wood also for heating and cooking. Deforestation was the result almost everywhere that an agricultural life was adopted. All of these practices took energy out of the system faster than it could regenerate and led to a long-term decline of the environment. Still, the land, the forest, and the animals all did regenerate, even if not as fast as necessary to meet all human needs.

Craft Industries

As civilization progressed and became more sophisticated, people learned how to make many products that made life more comfortable. Those that required special skills often also required access to special sources of energy. Those who worked with metals— blacksmiths, cutlers, weapons makers—all needed high levels of heat to smelt the metals they would fashion into products. Their furnaces needed a fuel that would burn at very high temperatures. Charcoal was often the chosen fuel, and to get charcoal a large number of trees had to be felled and then charred to remains that would re-ignite at the higher temperatures needed. More deforestation resulted. Some trades required only a steady source of power greater than what humans could supply. Sometimes this could be provided by animals, sometimes by running water or the wind. Tapping the wind and waterpower did little to disrupt the energy cycle since the demands were so small, though the disruption to the natural flow of water could disrupt the ecology downstream. In terms of sustainability, the main drawback of civilization at this level was that it improved the quality of life enough that the population rose to a point where more drastic measures had to be taken.

Coal

The powerhouse of the Industrial Revolution was the steam engine that ran on a totally different kind of energy, energy that had not been tapped before in the history of human civilization. These were fossil fuels. A fossil fuel is ultimately energy stored as chemical compounds that will readily ignite with oxygen to burn and produce heat. That stored energy comes from tropical forests that existed 250 to 300 million years ago—long before the first human beings appeared, and long before the continents drifted into their approximate present place. These forests became covered over when the continental plates smashed together and some of them got buried deep underground with the weight of huge mountains above them. Because they were originally tropical forests, they were rich in carbon compounds as all organic matter is. Carbon combines readily with oxygen to make carbon dioxide and releases a considerable amount of heat as the compound is formed.

Fossil fuels take several different forms. The early steam engines ran on coal. Coal deposits are found all over the world, some of them quite near the surface, making this a relatively easy fuel to obtain. For all sorts of reasons, the Industrial Revolution began in Britain, but one very convenient factor in the early days of industrialization was that the British Isles are particularly rich in coal. The large stationary steam engines, the railroad locomotives, and the steamships all ran on coal, and quite successfully.

A coal surface or strip mine.

Petroleum

Though steam engines became better designed and more efficient, and ultimately used a different source of fuel, they have been replaced as the major power producer by other machines that run on different fuels. Most mobile working engines are now internal combustion engines that burn a highly volatile fuel made from a petroleum distillate. Petroleum is also the source of kerosene, which was the main product of crude oil until the virtues of gasoline were discovered, but now has a much more limited market. Where there are petroleum deposits there is also natural gas, a major fuel used for heating and cooking.

Electricity

Electricity is not so much a source of energy as it is a conveyor of energy. We speak of a machine or an appliance as running on electricity, and so it does, but the electricity has to be generated somewhere, somehow, and then transmitted to the device that runs on it. Because electricity is so versatile, we can use it to run almost anything. But because there is some energy lost to usefulness whenever it is converted from one form to another, electricity is not necessarily the most efficient form of energy. One can heat a room with an electric space heater and cook food with an electric range, but to make the electricity, some other form of energy had to be used. That other form of energy might itself have been used to make heat, so why not use it directly. Hence, many homes are heated with natural gas or even a petroleum product, heating oil. The inconvenience of pumping the gas or delivering the oil may be less than the extra cost of making electricity from it and then using the electricity to make heat again.

A modern kitchen, such as this one, is filled with electric machines

Of course, many appliances and devices that are essential to our lives operate only with electric motors, so the electrical form of energy is essential. Still, it has to be made. We make electricity using every one of the sources of energy discussed so far. To manufacture electricity, it is only necessary to move a magnet in some regular fashion. The general procedure is to spin an electromagnet in the close vicinity of sets of wires and thereby induce an electric current. The energy that becomes electricity therefore had its source in whatever spun the magnet. Thus, any source of motion will do, even medieval waterwheels and windmills. With improved and modernized designs, these are still used.

Wind Power

In places with strong prevailing winds, windmills can still be useful power sources. They are sometimes used as water pumps, as they have been for centuries, but increasingly they are used to turn generators to make electricity. Only a small amount of the world's electric energy is produced this way, about one percent of the total, but that is growing rapidly. In 1980, only ten megawatts of electricity was generated by wind power; by 2000, the figure was over 18 000. In some countries, wind energy is a significant percentage of the total energy sources. The amount that can be produced will naturally depend on the strength of the prevailing winds, but even places with relatively mild breezes have been increasing their wind energy installations at a rapid pace. The great advantage of wind energy is, of course, that it is essentially completely renewable. The amount by which the windmills of the world slow down the natural airflows is so tiny as to be insignificant. Windmills can also be used in the most basic kind of installation in Third World countries as a way to provide a small amount of electrical power for a local use.

Solar Power

Since all our energy ultimately comes from the Sun, it makes sense to try to capture it first-hand and turn it into useful energy immediately, rather than wait until it has gone through many transformations. Solar photovoltaic cells is a relatively new technology, and one that is constantly being made more efficient. Light-sensitive cells are placed where the Sun shines on them for a considerable part of the day—on rooftops usually—and the energy from the Sun's light is used directly to make an electric current flow. This is another totally renewable source of energy that will become increasingly attractive as other non-renewable sources of energy become scarcer. Like wind power, the amount of solar energy being generated each year is rising rapidly—from seven megawatts in 1980 to 288 in 2000—and the reason is similar: government policies that encourage it.

Water Power

Generating electricity from water is a much more important source of electricity than either wind or solar power, and it is one of the oldest methods of producing electricity for general consumption. Any place with fast moving running water can generate huge amounts of electricity. For this we have a special name, *hydroelectricity*. In some places, the generation of electricity by falling water was so well established in the early days of electric utilities that all electrical power came to be known as "hydro," no matter how it was generated.

The principle of water generation is to force falling water through turbines, which will then rotate them quickly. The rotating motion of the turbines will spin electromagnets and induce electrical currents. Many of the great waterfalls of the world, for example Niagara Falls, have been harnessed to the production of electrical power, and where the water did not fall rapidly and dramatically enough, it would be made to do so by damming a river or a lake so that the water builds up at a high level and then is let out by running through turbines. Here, the capturing of part of the natural waterfall in turbines is relatively unobtrusive, but creating artificial waterfalls with dams can be very disruptive to the natural ecology of a region.

Coal and Oil

The major source of electrical power is the same as what drove the steam engines: coal. And actually, coal is still driving a steam engine. A coal-driven electric generator is really a steam engine harnessed to a spinning magnet. Coal is burnt to provide heat to boil water to turn to steam, just as in the older steam engines. The only new wrinkle is that the steam is now forced through turbines that spin the electromagnets rather than being used to push a piston back and forth. Coal was practical for that purpose and still is practical. It is also still readily available in huge deposits. There are two main objections to the continued wide use of coal for power generation: (1) burning coal produces a tremendous amount of pollution, and (2) it is a fossil fuel and therefore is ultimately in limited supply. Estimates vary on how much coal there is remaining on Earth, but natural processes are certainly not replenishing the supply.

In a more limited way, heating oil is also used occasionally for electricity generation where it is more readily available. It has most of the same drawbacks as coal. A better choice is natural gas, and it is used in places where it is readily available.

Nuclear Power

After the horror of the dropping of the atom bomb on Japan in 1945 had passed, thoughts turned to what constructive uses the incredible power unleashed in the atom bomb could be put. In the 1950s, atomic energy was seen to be the great hope for solving the world's energy problems. The power provided by controlled nuclear reactions could produce unlimited amounts of power in the form of electricity, and it would be so inexpensive that it would be "too cheap to meter." No longer would the public and its elected representatives have to worry about using up all of the world's fossil fuels; they would have a new source of power from the atom itself.

Nuclear power stations began to be built. The principle of nuclear powered electricity generation is much the same as the coal-fired plants after a certain point. The nuclear fuel is used to boil water and turn it to steam to drive a turbine, etc. That part is no different. The difference in the process is that the energy comes not from breaking chemical bonds in hydrocarbons and producing a new compound plus heat, but instead comes

The core of a CANDU nuclear reactor.

from breaking apart the nucleus of some of the heaviest, and therefore least stable, atoms, such as uranium. When the nucleus of an atom splits, it releases a number of neutrons from the nucleus, which then fly out in all directions, some of them striking the nuclei of other atoms and splitting them apart. This produces a chain reaction that can build very quickly and cause a tremendous explosion. But it can also be controlled so that the reaction takes place at a specified rate and has the effect of producing a very intense heat while not melting everything around it.

This is the principle of the nuclear reactor. Using specially prepared fuel rods containing a mixture of uranium and other materials to slow down any reactions, the rods are placed in an environment where they can heat a supply of water that surrounds them and turn that to steam. That steam is used to heat another adjacent supply of water, turning it to steam, which then is forced through the electricity-generating turbines. A great many safeguards are required to make the process work without undue danger to its employees or to the community around it. Partly because of the elaborate safeguards required, nuclear energy did not turn out to be remarkably cheaper than other forms of energy, but it was an alternative to fossil fuels.

Nuclear energy has proved to have a number of serious drawbacks: (1) it is very difficult to make a nuclear reactor that has fail-safe provisions for all kinds of malfunctions. This fact has been indelibly impressed on the public consciousness from a few very serious accidents at nuclear power plants. Because of those accidents and a few other minor incidents, public opinion turned against nuclear power and almost no new power stations have been built since then. (2) The other problem is a much longer-term one. Even if the reactors work perfectly as planned, there is still the problem of what to do with the spent fuel rods, which are highly radioactive and will remain so for a very long time.

Human Ingenuity

Meanwhile, world energy consumption continues to rise at an astounding rate. The developed countries continue to find new ways to use energy to improve their lives, and the developing nations in the Third World are scrambling to adopt a lifestyle more like that of the First World with all that that means for energy usage.

As a species, *homo sapiens sapiens* has certainly been very clever. We have not only learned how to transform the world to suit ourselves, extend our lifespan, fend off diseases, and make machines do the work for us, we have also found out how to get the power to do all of this out of grimy rocks and gooey gunk that exists in huge amounts under the surface of the ground. We can harness the winds and the flow of water to do work for us, and we can make dangerous heavy metals disintegrate and give us vast power, if only we can control it.

This ingenuity has given us the good life, much of which we now take for granted, even though it has only existed for a very short time. The pressing issue for humanity now is whether we should go on looking for new and better ways to make nature do our bidding, or whether we should turn our attention to assuring that it is not all taken away from us, because we have let it run amok.

A crowded marketplace in Yemen.

PART SIX

Population

One thing is clear. The world would not be facing most of its present environmental problems if there were not so many of us on the planet. It would not matter how abusive we were to our environment if we were few in number. Nature would restore itself and our assaults would hardly be noticed.

However, there are now over six billion people on the Earth, all needing to be fed from an agricultural system that continues to tax the ability of the soil to produce. Moreover, those of us in the industrialized nations consume vast amounts of irreplaceable natural resources. We reached these huge numbers by defeating our natural enemies in nature: famines, diseases, exposure to the elements. As we became masters of our own fate, we broke free of the restraints that control the populations of the rest of the living world. Along the way, we have also interfered with the natural controls on some of the other species as well, driving some to extinction and putting others in environments where they run riot.

We have attempted to understand what is happening to us and to try to head off what may be some very serious consequences in the not too distant future. We have had mixed success both with understanding our situation and with dealing with it. And we can't agree on whether we even have a problem with world population. The literature on population issues ranges in outlook from "the sky is falling" to "the more the merrier." These are controversial topics about which people have very strong opinions. For example, here are two opposing views:

Paul and Anne Ehrlich are among the most vocal and ardent advocates of massive world-wide birth control programs to halt the increase in world population before catastrophe strikes. Chapter One of their book, The Population Explosion, has the title "Why Isn't Everyone as Scared as We Are?" That chapter begins as follows:

> In the early 1930s. when we were born, the world population was just 2 billion; now it is more than two and a half times as large and still growing rapidly. ... Such a huge population expansion within two or three generations can by itself account for a great many changes in the social and economic institutions of a society. It is also very frightening to those of us who spend our lives trying to keep track of the implications of the population explosion. ... One of the toughest things for a population biologist to reconcile is the contrast between his or her recognition that civilization is in imminent serious jeopardy and the modest level of concern that population issues generate among the public and even among elected officials.

Contrast that with this quote from Bjørn Lomborg's The Skeptical Environmentalist. His first chapter is entitled "Things are getting better," in which he states:

> We are not running out of energy or natural resources. There will be more and more food per head of the world's population. Fewer and fewer people are starving. In 1900 we lived for an average of 30 years; today we live for 67. According to the UN we have reduced poverty more in the last 50 years than we did in the preceding 500, and it has been reduced in practically every country.... Mankind's lot has actually improved in terms of practically every measurable indicator.

Both books are chock full of facts and figures supporting their conclusions, which are often diametrically opposed to each other. The one thing they have in common is their insistence that these issues are of tremendous importance to us all and we need to know much more about them.

For Further Reading

Attrill, Rod and Moira. "Extinct is Forever." www.attrill.freeserve.co.uk/extinct.htm.

Boulton, Michael. *Extinction: Evolution and the End of Man.* New York: Columbia University Press, 2002.

Courtillot, Vincent. *Evolutionary Catastrophes: The Science of Mass Extinction.* Cambridge: Cambridge University Press, 1999.

Diamond, Jared. *Guns, Germs, and Steel: The Fate of Human Societies.* New York & London: W. W. Norton & Co., 1999.

Ehrlich, Paul R.. *The Population Bomb.* New York: Ballantine, 1968.

Ehrlich, Paul R.., and Anne H. Ehrlich. *The Causes and Consequences of the Disappearance of Species.* New York: Random House, 1981.

_____. *The Population Explosion.* London: Hutchinson, 1990

Ehrlich, Paul R.., Anne H. Ehrlich, and Gretchen C. Daily. *The Stork and the Plow: The Equity Answer to the Human Dilemma.* New York: Putnam, 1995.

Gordon, Anita and David Suzuki. *It's a Matter of Survival.* Toronto: Stoddart, 1990.

Lomborg, Bjørn. *The Skeptical Environmentalist: Measuring the Real State of the World.* Cambridge: Cambridge University Press, 2001.

Malthus, Thomas Robert. *An Essay on the Principle of Population, As it Affects the Future Improvement of Society.* London, 1798.

Meadows, Donella H. et al. *The Limits to Growth: A Report for the Club of Rome's Project on the Predicament of Mankind.* New York: New American Library, 1974.

Mesarovic, Mihajlo, and Eduard Pestel. *Mankind at the Turning Point: The Second Report to the Club of Rome.* New York: E. P. Dutton, 1974.

Oldstone, Michael B. A. *Viruses, Plagues, and History.* New York: Oxford University Press, 1998.

Ponting, Clive. A *Green History of the World: The Environment and the Collapse of Great Civilizations.* New York: Penguin, 1993.

Schumacher, E. F. *Small is Beautiful: A Study of Economics as if People Mattered.* London: Blond & Briggs, 1973.

Tuchman, Barbara. *A Distant Mirror: The Calamitous 14th Century.* New York: Alfred Knopf, 1978.

A highway scene in Australia in sheep country. There were no sheep at all in Australia before the end of the 18th century. Within 100 years, there were 100 million.

Chapter 24

Population Growth

If a balance of nature keeps the population of a species roughly within a certain range in a given area, it is because no radical changes occur in the ecological conditions that affect that species, such as temperatures, droughts, or floods, and no major changes take place in the food chain immediately above or below the species. In, say, a climax forest, which remains stable for hundreds of years, the food chain and the predator-prey relations settle into a routine interaction. However, if a flood or drought or severe winter kills off some essential part of the food chain, predators starve for lack of prey or prey multiply uncontrollably for lack of predators. These disturbances do happen all the time. Recall the elephant population in Tsavo Park or the moose on Isle Royale (Chapters 3 and 4).

Ideally, the predator-prey interactions keep both species within an acceptable range, as was the case with the wolves and the moose on Isle Royale. This was modeled in the Lotka-Volterra equations. But, recall from the discussion in Chapter 4 that it is dangerous to extrapolate from those situations where this interaction works neatly to assert that it is a general principle of nature. Just because stability exists in certain ecological systems in nature, there is no assurance that nature overall is stable, nor that it will protect the well-being, or even the existence, of any species. As the experiments of G. F. Gause showed, even slightly too many predators for the available prey in an environment can lead to the mass death of both, when the predators eat all of the prey and then starve.

What happens in an environment when a species has an unlimited amount of prey to feed on (which may be plants or animals) and no predators to keep them in check? On Isle Royale, we saw that the moose population skyrocketed until the introduction of timber wolves. The northern elephant seal population in the Channel Islands off the coasts of southern

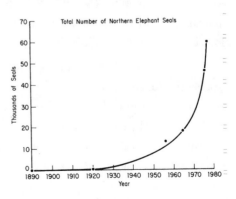

California and Mexico provides an even more dramatic illustration. These seals were hunted nearly to extinction in the 19th century. In 1890, only 12 remained. Then, left alone, they rebounded at a rate of about 9 percent per year. By the mid-1970s, the Channel Island area contained more than 60 000 seals. This is a phenomenal rate of growth that certainly cannot be sustained. Were that same rate to continue another 100 years, there would be 500 million seals by 2075 and over 4 billion by the turn of the century.

This projection, of course, assumes unlimited food and no danger from predators. Yet, it is a valuable exercise to bring home the point that populations do have a tendency to increase their numbers and are only kept in check by their interactions up and down the food chain and by the climate.

Exponential Functions

An exponential function is a mathematical term referring to a relation between two variables where the increase in one variable in any given period is a constant percentage of the amount of that variable in the preceding period. The most familiar example is compound interest. If a sum is invested at a compound interest rate of, say, 5 percent, then in each compounding period the increase added to the balance will be 5 percent of what is *then* the balance. Hence, the dollar amount of interest for any period will continually rise over time. What is surprising about compounding is how fast it builds up if it is left alone, a point that investment managers are always trying to impress on their clients.

One feature of exponential functions that helps a great deal in visualizing their effect is that all exponential functions will double at a characteristic rate. In the case of a 5 percent annual interest rate, the principal will double in about 15 years. Then it will double again in another 15 years, and so on. The elephant seal growth rate pretty closely approximated an exponential function at the rate of 9 percent per year. This would double every 8 years, which it did.

Generally, animal and plant populations do not really grow in the manner of a pure exponential function; too many other factors are at play—predator-prey relations in particular. But it provides a useful first approximation and reminds us that without the checks provided by nature, a population quite naturally does grow exponentially. Remove the danger either of predators or of starvation, and the total population in the next generation is very likely going to be directly related to how many potential parents there are in the present generation. This is a very important concept to understand intuitively, because so much of nature is the result of interactions of different species pushing to grow at exponential rates; without an intuitive understanding, it is very difficult to see approaching problems.

Some easily grasped illustrations of exponential growth are frequently used to get the main point across. The first is a very old fable that gets told in one of several versions. Here's one of the versions:

> At some time in the distant past, the Shah of Persia desired an ornate chessboard, so he commissioned a craftsman to make one for him. When the craftsman produced the board, the Shah was so thrilled with it that he told the workman that he would give him anything he wished for the board. The craftsman replied that his wants were simple. He could be paid in grain for each square on the board, one day at a time. The first day, he should be paid one grain of rice (or wheat) for the first square on the board. The second day, he should be paid two grains. The third day, four grains; the fourth day, eight grains and so on. Each day his payment would be twice the number of grains of the day before until he had been paid for all 64 squares of the chessboard. The Shah readily agreed, thinking that this was only a trivial amount. However, he had not reckoned on the compounding effect. To complete the agreed upon payment would require $2^{64}-1$ grains of wheat, or about 18 000 000 000 000 000 000 grains, a figure vastly more than the entire harvest of rice or wheat in the entire world.

The chessboard example illustrates how enormous and unwieldy a quantity can become, starting with a very small amount. Another example, often given, underscores how surprisingly fast a major change can take place from what appear to be small steps. In this version of the story, on a country estate, in a clear pond one day, a lily pad begins to grow. The owners call in an expert who tells them that lily pads double their numbers every day, and the pond will be completely covered over in thirty days. The owners decide that they have time to take action and elect to put off doing anything until the pond is half full of weeds. But when would that be? The answer is, on the 29th day. On the 28th day, the pond will be only one-fourth covered and on the 27th day—90% of the allotted time—the pond would be only one-eighth covered. Seven/eights of the growth happens in those last three days. This example is used to underscore how exponential growth patterns contain big surprises that leave no time in which to react.

Human Beings and the Balance of Nature

At the beginning of this chapter, two conditions were named as necessary for the balance of nature to be maintained: stability in the ecological conditions and no major changes in the food chain. If either of these factors are disturbed, the balance can be lost and a species can either become endangered or begin to grow out of control. Another consideration is particularly relevant when the species in question is *homo sapiens*. The species itself may adapt to new circumstances and gain new abilities, or be able to alter the environment to its advantage. Human beings have an amazing capacity to learn new skills, make new tools, and change their circumstances for their benefit. Because of these extraordinary abilities, people have altered the face of the Earth more than any other species could possibly have done, constantly increasing the food supply available to them, while reducing the threats to their survival.

Human beings have evolved through their learned capabilities to defeat all sorts of dangers. The entire history of humanity has been one of overcoming obstacle after obstacle, fighting malnutrition and infectious disease, and moving out around the world to occupy every available niche. The result of these efforts has been to overcome many of the forces that would keep our population more or less in check. The natural consequence is that our numbers continually increase, by something approximating an exponential function.

Even early hunter-gatherer societies had steadily rising populations. So long as they managed to figure out how to find more food, they were able to support higher numbers. The more sophisticated we became, the more technological problems we solved, the fewer obstacles stood in the way of our population growth. In fact, the world human population has been growing *not* at an exponential rate, which would have a fixed doubling period, but at a rapidly increasing rate, i.e., faster than exponential. The advances in sanitation, medicine, and nutrition of the last two hundred years have made possible a significant lengthening of normal life expectancy and a great reduction in infant mortality.

Differences in Growth Patterns Around the World

The human enterprise has taken different forms in different places throughout history. This has resulted in different patterns of growth across the globe. Moreover, vagaries such as severe epidemics, famines, and wars have knocked the population back in different ways at different times. The overall trend has been up everywhere, but the differences are striking and have important implications for the future.

Europe

The pattern in Europe was a fairly slow, but steady growth, with some fluctuations for diseases and famines, to a total population of about 140 million by the mid-18th century. Then, with the Industrial Revolution, the population jumped 80 percent to 250 million people by 1845; then rose another 80 percent by 1914, when the First World War affected it.

Through the 20th century, European population growth slowed. The earlier period of rapid growth is considered to be the result of lower mortality levels— people living longer and surviving illnesses better. In particular, infant mortality rates have fallen considerably. When the growth rate changed and began to moderate in the 20th century, it was primarily due to a fall in the birth rate: people were simply having fewer children.

Asia and Africa

The pattern in Asia and Africa begins much in the same way as that of Europe: slow beginning, steady growth, then a few giant steps backward due to disease, famine, and wars. Then, again comes a rapid rise, continuing into the 19th century. There the patterns diverge. Europe's population growth slows dramatically, while that of both Asia and Africa begins to skyrocket. The decline in mortality rates is similar in Europe, Asia, and Africa, but the different direction in population growth appears to be due to differences in the birth rate. In both Asia and Africa, the birth rate remained as it had been rather than falling, and, since, in addition, infant mortality declined with medical advances, the population soared.

There were exceptions: Japan and other highly industrialized countries in Asia followed the European model with a falling birth rate. The poorer countries, however, persisted in having many children.

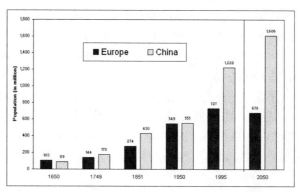

The Americas and Oceania

The population patterns in the Americas and in the ocean islands are much more complex. For much of the comparable period, they remained hunter-gatherer societies, with relatively low populations. Then came the European explorers, followed by colonization. Immigration came next, both of Europeans moving to the colonies and of slaves imported to work the plantations.

In North America, a period of tremendous growth occurred due to colonization from Europe, after which the North American (that is, Canada and the United States, but not Mexico) pattern reverted to the European one. South America's is much more like the rest of the Third World: a decline in mortality but no change in the birth rate, hence soaring population.

In the Pacific Ocean, Australia and New Zealand, both colonized by the British, followed the same contours of population growth as North America, but somewhat later. The remainder of the ocean islands lie somewhere between the Third World model of soaring populations and the hunter-gatherer model of a population contained by the natural environment.

All Populations Tend to Expand

It is simply a feature of biology that all living things leave more progeny than there are of themselves. Whether plants producing seeds, single-celled animals that reproduce by dividing in two, or larger animals that lay eggs or have live births, the number of offspring is greater than the number of parents. Were it not so, the species would die out, since disease and predators continually reduce their numbers.

In stable environments, where the population of any given species never breaks out of a certain range, the environment, which includes the predators, keeps the numbers from increasing exponentially. Recall the concept of the carrying capacity of a species (Chapter 4). If the environment is taken as unchanging, there is an upper limit to the population of any species in that environment. But the population will grow to that limit if not prevented.

Human beings have dramatically changed the environments in which they live, something other life forms cannot do. Moreover, the changes are ones that have added to the food supply and removed the dangers of predators and many diseases. If the concept of a carrying capacity for the human species is valid, that carrying capacity is surely much higher than it ever has been before. But the unanswered question is, what is that theoretical upper limit for humanity and what would life be like if we were near it?

What Happens to a Population without Predators

We have already seen the tendency to exponential growth exhibited by the elephant seals in the Channel Islands and the moose on Isle Royale, when a normal complement of predators is not available. These both provide good case studies because, being on islands, they can be isolated from other factors and the causes pinpointed. For many of the cases of populations out of control on larger landmasses, it is not easy to be sure exactly what the causes were, but more importantly, it becomes very difficult to rein in the runaway growth.

The settlement of the world brought with it the introduction of many species to parts of the world where they were not native and where their natural predators and other conditions that kept the population in check were missing. In most cases, this has led to serious disruption of the invaded land.

When Europeans, or for that matter, settlers from elsewhere, went to a new land, they often wished to recreate their home environment and would bring with them domesticated animals from home, or perhaps plants—either for food or for decoration—and, though it was inadvertent, would bring with those animals and plants (and with themselves) some unwanted pests clinging to or infecting the plants and animals or riding along onboard the ships. When the new land being colonized was in a new continent, the chances were that the ecological system was totally different from what it was at home. When the continents drifted apart millions of years ago, the flora and fauna on each separate tectonic plate began to evolve in isolation from those elsewhere. When a new species from a different continent was introduced into a system that had never contained anything like it, chances were that the species would either not survive at all or would balloon out of control for lack of predators.

The Americas were almost devoid of any animals that could be domesticated—one of the reasons that agriculture evolved so differently in those continents. When Europeans brought their standard draft animals into the Americas or into Australia and New Zealand, these populations quickly multiplied beyond all imagination. They would often be the offspring of a very few animals that escaped into the wild and began to reproduce. Some of the more dramatic examples are the sheep in Australia and New Zealand, introduced in the 18th century, and now one of the largest animal populations in either country. Columbus brought horses to the Americas in 1493; some got loose and went wild, and soon existed in large herds across both continents. The horse changed the way of life of the American native peoples, who until then had no domesticated animal that they could use for transportation. Another odd example is the camel, introduced into Australia in the 19th century to be a pack animal in its arid deserts. There are now more camels in Australia than in the Arabian Peninsula.

The Rabbits in Australia

Sometimes these introductions led to ecological imbalances that were far from what had been hoped for. In 1859, an enterprising farmer in Victoria, Australia, imported a few rabbits to raise as game. Inevitably, some got away, and, as rabbits are well known to do, bred prodigiously. Australia, of course, lacked the natural predators that might have kept them in check. In addition to breeding rapidly, the rabbits also ate a lot, a habit that farmers viewed with considerable alarm. They also got in the way of sheep farming—interesting, since sheep were another importation that had also gotten out of control, but unlike the rabbits, was by then an essential part of the economy.

A truck loaded with dead rabbits.

By the mid-1880s, government campaigns were launched to eradicate the rabbits. Nine million rabbits were killed in Victoria and New South Wales, with no sign of slowing their spread. The next plan was to wall them off so they could not reach the entire country. Between 1902 and 1907, a fence 1600 kilometers long, 120 centimeters high, and another 60 centimeters into the ground was built from the north to the south of the country to exclude the rabbits. This, too, failed as the rabbits found a way through in the 1920s. By 1950, there were about 500 million rabbits in Australia.

It was time for another approach. Australian scientists located a virus called *myxomatosis* that was native to Brazil and that appeared to keep the rabbit population in check there. The Australian government, happy for a solution at last, imported quantities of the virus and infected members of the rabbit population so that they would spread it among themselves. The virus was an effective killer. Almost all, 99.8% of the rabbits exposed to the virus, died. However, as with all communicable diseases, some members of the population with a natural immunity always survive. Since rabbits breed so quickly, even the tiny 0.2% of the population that survived was enough to start the population growing rapidly again—this time a population with natural immunity to *myxomatosis*.

Australia the Overrun

The rabbits, and the sheep and camels previously mentioned, are only a few of the species from elsewhere that were introduced into Australia and then ran wild. There seemed to be no way to stop this so long as European emigrants wanted life there to be like life back home. Anita Gordon and David Suzuki summarize the state of imported species in Australia and express their frustration as follows:

> As bad as they were, rabbits weren't the end. Practically every animal that was introduced to Australia over the past 200 years ran wild—pigs, donkeys, camels, to name a few. And plants such as the prickly pear, brought to create English gardens in the 1800s, overran the country in the 1900s. Through it all, Australians never learned the lessons of the ecosystem. In the 1930s, worried about insects devastating the sugar-cane crop, someone came up with the bright idea of importing the South American cane toad. No ordinary toad, this half-kilo dinner-plate-size solution became a heavyweight problem in itself. The sugar-cane beetles flew. The toads stayed on the ground. The two did not meet and both flourished. Today the cane toad has occupied 500 000 square kilometers of the state of Queensland, and nothing can stop it.

Cartoon courtesy Mount Barker Courier

> Time and again over those fateful 200 years, Australians have
> introduced a biological disaster. Today, Australia is a land
> transformed, or as the less charitable see it, grotesquely disfigured.
> The land has been overgrazed by 160 million sheep, 14 percent of
> all the sheep in the world. The precious topsoil is eroding 50 times
> faster today than it did before 1788. And Australians find
> themselves frantically trying to regreen a scorched earth.[1]

The Australian situation appears extreme, because its environment was so different from that of Europe when the settlers arrived, and everything they introduced from back home had no natural niche in any existing ecosystem there. Also, Australia is an island—a very large one, to be sure, but nevertheless cut off from the rest of the world, and life has evolved differently there.

No need to pick on Australia; it just offers stark examples. The story really is the same everywhere. Life is far more complex than we realize. When we make changes in ecosystems to achieve our purpose, we may get results that we had not anticipated. This is just part of the human enterprise, the same efforts that have brought us civilization itself.

We battle with the environment and find alternatives to our liking. These may bring us consequences we had not intended and do not want but also bring us what we do want. We now number so many ourselves that our very existence is threatened; meanwhile we have altered the ecology of the Earth and the balance of nature so much that it no longer provides the same support for our lives that it used to.

---

1.   Anita Gordon and David Suzuki, *It's a Matter of Survival,* (Toronto: Stoddart, 1990), p. 46.

"Triumph of Death" by Peter Bruegel the Elder, 1562.

Chapter 25

Famines, Diseases, and Death

The weather affects all elements of the food chain, from the lowest life form all the way to human beings. The size of the population, the health and longevity of its individuals, the availability of food, and the danger from predators are all very much influenced by climatic conditions. The Earth has gone through many cycles of colder and warmer periods that last sometimes hundreds, sometimes thousands, of years. These have produced major changes to the environments in which human beings have found themselves. How people have responded to these changes explains much of human history.

Average Temperature of the Earth

Scientists use various techniques to get fairly accurate readings of the prevailing temperatures in ages long past. For the oldest periods, obtaining this information involves the examination of deep ice cores extracted from the polar ice caps, some of them more than two kilometers long, representing 150 000 years of accumulations. Another technique is to drill deep into the ocean floor for sediment that may be tens of millions of years old. Other methods study these samples using isotope analysis, particularly the isotope carbon-14. These tools are used for the oldest periods. Other ways to date deposits include examining such phenomena as tree rings, growth differences in coral reefs, sedimentary layers in lakes, and the permafrost near the poles. Isotope analysis can also determine the temperatures existing at the time the layers were laid down. Volcanoes are also useful for fixing a record of conditions at the time of eruption.

What all this research has shown is that for almost all of the time that humans have existed, even going back as far as *homo erectus,* the average temperature of the Earth has been colder than it is now. Within that period, there have been warmer spells and colder spells, often called ice ages, and much of early human migration to different parts of the globe has taken place in response to those temperature changes. In the last 20 000 years, which includes the last part of the hunting and gathering era and the beginning of agriculture, a fairly consistent upward trend in temperatures has occurred. This would have been a great help to the establishment of farming and the settlement of the more remote parts of the Earth.

Much closer to our own era, a warming period occurred from about 800 to 1200, during which many new communities were settled in the north. For example, Iceland was colonized in 874 and Greenland in 986. The latter is an example of a settlement that was at the limit of what humans could inhabit successfully. When the warm period ended around 1200, the settlement in Greenland declined and then nearly disappeared.

From 1430 to 1850 was a much colder period, sometimes called the "Little Ice Age." Average temperatures were one to two degrees Celsius colder than at present. Although this does not sound like much, it was enough to make a significant difference in crops, many of which simply failed. Many people starved during this time. Remember that the tendency of the population was always to increase to the point where it was consuming all of the available food. Hence, any setback in harvests would immediately mean that there was not enough for all to eat.

The Dependence on Crops

Only relatively recently have major segments of society, in particular, the industrialized nations, eaten meat other than on rare occasions. In general, in an agricultural community, all the available land was needed to grow crops for humans to eat. Pastureland was at a premium. In any case, animals were primarily kept for their milk, or, in the case of sheep, for their wool, and most important of all, for their manure. Slaughtering animals was done reluctantly. And, compared to modern farm animals, those maintained in earlier times were far less robust. A medieval European cow produced about one-sixth the amount of milk and one-fourth the meat of modern cattle. Selective breeding has produced much larger and more robust animals than those that bred naturally.

Consequently, all the large civilizations relied primarily on plant food. In China, 98 percent of the calories in the diet came from vegetables, mostly rice and some millet. In Europe, the usual diet of the common person was some kind of gruel made from grain and/or bread. Only the upper classes had any regular access to meat or fish.

Famines

With populations always rising to the level of the food supply, any famines that struck were disastrous. All it took was a patch of bad weather, such as droughts, floods, or extreme temperatures, to cause crops to fail with starvation following. Throughout human history, there have been severe food failures, one of the major controls on the size of the population.

Famines have struck all over the world. Most of those in less advanced cultures were unrecorded and can only be inferred from indirect evidence. Of those for which records are available, some are particularly memorable for what they have to teach us about our vulnerability to nature and the likelihood that we will mismanage our way out of a crisis. Famines bring out the worst in human nature.

Here are two particularly gruesome famines from the history of Europe:

The Famine of 1315-1317

With the warm period that extended from 800 to 1200, the crops in Europe flourished and with them, so did the population. After 1200, the weather began to cool, the crops were poorer, and the population was near the limit of what could be supported. By the beginning of the 14th century, what was later to become the Little Ice Age was beginning. Barbara Tuchman's excellent book on this period describes it as follows:

> A physical chill settled on the 14th century at its very start, initiating the miseries to come. The Baltic Sea froze over twice, in 1303 and 1306-07; years followed of unseasonable cold, storms and rains, and a rise in the level of the Caspian Sea....

> This meant disaster, for population increase in the last century had already reached a delicate balance with agricultural techniques. Given the tools and methods of the time, the clearing of productive land had already been pushed to its limits. Without adequate irrigation and fertilizers, crop yield could not be raised nor poor soils be made productive. Commerce was not equipped to transport grain in bulk from surplus-producing areas except by water. Inland towns and cities lived on local resources, and when these dwindled, the inhabitants starved.[1]

---

1.   Barbara W. Tuchman, *A Distant Mirror: The Calamitous 14th Century* (New York: Alfred A. Knopf, 1978), p. 24.

Then came disaster in 1315. The rains fell incessantly throughout spring, summer, and fall. In winter, the torrent continued as snow. The traditional spring sowing failed, because the fields had become waterlogged and the ploughs could not penetrate the heavy mud. For the draft animals, the hay was neither ripe nor dry when harvested and stored, hence it rotted quickly. What crops there were—about half of the normal harvest—were of very poor quality.

By the beginning of the next year, food was in short supply all over Europe. The seed that should have been saved for next year's planting was being eaten to fend off immediate starvation. Again, the winter, the spring, and the summer were unseasonably wet. The next harvest was also about one-half the normal size. The price of wheat rose to three times its normal level in most places, and where storage was a special problem, the price rose by a factor of eight.

Food was simply not available. In all famines, the poor suffer first, but in this case, no one could get adequate food. One of the richest men of the time, the King of Bohemia, had to sacrifice thousands of sheep, because he was unable to buy feed for them. Everywhere across Europe, domestic animals were killed in huge numbers.

In such extreme circumstances, people became less than civilized. On a small scale, any known cache of food was raided. In the countryside, many peasants with no other recourse swarmed in packs looking for any hidden supply of grain or an animal to slaughter. Weakened animals died in huge numbers: two-thirds of the oxen and about the same proportion of sheep in certain areas succumbed to starvation or disease. Animals that had died of disease were eaten, causing outbreaks of fatal infections among the human population. To quote Barbara Tuchman again, "Reports spread of people eating their own children, of the poor in Poland feeding on hanged bodies taken down from the gibbet."[1] And, many other gruesome accounts were recorded, including bodies being dug up out of their graves and eaten.

It was an extremely difficult time. People were at a loss to solve their problems in any organized, coherent way. Living as close as they did to their carrying capacity for the technology and the environment of the time, it did not take much to cause a major disaster and reduce people to a very primitive state.

This kind of response to disaster happened all across the world when human civilizations found themselves in desperate circumstances. For example, when the

---

1.   Ibid.

inhabitants of Easter Island destroyed their environment and could no longer carry on with life as they knew it, they resorted to theft, murder, and even cannibalism. The crisis in Europe differed only in that such good records of it are available. It seems that what we call civilization breaks down very easily in the face of starvation.

The Irish Potato Blight

Lest we think that such barbaric behaviour occurred only in the distant past or within backward cultures, let us consider a much more recent European famine, one that had a noticeable effect on North American immigration patterns and still angers the descendants of those directly affected.

This is the potato blight that struck Ireland in the mid-19th century. As with the earlier famine of the 14th century, what made this crop disease a disaster was that the population was too close to the carrying capacity of the land, given the crops being produced. Ireland offered a classic case of a population rising to meet its food supply, with the resulting increased numbers causing a food crisis. The same problem drove the hunters and gatherers to agriculture during the Agricultural Revolution, but this event in Ireland happened much more quickly.

In the year 1500, the population of Ireland was about 800 000. By 1846, it had reached 8½ million, a ten-fold increase in about 350 years. Moreover, unlike England where landholdings passed intact from father to oldest son, in Ireland, the practice was to divide the land equally among all the sons. After several generations of such subdivision, the average plot of land available to a family was about one-fifth of a hectare. However, these were the lucky ones; about 650 000 labourers with no land holdings at all lived in permanent poverty. Most of the population lived in squalid, one-room cabins.

The only way to feed such a vast population from the limited arable land available was to find a crop that was highly nutritious and would grow in great abundance in a small space. The crop chosen was one of those brought back to the Old World when it had been discovered in the New World: the potato. A plot of one-fifth of a hectare planted solely with potatoes could provide enough food for a moderate sized family. The diet would be tedious, but the potato is nutritious enough that a person can survive on a steady diet of it.

By the early 19th century, the potato was the sole food of half of the population in Ireland. But the potato had some serious drawbacks as a crop to be relied upon. It originated in the South American Andes, where it grew at high altitudes in relatively dry soils. It was not well suited to the wet climate of Ireland and northwest Europe, where it also had been introduced. The climate made it all the more vulnerable to disease, and the practice of planting an entire field with the same species jammed together made the spreading of plant diseases easy.

There had already been some very serious crop failures in the 18th century, causing the deaths of hundreds of thousands of people, but there seemed to be no alternative to continue to plant the same crop and hope for the best. There were simply too many mouths to feed from too little land to consider any other options.

The inevitable disaster came in June 1845. Some potatoes imported from America were infected with a blight, a fungal disease affecting plants. The blight can destroy individual plants quickly, but more importantly, it spreads very quickly to other plants, both those in the ground and those already picked and in storage, especially in wet, cool conditions, as was typical of Ireland. As well as in Ireland, the potato was the major crop of the poor across Europe. The blight spread there as well, and soon there were no potatoes to be had anywhere in Europe.

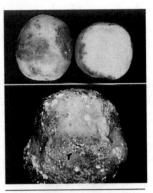

Potatoes in various stages of infection from the blight.

The Human Element

This was not 1315, but well into the Industrial Revolution. Transportation was available, and crops from elsewhere could have been imported to feed the starving, while seeking a more permanent solution. The problem that turned serious crop failure into an inhumane disaster was man-made.

In the 19th century, Ireland was under British rule so that all major policy decisions affecting the country originated in London. At the time, the British were convinced that the free market approach to commodities, as advocated by Adam Smith, was the only way to reach a viable solution to any problem of food supply. Therefore, they chose not to intervene in the crisis, except to the extent of protecting the property rights of those who did have something that the starving people might want. Curiously, while there were virtually no potatoes to be had anywhere in Europe, other sources of food existed, even in Ireland, that could have staved off the mass starvation that was soon to follow.

Because of the poor harvests across the British Isles, the British were allowing the import of grain from abroad, both into England and into Ireland. Ireland was even exporting some of its own grain. The grain that became available was wheat or corn, neither of which the peasants were familiar with. This grain was for sale on the open market. But the peasants had no money with which to buy it. The British government believed that it would have interfered with market forces to give them grain for nothing. Instead, government stock was sold only at open market prices, which were skyrocketing because of the shortages. Even if they did give the grain with no strings attached, the peasants did not have the utensils necessary for cooking wheat or corn and making it into an edible product.

It gets worse. One of the few ways that Irish peasants could raise some money to buy grain was to work in one of the government-sponsored public projects, such as road building. But under the circumstances, the British decided that these projects, which had been intended to provide temporary relief to the indigent, might turn into a permanent dependency on government welfare, so they were cancelled. Though there were some initiatives made to provide humanitarian relief, it was much too little and much too late.

When the blight finally ran its course and the worst was over, about one million Irish had died of starvation or disease. Another million had fled the country forever. By the end of the 19th century, a total of three million had emigrated, usually for North America. The remaining population in Ireland was about 4½ million people, just about half of what it had been before the blight struck.

What conclusions can be drawn from examining these two European famines? Both would not have occurred, or would not have been devastating, if the population was not already near the maximum of what the land could support. In the famine of the 14th century, a general disorganized panic led to some counterproductive actions and some barbaric behaviour as people became desperate. There was no effective government with sufficient power to intervene with a consistent policy that might have avoided some of the worst consequences. In the Irish potato blight, a strong government was in place that could, and did, impose its will to keep order and work toward a solution by following a consistent policy. Nevertheless, the policy was totally wrong-headed, and consequently even more people died than might have had there been chaos. There was food available, but it was withheld from those who needed it. It seems that in a crisis, people are capable of acting barbarously both individually and collectively through their government. This does not augur well for humanity if similar crises face us in the future.

Famines are regular events in the history of the world. They have affected the entire animal world, not just human beings, and sometimes they have been responsible for extinctions of whole species. Droughts and floods and other natural events have devastated the wild plants that many animals live on, with terrible consequences for those animals. We would view these as natural events, for which there is no particular cause other than the forces of nature. And if we are so inclined, we can call this nature's way of regulating the population, because a famine will certainly reduce the numbers of any species that was beginning to crowd its living space.

Famines affecting humans are different. To the extent that they are disasters, they are the ultimate result of some deliberate human action that put a strain on nature. Agriculture itself is an assault on nature, especially if the same crop is grown again and again in the same fields and if crops are planted right next to others of the same species, so that a disease that affects one plant can easily spread to others. They also are human-caused to the extent that we have forced nature to provide for our increasing numbers in ways that leave little room for the unpredictable.

Diseases

In the industrialized nations, famines are now rare. When crops fail due to unforeseen natural events, humanitarian aid can be flown in from elsewhere and a catastrophe averted. The Third World still has problems with famines, especially when population densities are very high or if the political climate makes effective delivery of aid problematic.

Disease is another matter. The health sciences have made enormous strides, especially in the last 150 years, to overcome some of the major debilitating diseases that have devastated human populations throughout history. But the battle is far from over. In fact the more we learn about disease, the greater seems the task of fighting it.

The Perils that Faced the Hunter-Gatherers

Looking back beyond the Agricultural Revolution to the hunter-gatherer era, the disease profile is quite different from the present day. Susceptibility to disease caused by malnutrition was rare, because the hunter-gatherer diet was more varied than that of agricultural communities, and until their population exceeded what their environment could support, their food consumption was high. Therefore, diseases resulting from deficiencies in the diet were rare, as is borne out by the fossil records (to the extent possible).

Present-day hunter-gatherers typically suffer from parasitical diseases, such as worms. These are most common in tropical climates where most of the remaining hunter-gatherer groups still live. But as humans moved out of Africa into the rest of the world, these problems likely faded as well.

Most likely, infant mortality and death in childbirth was high, though perhaps no worse than in later societies, even up to fairly recent times. General life expectancy was short, though some people did manage to live quite long lives. However, very few people would have attained the age of thirty.

Infection from Domestic Animals

Agriculture brought not just more food; it brought more exposure to disease. Once animals were domesticated, they lived in proximity to the people, often sharing the same living quarters. This radically increased the chances of contracting infections that would prove fatal. Animals, being another species, can easily be carriers of diseases to which they have a certain amount of immunity, but to which humans are totally at risk. Some diseases jumped unchanged from animal to human; others required mutations in the pathogens and then became true human diseases.

Many of what we consider specifically human infectious diseases are closely related to animal diseases, and may very well have originally developed in animal hosts before adapting to humans. To quote Clive Ponting:

> Smallpox…is very similar to cowpox and measles is related to rinderpest (another cattle disease) and canine distemper. Tuberculosis also originated in cattle as diphtheria. Influenza is common to humans and hogs and the common cold certainly came from the horse. Leprosy came from the water buffalo. After living for some ten thousand years in close proximity to animals, humans now share sixty-five diseases with dogs, fifty with cattle, forty-six with sheep and goats and forty-two with pigs.[1]

Just as agriculture arose at different times and spread at different rates in various parts of the world, so did these diseases. When a disease became endemic in a population, many in the population developed an immunity, or partial immunity, to it, so that it became less dangerous to the population as a whole, though still potentially fatal to many.

Societies that had no exposure at all to a disease also had no defences against it. An infectious disease that caused minor to moderate casualties in a society where it was

---

1.   Clive Ponting, *A Green History of the World: The Environment and the Collapse of Great Civilizations,* (New York: Penguin, 1993) pp. 225-226.

endemic could totally devastate one where it was unknown. The most notorious example of this is among the natives of the Americas. In the American continents, agriculture had developed without the domestication of animals, there being no suitable species available locally. That also meant that the native Americans had developed no immunity to diseases that such animals might have carried and transmitted. Smallpox and measles, in particular, were unknown in the New World until brought by the Europeans. These diseases raced through the native communities in both North and South America, leaving huge numbers dead.

Infection from Human Waste

As agriculture advanced and towns became organized, people began living permanently in one circumscribed area, not moving about as the nomadic hunter-gatherers had done. Thus arose a predicament common to all animal species: how to stay clear of one's own waste matter. The problem was not serious for the hunter-gatherers because their population density was lower, and they moved on soon enough. But for settled people, disposing of human waste was a major headache. Most early societies, and indeed many backward contemporary ones, did not manage to keep human excrement from infecting their drinking water. The early societies made no effort to do so because they had no understanding of the consequences. But even those who did intuitively understand that what they ingest should not be mixed with what they excrete did not take adequate steps to prevent problems. Nor did they know what steps would be adequate.

For most early societies, one and only one watercourse served as both a sewer and as drinking water. In this environment, such intestinal parasites as worms flourished and then were consumed. Other water borne diseases, such as cholera and dysentery, were endemic in these early societies—and still are a major problem in the Third World.

Infection from Other People

When people settled down to live in one place, they chose to live close to each other, further increasing the likelihood of the spread of infectious disease. Many infectious diseases cannot survive unless a minimum number of human hosts are available. For example, measles has died out on islands with a population of less than half a million. This is a number that would have been exceeded in Mesopotamia, not in one city perhaps, but collectively in several that had frequent contact with each other.

Infection from Irrigation

Agriculture soon moved from sowing seeds and hoping for the best to intensive methods involving artificial irrigation. Irrigation ditches tend to have slow moving water that made excellent breeding grounds for parasites. *Schistosomiasis* is caused by a blood fluke that has a life cycle involving both human hosts and water snails, which lived in the irrigation ditches. People who worked the ditches, standing in them much of the time, were prime targets for the fluke. The disease got a firm footing soon after the establishment of intensive farming in Egypt and Mesopotamia. Today over 100 million people suffer from schistosomiasis, mostly in Africa.

Infection from Land Clearance

The process of clearing land for future planting upsets the natural ecology of an area so that an unwanted pest that was not there before can get a footing. In particular, the swidden "slash and burn" system created pools of stagnant water that then became breeding grounds for mosquitoes. Mosquitoes can transmit many debilitating or even fatal diseases. In tropical climates, the worst and most widespread disease spread by mosquitoes is malaria. In many cases, the spread of malaria around the world can be tied to the introduction of farming or irrigation into an area.

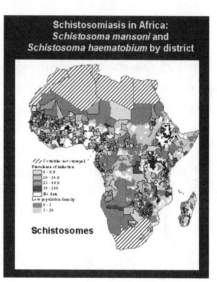

Schistosomiasis in Africa: *Schistosoma mansoni* and *Schistosoma haematobium* by district

Plague

The term "plague" is now generally reserved for bubonic plague, but it has been widely used through history to mean any sort of epidemic. Many of the "plagues" reported in ancient cultures could have been one of any number of virulent infectious diseases, such as smallpox, yellow fever, cholera, or influenza. These are all devastating to a population, especially when the causes are not understood and no sensible way can be devised to contain the disease. Some of these diseases have been defeated, at least in the industrialized nations. Medicine has identified the cause of the disease and been able to prevent its spread and treat infected individually successfully.

Those of us who live in a modern society with a first-class health care system have a very difficult time understanding how vulnerable human populations have always been to runaway infectious diseases that decimate a population before anyone has time to react. These diseases were just part of the precarious risks of life before science began to understand microbes and the transmission of disease. The developments in the last 150 years in medicine have transformed life in the developed countries. Unfortunately, many of these same diseases are still out of control in parts of the world with inadequate health care.

The Black Death

Any of a number of serious infectious diseases could be used to illustrate the profound effect that epidemics have had on individual societies and indeed on the course of history. One stands out as particularly significant in its cruel virulence, its decimation of the population, and the surprising effect on society in its aftermath. That is the epidemic of bubonic plague that struck Europe in the 14th century, known among the people as the *Black Death*.

 It started in 1347 in the port cities around the Mediterranean where trading ships put in from various Asian locations. These ships came from areas in which the bubonic plague was endemic and had been so for some time. On board these ships, as on all ships of that time, were rats that had gone along for the ride and for access to the food stored on board. These rats, naturally, were infested with fleas. The rats carried the bubonic plague. The fleas bit the rats, which were soon dying. Then the fleas jumped to people: first, of course, the sailors on board the ships, many of whom arrived in port deathly ill if not already dead. Inevitably, the rats and fleas got into the port cities, and the disease spread like wildfire. In just 18 months, fully one-third of the population of Europe is estimated to have succumbed to the plague. It was called the *Black Death*, because the sores and lesions produced turned black, as well as everything produced out of the bodies of the ill.

In her book on the 14th century, historian Barbara Tuchman describes vividly what it must have been like for those who experienced it firsthand:

> In October 1347, two months after the fall of Calais, Genoese trading ships put into the harbor of Messina in Sicily with dead and dying at the oars. The ships had come from the Black Sea port of

Caffa (now Feodosia) in the Crimea, where the Genoese maintained a trading post. The diseased sailors showed strange black swellings about the size of an egg or an apple in the armpits and groin. The swellings oozed blood and pus and were followed by spreading boils and black blotches on the skin from internal bleeding. The sick suffered severe pain and died quickly within five days of the first symptoms. As the disease spread, other symptoms of continuous fever and spitting of blood appeared instead of the swellings of buboes. These victims coughed and sweated heavily and died even more quickly, within three days or less, sometimes in 24 hours. In both types everything that issued from the body—breath, sweat, blood from the buboes and lungs, bloody urine, and blood-blackened excrement—smelled foul. Depression and despair accompanied the physical symptoms, and before the end "death is seen seated on the face."

The disease was bubonic plague, present in two forms: one that infected the bloodstream, causing the buboes and internal bleeding, and was spread by contact; and a second, more virulent pneumonic type that infected the lungs and was spread by respiratory infection. The presence of both at once caused the high mortality and speed of contagion. So lethal was the disease that cases were known of persons going to bed well and dying before they woke, of doctors catching the illness at a bedside and dying before the patient.... The malignity of the pestilence appeared more terrible because its victims knew no prevention and no remedy.[1]

In Europe, no one had any natural immunity to the disease, and because of the crowding in the port cities, the infection spread quickly there. The ports were the central nodes of the economy and were where a high proportion of the wealthy lived. As mentioned in Chapter 2, Venice lost 60 percent of its population to the Black Death. The original outbreak settled down eventually, but another major outbreak of bubonic plague occurred every 11 to 15 years somewhere in Europe for the next three hundred years.

The antibiotic cure for plague was developed only in the 20th century, but long before then people realized that the disease spread more quickly where people were in close proximity. Thereafter, in any outbreak, major institutions closed and people dispersed into the countryside, which proved to be an effective containment policy. In the

---

1.   Tuchman, *Op. cit.,* pp. 92-93.

history of science, one famous case of fleeing to the countryside to avoid the disease was particularly memorable. In 1666, when Isaac Newton was a young man recently graduated from Cambridge University, the plague struck England. Newton had planned to stay on at Cambridge for further studies, but the university elected to close completely for the duration of the plague. Newton therefore returned to his family home in Lincolnshire to sit it out. It was while he was there, with plenty of time to think about the scientific concepts that were still foremost in his mind, that Newton had some of his most important insights. He worked out the principles of a new branch of mathematics, the calculus; he performed crucial experiments to determine the composition of light; and, if we can believe Newton's own recounting many years later, it was then and there that Newton saw an apple fall in his orchard that gave him the basic idea of universal gravitation.

As an insight into how civilizations develop, with advances and setbacks, nothing is more revealing than to look at what happened to Europe after the plague of the 14th century. As already discussed in Chapter 11, the plague cleared the way for renewed growth and prosperity. The terrible and unjust swath of death left by the plague also gave Europe a new beginning and new vitality.

The extinct Dodo.

Chapter 26

Extinction

Among the most surprising discoveries of the late 18th century by naturalists were fossilized bones that resembled no living creatures on Earth. The surprise was that no one expected that species of animals (or plants) could have existed in the past that were no longer found on earth. It made no sense. God's creation was believed to be perfect. How could it change? Had God made a mistake? These issues were seriously debated in the early 19th century.

As a result of the many excavations carried out in Europe in order to dig canals and lay railroads for the Industrial Revolution, the number of mystery fossils began to accumulate to such an extent that they could no longer be explained away. It became clear that many animals had existed in the past, but were no longer alive anywhere on Earth. They were extinct. The most troubling of these were the huge lizard-like skeletal remains that were soon called dinosaurs. These were no ordinary creatures; they were monsters that would have terrified any human population that had ever come in contact with them.

Aside from the dinosaurs, there were the remains of other large animals that were nowhere to be seen in the 19th century. In Paris at the *Muséum d'histoire naturelle*, Georges Cuvier founded a new science of comparative anatomy through which he was able to reconstruct the probable bodily structure of the extinct animals on the basis of a few scattered bones from an excavation. For many, Cuvier's work clinched the matter, and after the publication of Darwin's *Origin*

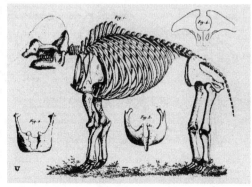

The American Mastodon, reconstructed by Georges Cuvier.

of Species in 1859, few remained who did not accept that many very different creatures had been alive on Earth in the distant past who were no longer extant.

For the dinosaurs, and for quite a few of the other extraordinary creatures, it was reasonable to suppose that they had ceased to exist long before human beings appeared on Earth. Whatever made them go extinct had nothing to do with human beings. But since the time that extinctions were first understood, we have also come to understand that many extinctions have been the direct result of human actions.

Affecting Animal Habitats

A *habitat* is the environment in which an animal normally lives and flourishes. The habitat of an animal is an ecological niche that contains under normal conditions an adequate food supply, the right number of predators to keep the population in check, and the environmental conditions that suit the particular species. Habitats evolve over millions of years. With the exception of human beings, very few animals can readily shift to life in a different habitat without serious consequences.

Extinctions Due to Hunters and Gatherers

Hunting and gathering communities generally did not upset the existing habitats of animals, even those they hunted. However, some extinctions of large mammals in areas populated by hunting and gathering groups do suggest that they may have been hunted to death. Alternatively, at least over-hunting during a time of a climate change may have pushed a weakened animal population into extinction. Where this explanation is most convincing is in parts of the world where hunters and gatherers have remained for much longer, for example, in Australia and the Americas.

It has been estimated that over the last 100 thousand years, 86 percent of all the large animals in Australia have become extinct. This is in an area where very few fluctuations in the climate that might have threatened a species have occurred. How could this decimation have happened? One possibility is that the Australian Aborigines hunted them to death. Or, even if they did not hunt the large animals to death, they may have altered the habitat of the animals so much that the animals could not survive.

In the Americas, the comparable figures are an 80 percent loss in South America and a 73 percent loss in North America. Most of these extinctions happened well after the end of the ice age, suggesting that climatic change was not the cause.

Agriculture Destroys Habitats

Once people turned to agriculture, they deliberately altered many ecosystems, and those changes destroyed many animal habitats. Forests are habitats for many different creatures, from very small to very large animals. Clearing forests for pastureland and for planting destroys the habitats of those creatures that lived there. Likewise, the draining of marshes, which are delicately balanced ecosystems. Another human practice that frequently has had disastrous results is the deliberate introduction of a plant or animal species into a new ecosystem.

Most of this damage has been done since the beginning of the period of colonization when settlers fanned out all over the world, determined to make life elsewhere as close as possible to the life back home that they had left. But the European settlers were not the first to display thoughtlessness toward their fellow creatures. It was long established in human civilization from the outset.

Ancient and Medieval Extinctions

For periods after the invention of writing, descriptions exist that can help pinpoint when an animal became extinct in an area. In ancient Egypt the conversion of all the cultivatable area on both sides of the Nile into farmland took away the natural habitat of elephants, rhinoceroses, and giraffes that had relied on access to the Nile, driving the animals from the country. There are some detailed reports on slaughters, often for purposes of celebration that would have affected the local populations of animals. In Greece, for example, by 200 B.C.E. the lion and leopard were extinct both on the mainland and across the Aegean Sea in what is now Turkey.

The Romans appeared to have especially savoured the killing of large animals for display. When the Coliseum in Rome was completed, in a one hundred-day celebration nine thousand captured animals were killed. And when Emperor Trajan conquered the province of Dacia, another 11 thousand were sacrificed.

Some extinctions were the result of wanton over-hunting of prey that lived in abundance, because they had few predators until discovered by people. Flightless birds are always vulnerable to this sort of attack. Along the coasts of Scotland and Iceland, there used to be huge colonies of the great auk, a flightless seabird. These were easy kills and made good food. There is a report that in 1540, two ships pulled in to one of the nesting areas and filled both vessels with freshly killed auks in just 30 minutes. Their eggs were also a delicacy and were much sought after, though the auk laid only one egg per year. With such excessive raids, it did not take long before the auk was a rarity in its former habitat. The last known pair was killed in Iceland in 1844.

Animals as Pests

Many animals were deliberately hunted down and exterminated because they were viewed as pests that interfered with human life. Wolves, for example, were common throughout Europe until about 500 years ago. Even cities like Paris had roaming wolf packs, even in daylight. In Britain, the wolf was viewed as such a pest that full-scale hunts were organized to rid the land of them forever. They succeeded. The wolf is now extinct in Britain.

The British were very organized about their campaigns against unwanted animals. In 1533, the English Parliament passed an act requiring all church parishes to have nets to catch rooks, choughs, and crows—birds that were viewed as nothing but trouble. Then in 1566, the churchwardens were authorized to pay a bounty for delivered corpses of virtually all undesired animals: foxes, polecats, weasels, stoats, otters, hedgehogs, rats, mice, moles, hawks, buzzards, ospreys, bluejays, ravens, and kingfishers. Policies like these continued until even into the 20th century.

The Grass is Greener Elsewhere

Not surprisingly, when Europeans began exploring the rest of the world, their own land had been decimated of the abundance of nature. This was part of the reason for the exploratory voyages in the first place. The homeland had been used to the point that it could no longer comfortably support the rising population. The explorers were astounded by the richness of life that they found in the faraway lands. It does not seem to have occurred to any of these explorers that Europe had once been the same, that it was no longer so because of human actions, and that if they showed the same disregard for nature in the newly discovered lands, the results would be the same as at home. How could they have realized all this? Those effects had taken hundreds of years to appear.

A steady stream of European explorers to the Americas and Australia sent back reports of fish in such abundance that they broke the fishing nets put in the water to catch them, and of birds, both flighted and flightless, that were easily caught in droves or whose nests were easily raided for eggs.

But it took surprisingly little time for the organized hunting with guns, nets, and traps to devastate the populations of some species that had seemed without limit. Islands were especially hard hit, since there was no place for the animals to escape to. On many islands flightless birds flourished where there were no natural predators that would have hunted them to death long ago. Fully 90 percent of all bird extinctions have occurred on islands.

The Dodo

Special mention has to be made of the *dodo*, which has become the symbol for all extinctions. The dodo is merely one of the many examples of flightless birds on islands that were hunted to death after the arrival of European settlers. The bird was rather peculiar looking and therefore a conversation piece of sorts. Its existence and its demise were widely reported across Europe at a time when the idea of the possibility of extinction was still a novelty. Here, in the words of Rod and Moira Attrill, is what happened:

> The Dodo was a strange looking bird. Said to look more like an overweight Vulture than its relatives the pigeons, it had no natural enemies on the island of Mauritius—at least until the Dutch came in 1598 with their dogs, their stowaway rats and their own voracious appetites. Slow and clumsy, the Dodo had no means of escape. The birds offered no resistance to the settlers who clubbed them to death. By 1638 few remained. An English traveller saw the last living Dodo disappear into the bushes in 1681![1]

---

1.   Rod and Moira Attrill, "Extinct is Forever," www.attrill.freeserve.co.uk/extinct.htm.

The Passenger Pigeon

In 1858, the naturalist Alfred Russel Wallace wrote a paper summarizing his views on the evolution of species by natural selection. It was this paper that finally prompted Charles Darwin to settle down and commit to print the work on evolution that he had been steadily doing for over 20 years. Wallace gave many examples of different species and how the predator-prey relations in their particular environments tend to keep their populations within a certain range. Meanwhile, the effect of predators culling the weak from the herds and the competition for food would constantly nudge the population toward characteristics that would better suit it to its environment.

A model of the now extinct passenger pigeon.

Wallace wished to show that even a low birth rate in a species would still result in an exponential growth pattern that would soon reach unimaginable proportions were there not something external that keeps it in check. To prove the point, he cited the case of the *passenger pigeon*, one of the most abundant bird species in the United States, which nevertheless has a very low birth rate. It was an ironic choice of species to use for this illustration. Here is the excerpt from Wallace's paper that discusses the passenger pigeon:

> [A]s far as the continuance of the species and the keeping up the average number of individuals are concerned, large broods are superfluous. This is strikingly proved by the case of particular species; for we find that their abundance in individuals bears no relation whatever to their fertility in producing offspring. Perhaps the most remarkable instance of an immense bird population is that of the passenger pigeon of the United States, which lays only one, or at most two eggs, and is said to rear generally but one young one. Why is this bird so extraordinarily abundant while others producing two or three times as many young are much less plentiful? The explanation is not difficult. The food most congenial to this species, and on which it thrives best, is abundantly distributed over a very extensive region, offering such difference of soil and climate, that in one part or another of the area the supply never fails. The bird is capable of a very rapid and long-continued flight, so that it can pass without fatigue over the whole of the district it inhabits, and as soon

as the supply of food begins to fail in one place is able to discover a fresh feeding-ground. This example strikingly shows us that the procuring a constant supply of wholesome food is almost the sole condition requisite for ensuring the rapid increase of a given species, since neither the limited fecundity, nor the unrestrained attacks of birds of prey and of man are here sufficient to check it.[1]

Wallace had chosen what he believed was such an extreme example—a bird that lays only one or two eggs a year, but nevertheless had achieved a huge population—that it would illustrate his point that survival depends more on food supply and on predators than on reproduction, which will always be adequate. The passenger pigeon had a huge population in the United States. An early settler in Virginia wrote that the birds were so thick that they shadowed the sky. Some of the flocks were described as a mile wide and taking four or five hours to pass overhead. Because of this abundance and the tendency of the birds to fly together in large flocks, capturing them was easy. A net need only be swung into the air from a high point as a flock passed over, and it was sure to bring down a fair number of birds. Before the European settlers arrived, the native people were capturing passenger pigeons this way. With colonization, European immigrants learned similar methods, and the rate of harvesting the birds picked up considerably. Still, by the time that Wallace was writing in the mid-19th century, the population was still several billion strong.

This was about the time that a commercial operation was begun to capture the birds and sell them for their meat and feathers to the large metropolitan areas. When railroads were built linking the east coast of the United States to the Mid-west, it became possible to ship large numbers of dead birds to market. Since this was a commercial operation, fairly detailed records are still available to help judge the success of these efforts. One report states that on July 23, 1860, a total of 235 200 passenger pigeons were put on a train to the east from Grand Rapids, Michigan. In 1869, Van Buren County in Michigan recorded seven and one-half million birds sent east during the year.

This magnitude of hunting quickly got ahead of the ability of the passenger pigeon to regenerate. By the 1880s, the size of the flocks had diminished considerably, and the great commercial bonanza came to an end. The last wild passenger pigeons were seen in

---

1.   Alfred Russel Wallace, On the Tendency of Varieties to Depart Indefinitely from the Original Type, *Journal of the Linnean Society, Zoology* (1858) III, 45-62.

the eastern United States in the 1890s, and the last surviving bird of the species died in captivity in 1914.

Local Extinctions

The dodo and the passenger pigeon are examples of species that are gone forever. They no longer exist anywhere on the planet that we know of. Human beings can be held responsible for total extinctions like these where a species existed only in one environment, and it was hunted to death there or its habitat totally destroyed.

There is another category that people sometimes call extinctions. These are local events, where a species that was common in one area is decimated to the point of non-existence in that region, but might exist elsewhere. Much of the commercial market in fish, furs, and certain game animals has been subjected to this sort of extermination. Generally, when people find a highly efficient killing process that can harvest a great many individuals at once, species are driven to local extinction. Because these extinctions are only local, it often is of little concern to the industry that lives off the species, because they can always move their hunting grounds somewhere else. Think of this as a highly advanced and efficient version of the nomadic hunter-gatherer that moved on to new territory when one area was exhausted of food.

Consider fishing. This is one of the industries that has become very mechanized and efficient in the last several decades. Because of this, it threatens to destroy the very stocks for which it fishes. In past times, it seemed inconceivable that fishing could deplete the stocks of the waters of the Earth. There were just too many fish and too few fishermen with too primitive methods of catching them to do any real harm. An example familiar to Canadians is the cod fishing industry. Cod fishing came to the Grand Banks off Newfoundland when European stocks were running low from over-fishing there in the 16th century. When fishermen first went to the Grand Banks, they reported that the fish were so plentiful that they could simply be scooped out of the sea with buckets. The fish in the oceans seemed inexhaustible.

The stocks began to be threatened when steamships became common in the later 19th century. After the Second World War, a new technology enabled fishermen to exhaust an area much more quickly: the mechanized fish factory ship. These ships not only caught the fish, they carried out all the steps of processing the fish for market, including what was necessary to keep the fish fresh, thus making frequent trips to shore unnecessary. Within ten years, the stocks of fish in this once plentiful area were being depleted. The response of the fishing industry to this problem wherever it occurs generally is to leave when the catches fall below an acceptable level and head to unexploited areas. Thus, over time, the fishing industry can systematically decimate a population area by area.

The same is true of the fur trade. In the Middle Ages, when little or no indoor heating existed, the wearing of garments made from animal furs in northern climates was certainly desired, though not always possible. Fur coats became a status symbol in Europe. Any animal fur could keep a person warm, though usually many pelts were needed to make a garment of any size. Some pelts were more prized than others and fetched higher prices, particularly beaver pelts. In the Middle Ages, beavers were common all over Europe, but trapping had severely reduced their numbers by the Renaissance. One of the great attractions of Canada to the European settlers and traders was the prodigious number of beaver just waiting to be trapped. The Hudson's Bay Company, one of the first joint stock companies in the world, was formed in 1682 in part to exploit the beaver population in Canada.

There are other examples of species being brought near to extinction by voracious hunting. Seals, whales, and bears all come to mind. All these decimations of animal populations have one feature in common: the animals are wild, so no one can lay claim to them and no one can prevent others from attacking them; since the animals belong to no one group, no one has any particular incentive to reduce hunting in order to help the population sustain itself. After all, if any one hunter refrained from killing an animal, other hunters could just come along and take it for themselves. The only rational action from the "economic" viewpoint is to get there first and make the kill.

The Reverend Thomas Robert Malthus.

Chapter 27

World Models

If the human population of the world keeps on rising at an alarming rate while the resources we consume to maintain our way of life continue to be depleted and the quality of the environment becomes less hospitable, perhaps it would be a good idea to try to look ahead and plan for a future that will be sustainable. If human beings are so clever, they should be able to avoid the fate of some of the species that they have seen become extinct.

The notion that we may have to plan our future in order to avoid a disaster is a hard sell if the dominant attitude in a society is that things are always getting better and better. The idea of progress that the Industrial Revolution so helped to establish in the mainstream of thinking runs counter to the thought that there may be something wrong with going full steam ahead toward a grander standard of living. Yet, not everyone merely jumped on the bandwagon of progress without some thought of the consequences.

The Essay on Population

At the end of the 18th century, when the Industrial Revolution was in full swing, a British clergyman and economist, the Reverend Thomas Robert Malthus, published a book that predicted that a future time would come when some very unpleasant decisions would have to be made by society. His book, *An Essay on the Principle of Population, As it Affects the Future Improvement of Society*, published in 1798, alarmed many and became a topic of concerned discussion among intellectuals through the 19th century. Basically, Malthus predicted that at some point in the not too distant future, the world, or at least Britain, would not have enough food to feed its growing population.

The First World Model

Malthus' book probably qualifies as the first of a series of studies that have come to be called *world models*. A world model is an analysis of certain global trends in different but related areas projected into the future in order to make predictions. A world model is necessarily extremely sketchy. A handful of important statistical measures are gathered for some period in the past. These might be, for example, population size, birth and death rates, resources available and their rate of usage, food production and its consumption, pollution, disposable income, cost of living, and capital investment. Rules are then drawn up to predict how these variables affect each other. In a good model, the predicted results will not be too far off from the actual ones.

Actually, what is described above would be a fairly sophisticated model that would require some high-powered calculating power to work with. The world model that Malthus expounded was simplicity itself.

The Malthus Thesis

Malthus' model is very straightforward and easy to grasp. Nevertheless, it took him over 200 pages of text to propound it to his satisfaction. That is because despite the conceptual simplicity, Malthus wished to go to great lengths to show that all his assumptions were reasonable and not just some crazed notion. Remember, this was at the height of the reign of the idea of progress.

The argument rests on four assertions. Here they are in Malthus' own words. First are his postulates:

> 1 That food is necessary to the existence of man.

> 2 That the passion between the sexes is necessary and will remain nearly in its present state.

These seem reasonable enough. Malthus asserts them without much justification. The upshot of these is that people need to eat and they have an urge to procreate. Then he goes on to his "lemmas." or preliminary theorems that he needs to establish before going further. These are:

> Lemma 1. Population, unchecked, will increase in a geometric ratio.

> Lemma 2. Subsistence will increase in an arithmetic ratio.

The first "lemma" is the assertion, familiar enough to us now and confirmed by repeated observation and experiment, that populations increase exponentially (being the meaning of a "geometric ratio"). In Malthus' time this was not well understood, so he went to some lengths to explain it, pointing out that if two parents have on average more than two offspring who themselves marry and have children, then the total size of the population will expand exponentially.

The second "lemma" is not so easily confirmed, and it is the weakest spot in his entire argument. By "subsistence," Malthus means the products of agriculture, whether crops or meat, and in both cases, the amount available depends on the amount of land under cultivation or cleared for pasture. Malthus was not aware that changes in agricultural technology might increase the output of food per unit of land, so the only way he could imagine getting more food was by farming more land. But the amount of land that could be cultivated was finite, just as the Earth itself was finite. For population growth, he could conveniently express the principle at work with an exponential function, or, in his terminology, a "geometric ratio."

How could he get at the problem of the availability of land with a mathematical formula? Surely it takes people to clear land for pasture and to cultivate it. If there are more people, there will be more potential farmers, so there can be more farmland. But that fails to take into account that the amount of land available is constantly diminishing, so the closer one gets to the limit of available land, the slower will be the increase. What Malthus needed was something like the logistic S-curve used to model carrying capacity (see Chapter 4), but that was mathematically beyond his (and his readers') reach, so he settled on the approximation of a straight line. This is the meaning of his "arithmetic ratio."

He could imagine the amount of land being put under cultivation rising at a steady amount, presumably forever, but the population growing by an ever-increasing amount. No matter where you start and no matter what the assigned rates of increase are (as long as they are positive), sooner or later, the exponential function gets ahead of the straight line. It's really that simple, and that is all that Malthus was trying to demonstrate. But to fix ideas with some real data and real numbers, he gave particular examples and made predictions. Since he had not foreseen all the possibilities, his predictions were off the mark. As a result, many people came to the conclusion that he was wrong and everything he said was misconceived.

Malthus made all of his projections based on Britain, treating it as a separate entity isolated from the rest of the world. Given the technology of the time, this was probably fair. Food imported from abroad was a novelty and restricted to items such as tea and sugar that could not sustain a population. Also, emigration out of Britain to the colonies was underway, but the total numbers were not enough to affect the general rate of population growth in Britain.

Malthus then needed some estimate of the "natural" growth rate of human populations where there were no hindrances to growth. In other words, he needed to know how fast people reproduce when they are living with an unlimited abundance of resources. He needed a situation rather like that which scientists found later for the elephant seals in the Channel Islands (see Chapter 24). Where was a land of plenty where people could freely exercise their instincts? He chose the American colonies, which had not too long before become the United States.

In America, there were some rough census estimates of population growth—enough for Malthus to get a working figure. What he concluded was that in America, the population could double every twenty-five years. This is truly an extraordinary rate of increase for a human population, but Malthus, for purposes of illustration, took this as his "natural" rate.

Now, what about food production? Here Malthus became somewhat arbitrary. He decided that if the population doubled during a 25-year period then possibly food production could keep pace for the first period, but thereafter it would only be able to continue increasing by the same amount.

Returning to the situation at hand in Britain, Malthus noted that the population of Britain in the year 1800 would be about seven million. Following this logic, if there were plenty of food available then, the population might grow at most to double that, or 14 million, by 1825. And if there was, say, just enough food to satisfy all demands in 1800, then there might be an increase by 1825 so that there was just enough food for all 14

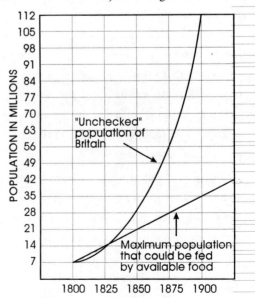

Illustrative example by Thomas Malthus of how population outstrips food supply. The exponential curve representing the "unchecked" population of Britain must eventually cross the straight line representing the maximum population that could be fed with the available food. When this happens famine will result. Malthus argued that such a grim fate was inevitable unless something was done to "check" the growth of the British population.

million. But thereafter, the population will strive to double again to 28 million by 1850, while the best the land can do is provide food for another seven million—i.e., grow at the same rate as it did in the first 25 years. The result is that there will be conflict, fighting over the food. As Malthus expressed it, there would inevitably be either *misery* or *vice*. Misery would be caused by people preventing population growth by curbing their natural instincts (remember postulate #2), that is, by practicing some sort of birth control or celibacy. Vice would be caused by some people forcibly taking food away from others. Malthus imagined that wars would be fought or there would be massive civil disobedience.

Malthus Engenders Fright, Then Disdain

The reaction to Malthus' *Essay* can serve as a lesson to all those who take it upon themselves to alert the public about dangers ahead. When his book first appeared, it caught the public by surprise, but then got their attention and was discussed in many circles. At first his logic seemed airtight. After all, he had couched it in mathematical terms and presented it in the systematic format that had become the model for scientific theories of all sorts since Isaac Newton's *Principia Mathematica*. The population would exceed the food supply and there would be either starvation or conflict. If his purpose was to get the public to consider these issues, instead of just put their faith in eternal progress, then he succeeded, at least with a portion of the population.

But his Achilles heel was that he made his mathematical model too precise, and he committed numbers to it. Once he did that, he had made a prediction and would be held to it. In the first place, the population of Britain did not rise as quickly as his illustration suggested. But more damning was that the food supply did increase at a rate faster than the steady "arithmetic rate" that he had projected. There were considerable improvements in agricultural methods in the 19th century, including both the efficiencies of mechanization and of fertilization. Also, food began

An early steam-powered tractor. Advances in farm machinery have historically allowed for greater increases in food production.

to be imported from elsewhere in the world with lower population densities. The food supply continued to be able to stay ahead of the population. Malthus must have been wrong.

None of the charges leveled against Malthus need have stuck had Malthus not committed himself to an illustration of his principles and had he not forced the model of growth of food supply to a straight line, which it was not. Take away these, and his basic assertion stands. Populations will expand until they hit a barrier caused by lack of food. Food is limited in any area, because ultimately it comes out of a fixed amount of land.

In the 20th century, when human populations began to show signs of uncontrollable growth, Malthus came to be regarded more positively and was forgiven for some of his overstatements. But meanwhile, those who chose to ignore his warnings had armed themselves with the proof that he was wrong and therefore that his ideas need not trouble them.

Curiously, Malthus' most important influence may have been on two naturalists who saw his point clearly enough and then focused on the very conflict that Malthus had warned about. Their work got much wider acceptance, including acceptance by some of those who vehemently opposed Malthus. These two were Charles Darwin and Alfred Russel Wallace. To both of them, Malthus' idea of an inevitable struggle over resources struck a chord. Both Darwin and Wallace saw that a population of any species produces many more offspring than the parent generation, yet the general number living from one generation to the next does not change that much. That is because the other forces of nature that work against them, for example, predators, continue to cut their numbers back. There is therefore a struggle for existence that is won by those who are most adapted to their environment. This is the principle of natural selection.

The passage quoted in the Chapter 26 on the passenger pigeon by Alfred Russel Wallace served much the same purpose as Malthus' argument about population pressures. Wallace had just read Malthus' *Essay* and it set him to thinking about the world of animals and plants. The same had happened to Darwin about 20 years before when he too read Malthus' *Essay*, though Darwin held back publishing his views until he had mountains of confirming data. But they really demonstrated and documented the same principles that Malthus had done for human populations.

Feedback

What Malthus lacked in his model that would have made it more realistic was some way to take into account the natural interactions between a population and its food supply. The hypothetical example that Malthus cited, depicted in the graph shown above, leads to an impossible situation. Once the year 1825 is reached, the population would exceed the food supply. To make his point, Malthus asks us to consider how 28 million people would be fed if there were food for only 14 million people. But this is not what would happen in any case. If there were no longer enough food to go around, then the dire consequences that Malthus warned about would already start kicking in. People would begin to starve or kill each other or endure the "misery" of having no more children.

This interaction is called *feedback*. It was not a notion that had been studied much in Malthus' time, but it had already had a significant application in the Industrial Revolution. Just a few years before Malthus was writing, James Watt introduced a new innovation in his steam engine that made it run much more smoothly. It was a device that determined how much steam to pump into the machine, based on how fast the machine was actually running. It produced an interaction between the input of steam and the output of a flywheel turning.

Watt's innovation was the *governor*. It was a purely mechanical device. A spindle was attached by gears to the flywheel of the steam engine. The faster the engine turned the flywheel, the faster the spindle turned. On the spindle were two metal rods, attached on one end near the top of the spindle so they could pivot easily. At the other end of the rods were attached two heavy weights ("flyballs"). As the spindle turned, the flyballs were swung out by the centrifugal force of the rotation. The faster the spindle turned,

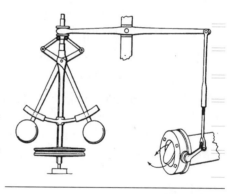

James Watt's flyball governor.

the farther the flyballs were thrust outward. The other ends of the rods were connected to a lever that was pulled down when the flyballs went outward and let back up as the flyballs sank back toward the axis of the spindle. The lever was connected to a valve that controlled the amount of steam that was pumped into the engine. The faster the engine turned, the more the flyballs were thrust outward, the more the lever was pulled down, and the less steam was admitted into the engine. Conversely if the engine slowed down, it was given more steam.

The device was called a governor, because it governed the speed of the engine, tending to make it run more smoothly. This is an example of what is called *negative feedback*. An increase in one quantity causes a decrease in the other quantity, and vice-versa. The overall effect is to tend to maintain the status quo. This is likewise the principle of steering. If a vehicle or a vessel is drifting off course to the right, the person steering directs it back to the left. In fact, the word governor is derived from a word meaning "steersman." The direct root of the English word "governor" is the Latin *gubernator*, which itself is derived from the Greek κυβερνετες (*kubernetes*), meaning the steersman.

The opposite effect from negative feedback is achieved when a change in one quantity produces a change in another quantity in the same direction. This is called *positive feedback*, and is what is at work in Malthus' population-food interaction. In Malthus' model, if population had unlimited food available, it would increase at its maximum rate. But if the food supply could not keep pace, the population's rate of increase would fall back. The change in population is in the same direction as the change in food supply. Had Malthus been able to incorporate this into his model, it would have been much more believable—though he might have then been speaking over the heads of his main audience, which was not accustomed to such abstract notions.

It's one thing to have a mechanical device to govern the speed of a steam engine; it's quite another to work all this out on paper and take all the interactions into account in mathematical formulae. That is another aspect of the problem that Malthus addressed that made it very difficult for him to be more realistic. To carry out the kinds of calculations required and at the same time take into account enough variables, all with their own interactions, you really need a computer.

The Limits to Growth

Midway through the 20th century, the problems that Malthus had alerted the world to were becoming easier to see and harder to deny. Not only was the population soaring and the food supply failing to keep pace, but the industrialized world was using irreplaceable natural resources at an ever increasing rate, and the environment was becoming degraded with pollutants. In 1968, a meeting was held at the august Italian scientific society, the Lincean Academy of Rome. A group was formed there to look into the growing world problems and see what could be done about it. The membership of the group included thirty individuals from ten countries—scientists, educators, economists, industrialists, and civil servants. It came to be called the Club of Rome. The Club commissioned studies that would attempt to do what Malthus did not have the means to do: create a viable world model and make reasonable predictions from it based on historical data and established trends.

The first report commissioned by the Club of Rome appeared in 1972, called *The Limits to Growth*. As the title suggested, the report argued, rather like Thomas Malthus, that there was a limit to the growth of the population that would be imposed by the environment. Unlike Malthus, they considered many more variables: population, food supply, natural resources, capital investment, industrial output, and pollution. They spent much time and effort establishing the feedback relationships among all of their variables, for example, the interaction between the natural resources necessary to make chemical fertilizers and agricultural output. Compared to Malthus, their report was of a totally different level of sophistication.

The Population-Pollution Interaction

To give an idea of how their model works consider the input/output diagram shown. This diagram shows population is affected by pollution and how pollution affects population; also, it models what the effect might be of a birth control campaign. In the top center is the population level. It is affected positively by the number of births per year, shown as the arrow going from the births balloon to the population level balloon. The population level positively affects the number of births, too, since the more people there are, the more babies will be born. That is shown as the arrow going from population level back to births. These together make a positive feedback loop; an increase in each one leads to an increase in the other. On the top right is the number of deaths per year. Deaths reduce the population, so the arrow going toward the population level from the deaths balloon has a minus sign over it. However, an increase in the population level means there are more people who might die, so the arrow going back to deaths is positive. Hence, deaths provide negative feedback to population, but population provides positive feedback to deaths. Taken by themselves, this is a negative feedback loop.

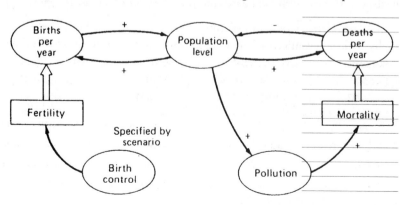

Returning to the left side of the chart, there is also a fertility rate, which expresses the rate of births as a percentage of the population. This might be considered an independent variable, but the study wished to consider the effect on their projections if that rate could be changed by the institution of a concerted social program of birth control.In this model, population also affects pollution. The more people there are, the more mess we make, and the higher the pollution level. Hence the arrow from population to pollution is positive. The pollution level also affects the quality of life, and ultimately will have an influence on the mortality rate, the percentage of the population that dies in any given year. That effect is positive: more pollution raises mortality. If the mortality rate goes up, then the number of deaths will go up.

Altogether, this is a complex interaction, requiring careful measurement to measure the effect that one variable has on another. Yet this is a tiny piece of the entire study, which mapped interactions between all of the variables that were listed above. There was no way that these calculations could have been done before the availability of computers. However, with computers the model can be run again and again, tested on historical data to validate it, and then run with different scenarios of possible actions and eventualities for the future. It was quite a project.

The Standard World Model Run

The first scenario run after they had finished all their testing and decided that the model was sound was what they called the *Standard World Model Run*. This simply let the model calculate what to expect if all their parameters were correct and no particular external interventions were made to change any of the feedback relations. It predicts disaster sometime in the mid-21st century.

This the description of the standard run from the *Limits to Growth* report:

> The "standard" world model run assumes no major change in the physical, economic, or social relationships that have historically governed the development of the world system. All variables plotted here follow historical values from 1900 to 1970. Food, industrial output, and population grow exponentially until the rapidly diminishing resource base forces a slowdown in industrial growth. Because of natural delays in the system, both population and pollution continue to increase for some time after the peak of

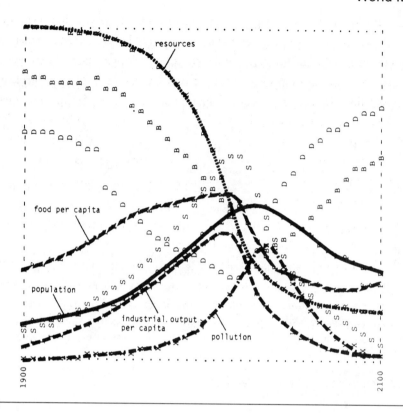

Standard World Model Run. The time period covered in the chart is from 1900 to 2100. The first 70 years are historical data; thereafter the values are predicted by the computer simulation. The variables mapped are: total world population, industrial output per capita in dollars, food per capita in kilogram-grain equivalents per person per year, pollution as a multiple of the 1970 level, non-renewable resources as a fraction of the deemed remaining resources in 1900, the crude birth rate overall—births per 1000 persons per year (represented as B), the crude death rate overall—deaths per 1000 persons per year (D), and services per capita in dollars (S).

industrialization. Population growth is finally halted by a rise in the death rate due to decreased food and medical services.[1]

The standard run worked with 70 years of historical data but made a number of assumptions about the future, namely that there would be no major disasters, no technological breakthroughs to prevent pollution, no discoveries of additional natural

1.   Donella H. Meadows, et al., *The Limits to Growth: A Report for the Club of Rome's Project on the Predicament of Mankind.* (New York: New American Library, 1974), p. 129.

resources, and no changes social behaviour. Any of these would materially affect the interactions on which the model is based. Then the model was run with a variety of other possible scenarios. What was surprising was that almost all other runs came to the same end: the rising population would continue to deplete resources, cause more pollution and eventually bring the entire system down, though perhaps at a different time.

To give one example: the authors of the report tried another run, nearly the same as the standard run, but they arbitrarily doubled their estimate of the amount of natural resources that were available at their starting point, the year 1900. That is, they left the rest of the model the same, but chose one variable that would have an enormous effect and assumed that they had very seriously underestimated it. Here is their description of what happened in that run:

> Now industrialization can reach a higher level since resources are not so quickly depleted. The larger industrial plant releases pollution at such a rate, however, that the environmental pollution absorption mechanisms become saturated. Pollution rises very rapidly, causing a slight increase in the death rate. Finally, a decline in food production results when the falling industrial output can no longer sustain capital-intensive agriculture. At the end of the run resources are severely depleted in spite of the doubled amount initially available.[1]

And there were many other "runs" representing different assumptions: pollution under control, agricultural output vastly improved, unlimited natural resources discovered, and others. All led to disaster sooner or later as one or another of the variables got out of control and brought the others down.

The *Limits to Growth* report emphasized that they were not certain of any of the scenarios they ran. There could be large variations in the input data and the interactions that they assumed. But, they emphasized, since they all lead to the same disaster scenario sometime in the 21st century, it didn't really matter what the details were.

One and only one scenario showed stability for the foreseeable future. That one assumed that the birth rate could be curbed, presumably by a massive program of birth control, so that the world population would stabilize, and quickly. Also, the per capital industrial output must be held to 1975 levels, goods must be recycled, and pollution controlled.

---

1. Ibid., p. 133.

Reaction to Limits to Growth

In a way, the reaction to the *Limits* study was very much like the reaction to Malthus' *Essay*. Many people were taken by surprise at first, then were devastated by it. They found the arguments convincingly airtight. Doom was most certainly just around the corner, and only a radical change in human habits could forestall the inevitable catastrophe. Others were skeptical from the start and refused to be distracted by the report. And just as happened to Malthus, the particular predictions made in *Limits to Growth* were held against them when they did not happen. Among those predictions—from the standard model—were that the world would run out of gold in 1981, out of silver and mercury in 1985, and out of zinc in 1990. None of these happened, indeed more deposits have been discovered, so now the reserves stand at higher levels than *Limits* took as their starting point. This is the familiar case of confusing the illustrative data with the integrity of the model itself. Indeed, as the *Limits* study itself maintained, they could be wildly wrong on their assessment of natural resources, but if their methods were correct, the disaster would still happen, though perhaps at a different time.

Mankind at the Turning Point

There were also major objections from another quarter altogether. One of the ways in which the *Limits* study was particularly clumsy was that the variables they used were all worldwide figures. Population was world population; resource usage was worldwide, and so on. People from Third World countries objected vehemently that *they* were not the ones overusing the world's resources nor causing pollution nor eating sumptuous meals. They should therefore not be lumped together with the industrialized nations and told to cut back. Instead, the industrialized nations should stop their excesses and begin to act more responsibly. The rejoinder to this from the industrialized nations was that the biggest problem is runaway population growth. In the developed countries, the birth rate has fallen as affluence has risen. In the undeveloped world, the better nutrition, better sanitation, and modern health care has simply increased the birth rate. Any way you look at it, the problems of the world were different in different places.

To address this failing in the *Limits* study, a second report to the Club of Rome appeared two years later, in 1974, entitled *Mankind at the Turning Point*. The *Turning Point* study began by dividing the world into ten separate regions with similar economies.

The fault of *Limits* was immediately seen, no matter what one thought of the particular divisions in *Turning Point*. The world did not act as a unit, so why should a world model. An interaction that worked one way in one part of the world might have a completely different effect elsewhere.

Consider just the issue of population. In the equivalent of the standard model run of *Limits to Growth*, the projection in *Turning Point* that assumed no changes in current trends predicted that in 50 years—that would be 2024—the increase in the population of North America would be an additional four people per square kilometer. In South Asia, it would be an additional 160 more people per square kilometer. Clearly North American birth rates are well under control while South Asian rates are at a crisis level.

Like *Limits to Growth, Mankind at the Turning Point* ran several scenarios predicting different results, depending on the actions taken to deal with the crisis. The *Turning Point* recommendations focus on massive foreign aid from the developed countries to the undeveloped world to raise their standard of living, coupled with a vigorous birth control campaign to combat the debilitating effects of too many mouths to feed. The working

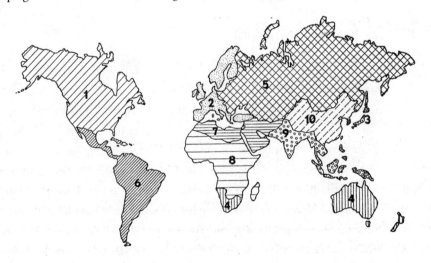

The ten regions of the world system in *Mankind at the Turning Point*. (1) North America, (2) Western Europe, (3) Japan, (4) other capitalist economies (Australia, New Zealand, South Africa, Israel), (5) Eastern Europe and the U.S.S.R., (6) Latin America, (7) North Africa and the Middle East, (8) Tropical Africa, (9) South and Southeast Asia, (10) China. This was, of course, before the fall of the Soviet bloc and the return of South Africa to the control of native Africans. Note also some of the now highly industrialized Pacific Rim countries are just lumped in elsewhere. This shows this difficulty of making any arbitrary categories in such studies.

assumption is that with a higher standard of living, including education, health care, and a healthy infrastructure, will come a willingness to have fewer children. The developed nations would have to curtail their own consumption patterns in order to afford all the foreign aid that would be necessary.

There are interesting aspects to these recommendations. In the first place, they have as a goal reducing the wealth disparity between the developed and the undeveloped nations, but they stop far short of advocating equality. In fact, the stated goal was to achieve a per capital income level in the undeveloped nations that was one-fifth that of the developed nations. Where *Turning Point* shows its greatest weakness is where the recommendations of all such world models do: they rely on cooperation and goodwill of too many different people with different priorities.

Turning Point did not cause the stir that *Limits to Growth* did. It was too complicated for one thing. It was also pretty obviously unworkable. Like Malthus' *Essay* and *Limits to Growth*, it made some pretty poor predictions, such as world population levels reaching 12 billion people by 2010, double the figure reached in 1999.

The Fate of World Models

There have been many world model studies since *Limits to Growth*, 28 of them from the Club of Rome. With greatly increased computing power available, they are becoming more and more sophisticated. Moreover, many are now taking on more manageable tasks, trying to predict more limited results in restricted regions of the world or for much more limited time-periods. There can be no doubt that they are getting better.

But all world models suffer from the same general flaw: over-simplicity. Unlike the laws of physics that can accurately predict the motions of bodies in space for extended periods of time within a very small margin of error, the "laws" that govern interactions within a world model are not more than roughly accurate for even short periods of time. Despite the increasing sophistication of computer technology, a world model still has to reduce a system of extreme complexity to a small number of measurable variables and ignore everything else. Moreover, one would not be able to predict anything at all unless the data were treated as being reliable, despite the fact that much of it is dubious. Try as they may, world models cannot really anticipate the unknown: technological breakthroughs, epidemics, natural disasters, wars, etc. But they have their place as a tool that will help us plan for the future.

Chapter 28

The Green Revolution and Appropriate Technology

In his *Essay on Population*, Thomas Malthus predicted that the population would inevitably outstrip the food supply, and the consequences would be most undesirable. Malthus was wrong about the timing of the disaster he had foreseen, because of the vast improvements that were made in agriculture after 1798 when he published his study, but his general conclusion was bound to come true sooner or later if the population continued to rise exponentially unless, somehow, agriculture could continue to improve forever.

In the 1940s, it looked like the misery that Malthus had predicted was going to settle permanently on the Third World, where the population was continuing to inflate and where modern agricultural techniques had not been adopted. Famines were becoming common, with serious death tolls.

In the industrialized nations (despite there being a world war in progress), a number of scientists and laymen with humanitarian concerns for the starving people decided that there must be a scientific and technological solution to the problem of feeding these masses.

The Green Revolution

Studies were undertaken to try to find better crops that could feed more people. The center of activity was the International Maize and Wheat Institute in Mexico, beginning in 1943. There, over a period of a few years, plant biologists worked with multiple species of corn, wheat, and other grains trying to breed a hybrid that would have a greater yield than the traditional crops grown in most of the Third World.

They succeeded in developing a new wheat that held great promise. This hybrid strain had a yield for a given area up to twice that of ordinary strains of wheat. It was rapid growing and less light sensitive. One of the features of the improved wheat was that more of the plant was the edible grain and less was the stalk, which just became chaff. In the 1960s, a similar effort at the International Rice Research Institute in the Philippines produced a superior rice.

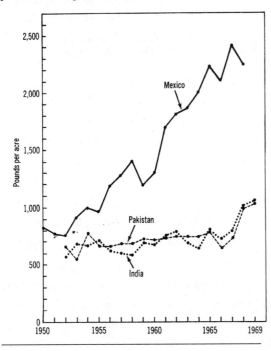

Wheat yields in Mexico, Pakistan, and India.

It was a great success, especially in Mexico, where wheat production leaped to meet the food crisis. Famines were averted. But there was a catch. This was intensive farming, just like every other development in the history of agriculture that got more food out of a fixed area. All intensive farming takes its toll somewhere. These new varieties of wheat and rice were being given to people who lived on small farms and cultivated them in a very old-fashioned way, with the simplest of tools and in many cases with no special irrigation other than what rain provided—what is called "dry" farming. This had worked for them for centuries; the skills required were passed down from one generation to the next. Their crops had sufficed all those years to feed them as best they could and now were only falling short because their population had reached its carrying capacity in their part of the world.

The new improved varieties required a whole new approach: first, they needed a very high input of chemical fertilizer; second, they needed irrigation; third; they had to fend off destruction with heavy doses of expensive herbicides, fungicides, and insecticides. This was a totally foreign way of farming to the people most in need of these new varieties. And in the long run it was a strain on the land as well.

One of the problems came from the feature of the new breeds that gave them their higher yields in the first place. This was the ratio between seed and stalk. Ordinary wheat is a grass with a long stem and a "flower" of seeds at the end. The seeds are the edible grains and are separated from the rest of the plant, which either remains on the ground or is used to make straw to feed animals. In the new plants, the stalk was much shorter and the seeds grew bigger. This is exactly what was desired.

But unfortunately, that discarded stalk had a purpose. It tended to hold the ground together with its roots, and when it decomposed it returned nutrients to the soil. Without its full complement, the soil could more easily erode and become depleted.

Another problem came from all the apparatus necessary to tend the crops—the tilling, the irrigation, and the application of fertilizers, herbicides, fungicides, and insecticides. This all required equipment and training. The result was that soon only the larger farms could cope, and they began to take over the small farms. Instead of relieving the poverty of the people, the new techniques tended to concentrate wealth in the hands of a few. As a result, the Third World began to develop an unemployment problem that it had not known before.

And then there was the question of how to pay for all this. Originally, the new seeds were distributed to the needy countries as humanitarian aid sponsored by the rich countries, but the expectation was that the needy countries would become self-sufficient once they had enough to eat. No one seemed to take into account that all the required inputs—the fertilizers, the pesticides, the seeds themselves—had to come from commercial operations in the developed nations.

These companies expected to be paid for their products. But that required foreign currencies, which the needy countries did not necessarily have. The only way these countries could raise foreign currency was to come up with something to sell to the developed nations. There were basically two options: find a natural resource to sell off, as the Third World had been doing ever since it became the Third World, or start up a manufacturing facility, making some product to sell abroad. In neither case would the result be to help establish an economy in these countries that might some day be independent. It merely deepened the dependency, now to include food itself.

The Green Revolution was a mixed success. It certainly did solve the immediate problem of staving off hunger in countries where famines were imminent. But the cost was to introduce a long-term dependency that became more and more difficult to reverse. The well-meaning scientists and philanthropists who came to the rescue with their wonder crops may have made an even bigger problem for later on.

To cite one example: Mexico, where the Green Revolution had its greatest success, quickly moved in the 1950s from being dependent on increasing imports of wheat to being an exporter. Grain production increased four-fold by the mid-1980s. Then, as always happens, the population caught up, and Mexico once again faced a food crisis.

There were new problems to deal with. Mexico had a huge foreign debt on its hands, some of it to pay for the new food technology that it was then committed to. The country had been producing hard currency to pay its debts by selling oil, but in the 1980s the skyrocketing oil prices of the 1970s collapsed and Mexico could not raise the cash it needed. Meanwhile, ten percent of its grain-producing farmland had been lost to other uses as the population expanded. Even so, Mexico's situation is not as desperate as much of southern Asia, where there is just not much hope of getting more food out of the available land. There are still options, including not devoting so much farmland to producing cash crops for export. But no matter what steps are taken to produce more food, the population soon grows to where there is again a shortage.

Appropriate Technology

The Green Revolution solved a short-term problem in the Third World with a solution best suited to the First World. Seen in the context of the whole progress of agriculture since its beginnings alongside the development of civilization, this was a logical next step. It was one more form of intensification to get more out of the soil. It relied on all the apparatus of modern chemical and agricultural technology to pull it off. But it may not have been the appropriate solution for the Third World.

When the drawbacks of the Green Revolution began to become apparent, another set of concerned First World citizens began to question the wisdom of saddling Third World countries with First World technology when they lacked all the infrastructure necessary to make it work. In 1965, a small group of people met together in London, England, to discuss these matters and formed an organization they called the Intermediate Technology Development Group to help people in the Third World develop appropriate technology for their cultures. This quickly grew into a worldwide movement. Part of the goal was to scale down large technologies to fit rural usage.

The term coined by this group was *Intermediate Technology*, meaning technology that was not at the advanced level of the industrialized nations but was a step in that direction that best suited the undeveloped countries that needed it most. Another term coined that in effect had the same meaning was *Appropriate Technology*, emphasizing that the technology must suit the culture in which it was to be implemented. An essential component of these technologies was that they must be on a scale that can be implemented and sustained in the Third World with local resources and local expertise.

Small is Beautiful

The Appropriate Technology or Intermediate Technology movement was fortunate to have an eloquent spokesperson to explain it to the rest of the world. That person was E. F. Schumacher, who in 1973 published a book that became the rallying point for the new movement. This was *Small is Beautiful: A Study of Economics as if People Mattered*. Schumacher took apart the philosophical basis of the well-meaning foreign aid programs of the developed nations and argued that a different approach was needed, one that took people from where they were and helped them reach the next step, not one that came in and tried to institute the most efficient high technology solution to all their problems.

Schumacher illustrated the mismatch between the stated goals of foreign aid programs in the developed countries and the results that followed from these programs. Citing an earlier British Government White Paper on Overseas Development, he quoted the government's stated aim:

> To do what lies within our power to help the developing countries to provide their people with the material opportunities for using their talents, of living a full and happy life and steadily improving their lot.[1]

Unfortunately, Schumacher continued, the "full and happy life" seems to be getting no closer to happening than ever. Part of the reason is that the foreign aid programs have encouraged more and more people in the developing countries to leave the countryside and migrate to the cities, where they remain unemployed and in dire poverty. The problem, he said, is not so much that the amount of aid is inadequate, but that it is directed to the wrong places. In virtually all developing countries, a "dual economy" has emerged,

> ...in which there are two different patterns of living as widely separated from each other as two different worlds. It is not a matter of some people being rich and others being poor, both being united by a common way of life: it is a matter of two ways of life existing side by side in such a manner that even the humblest member of one disposes of a daily income which is a high multiple of the income accruing to even the hardest working member of the other. The

---

1. Quoted in E. F. Schumacher, *Small is Beautiful: A Study of Economics as if People Mattered*, (London: Blond & Briggs, 1973), p. 136.

social and political tensions arising from the dual economy are too obvious to require description.

> In the dual economy of a typical developing country, we may find fifteen per cent of the population in the modern sector, mainly confined to one or two big cities. The other eighty-five percent exists in the rural areas and small towns. ...[M]ost of the development effort goes into the big cities, which means that eighty-five per cent of the population are largely by-passed. What is to become of them? Simply to assume that the modern sector in the big cities will grow until it has absorbed almost the entire population—which is, of course, what has happened in many of the highly developed countries—is utterly unrealistic.[1]

The course of action that Schumacher proposed was that foreign aid should instead concentrate on the 85 percent or so of the population that lived in rural areas, creating workplaces for them where they live, not in the metropolitan areas. The workplaces should not call for great capital expenditure to set up. Rather, the most important consideration is that they should be created in large numbers and capable of employing many people. Whatever skills are required should be as simple as possible so the local population will be able to run it all themselves, including not just production, but also organization, finance, marketing, etc. And it should work with local materials so far as possible.

Inappropriate Technology

Most efforts that have been made by the developed nations to help developing countries are based on what would be effective in the First World. The assumption behind these projects seems to have been that if these projects are what made the developed nations rich, putting them into the poor countries can only help them get a step up. Most of these projects are large and capital intensive. Typical projects would be: steelworks, chemical works, dams, airports, and power stations—all hallmarks of the highly industrialized nations and all entailing a high level of trade in hard currencies with the developed nations. The idea was that such projects would give the developing countries some way of producing a product or service that they could sell to raise cash which they could then use to build their own economies. Unfortunately, these projects

---

1. *Ibid.*, pp. 136-137.

tended to produce islands of development, employing a very small number of people, amid a surrounding environment of extreme poverty where the great majority of the population lived and remained destitute.

These projects and this type of aid is what Schumacher and the others in his movement called "Inappropriate Technology." This would only lead to a greater divide in the poor countries and would virtually guarantee that the impoverished in the countryside—or, even worse, those who migrated to the cities and found no work— would remain poor without any hope of changing their circumstances. Appropriate, intermediate technology was instead proposed as a means to give these poor nations some hope of improving their lives.

Success Stories of Appropriate Technology

To see that Appropriate Technology actually works, one does not need to search among the smaller Third World countries to find some economy that has pulled itself up using the approach recommended by Schumacher et al. The best example is the world's strongest economy: the United States. Another example, with a rather different twist is the world's largest country, China.

Going for the Cheap in the U.S.A.

Consider the U.S. position in the 19th century: Britain was the world leader of the Industrial Revolution and Europe represented the rest of the industrialized world. The U.S. was economically dependent on British trade in much the same way that Third World countries are dependent today on the industrialized nations. The U.S. (and likewise Canada) was largely a supplier of resources to Britain and the rest of Europe. It had little indigenous industry that helped it build its own economy. However, from the time of the American Revolution in the late 18th century, the U.S. had begun taking steps to set up its own manufacturing industries in a way suited to a largely unpopulated, rapidly expanding frontier country.

An example is the railroad industry. In Britain, where the railways were first developed, the distances from one center to another were relatively short. The British engineers built excellent locomotives with superb engineering. They also laid track in the straightest and shortest possible route from one point to another, building bridges and tunnels as necessary. Their service was good and reliable, and was a model for everywhere else in the world. In the United States, railroads were originally built on the British model, and the locomotives were imported. It was not long before the Americans realized that they had somewhat different priorities.

Aside from the main centers on the east coast, the distances that American railroads needed to traverse to get from one point to another were much greater than those in Britain. The British model would be prohibitively expensive to implement across the United States. The first compromise was to lay track *around* natural obstacles instead of forcing the line to go straight through them. It was a lot less expensive to go around a mountain than to tunnel through it. If then the train took a little longer to get to the destination, that did not matter as much, given the savings on construction and maintenance. Having decided on routes with more curves and more changes in elevation, the next problem was the choosing the appropriate types of locomotives.

British locomotives in the early 19th century were all built with just four wheels, which was ideal for the British tracks. However, in the U.S., these locomotives did not do at all well on the many sharp curves and inclines. Americans took on the problem of building locomotives that would suit their situation. The result was a uniquely American design. The drive wheels of the locomotive were at the back while the front rested on a separately hinged "bogie" that could turn with the track and prevent derailment. In addition, the front of the engine was equipped with a large V-shaped grate that cleared the track of obstacles that might wander in the way and cause severe accidents. These were nicknamed "cow-catchers," which pretty well explains their function. Altogether, the American design was, by British standards, slapdash and of clearly inferior workmanship. But it suited the problems of North America in a way that designs for Europe could not.

A locomotive in use in 1879 in the state of Wisconsin, with a bogie and a cow-catcher.

The railroad may not seem like the most convincing example of Appropriate Technology, especially if its connotation of "intermediate" technology is kept in mind. Railroads were the cutting edge of technology in their day. The main point here is that the Americans did not try to emulate the top-notch engineering of the Europeans, but instead, found what worked for them. Nor did they attempt to reproduce the high level of craftsmanship for which the British were so well known and respected. That was the product of a long tradition going back to the Middle Ages. It was not something that could be reproduced in an environment that was just breaking its colonial dependence. Instead, the Americans pioneered a new way of manufacturing, so distinctive that it gained the name abroad of the "American system of manufactures."

Until the middle of the 19th century, quality machines and tools were made one at a time, in the workshop of a single craftsman who made every part and fit them to each other. This required great skill, which was not found in abundance in the United States. The new approach that the Americans introduced was to have each part of a machine or any other complex device made by a single person or team. The part would be made to very careful specifications, and every part made had to be virtually identical to every other. Then, when all the parts had been made, the device was assembled into the finished product. The virtue of the system was that the craftsmen only had to master making one thing. Even more important, the finished product was merely an assembly of interchangeable parts. Thus, if any one part failed, it could be replaced by an identical component right from the factory. In the older system, a defective part had to be re-engineered and retooled to fit the single device in which it was to be used. Some of the best examples of this new manufacturing scheme were the Colt revolver, Eli Whitney's cotton gin, and the McCormick reaper. All of these were essential to the American economy, and all were used far from the workshops in which they were made. Interchangeability had a particularly important function in America that it did not have in more densely populated Europe. Nevertheless, it caught on worldwide anyway.

Walking on Two Legs in China

The example from China is more recent. In communist China of the mid-20th century under the leadership of Chairman Mao Zedong, the country was building up a heavy manufacturing and processing industry, based on the Russian model with the guidance of Russian expertise. It was perhaps not what the largely agrarian Chinese society needed most. In 1960, China severed its close ties with the U.S.S.R. and began to change its focus more toward decentralization and self-sufficiency instead of making industrial products more suitable to a different economy. However, the heavy industry was already in place and was a major contributor to the economy. The task was to find a way to address the needs of the Chinese people that were not being met by premature industrialization, and also to take advantage of the very long tradition of Chinese workmanship and organization that long predated the Russian culture with which they had more recently aligned themselves.

In his announcements of this new emphasis for China and the plan to make the best of both worlds, Mao used the phrase "walking on two legs." It would not throw out the huge and often inefficient Russian-style industries, but instead would build up others, more "Chinese," around them. In practice, this included establishing smaller factories or power plants in the countryside and reviving older technologies of manufacturing and traditional Chinese medicine. Some of these initiatives were very successful in pulling the Chinese economy into self-sufficiency. On the other hand, some of them were great disasters, attractive ideologically but proving not to be practical ventures. For example, small iron production facilities were re-opened, using small-scale blast furnaces of a kind developed by the Chinese over a thousand years before. These were extremely inefficient and became environmental disasters since they ran on charcoal. These excesses were part of what are sometimes referred to as the follies of the "Great Leap Forward," but overall the plan has worked. China has built up economic independence by falling back on local talent and locally available materials, using methods that would be considered totally outdated elsewhere.

The Aims of Appropriate Technology

There is an important difference between the aims of Appropriate Technology and the broader humanitarian outlook typified by the statement of purpose of the British Government cited by Schumacher above. Appropriate Technology does not seek to make Third World countries into copies of First World nations. Instead, it tries to help these countries find a long-term sustainable future on their own terms and with their own means—and, importantly, loosen the economic ties to the developed nations that have kept them mired in their untenable position. This should be achieved by employing local skills, local materials, and local finances, if possible. Whatever help is proposed will work only if it is compatible with the local culture and satisfies the actual wishes and needs of the people. The countries in need of assistance have no room for failed experiments. They live at all times very close to disaster in the form of famines or epidemics.

Appropriate Technology Equipment

The sort of equipment appropriate for use in the poorest of countries is that which will help them conserve essential natural resources, such as water, or harness a readily available source of power, such as with a windmill, or produce a fuel out of existing materials, such as bio-gas. It must be simple enough to be readily understood and repaired if necessary and must fit the local social structure. Superbly engineered simple windmills can still fail if they have a low tolerance for misalignment and can only be repaired by a qualified engineer. A bio-gas conversion device that produces a combustible gas for cooking from human and animal waste products can be a great boon to societies where no other fuel for cooking is readily available. But these devices require careful tending, and the equipment can be misused.

When the necessities of food and shelter have been addressed, some help can be given toward establishing viable local industries. Here care needs to be taken that the industries will provide jobs for many, not replace what had been done by human labour, thereby leaving more unemployed. Too many projects begun with support from the industrialized nations rearranged the economies of the countries where they were introduced by making a few people richer and removing the last shred of self-sufficiency of the majority.

How All This Happened

To understand the plight of the poorest Third World countries, we need to consider how they fit into the whole history of human society since the beginnings of civilization. The population of the world has increased over time from a small number of human beings living by finding food where they could and moving on when they couldn't, to a vast number of people crowding almost every corner of the Earth. Since we are a clever species, we have found ways of getting the better of our environment, fending off predators (including diseases) and developing more food. That has allowed us to increase our numbers, more or less exponentially, allowing for the occasional setbacks due to famines, wars, and epidemics.

But we have not all proceeded along the same path, and we have had different levels of success in improving our lot. Population pressures have been a great motivator, encouraging people to find new and better ways of doing things. Agriculture itself, from its very beginnings, was an answer to the problem of how to feed everyone from the resources locally available. The success of agriculture was very much dependent on where one lived. The first societies to settle down and make a success out of farming were those that lived on or near rich, loose soils that were naturally irrigated by rivers bringing further nutrients to the land. These people soon found that they could raise crops that were in excess of their immediate requirements. That gave them wealth.

It also gave them the ability to support more people, and without fail, more people were soon on hand, requiring more food. That encouraged more innovation in farming methods and prompted the spread of the population into other lands. This is how civilization began and developed, always endeavoring to keep ahead of the basic necessities of life. Along with the provision of a secure supply of food and safe shelter, the institutions of culture developed, totally setting us apart from other species. Just as agriculture developed differently in different parts of the world, human civilization developed in many forms.

Always, the population kept rising to meet the food supply, or at least it did so until those basic necessities were so well covered that the other aspects of human life became more important. During the Industrial Revolution, life changed dramatically for people living in the countries that did industrialize. Part of that change was a vast improvement in nutrition, sanitation, and health care that served to increase life expectancy and raise the conditions of life. These fundamental changes to the nature of human life are primarily confined to the industrialized nations. In these nations, a remarkable change took place in the human propensity to procreate and increase the population to its limit. People found that life was better without so many children to support. Women found that there was more to life than being pregnant and raising young. The birth rate began to fall.

But the falling birth rate occurred only in those countries that had experienced these changes in their way of life. For the ithree-fourths of the world that has not become industrialized, the pattern of life is still much like what it was before the Industrial Revolution. Most of life is concerned with acquiring food and shelter. But there is a difference in their lives compared to what it was before the Industrial Revolution. Now, most of the world has the benefit of at least some of the improved sanitation and health care that so changed life expectancies in the industrialized world. What that benefit has done is remove some of the checks that have held back population increases in those lands.

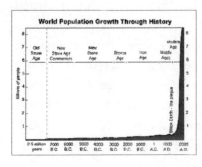

In those countries where none of the other ibenefits of industrialization have penetrated, there is little incentive to refrain from having children. Now, with lowered infant mortality and safer birth procedures for the mothers, more and more children are being born—in the very countries that are least able to support them.

As mentioned above, for most of history, the world human population has increased at an exponential rate. That means that it has a fairly constant doubling period. However, in the last hundred years or so, the doubling period has been getting shorter, which is to say that the population is increasing at faster than an exponential rate. Yet, in the industrialized nations it is hardly increasing at all.

This is an unbalanced and bizarre situation that defies an easy solution. If no steps are taken, then the poorest countries will probably continue to overpopulate and soon have food requirements way above the most optimistic estimate of possible supplies. This is unacceptable to the citizens of the industrialized nations who do not wish to stand idle while hundreds of millions of people starve. Less altruistically, a very real fear is that if a collapse occurs in the Third World, the economy of the entire world will go down with it. The Green Revolution was a program to meet that need for food with all the power of modern technology. Aside from all the ireasons why the Green Revolution in its initial form was unworkable, if it had done everything it set out to do, the effect would have been to foster an even higher population within a few years.

The Appropriate Technology movement recognized that in some sense the problems of the Third World have to be solved by the Third World, and the best that we can do is give them help getting started toward a viable solution. The premise of the Appropriate Technology movement seems to be that if a stable, albeit simple, economy can be established in a Third World country, one that has nearly full employment and a certain amount of dignity of life and self-reliance, then the citizens of such a country will raise their ambitions, seek education and training, and find ways to keep their populations within manageable limits. The evidence that supports this all comes from the First World, where those things did happen.

The difficulty is that the Third World countries with the most serious population problems are those least able to turn themselves around. The optimists are those who think it will be possible to increase the food supply in the nations that need it most, institute a massive and effective birth control program in those countries, instill a sense of dignity and a means of self-sufficiency in the destitute nations, and accomplish all this before the crisis breaks all around us. The pessimists are those who think that these goals are unattainable and instead are preparing for the worst. The vast majority, at least in the developed countries, don't think about any of this at all.

PART SEVEN

Fouling Our Nest

Throughout the history of human civilization, two trends have continued steadily, with only a few reversals. These are: (1) greater and greater technological invention, leading to a more comfortable and interesting life, and (2) greater health and nutrition, leading to more and more people. The technological invention succeeds by using more and more natural resources and leaving behind more rubbish in its wake. The greater number of people crowd the livable space on the planet and make more demands on the environment. Inevitably, if we learn to produce poisons for some human purpose, those poisons have to go somewhere when they have done what they were intended to do. For most of human history, where the refuse and the discards went was of little concern. There was always another place to go to. In fact, during the Industrial Revolution, it was a sign of progress to be living amid disfigured land, undrinkable waters, and choking air. By the 20th century, this no longer seemed a source of pride.

The awareness of the environment we live in suddenly came to the attention of the public in the last half of the 20th century when it was pointed out that disasters were just around the corner if we did not begin to control what came out of and went into the environment we lived in.

So much of that public awareness is attributable to one person, Rachel Carson, that a chapter is devoted to discussing what she started. The rest of Part Seven is a look at some of the ways that we have been maltreating our environment: our water, land, and air.

For Further Reading

Anderson, Stephen. O. and K. Madhava Sarma. *Protecting the Ozone Layer: The United Nations History*. London: Earthscan Publications, 2002.

Ashworth, W. *The Late, Great Lakes: An Environmental History*. New York: Knopf, 1986.

Bojkov, Rumen D. *The Changing Ozone Layer*. New York: World Meteorological Organization and United Nations Environment Programme, 1995.

Burger. Joanna. *Oil Spills*. New Brunswick, NJ: Rutgers University Press, 1997.

Byrne, John, and Daniel Rich, eds. *Energy and Environment: The Policy Challenge*. Energy Policy Studies Series, Vol. 6. New Brunswick, NJ: Transaction Publishers, 1992.

Carson, Rachel. *Silent Spring*. Boston: Houghton Mifflin, 1962.

Cook, Elizabeth. *Ozone Protection in the United States: Elements of Success*. New York: World Resources Institute, 1996.

Department of the Environment; Central Directorate on Environmental Pollution. *Chlorofluorocarbons and Their Effect on Stratospheric Ozone*, 2nd report. Pollution Paper No. 15. London: Her Majestyís Stationery Office, 1979.

Environment Canada. *The Ozone Primer (La couche d'ozone)* Ottawa: Environment Canada, 1999..

_____. *Providing Cleaner Air to Canadians (De l'air pur pour les Canadiens)* Ottawa: Environment Canada, 2001..

Gordon, Anita, and David Suzuki. *It's a Matter of Survival*. Toronto: Stoddart, 1990.

Glasstone, Samuel, and Walter H. Jordan. *Nuclear Power and its Environmental Effects*. La Grange Park, IL: American Nuclear Society, 1981.

Gribbin, John. *The Hole in the Sky: Man's Threat to the Ozone Layer* New York: Bantam, 1988..

Harris, Jeremy. *Chemical Pesticide Markets, Health Risks and Residues*. Biopesticides Series No. 1. New York: CABI Publishing, 2000.

Hester, Ronald E., and Roy M. Harrison. *Causes and Environmental Implications of Increased UV-B Radiation*. Issues in Environmental Science and Technology, No. 14. Cambridge: The Royal Society of Chemistry, 2000.

_____. *Environmental Impact of Power Generation*. Issues in Environmental Science and Technology, No. 11. Cambridge: The Royal Society of Chemistry, 1999.

Hostetter, Martha, ed. *Energy Policy*. The Reference Shelf, Vol 74, No. 2. New York: H. W. Wilson, 2002.

Hynes, H. Patricia. *The Recurring Silent Spring.* New York: Pergamon Press, 1989.

Kandel, Robert. *Our Changing Climate.* New York: McGraw-Hill, 1992.

Litfin, Karen T. *Ozone Discourses: Science and Politics in Global Environmental Cooperation.* New York: Columbia University Press, 1994.

Livernash, Robert, and Eric Rodenburg. *Population Change, Resources, and the Environment.* Population Bulletin, Vol. 53, No. 1 (March, 1998).

Lomborg, Bjørn.*The Skeptical Environmentalist: Measuring the Real State of the World.* Cambridge: Cambridge University Press, 1998.

Mangun, William R., and Daniel H. Henning. *Managing the Environmental Crisis,* 2nd ed. Durham, NC: Duke University Press, 1999.

Marco, Gino J., Robert M. Hollingworth, and William Durham, eds. *Silent Spring Revisited.* Washington, D.C.: American Chemical Society, 1987.

Melosi, Martin V. *Effluent America: Cities, Industries, Energy, and the Environment.* Pittsburgh: University of Pittsburgh Press, 2001.

Outwater, Alice. *Water: A Natural History.* New York: Basic Books, 1996.

Pimentel, David, and Hugh Lehman, eds. *The Pesticide Question: Environment, Economics, and Ethics.* New York: Chapman & Hall, 1993.

Pompe, Jeffrey J., and James R. Rinehart. *Environmental Conflict: In Search of Common Ground.* Albany, NY: State University of New York Press, 2002.

Ponting, Clive. *A Green History of the World: The Environment and the Collapse of Great Civilizations.* New York: Penguin, 1993.

Owen, Lewis A., and Tim Unwin, eds. *Environmental Management: Readings and Case Studies.* Oxford: Blackwell Publishers, 1997.

Ragsdale, Nancy N., and James N. Seiber, eds. *Pesticides: Managing Risks and Optimizing Benefits.* ACS Symposium Series, No. 734. Washington: American Chemical Society, 1999.

Ponting, Clive. *A Green History of the World: The Environment and the Collapse of Great Civilizations.* New York: Penguin, 1993.

Reid, Stephen J. *Ozone and Climate Change: A Beginner's Guide.* Amsterdam: Gordon and Breach Science Publishers, 2000.

Van Kooten, G. Cornelius, Erwin H. Bulte, and A.R.E. Sinclair, eds. *Conserving Nature's Diversity: Insights from Biology, Ethics, and Economics.* Aldershot, Hampshire, England: Ashgate Publishing Limited, 2000.

Whorton, James. *Before Silent Spring: Pesticides and Public Health in Pre-DDT America.* Princeton: Princeton University Press, 1974.

Worldwatch Institute. *Vital Signs 2001: Trends That Are Shaping Our Future.* New York: W. W. Norton, 2001.

Rachel Carson, author of *Silent Spring*.

Chapter 29

Silent Spring

Public awareness of environmental issues started with a jolt in 1962 when a modest marine biologist named Rachel Carson published a book entitled *Silent Spring.* Carson had previously published two bestsellers on marine life, *The Sea Around Us,* in 1951, and *The Edge of the Sea,* in 1955. Once the financial success of the first of these was clear, she resigned her position as a scientist with the U.S. Bureau of Fisheries to devote herself to writing full time. When her next book was ready for publication, her publisher, Houghton Mifflin, realizing that it would be another bestseller arranged for part of it to appear serialized in *The New Yorker* magazine in the summer of 1962, followed by the publication of the book in October. It would then be the October selection of the Book-of-the-Month Club. This maximum level promotion assured that her book would come to the attention of the largest audience possible, and the preview chapters in *The New Yorker* meant that it would already be being discussed before it was in the bookstores.

Silent Spring took aim at the overuse of pesticides in America, claiming that their use is extremely dangerous to the health of everyone, not just the pests they are supposed to kill. Since the basic gist of her argument was clear from her *New Yorker* articles, the chemical industry had time to prepare its defence before the book was published in the fall. An article in the *New York Times* on July 22, 1962, reported

> The men who make the pesticides are crying foul. "Crass commercialism or idealistic flag waving," scoffs one industrial toxicologist. "We are aghast," says another. "Our members are raising hell;" reports a trade association.
>
> Some agricultural chemicals concerns have set their scientists to analyzing Miss Carson's work, line by line. Other companies are preparing briefs defending the use of their products. Meetings have been held in Washington and New York. Statements are being drafted and counter-attacks plotted.[1]

---

1. John M. Lee, *"Silent Spring is now Noisy Summer,"* New York Times, July 22, 1962.

When the book did appear and its sales skyrocketed, the American television network, CBS, scheduled an hour-long program to discuss it. Two of the program's regular sponsors withdrew their financial support, but the network went ahead anyway. The U.S. President, John F. Kennedy, discussed *Silent Spring* at a press conference, and Congress started holding hearings on the uses and hazards of pesticides.

There are only a few books that can be said to have started a whole movement of social reform and *Silent Spring* is one of them. Another book to which it has often been compared is Harriet Beecher Stowe's *Uncle Tom's Cabin* that dramatized the plight of the slave workers on southern plantations in the American south. Some people go so far as to say that Stowe was responsible for galvanizing the American people to reject slavery, leading to the American Civil War. It seems that President Abraham Lincoln agreed with this assessment. When he met her during the height of the war, he is said to have greeter her with, "So you're the little lady who started this whole thing." In an echo of that, when Rachel Carson was called to testify before Congress in 1963, Senator Abraham Ribicoff welcomed her to the session with the words, "Miss Carson, you are the lady who started all this."

What she started was the environmental movement, a general consciousness and awareness by the public of the dangers of products and practices in modern industrial life that can have unforeseen side effects that may be worse than their advantages.

DDT

If *Silent Spring* is remembered for one thing alone, it is that it led to the banning of the pesticide DDT in the United States. Much of Carson's book is a vigorous and concerted attack on what was then considered to be a wonder chemical that made the world safe from insects of all sorts.

DDT is the acronym for dichloro-diphenyl-trichloro-ethane. It is one of those amazing synthesized chemicals that arose from the laboratories of the chemical industry and proved to have very strong effects. First synthesized in 1874, it was not until 1939 that it was discovered to be a powerful insecticide. When that happened, there was a rush to use DDT widely to control all sorts of insects in virtually every setting. The power of DDT was welcomed and considered to be a great step forward in civilized life. Dr. Paul Müller of Switzerland, who discovered the deadly effects, was awarded the Nobel Prize.

In the Second World War, DDT was used to control lice on soldiers and displaced persons. It was applied liberally in a dust form to the bodies of thousands of people. It killed the lice and appeared to have no ill effect on the people. As a result, DDT was deemed to be harmless to humans. Rachel Carson pointed out that the skin does not readily absorb DDT in powder form, and that is why it did the soldiers little or no harm. But in later uses, DDT was generally applied as a spray, dissolved in oil. In that form, it is highly toxic.

DDT was used to control insects everywhere. Since it was considered harmless to humans, no precautions were taken to prevent human contact. Public beaches, playgrounds, parks, and city streets were all sprayed regularly to rid them of mosquitoes and other pests. Children often followed the spray trucks right into the areas sprayed; sometimes they even ran through the spray for fun.

DDT was sprayed in an oil solution because it would then adhere to whatever it landed on, or

Mosquito control with DDT. Jones Beach State Park, New York, 1945. The sign on the truck begins: "D.D.T. Powerful Insecticide, Harmless to Humans."

that landed on it, and would have time to do its damage. But substances that are soluble in oil rather than in water also do not pass easily through the body. If a human being swallows DDT, it will be absorbed into the body and stored in the fatty tissues of the body for extended periods. Small amounts can therefore accumulate to become large amounts and tend to lodge in the liver and kidneys. Moreover, anything stored in the body's fatty tissues becomes more concentrated than it was when it entered the body, perhaps 10 to 15 times more concentrated. Given that even after washing, minute traces of DDT were present on most foods that had been sprayed with the chemical by farmers, these traces could accumulate in the body and quickly reach considerable concentrations.

Any substance that lodges in the fatty tissues will also remain there if that animal becomes food for another, higher up the food chain. Carson gave the following example:

> …fields of alfalfa are dusted with DDT; meal is later prepared from the alfalfa and fed to hens; the hens lay eggs which contain DDT. Or the hay, containing residues of 7 to 8 parts per million, may be fed to cows. The DDT will turn up in the milk in the amount of about 3 parts per million, but in butter made from this milk the

Spraying for mosquites in Florida.

concentration may run to 65 parts per million. Through such a process of transfer, what started out as a very small amount of DDT may end as a heavy concentration.[1]

DDT was the most widely used of the pesticides that Carson analyzed, but it was not the most toxic. Several others were also in wide usage for special purposes, ranging from getting rid of aphids in the garden to eliminating nasty infestations of insects in living quarters. Carson recounted the features of each of a number of these poisons, enough to give anyone pause who persisted in using them. One of the most horrific stories was the following about endrin, another compound chemically related to DDT, but more toxic.

> In one of the most tragic cases of endrin poisoning...efforts had been made to take precautions apparently considered adequate. A year-old child had been taken by his American parents to live in Venezuela. There were cockroaches in the house to which they moved, and after a few days a spray containing endrin was used. The baby and the small family dog were taken out of the house before the spraying was done about nine o'clock one morning. After the spraying the floors were washed. The baby and dog were returned to the house in midafternoon. An hour or so later the dog vomited, went into convulsions, and died. At 10 p.m. on the evening of the same day the baby also vomited, went into convulsions and lost consciousness. After that fateful contact with endrin, this normal, healthy child became little more than a vegetable—unable to see or hear, subject to frequent muscular spasms, apparently completely cut off from contact with his surroundings.[2]

Because of the slow accumulation of DDT and related toxins in the fatty tissues of the body, the harmful effects may take a long time to show up, but when they do, they

1. Rachel Carson, *Silent Spring.* Boston: Houghton Mifflin, 1962, pp. 23-24 of the 1994 edition.

2. *Ibid.*, p. 27.

may be irreversible. Carson reported another case of a housewife who wished to rid her home of spiders. She obtained an aerosol spray of DDT and sprayed her house thoroughly, especially the basement. Though she felt ill afterwards, she recovered in a few days, and then a month later repeated the spraying, falling ill again, and then recovering. She did this one more time some weeks after that and got more seriously ill. She was diagnosed with leukemia and died the next month.

Pesticide Runoffs

One of the surprises that Rachel Carson had for the public in *Silent Spring* was the disturbing news that pesticides used on farmers' fields or in cities to control insects or lawn weeds enter the water supply, and from there, end up in our bodies. Carson documented cases of drinking water found to have pesticide residues sufficient to kill test fish in a laboratory in four hours, or of water downstream from sprayed fields that had gone through municipal water treatment purification and still was toxic enough to kill fish further downstream.

Among her more convincing arguments was her explanation of how pesticide residues become more and more concentrated as they move up the food chain. Even very dilute quantities of a poison, not enough to harm anything larger than an insect, can easily be lethal to much larger creatures as one animal eats another which has poisons remaining in its fatty tissues. One of her dramatic stories concerned the efforts to combat gnats at Clear Lake, California, a lake north of San Francisco that was popular with fishermen. It was also popular with a small gnat that inhabited the lake in great numbers, much to the annoyance of the fishermen and the cottagers around the shore.

In 1949, a program to rid the lake of gnats was instituted, using the pesticide DDD, a product similar to DDT but deemed less dangerous to fish. The insecticide was applied to the lake at the very dilute rate of one part chemical for 70 million parts of water. Five years later, a second treatment was applied at the rate of one to 50 million parts. These rates were considered so tiny that nothing larger than an insect was believed to be affected by them. Nevertheless, within a few months, the western grebes, a fish-eating bird, began to die. In 1957, after yet another application of the insecticide at the rate of 1 to 50 million parts of water, the dead grebes were found to have DDD in their fatty tissues at a concentration of 1600 parts per million—80 thousand times the concentration applied to the water! On further investigation, it was discovered that the fish that the grebes fed on (and that human beings caught and ate) also had significant DDD residues. The lake had a complete food chain, from plankton to small fish to large fish to the birds. At each stage the concentration of DDD was enormously higher than the previous stage. Meanwhile, no trace of DDD at all remained in the water of the lake, even shortly after the last application.[1]

This example was a case of deliberate application of a pesticide to water, though in a miniscule concentration. Other examples Carson cited were totally unintentional, where spraying of a field with a pesticide resulted in a contamination of the groundwater, or even worse, where a combination of industrial chemicals accidentally present in the same place had spontaneously formed a lethal poison and leaked into water supplies.

Carson's illustrative horror stories made the problem of water pollution by pesticides understandable to the public and also prompted professionals to look more closely at issues of water quality, particularly of drinking water and waters where edible fish spawn. Even though the worst of the chemicals that she wrote about have now been banned from North America (but not from the Third World), some of their residues remain and have accumulated to higher concentrations. Moreover, there are now more pesticides in use than at the time of *Silent Spring*, and the quantities used are greater than ever. Their application may be better targeted and their side effects minimized, but the dangers are greater than ever.

Killing the Soil

It must surely seem surprising to biologists, especially botanists, how little the public understands about the biology of plant growth and the function of the soil. Perhaps the public consciousness has never gone much beyond the ancient idea of four elements: earth, air, fire, and water. Earth is often taken as a given. It may be rocky, sandy, loose, packed, or have other visible and palpable characteristics that the ordinary person can fathom, but rarely is it understood that what we call earth, or dirt, or soil, is a teeming mass of life, and if it were not teeming, it would not serve its purpose.

In the 19th century, Charles Darwin was fascinated with the formation of soil and wrote an entire book about the role of earthworms in the soil. His book, *The Formation of Vegetable Mould, Through the Action of Worms, With Observations on Their Habits*, opened the minds of readers interested in the details of nature to the complexity of the soil and its delicate formation. Darwin calculated that earthworms alone might add three to five centimeters of soil to an area every ten years. This is in addition to their important

---

1. *Ibid.*, pp. 46-48..

functions of breaking up and aerating the soil, which keeps it loose enough for plants to root. Soil itself is an organic product composed of a mass of living things. Bacteria and fungi make up most of the weight of soil, and much of the rest of it consists of masses of microscopic insects such as mites and springtails. It is all of these minute life forms that make the soil a medium for growth. Were they not present, soil would be so much pulverized mineral, incapable of nurturing anything.

Spraying pesticides.

What then happens when a pesticide is sprayed on a farmer's field or a homeowner's garden for the purpose of controlling certain insects that destroy crops and flowers, or weeds that crowd out the desired plants? This is a question that Rachel Carson put to her readers. Pesticides have a broad spectrum. That is, they kill anything in sight. To cover a field with an insecticide, such as DDT, or a herbicide, such as 2,4-D, will not just affect the target organism; it may kill so much else that the soil loses all resilience. Carson asked, "Is it reasonable to suppose that we can apply a broad-spectrum insecticide to kill the burrowing larval stages of a crop-destroying insect, for example without also killing the 'good' insects whose function may be the essential one of breaking down organic matter?"[1] What seemed the most astounding is that in the rush to use the new wonder chemicals, these consequences were not given much thought. Carson was only able to cite a few studies of the effect of pesticides on soils, because only a few studies had been done. However, she did effectively sound the alarm.

Poisons For Sale in the Supermarkets

It was not just the existence of these dangerous toxins that bothered Carson; it was also their ready availability for anyone to purchase whether they knew what they were buying or not. Supermarket shelves were stocked with deadly pesticides "with the pickles and olives across the aisle and the bath and laundry soaps adjoining." Many of the insecticides were sold in glass containers, which, if dropped and smashed on a supermarket floor could splash on anyone nearby and easily send them into convulsions.

---

1. *Ibid.*, p. 56.

Moreover, many convenience products were made for the kitchen(!) to keep insects at bay, for example, shelf paper with impregnated insecticide on both sides. Floor waxes were sold containing enough poison to kill any insect that walked across it. Blankets were routinely mothproofed by being impregnated with the deadly insecticide dieldrin.

Home and garden pesticides were a regular part of the arsenal of every household. The four pesticides shown here were discovered lurking in the back of the author's basement cupboard.

Home gardeners were *expected* to use all kinds of lethal sprays and dusts to keep their gardens free of pests, otherwise they were viewed as irresponsible. Gadgets were sold (and still are) to attach to garden hoses that will spray a fine mist of chlordane or dieldrin or another lethal poison across the lawn or garden. These were extremely dangerous to the person using the attachment and were also a menace to the groundwater. There were even attachments to power lawnmowers that sent up a mist of poisons as the homeowner mowed his lawn. And yet none of this was distributed with warnings about their dangers, or if they were, it was hidden in fine print.

And this is but a small sample of the terrifying enumeration of dangers that Carson recounted. Others included massive deaths to the robin population in areas that had sprayed for Dutch elm disease, and rivers nearly devoid of their usual healthy salmon population because of runoff from fields sprayed with insecticides. Her examples and her forceful writing got the point across to a concerned public.

The Chemical Industry Fights Back

The pesticide industry had annual sales of about $300 million. If the public suddenly turned against them, they would be in deep trouble. Moreover, the many scientists who worked with pesticides had a different view of the situation. They believed that they understood the risks and had weighed them against the dangers from insects and weeds and made the right choices. There was a vigorous rebuttal of *Silent Spring* underway even before the book was officially published.

One of the spokesmen for the pesticide industry, Dr. Robert White-Stevens went on record as follows:

The major claims of Miss Rachel Carson's book, *Silent Spring*, are gross distortions of the actual facts, completely unsupported by scientific, experimental evidence, and general practical experience in the field. Her suggestion that pesticides are in fact biocides destroying all life is obviously absurd in the light of the fact that without selective biologicals these compounds would be completely useless.

The real threat, then, to the survival of man is not chemical but biological, in the shape of hordes of insects that can denude our forests, sweep over our crop lands, ravage our food supply and leave in their wake a train of destitution and hunger, conveying to an undernourished population the major diseases scourges of mankind.[1]

The defense of the chemical industry was clear: without pesticides, insects would take over and that would be far worse. There is no reason to think they did not firmly believe this. Moreover, Carson herself was not advocating that all pesticides be banned, only that their use be controlled much more and that other alternative controls be thoroughly investigated.

The Start of the Environment Movement

What Rachel Carson accomplished with *Silent Spring* was to involve the public in the consideration of matters that do and will affect all of us and the world we live in, instead of leaving all such questions for the experts in various fields, who might have been working at cross purposes. She got the attention of President Kennedy and of the U.S. Congress. After a number of hearings, Congress did act, banning DDT from use in the United States. (It is still widely used in the Third World.) A few years later, in 1970, a large public event was held in the United States to raise consciousness about environmental issues. This was Earth Day, when many speeches were made and loose commitments given to start thinking about environmental consequences and to pass laws making environment abuse punishable by fines or imprisonment. That same year, the U.S. organized the Environmental Protection Agency to oversee the uses of pesticides and pass judgement on other commercial projects that might impact on the environment.

---

1. Jonathan Norton Leonard, "Rachel Carson Dies of Cancer; *Silent Spring* Author was 56," *New York Times*, April 15, 1964.

As so often happens with people of great influence, Carson's own writings are carefully thought out and measured, saying only what she could support and not railing against those who disagree with her. But once said, her ideas came to be either worshipped or reviled by followers and foes, and on both sides were overstated and oversimplified. She might have been able to correct some of this misconception in the next few years as the environmental movement got underway, but unfortunately, she succumbed to cancer in 1964, just two years after the publication of *Silent Spring*.

The environment movement has suffered from an antagonism between those who are demanding a halt to all technological change and those who deny that there is a problem. Much of this antagonism remains—more about that in the final chapter—but a great deal has been done by saner minds to find better solutions to nature's challenges. *Silent Spring* was an effective wake-up call to the world, reminding us that despite our great technological triumphs, we don't really know enough to make nature do our bidding. That message, at least, does seem to have taken root. As an illustration of this, in his introduction to the 1994 edition of *Silent Spring*, then Vice-President Al Gore quoted pesticide industry spokesman, Dr. Robert White-Stevens in one of his more intransigent comments about the book:

> The crux, the fulcrum over which the argument chiefly rests, is that Miss Carson maintains that the balance of nature is a major force in the survival of man, whereas the modern chemist, the modern biologist and scientist, believes that man is steadily controlling nature.[1]

That sort of hubris has the ring of the early Industrial Revolution when it seemed that nothing could stand in the way of human ingenuity. It no longer represents the mainstream of opinion in science and technology. As Al Gore commented, "The very absurdity of that world view from today's perspective indicates how revolutionary Rachel Carson was."[2]

---

1.   Carson, *Silent Spring*, p. xvii.

2.   Ibid.

This photograph taken at the Wheeler
National Wildlife Refuge in the 1980s
shows the lingering effects of DDT.
Although the chemical is now banned, it
continues to contaminate the soil in certain
areas.

Paint in the water supply.

Chapter 30

Abusing the Water

The legacy of *Silent Spring* was the beginnings of a concerted effort by governments in all the industrialized nations to attend to their growing environmental problems. Using the power of laws and regulations, governments began to institute practices and bring about compliance intended to halt and perhaps even reverse the daily damage done to the environment by both industry and individuals. In the United States, the Environmental Protection Agency was formed in 1970, and two years later Congress passed the Federal Water Pollution Control Act—the "Clean Water Act."

Just the year before, the seriousness of the water problem in the United States was dramatized in a most embarrassing way for the city of Cleveland, Ohio. Cleveland is located on the Cuyahoga River, a major artery for freighters from Akron, Ohio to Lake Erie, into which it empties. On June 22, 1969, the river caught fire. It was so polluted with oil slicks and floating debris that a small flame that should have been extinguished immediately in water actually started a considerable blaze right on the river and had to be extinguished by fireboats. Cleveland, and with it the rest of the industrial United States, became an international joke.

The purpose of the Clean Water Act was to restore the waterways of the United States to something like their natural state. To be sure, one of the immediate problems with such intentions was to define what a "natural" state was. Almost every human action since the beginning of civilization has altered in one way or another the waterways beside which people live, so how do we now decide what is natural? The criterion settled upon was marvelously anthropocentric: natural meant what was most desirable to most people. What this came down to was that the rivers, streams, and lakes were to be safe for swimming and productive for fishing. To give credit, much progress was made toward those ends in the next decades, and some of the worst excesses were cleaned up. In Cleveland, for example, the Cuyahoga now has a considerable amount of recreational boating, along with waterfront bars and restaurants near the mouth of the river, where before only freighters and sewage could be seen.

Beavers

If a "natural" state of waterways is taken to mean the condition that waterways might remain in for a long time without human interference, one way to understand its characteristics is to consider the condition of the rivers, lakes, and streams before a significant number of people came to settle by them. For the Old World, it would be very difficult to reconstruct a setting before human settlement began to make major differences in the terrain. But, for the New World, one need only go back to the time before the huge influx of Europeans arrived, when there were relatively few people and those that there were did not live by farming and commerce.

In a very interesting book all about water,[1] Alice Outwater tries to reconstruct what the waterways of North America were like before European settlement and what happened to them during the colonial period and beyond. To illustrate the complex interactions of a natural environment, she focuses on the functions of one animal species, the beaver, and how that was disrupted by the settlers.

Beaver Pelts

A beaver.

The saga of the beaver is crucial because North America had many beavers, which lived and affected the rivers and streams everywhere and which were in great demand for their fur. The popularity of beaver pelts in Europe led to the growth of an industry in the New World that eventually decimated the beaver population and changed the character of the waters in which they lived.

To put this story in context, first consider the general conditions of life in Medieval Europe. Northern Europe was a cold place and indoor heating was either non-existent or woefully inadequate. All those who could afford to dressed in fur garments and slept under fur covers to keep warm. These garments became status symbols, with the more expensive and more desirable furs restricted to royalty and the wealthy. However, even the poor often wore some fur. Outwater comments that more furs were worn in the Middle Ages than at any time before or since.

---

1. Alice Outwater, *Water: A Natural History* (New York: Basic Books, 1996).

The fur trade was quite robust and very well organized throughout the Middle Ages. However, by the end of this period, about the time of the first European voyages of discovery across the ocean, fur-bearing animals across Europe had been hunted to near extinction. European furs were so difficult to find that trappers had moved into fRussia, trapping there and exporting pelts back to Western Europe. Outwater illustrates the enormous extent of this activity by citing two surviving records of the fur trade from the end of the 14th century. These records both refer to furs imported to England from the Baltics. Between July and September in 1384, a total of 382 982 furs were imported, and from March to November in 1390, another 323 624 were brought in. It was not long before fur-bearing animals were scarce even in Russia.

The beaver pelt was particularly prized because its fur was very dense and therefore suited the felting process for making hats. Beaver fur locks together to make an impermeable coat to protect the beaver in the cold waters they must endure, making these fur garments or hats waterproof. In addition, beavers were especially easy to trap because they settled in one location, building dams and constructing lodges there in which to raise their young.

When Europeans first arrived in the New World, they encountered native people basically living in a Stone Age civilization, using primitive tools made of flint, bone, and stone. Europeans had iron tools. As soon as the native Americans saw the superiority of these tools, they wanted to own them and were willing to provide whatever the Europeans wanted in order to get them. What they could provide that the Europeans wanted very badly were animal pelts, beavers in particular.

In Europe, beaver hats had gone out of fashion because no beaver pelts were available, but as soon as the supply from the New World started coming in, they became all the rage. By 1700, beavers were almost extinct in New England. However, in Canada, the supply of beavers was better managed. The Hudson's Bay Company had jurisdiction over a vast area and was able to impose hunting restrictions so that the supply of fanimals was able to regenerate between hunts. Nevertheless, the demand for beaver pelts was almost limitless, but the supply was finite. The native tribes doing the hunting became dependent on the beaver trade for their livelihood and soon enough began killing all they could find.

The Beavers and the Wetlands

The preoccupation of beavers, at least those in North America, is to build dams and to maintain them. This is what they do with their lives. That, and raise their young to do the same thing. They choose a site for a dam on a stream where the water is not too deep and the bottom is firm enough to seat tree trunks securely. They then fell trees in the vicinity with their very sharp teeth and push the trunks into position, securing them with mud. The dams slow the flow of water enough that, upstream of the dam, the beavers can build a lodge of sticks in the stream where they can safely raise their young. Built on a platform of tree trunks and branches, the lodge sits slightly above the water. The entrances to the lodge are, however, steep ramps that go underwater in order to prevent the main (non-human) predators, lynx and wolverines, from reaching the beavers. The dams must be maintained in order to assure that the water level always remains high enough to cover the entrances to the lodges.

A beaver lodge near the author's cottage.

That's what the beavers do, and why they do it, presumably. In addition to creating their safe homes, their activity creates what are called *wetlands*. The water blocked by the dams eventually backs up and floods the land, providing a shallow layer of swampy water, teeming with insect, animal, and plant life, especially algae. The city dweller may regard this as an unpleasant mess to be cleaned up. Certainly, it is a breeding ground for countless insects. However, the algae and other plankton clean the water of impurities, and the sediment formed provides a sink for other impurities. The wetlands also make a sort of reservoir that absorbs water during spring flooding and then leaks it downstream throughout the year. Slowing the water flow also slows soil erosion. Without the wetlands, water would rush too quickly out to sea. Thus, wetlands are a major contributor to the richness and productivity of the land all around them. The decimation of the beaver population led to a decrease in the wetland area and affected the ability of the wetlands to regenerate itself.

The Forests

Another essential part of a natural water system is forestland. As well as holding the soil in place and preventing erosion, trees in a climax forest, where they have a life cycle of perhaps hundreds of years, also have a effect on the water system. Like the wetlands, a mature, thick forest is teeming with life that exists nowhere else and that serves a function in the processing of water. When trees die a natural death, they fall to the ground and become a habitat for all sorts of life forms. When a dead tree falls into a flow of water, it slows the water and diverts it away from the rush to the sea. The fungi and lichens that grow on the tree serve some of the same purposes as those of the wetlands.

But the march of civilization brings with it deforestation surrounding human settlements everywhere. Europeans had already devastated much of their home continent's trees before crossing the ocean and were awed by the great forests they encountered. As did the Europeans, who pushed into and cut down the forests of Eastern Europe (see Chapter 12), the American settlers saw the forests as something to be removed. Alice Outwater found the perfect expression of the attitude of the new United States in the preface to the 1810 census report, which she quotes as follows:

> Our forests encumber a rich soil, an hundred or two hundred miles from the sea, and prevent its cultivation… [To get rid of the trees, we should] erect iron works, which require charcoal; of the maple trees we make sugar and cabinet wares; of the walnut and wild cherry, we make furniture and gun stocks; of the general woods we make potash and pearlash, of the oak, casks, and of the various trees, we make boards, joists, scantling, shingles, charcoal and ordinary fuel.[1]

Following this policy, the great climax forests of North America were demolished in a short time. Though the attitude toward forests and natural habitats did change toward the end of the 19th century, much of the original woodland had already been removed, and with it, the ideal means of renewing and cleansing the water supply.

Farming on the Prairies

The very earliest civilizations proved that agriculture is destructive to the environment. Planting the same crop over and over again in the same soils surely depletes that soil of some of its essential nutrients which then take much longer to regenerate, even when fertilizers are brought in. In addition, over-irrigation destroys the viability of the soil by making it waterlogged and too salty. This was proven in the very first agricultural civilization, Sumer. (See Chapter 10.) In the post-Industrial Revolution world of mechanized agriculture and large farms, another hazard exists: using up the water. This would have been impossible in earlier civilizations that could, at best, dam

---

1. *Ibid.*, p. 41.

water sources and divert them unnaturally. But they could only work with the water that was at hand. This all changed with big agriculture in the North American prairies.

It was government policy in the United States in the mid-19th century to encourage the development of the vast prairies of the Midwest as farmland. The prairies were the huge swath of grassland that extended from Canada down to the Gulf of Mexico between the mountain ranges of the east and the Rocky Mountains in the west. These had been grazing-land for the great herds of bison before being hunted to near extinction. Next, they became grazing-land for wild horses, and then vast cattle ranches. In the 19th century, the population of the cities in the east was reaching levels greater than their economies could support. In response, the U.S. Congress passed a law to encourage migration further west. The Homestead Act of 1862 granted all American citizens over 21 years of age 160 acres of land, provided that they lived on it, worked it, and improved it, over a five-year period.

The prairies promised to be good farming land, and some of it was. There were neither trees to clear out of the way nor troublesome stones. The terrain was flat or rolling. It suited ploughing and the new John Deere steel mouldboard plough did that very well. However, moisture was a problem.

There were basically three kinds of prairie lands: those that grew tall grasses, those that grew mixed grasses, and those that grew short grasses. The tall-grass prairies had low total rainfall, which tended to be torrential when it came, along with high winds, hot summers, and low humidity. Just enough moisture remained after the winds and the evaporation to grow good crops of corn and wheat, because the soil was so rich. On the mixed-grass prairies, the conditions were similar, but with even less rainfall. There were not enough natural streams and rivers to provide irrigation water for everyone. Farmers who lived near waterways tended to hog the water by making dams and diverting the flow.

There was only one solution for the farmers on the mixed-grass prairies. That was to dig wells and bring up water for irrigation. Windmill pumps operated the wells. This did work, but the amount of water produced was only enough for a small farm. Fortunately, periods of several years of rainy seasons made farming viable, but they were interspersed with drought years, attended by plagues of locusts and grasshoppers that destroyed the crops.

With the 20th century came gasoline-powered farming equipment that allowed farmers to do a more thorough job of tilling soil and manage much larger farms. From

1914 and 1929, most of the prairies was settled and put to the plough. Unfortunately, ploughing churned up the soil and destroyed the grasses that had held it in place. When droughts hit again in the 1930s, the soil was too loose, and the infamous Dust Bowl began in both the United States and Canada. The "dust," which was the most productive topsoil, blew all the way to the East Coast and hundreds of kilometers out to sea. Since this was during the Great Depression, when farmers were already in financial peril, the loss of topsoil was ruinous for many of them.

The Ogallala Aquifer

The Ogallala Aquifer.

One surprising result of the disastrous Dust Bowl was the discovery that there was water—a lot of it—below ground, if only you dug deep enough to tap it. What was found was what has come to be called the *Ogallala Aquifer*, a huge underground sea of fresh water, the size of Lake Ontario, running from the state of South Dakota well into the Texas Panhandle. An aquifer is water trapped underground from the ice ages millions of years ago before the ground shifted once again, sealing in the water and also cutting it off from regeneration by rainfall and spring floods.

The homemade windmill pumps that the farmers had used in the late 19th century worked on the principle of suction, hence they were not able to raise water more than about 10 meters. But newer pump technology and gasoline engines made deeper wells feasible. The effect was miraculous. Land that was marginal at best and always in danger of being blown away in another dust storm could now be adequately irrigated from water deep in the ground. The Ogallala now irrigates 9 million hectares of farmland. The only problem is that this is not ordinary groundwater. It is water that was sealed in millions of years ago, and when it is gone the land will be dry and marginal once more. This land is a significant part of the great breadbasket of the United States, and is partially responsible for the vast surplus of food on which the U.S. has built its horn of plenty. The Ogallala now has about one-half of its water left. What remains will last another 25 years or so at present rates of consumption. It is hard to imagine what will happen to this land when that water supply is no longer available.[1]

Dams

The third type of prairie is short-grass land, which is too dry for ordinary farming and which has no underlying aquifer to tap. Farming is only possible with significant irrigation. Most of this land is farther to the west, near the Rocky Mountains. There were rivers, large ones, down which huge amounts of water flowed, but the land that it flowed through was arid. To make the land fertile, it would be necessary to divert some of these rapidly flowing rivers to irrigation. To do that required dams. Unlike the dams that beavers could build or even that individual farmers could construct on small streams, the dams that would be effective on these rivers had to be enormous—capable of holding back a tremendous flow of water trying to reach the sea.

In the early 20th century, another major U.S. initiative was to build dams on the major western rivers for the purpose of "reclaiming" the deserts and making them viable farmland. One after another, giant dams were built to irrigate otherwise uninhabited land, and the projects were viewed as great successes. As time went on, the dams got larger and more expensive. They were not financially self-sustaining. The farmers who received the water could not afford to pay fees that covered the real costs, so the dams were heavily subsidized. Nevertheless, they allowed this part of the country to become settled, and that was enough. Dams also could be used as electrical power generators and as effective controls for drinking water supplies for the growing populations.

These were great triumphs of American engineering, admired all over the world. They assured fertility of the soil and ample electrical power for a very high standard of living. What began as a few dams quickly mushroomed into many, as their advantages

---

1.   There are aquifers at various places all over the world and they are often used for agriculture. Unlike the Ogallala, they are not all not cut off from replenishment by rainwater, but their source of replenishment may be far from where they are tapped for irrigation. This can lead to considerable tension between nations where the source of the water lies in one jurisdiction and the use in another, especially in arid climates where water is at a premium. To give a single example, much of the water that irrigates Israel's highly successful farmland comes from aquifers that are replenished from rainfall on the West Bank area, but are used in Israel proper or in the occupied territories. This is a major source of tension between Israel and the Palestinians. For more information see Peter H. Gleick, "Water, War and Peace in the Middle East," *Environment* 36, no. 3: (1994) 6-15, 35-42.

were recognized. In the United States alone there are now about 50 thousand dams, and of these, a thousand are huge, what engineers refer to as "major works." This was considered of such importance for economic development that dams for irrigation and hydroelectricity were among the main projects supported by public funds in the mid-20th century. To quote Alice Outwater about the United States,

> Over a period of eighty-six years—from 1905 to 1991—the Bureau of Reclamation and its predecessor built 339 reservoirs, 154 diversion dams, 7,670 miles of irrigation canals, 1,170 miles of pipelines, 270 miles of tunnels, 267 pumping plants, and 52 hydroelectric power plants. With the help of $18 billion in capital outlays, over 14,000 square miles of farmland received water, and the West bloomed and prospered. Water made much of this land intensely productive, and advocates of reclamation saw public irrigation as a miraculous font of free riches.[1]

The American model was copied across the world: the James Bay project in Quebec, the High Dam at Aswan in Egypt, and most recently the enormous Three Gorges project on the Yangtze River in China that by 2009 will submerge 21 cities and counties—a total of about 632 square kilometers, about one-third the size of Lake Ontario. It will also submerge the sites of some of the world's oldest archaeological treasures. In response, archaeologists from all over the world have begun what will probably be the largest archaeological salvage mission in history.[2]

The location of the Three Gorges dam and resevoir on the Yangtze River.

---

1.   Outwater, *Water*, p. 104.

2.   Chen Shen, "The Great Rescue Project of China," *Rotunda: The Magazine of the Royal Ontario Museum*, 35: no. 3 (2003) 20-31; Fred Pearce, "The Biggest Dam in the World," *New Scientist* (January 1995), 25-29.

The giant statues at Abu Simbel that were moved because their original site was going to be flooded during the construction of Lake Nassar and the High Dam at Aswan.

When the High Dam at Aswan was being built, a similar archaeological disaster threatened, one which would completely submerge the statues and temples of Abu Simbel built by Pharaoh Ramses II in the 13th century B.C.E. However, in a remarkable project costing $36 million dollars in donated funds, the entire site was cut into large chunks, numbered, and reassembled at a nearby higher elevation. The High Dam achieved its goal of producing electricity through twelve hydroelectric generators and reclaiming more than 40 000 hectares of desert land for cultivation and also made one or two extra crops possible on another 300 000 hectares.

What these huge dams do is give people much greater control over the flow of water downstream from the dam. As the entire system is artificial, it therefore can be manipulated to achieve human goals. Floods, as well as droughts, can be prevented, and instead of the more natural sudden changes of temperature and flow, constancy is achieved. This may meet human needs but destroys the natural processes through which a water system cleanses itself. A river normally carries silt and other sediment downstream, part of the normal process through which agricultural land is renewed. However, a dam holds all the sediment back and prevents it from reaching downstream. This was ruinous for the agriculture of the Nile valley, which had been self-sustaining for millennia. After the High Dam was completed, Egypt needed to import artificial fertilizers to make its lush soil productive again. Sediment also retards erosion. Waters downstream from a major dam now are so free of sediment that serious riverbed erosion is a problem.

All these changes also have major consequences for aquatic life that has evolved to live in the more natural environment. The most notorious of these consequences is the near destruction of salmon runs on both coasts of North America. In recognition that fish such as salmon go upriver to spawn, many dams are now built with "fish ladders." These make it possible for fish to ascend an artificial waterway to the top of the dam and continue on their way, but have had only mixed success. Alice Outwater explains:

> Young salmon live in the ocean, feeding on zooplankton, small fishes, and squid…. When a salmon is four or five years old and has traveled 10,000 miles or more in its circuits of the great oceanic grazing grounds, it puts on weight and heads inland to spawn…. Although the salmon's life path was never easy, it has become unspeakably difficult…today. If a salmon needs to ascend (for example) the Columbia to find its natal stream, it has to start with the Bonneville Dam. Fish mill about at the bottom of the dam waiting their turn at the fish ladders, bottlenecked in the odd-quality water straight from the reservoir. At the top of the Bonneville ladder, they are confronted with 40 miles of warm, placid water, very different from the cool, oxygen-filled waters of the rapids and river currents it replaced. After the Bonneville Dam comes the Dalles and then the John Day and the McNary—each a major barrier to fish migration and each a major lake to swim through. Next come the Priest Rapids Dam, the Beverly Dam, and the Rock Island Dam, for the Columbia is no longer a river but a series of slackwater lakes.[1]

Effluent

Modern industry makes a lot of waste. Virtually every manufacturing process leaves behind a mountain of discarded, useless trash that does not become part of the finished product. This unwanted remainder has to be disposed of, somewhere, somehow. Over the course of the history of civilization, our choices of where and how to do so have often been very poor.

Among the very worst industries for producing waste that is both plentiful and hazardous is the chemical industry. Many of the products used in chemical processing are extremely caustic or toxic. When they have done their part in the manufacture of a product, they have to be disposed of somewhere. The chemical industry as a whole has a very poor record of its choice of methods.

---

1.   Outwater, *Water*, pp. 109-110.

Since the earliest civilizations, the preferred method of disposal for liquid waste of any form has always been to dump the waste into the water supply. The idea was that such waste eventually would flow away through streams and rivers into the oceans to be absorbed there. As civilization became more advanced, industry more complex, and populations in any area higher, the safe disposal of waste grew more difficult.

Many chemical-manufacturing plants are located around the shores of the Great Lakes. It is a natural location both because these industries all need a large source of water in their processing and because the freighters that transport their products out to markets travel out through the Great Lakes. Inevitably, many chemical companies routinely dumped their effluent waste into the lakes, counting on it becoming sufficiently diluted to do no one any harm.

Polychlorinated Biphenals

Rachel Carson sounded the alarm on the dangers of contamination of the waterways from pesticides, particularly DDT and its relatives, but pesticides are only one category of pollutant that has wreaked havoc in otherwise clean water. Many chemical products, like DDT that were considered miracles of modern chemistry with huge benefits to humankind, were found later to have some very serious drawbacks, often after they had become spread widely in the environment. A good example is the class of wonder chemicals called *polychlorinated biphenals* or *PCBs*, for short.

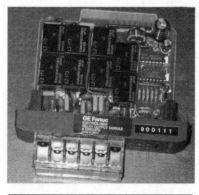

Before 1976, common electrical transformers like the one pictured above would likely have contained PCBs.

First manufactured in 1929, PCBs were found to have wonderful properties. They are relatively insoluble in water, they do not degrade under high temperatures, they are inflammable, and they make excellent electrical insulation. They were used at first in the manufacture of plastics and then as an additive to paints. They were particularly useful as insulators in electrical transformers where high temperatures were a particular problem. They were used as a coating in carbonless copy paper, which was widely used before the photocopy machine became ubiquitous. As well, they were used in many products that found their way into homes, such as resins for wood composites and other protective coatings. But like so many wonder chemicals, they had unwanted properties as well. Even when they were identified as toxic, it was not a special worry because it was not envisaged that they would be released into the environment in a form that could do any harm. Yet the reality was that it was inevitable that they should find their way into the air, water, and soil.

Workers at the Stelco plant in Hamilton, Ontario, recalled working with PCBs was like before their use was suddenly curtailed in 1977:

> Joe Choscinski, Chief Health and Safety representative for the electrical department…remembers what a shock it was. "PCBs had been everywhere—in all kinds of walkways…. Sometimes workers would spill PCB oil all down the front of them as they tested transformers. Often, they would eat on the job without cleansing their hands of them." Gary Knox, Joe's predecessor in the electrical department, says he thought nothing of reaching down into a transformer, PCB solution up to his armpit, and changing the diodes.[1]

Like so many of the wonder chemicals that were developed in the early decades of the 20th century, PCBs were thought to be harmless to humans in the concentrations to which they might become exposed. But as with DDT, the effect of PCBs can accumulate and remain persistent for a long time. Most natural chemical products, even those which are toxic, decay over time. But some, like PCBs, resist natural decomposition—which is why they are so useful. For that reason, if they do find their way into the waterways or into the soil, they remain for a long time and have more opportunity to be taken up the food chain to become increasingly concentrated. PCBs that were intended to be forever sealed in electrical transformers end up somewhere else when the transformer comes to the end of its life and has to be junked. While the manufacturer may realize that the PCBs need special care, the worker whose job it is to dispose of outdated equipment is more likely to just dump it in the nearest location. PCBs, being liquid, tend to make their way into the water system.

In 1966, a scientist in Sweden published a report of a study, in which he found traces of PCBs in nearly every place that he looked. Other scientists followed his lead and reported that there was virtually no place on Earth where PCBs were not found, including in the fat cells of arctic polar bears, far from any place where PCBs were

---

1. Byron E. Wall, ed., *Science in Society: Classical and Contemporary Readings* (Toronto: Wall & Thompson, 1989), p. 326.

actually put to use. PCBs cause a variety of dysfunctions in animals and are fatal even in very small concentrations to fish and invertebrates. They may be carcinogenic in humans.

In 1976, the United States banned the manufacture of PCBs, and other countries soon followed. However, by this time, one and a half billion kilograms had been produced and much of it was already loose in the environment. Though the ban prevented the manufacture of more PCBs, that which already existed continued to function in applications such as transformers and electric ballast.

Mercury

Not only wonder chemicals caused problems when disposed of. Sometimes, ordinary elements and compounds not normally encountered in the water did so as well. Mercury, for example, was widely used by industry as a catalyst in the production of caustic soda. In a process used in the 1940s, 170 grams of mercury was discharged into the water for each tonne of caustic soda produced. Mercury was also used in many other manufacturing processes and products. Since mercury is one of the heaviest elements, it was expected to sink to the bottom of the lake or river where it was dumped and remain inert there. No one realized that certain bacteria living in the bottom sediments of large bodies of water consumed the mercury and from it made an organic compound that made its way up the food chain.

The horror story that has marked this environmental problem took place in Japan, in a region called Minimata. There, in 1932, a local chemical plant began making acetaldehyde, and as part of their processing discharged mercury into the nearby ocean. Generally, discharges into the ocean are considered the safest of all since the amount of dilution any pollutant is immediately subject to is enormous. In the 1950s, this same company stepped up its production of acetaldehyde and hence its discharge of mercury. In 1956, a sudden outbreak of disease hit the local population of Minimata. Children in great numbers showed up in hospital with brain damage. Unexplained deaths occurred among the local cats. After a time, consumption of the local fish was found to cause the illness, due to the high concentrations of mercury in their bodies. Their sale was prohibited. In time, the chemical factory was identified as the source and culprit. After a long legal battle, the company finally was ordered to pay compensation to more than three thousand brain damaged victims.

Detergents

Not all pollutants let loose into the waterways came from industrial processing. Plenty came right from the homes of ordinary people. One of the worst offenders is a once highly prized, but now taken completely for granted, consumer product that makes life so much easier: detergent. Detergents came on the market just after the Second World War as an alternative to soap. They are much more efficient and effective cleaning agents than soap. Their use paralleled the adoption of the washing machine in industrialized countries.

The effectiveness of detergents as cleaning agents is the result of their peculiar molecular structure that attracts dirt. Unfortunately, most detergents make long-lasting suds that appear in public waterways. Many detergents also contained phosphates to improve their effectiveness. Phosphates increase the plant growth in water and have led to excess growth of algae on lakes that choked all other life. The worst example of this was Lake Erie, the shallowest of the Great Lakes, which became a symbol of carelessness about water resources. It was so polluted with effluent and choked with algae that almost all normal marine life had disappeared and the lake was pronounced "dead."

Oil Spills

The modern industrial world runs on oil. Petroleum products provide our chief transportation fuel on land, air, and sea. Plastics are made from petroleum, as are many other consumer and industrial products that we would be hard pressed to do without. But oil is not evenly dispersed around the world; therefore, a very large industry exists to transport crude oil from its sources to where it will be refined and used. Inevitable accidents occur during transportation, resulting in some spills of oil into the environment. But, even aside from the

This dirty iceberg is smeared with oil from the crash of the oil tanker *Exxon Valdez.*

outright accidents, quite normal spillage occurs in regular transportation. Both are causes for concern.

A crude oil barge and tug boat.

Tanker Accidents

Much of the crude oil of the world is extracted from the ground on one continent and then sent by sea to another continent in ships we call tankers—basically huge floating cans of oil. It is unlikely that accidents could be avoided while moving these around and that those accidents would not result in crude oil spilling into the ocean. For reasons of economy, beginning in the 1960s, the size of the tankers shipping oil grew from the relatively small to the very large size we now call *supertankers*. One of the distinguishing features of supertankers is that they are very difficult to maneuver in the water, typically requiring many kilometers to come to a stop. Great care must be taken to avoid even the possibility of getting too near any possible obstruction in the water since a rapid change of course is out of the question. Since the greatest number of dangerous obstructions lie near shore and since the supertankers do have to start and finish their voyages at shore ports, there is no avoiding these perils. At the same time, any accident with a tanker resulting in an oil spill will do the most damage if it is near enough for oil to be carried ashore.

Supertanker accidents are big news and get much public attention when they happen. The greatest attention is given to spills in coastal waters—because of the impending shore damage—and, in particular, those spills occurring in North America and Western Europe—because the free press makes such reporting possible. There are many other oil spills and other environmental catastrophes that happen in other parts of the world but that either never reach the public consciousness or are reported in rather less detail. Accordingly, the disastrous oil tanker accidents we know best are those closest to home.

The first big accident with a supertanker happened off the coast of England in March, 1967, when the tanker *Torrey Canyon* carrying oil from Kuwait ran aground on rocks while trying to steer between offshore islands. The ship broke open and nearly a million barrels of oil leaked out. The first response was to try to save the tanker, but this proved fruitless. Finally, the British sent jet planes to bomb the tanker and set fire to the remaining crude to try to prevent it coming ashore. They then dumped 10 thousand tonnes of detergent on the oil as it neared the shores of Cornwall in an attempt to break up the oil and disperse it. However, the detergent was lethal to shore birds, thousands of which died. Eventually, the oil crossed the English Channel and threatened French beaches. The French had more time to consider the best course of action and instead opted for dumping powdered chalk on the oil slicks, which would adhere to the oil and cause it to sink. This proved to be a better solution. Henceforth, it was realized, if such accidents ever occur again, a team of scientists should immediately be convened to find the most appropriate solution. This recognition of the complexity of these disasters has helped to contain the damage that might have occurred from some later, much larger oil tanker accidents.

Over the next two decades the world experienced about half a dozen major oil spills involving tanker accidents. These have proved to be the largest accidental spills in history, to date. Through this period, methods were learned to contain the spread of oil slicks, to improve cleanup, and to determine legal responsibility. But little was done to prevent further accidents.

New methods discovered for containing and cleaning up after oil spills are much less damaging to the environment than those use in 1967.

However, accidental oil spills remain a problem that will not go away. Almost all supertanker accidents can be traced to human error at some point. It's hard to see how this can ever be eliminated. What can be done is to improve the design of tankers—a double hull would help—and to find better ways of transporting oil. But this is managing rather than solving a problem. Twenty-two years later, North America had to cope with the foundering of the *Exxon Valdez* in Prince William Sound, Alaska, in March of 1989. The *Valdez*, a considerably larger tanker than the *Torrey Canyon*, had just taken on a full load of Alaskan crude oil and was being guided out to sea, first by the port pilot, then by the captain, and then by the third officer. There may have been a misunderstanding of orders, but in any case, the vessel did not alter course to avoid shoals until too late, and the 430-meter long tanker crashed into a reef. Within a short time, it lost over a quarter of a million barrels of oil into the sea, about one-fifth of its load. Though this was considerably less than the loss of oil from the *Torrey*

Canyon, the damage was greater because the prevailing winds and currents blew the oil onto a long stretch of pristine Alaskan shoreline that was home to a tremendous amount of wildlife. The damage to life and to the ecology of the area was enormous, and for some of the native people, who continued to live by hunting and fishing, it destroyed their way of life forever. On a slightly more positive note, the efforts to fight the damage did proceed much more quickly and were better organized than in previous spills, and despite the ghastly damage, a better accounting of it was made which was useful for latter assessment. The Exxon Company was held responsible for the damage and ultimately paid out a billion dollars in compensation.

Intentional Oil Spills

It may surprise the reader to learn that the great supertanker oil spills that make front-page news are actually a small part of the oil pollution of the waterways. When tankers deliver their load of crude oil to its destination, they must take on seawater to provide ballast for the return journey. However, the holding tanks still contain a small amount of oil clinging to the walls. The ballast is ultimately dumped at sea, along with the oil residue. The total amount of oil discharged this way is only about 0.4 percent of the total cargo of oil, but it does occur on every voyage. Given the large number of tankers at sea, this adds up to a considerable pollution problem. In the 1960s, a number of international agreements were signed to regulate these discharges. However, the thrust of most of the legislation is to require that the discharges not take place within a certain distance from shore. Other regulations required a different technology to be used for cleaning the tanks that would produce considerably less discharge into the sea. The difficulty with all such regulations is that, being international in character, it is difficult to get agreement on what should be required or to agree on penalties for non-compliance, and virtually impossible to police.

Whatever the tanker captains do to maintain their vessels, there is no reason to suppose that they seek to pollute by what they do. However, deliberate assaults on the environment are not out of the question, and oil pollution is an effective way of achieving that. The worst oil disaster the world has ever seen was deliberately caused. In the Gulf War of 1990-1991, the retreating Iraqi troops set fire to two-thirds of Kuwait's oil wells and opened pipelines that gushed into the sea. By the time that the fires were put out, the wells capped, the pipelines closed, and the oil slicks contained, the amount of oil dispersed into the environment approached six million barrels, far beyond any of the worst tanker accidents.

Sewage

One of the clearest measures of the cultural advancement of a civilization is how well it cleans up after itself. In particular, how it handles that most unpleasant task of dealing with human waste. Throughout history this has been critical for the health of a community (see discussion in Chapter 25).

In some of the more successful early civilizations, there were separate watercourses for drinking water and for excrement, but for most of human civilization the two have become mixed, usually with unfortunate consequences. Europe, after the fall of Rome, was particularly unclean. The Romans had had a complex system of aqueducts to bring fresh water into their cities, with the waste matter flushed out a different way. Europe in the Middle Ages had fouled city wells, which were continually contaminated with both sewage and rotting corpses from graveyards near the local church. The American colonies followed the same practice and soon began to foul their own otherwise pristine well water. The habit of emptying chamber pots out the nearest door and dumping garbage in alleys only added to the difficulties. As cities became more populous, they also had more horses, which deposited manure all over the streets.

Some of the earliest concerted efforts to clean up the water supply came out of a concern that epidemics, such as yellow fever or cholera, may be spread by water or by "miasmas" that rise up out of foul water.

The Toilet

The flush toilet was invented in the late 16th century, but it was not until the 19th century that it came into wide usage, and then at first only in the homes of the wealthy and in hotels and public buildings. Flush toilets only were practical when a steady supply of water was piped into cities. The early toilets used phenomenal amounts of water on each flush. Homes with indoor flush toilets used much more water than those without them. The toilet and then the bathtub were responsible for causing the demand for fresh water in the home to skyrocket. But with the water supply systems and the prodigious water usage came a higher and more comfortable standard of living.

Toilets flushed into sewers—another new addition to the infrastructure of the cities. But sewers were first created without the thought of the toilet. The sewers emptied into the nearest river, which may have been the source of drinking water for the same city, or if not, it probably was the source for a city further downstream. Even if drinking water came from elsewhere, raw sewage in a river running through a city can be very offensive.

One of the best-documented cases of the effects of sewage was in the Thames River in London, England, in the mid-19th century. The year 1858 was called "The Great Stink"; the smell was so bad in central London that the House of Commons ceased to sit. Private water companies were taking water supplies from the Thames and delivering contaminated water to their subscribers.

The answer to this problem has not been to separate the source of fresh water from the dumping grounds of sewage, since that would be next to impossible. Instead the solution has been to sanitize water in treatment plants. Almost all water supplies in heavily populated areas of the world comes from sources that are too contaminated to be used without some sort of filtering.

For cities on the coasts or at the mouths of rivers, sewage is often dumped directly into the water with the expectation that it will be carried safely away out to sea. Venice, Italy, adopted this solution hundreds of years ago and now has had to add complex barriers to prevent the sewage from returning with the tides. (See Chapter 2.) Boston has adopted a system of sending its sludge out to sea via a long pipe that disgorges it a considerable distance from shore. Nevertheless, it has had to cope with some of that returning to shore as well.

Swimming is Dangerous to Your Health

Beaches near large populations everywhere are used for recreation by the local residents, and, depending on the location, by significant numbers of tourists and vacationers, who come to take in the sun, go for a swim, or spend time on the water in different ways. For some Third World countries, tourist dollars are essential and their beaches are among their most important economic resources. For Europe, especially in the Mediterranean area, tourism is also essential for a sagging economy. Yet, in many of these places, the beaches are not healthy places to be. The level of dangerous bacteria in the water from sewage can cause infections, hepatitis, dysentery, or even cholera.

One of the main problems is that the pollution is caused in one jurisdiction and then experienced in another. To take the Mediterranean as one example, it is a large body of water with a relatively small opening to the Atlantic Ocean. It also has an exchange of water with the Black Sea, though that is even more polluted than the Mediterranean. For millennia, it was fed by the freshwater flow of the Nile, but now that is all used for farming. Other rivers that normally fed into the Mediterranean are either also diverted for irrigation, or used as conduits for sewage and refuse. Venice is a good example of this.

The combination of fecal matter, detergents, industrial effluents, and pesticides flow in from all sides and have a hard time getting out. Plastic rubbish, oil slicks, dead fish, and algae plague the famed beaches of the south of France. Swimming invites serious infection. And yet the local economies desperately need the tourists. Though the Mediterranean countries banded together in 1975 to form the Mediterranean Action Plan to clean up the sea, progress has been slow to non-existent.[1]

Much more is known now about water conservation, what is possible and what is not, what makes matters worse and what makes them better. Some progress has been made to curtail some of the worst excesses that have polluted our waters. But the problem that water goes everywhere makes control difficult. Precious resources can be used by those who can get to it instead of shared for all, or even saved for the future—as for example with the aquifers that are being rapidly drained. We cannot help but produce a tremendous amount of waste and pollution, but it does not necessarily have to be dumped in the nearest river with no thought of what happens downstream.

1.   Fred Pearce, "Dead in the Water," *New Scientist*, February 1995, pp. 26-31.

Chapter 31

Abusing the Earth

We don't just dump our waste into the waterways of the world, we dump it on land—anywhere we can. And, particularly in the industrialized nations, we produce a lot of it. The more technologically advanced a civilization is, apparently, the more garbage it produces.

In their 1990 book *It's a Matter of Survival*, Anita Gordon and David Suzuki cite some statistics on garbage production:

> North Americans are the most wasteful people on the face of the Earth. In Rome, people put out a little over 650 grams of trash a day; in Nigeria, it's about 450 grams. In North America, every day, each person throws out almost 1800 grams of waste. Over the course of a year, that's almost a ton of garbage a person.
>
> A typical North American goes through and discards 7 kilograms of junk mail and 54 kilograms of newsprint each year. Each day, North Americans use hundreds of thousands of plastic tampon holders. Each hour, we throw away more than 2.5 million non-returnable, non-recyclable plastic bottles....
>
> We put our babies in disposable diapers, enough of them each year to stretch to the moon and back several times. Worldwide, one billion trees annually are cut down for those fluffy liners in disposables.... Modern life is a garbage maker's perpetual-motion machine: every year 1.6 billion pens, two billion razors and blades, and 246.9 million scrap tires are discarded; and every three months, Americans throw away enough aluminum to rebuild the entire U.S. commercial airline fleet.[1]

---

1.   Anita Gordon and David Suzuki, *It's a Matter of Survival* (Toronto: Stoddart, 1990), pp. 184-186.

Not in My Backyard

And where does all of this garbage go? No one is particularly happy about living near garbage. Those who produce the greatest amounts of it are in the worst position. They live in cities with air pollution and dubious water supplies. Their food is imported from some distance away because all around them is concrete and other housing. As the cities expand, the garbage dumps get farther and farther away. And when all the land that a city controls has been allocated for other uses, the city goes begging for a place to send its waste.

The most infamous example of this, cited again and again in books about solid waste problems, is the garbage barge named Mobro. On March 22, 1987, it left New York City, fully loaded, seeking a landfill site where it could unload its cargo of refuse from the Big Apple. North Carolina, Louisiana, Alabama, Mississippi, Florida, Mexico, Belize, and the Bahamas were all on the list of possible places, but the governments of each jurisdiction banned the barge from unloading. Eventually, the barge returned to New York, still fully loaded.

A Washington State landfill.

Landfill

In most of the industrialized world, garbage is collected and then trucked to a dumpsite, which will eventually in time become "land fill." As if that term is not innocuous enough, these places are often called "sanitary landfill sites." Such a site is an area that is deemed to be of marginal ecological value and which could be improved, or at least not made worse, by being "reclaimed" through filling it in with solid waste. The rationale is the same as that which viewed a drained swamp as a positive addition of land with no adverse consequences. Despite the optimism that accompanied this solution to the garbage problem, and despite the endorsement of organizations such as the Sanitary Engineering Division of the American Society of Civil Engineers, the public was not convinced that a landfill site was anything other than a dump.

No matter how sanitary the site was intended to be, if it is filled with garbage, it will attract and breed insects and rodents, and birds and scavenging animals may pick up pathogens that can be thereby be spread into the surrounding area. And unless the site is extremely well lined and protected, it can leach into the ground water and pollute it irreparably.

And then what happens when the site is filled? It is covered over and becomes "reclaimed" land. That land can then be used for construction projects, perhaps housing subdivisions or hospitals or golf courses. Yet, if the site does contain materials either that are, or that in time can become toxic, then the land can have some unwelcome surprises for those who unwittingly live over it. Municipal jurisdictions are finding it harder and harder to find another place that is willing to accept their garbage, no matter what the financial inducement.

Incineration

What are the alternatives? Not producing the garbage in the first place would be the best solution to the problem, but this seems unrealistic. Consider for the moment that the existence of the garbage is a simple matter of fact. What can be done with it?

One alternative is to burn it—reduce it to ashes, which will certainly take up much less room to store anywhere and which will eliminate the possibly harmful pathogens that make a landfill site so unpalatable. This sounds promising, and it does have its enthusiastic supporters, but it has always had two serious drawbacks: cost and pollution.

Compared to just dumping garbage in a landfill site, building and operating large incinerators for municipal solid waste is very costly. It is a solution that communities are driven to when the cheaper alternatives cease to be available. As a technology, garbage incineration has been around for over a century, but adoption has been slow. Yet, recently it has been revived and probably will continue to grow. In the United States—the country with the biggest solid waste problem—only three percent was being incinerated in 1988, but ten years later, that had jumped to 15 to 17 percent.[1]

Some incinerators just burn the easily combustible parts of solid waste to reduce the overall volume; then the whole remainder is sent to a landfill site. The newer technology does more thorough burning and, in addition, uses the heat produced to generate steam for the production of electricity. This sounds like a positive step, producing needed energy out of otherwise unwanted garbage. There are problems with both types: much of

---

1. Martin V. Melosi, *Effluent America: Cities, Industries, Energy, and the Environment* (Pittsburgh: University of Pittsburgh Press, 2001), p. 79.

what they burn is emitted into the atmosphere as pollutants. As one environmental expert put it,

> Garbage burning generates a range of pollutants, including gases that contain heavy metals and dioxins and that contribute to acid rain. Moreover, incinerators require a new breed of secure landfills that accept only the toxic ash they generate.[1]

Ironically, environmental groups are the most vocal objectors to landfill sites and also oppose the most viable solution to avoid excessive landfills, incineration.

Recycling

The solution receiving the most attention and the support of both environmentalists and local governments is recycling, the only solution that garnered general praise. The government policy makers could demonstrate that they were on the side of conservation. The environmentalists saw that materials that went into products for a single use could now be reprocessed and reused, placing less demand on existing natural resources. Perhaps, most important, the ordinary citizens had a way to participate directly in an environmental issue, thus increasing general awareness of environmental concerns. The now familiar recycling "blue boxes" are a reminder that we do use up a tremendous amount of raw material every day, some of which can be effectively reused. All schoolchildren now get "reduce, reuse, recycle" drilled into them. By the time they reach young adulthood, they are prepared to sort through garbage in food courts and other public places and put each of glass, plastic, metal, newspapers, and trash in separate containers. This level of public consciousness and cooperation would have been unthinkable a generation ago.

Still, recycling has its critics, from both sides. There are those who object to the high costs of maintaining recycling programs. They claim that the energy expended on making some materials reusable in other products outweighs the savings in materials, with the result that the entire program of recycling produces no net gains whatsoever. In *The Skeptical Environmentalist,* Bjørn Lomborg makes just this point.

> ... [W]e must...consider whether recycling to avoid waste is a good investment of resources. Possibly, we may be able to save more resources by burning old paper at incineration plants, making use of

---

1.   Allen Hershkowitz, "Burning Trash: How It Could Work," *Technology Review* (July 1987): 27.

the heat produced and felling more trees, instead of using energy to collect the old paper to be sorted, prepared and filtered. New studies seem to indicate that it actually costs more to recycle paper than to produce new paper.[1]

On the other side, some environmentalists who assert that recycling programs do save significant amounts of natural resources also worry that the public has become complacent about its profligate usage of resources in the first place. To quote Richard Gilbert of the Canadian Federal Task Force on Packaging,

> Recycling is just a sophisticated twist in the throwaway society. It's number three on anybody's waste-management list. It's deceiving us. It's saying you can still continue to consume as much as before, you just have to throw the stuff into your garbage can in a slightly different way. ... Recycling is just reinforcing the throwaway society."[2]

Yet all of these coping methods concern only ordinary, run-of-the-mill household and industrial garbage, not materials that are clearly and unambiguously hazardous. Those have presented even more difficult problems.

Hazardous Waste

The public consciousness of the dangers of landfill sites was raised by a particularly appalling case of a site gone bad. This site was not an ordinary sanitary landfill of domestic garbage, but a site containing clearly dangerous chemicals. But the incongruity of this was that those affected never knew that there were any special dangers. This is the story of Love Canal.

Love Canal

Love Canal was the name of a residential neighbourhood in Niagara Falls, New York. In the 1940s and '50s, the Hooker Chemicals and Plastics Corporation plant nearby had, with permission, used an incomplete canal trench (the Love Canal) as a dump site for nearly 20 000 tonnes of chemical waste, including PCBs, dioxins, and pesticides. After

1. Bjørn Lomborg, *The Skeptical Environmentalist: Measuring the Real State of the World* (Cambridge: Cambridge University Press, 1998), p. 209.

2. Cited in Gordon and Suzuki, *It's a Matter of Survival*, p. 189.

the plant closed down, the site was covered over and donated by the company to the city of Niagara Falls, which was then expanding rapidly. With the best of intentions on all sides, the city allowed residential housing to be built on what had been the former dumpsite.

An aerial view of the Love Canal housing development in the 1960s.

A suburban housing development was built on the site, and people moved in and raised families. In the 1970s, some of the local residents began to complain about bad odours throughout the neighbourhood. Investigations by state officials detected toxic chemicals leaking into the basements of homes throughout the area. Then it began to be noticed that much more than smells were wrong. There was an abnormally high incidence of cancer in children and miscarriages among pregnant women.

The state of New York took action, evacuating the area and relocating the residents, but only after considerable damage had been done to their health. The Occidental Chemical Corporation, which had taken over Hooker Chemical, was held responsible. It and the city of Niagara Falls agreed to pay $20 million in damages to about 1300 former residents of the area.

The toxins were still in the ground and were still contaminating the surface above it, and doubtless also contaminating the groundwater around it. One way or another the problem had to be addressed. However, the solutions to a problem such as this were not obvious. If the site were dug up, what would be released into the atmosphere and onto the surrounding land because of disturbing the toxic materials? Several plans were proposed, including covering the entire site with an airtight tent before digging commenced, as well as several other technological solutions. And then, what should be done with the toxins? Incinerate them into the atmosphere? Carry them somewhere else and dump them there? Or, just try to bury them there more effectively.

What did happen was a combination of these plans with an emphasis on containing the toxins in their original site. By the early 1990s, New York State had completed its cleanup and once again declared that the area, or at least parts of it, was safe for habitation. Occidental Chemical paid the state and federal governments additional sums to offset some of the costs of cleanup.

Meanwhile, Love Canal became the point of reference for discussions of the perils of chemical wastes and of trusting too much in one's municipal government to protect its residents from unforeseen dangers. Love Canal was a situation to be avoided by industry and citizenry alike. Another way had to be found to deal with hazardous waste.

Koko

Not surprisingly, another method that came easily to hand was to export the problem to the undeveloped nations. The Third World was already being used as a dumping ground for products that could no longer be sold profitably in the industrialized countries—old technology, extra food, pharmaceuticals that didn't meet the standards of the home countries, and, of course, the pesticides that were banned at home when they were found to be too dangerous.

Barrels of imported radioactive waste in Nambia.

As usual, there are a few classic cases repeatedly cited to show how outrageous this practice can become. Here is one about Koko in Nigeria, reported by Andrew Lees of the environmental group, Friends of the Earth.

> You approach the village of Koko through bush where quite a lot of palm nuts are being grown. It's hot. Everything looks quiet and peaceful, but then you see a rickety wire compound behind somebody's house. In that compound are vast stacks, three or four high, of 200-liter oil drums. We estimated there were about 10 000 drums of chemicals.... Many of the containers were bulging in the hot sun.... You could actually hear a menacing hiss.[1]

The drums contained PCBs, lead, mercury, solvents, and radioactive waste. They had been smuggled into Nigeria on forged papers by an Italian construction company, after being collected from all over Europe. When the Nigerian government found out about it, they were sent back to Italy, but this was only one of many such incidents where poor

---

1.   Cited in Gordon and Suzuki, *Op. cit.*, p. 136.

people can be persuaded to take enormous risks that they do not understand for a small payment of hard cash.

Nuclear Waste Disposal

Even though nuclear power plants have become less popular after the disasters at Three Mile Island in Pennsylvania and at Chernobyl in the Ukraine, a lot of nuclear plants are still working, and there are plans for more. It is a proven method of obtaining more electricity at a reasonable cost. For countries lacking indigenous fossil fuels or the possibility of hydroelectric power plants, it is one of the few ways to assure a power supply without being dependent on imported fuels. Until such a time comes that alternate sources of power are available in very large amounts, nuclear power plants will continue to exist.

Where there are nuclear plants, there is nuclear waste. A nuclear reactor operates by provoking and then controlling a nuclear chain reaction in uranium. The fuel that runs a reactor comes prepared in pellets containing uranium oxide and other materials to insulate and protect the active fuel. The pellets are assembled into rods. Before they are used in a reactor, these rods are safe enough to handle, but after they have been used to make a chain reaction and produce enormous amounts of heat, they are dangerously radioactive. Disposing of spent uranium fuel rods is the most challenging waste disposal problem for civilization.

To say that spent fuel rods are dangerous would be a gross understatement. Terry Lash put it succinctly:

> Unlike the disposal of any other type of waste, the hazard related to radioactive wastes is so great that no element of doubt can be allowed to exist regarding safety.... In general, the complex behavior of radioactive materials in the often subtle interrelationships among the various life forms and their physical environment makes prediction of the harm caused by releases of radioactive wastes highly uncertain.[1]

---

1. Terry Lash, "Radioactive Wastes," *Amicus* (Fall 1979): 26-27.

There are two main problems with radioactive nuclear fuel waste. First, these wastes do have some potential for use in the manufacture of nuclear weapons. Therefore, extreme care must be taken in where and how they are disposed of, lest these materials fall into irresponsible hands. Second, the spent fuel rods are not only highly dangerous when they have reached the end of their useful lives, they remain so for a period of time that is almost unimaginable in present-day society.

The measure of the persistence of danger from radioactivity in a substance is its *half-life*, the amount of time required for half of any amount of the substance to have decayed and ceased to be harmful. Some of the by-products of a nuclear reactor have half-lives of about 25 000 years. That's about five times as long as the entire period of recorded history. And that is just for half of it to decay. The other half remains just as potent. A small amount of plutonium can remain fatally toxic to human beings for 500 000 years.[1] We can hardly even conceive of such an amount of time.

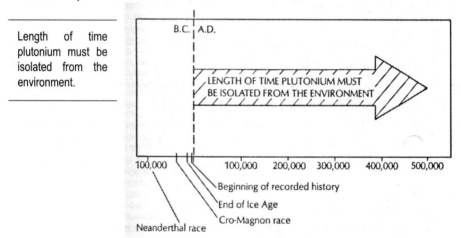

Length of time plutonium must be isolated from the environment.

Yet the countries of the world that have nuclear power plants have all contemplated such spans of time and considered a variety of options for dealing with the waste. While the considering has been going on, nuclear fuel waste has been accumulating for as long as there have been nuclear reactors producing electricity. What has happened is this: the fuel rods remain in the reactors for a period of three to four years, after which they must be replaced. These rods will not explode, but they are so radioactive that any human contact with them whatsoever would be fatal. However, water shields the radiation. So

---

1.   Fritjof Capra, cited in Byron E. Wall, ed. *Science in Society: Classical and Contemporary Readings* (Toronto: Wall & Emerson, 1989).

long as the fuel rods are kept is a very carefully maintained cooling pond, they do no damage. Hence, the spent rods are transferred to stainless steel lined concrete water tanks adjacent to the reactors. This was to be a temporary holding spot, but there they remain.

This much was thought out before nuclear reactors were built in the first place, but the issue of what to do with the spent rods after that was put off for later consideration. The chairman of the State of Nevada's nuclear waste commission, Grant Sawyer, compared this to "sending [Astronaut] John Glen into orbit without figuring out how to bring him down."[1] Since the cooling tanks were planned to be temporary way stations, they had limited capacities. Most of the cooling ponds are now full or close to full—or, when necessary, more rods were put in them than they were designed for. All of the spent rods give off heat constantly. After 10 years, a fuel rod still emits about 10 kilowatts of energy, which makes cooling that much more of a problem.

The Grand Plan

There are only so many possibilities for how to dispose safely of the nuclear fuel waste. Wherever it is put, it has to remain there, neither contaminating any underground water supplies, nor be disturbed by the normal geological activity of the tectonic plates, including volcanoes and earthquakes and just plain continental drift. And, despite our very incomplete knowledge of all the normal forces of nature and our total ignorance of random events to come, this must all hold for thousands and thousands of years.

Several possibilities have been seriously considered. One is to bury the waste deep in the ocean seabed. A site would be chosen where the ocean is very deep, where there has been no seismic turbulence, and where the waters are beyond the circulation of normal ocean currents. The waste matter would be encased in an impermeable container and then buried in the rock of the ocean bed. Another idea is to go to the polar regions—far from human habitation—and bury the waste in the polar ice sheet. Both of these schemes suffer from the problem of our just not knowing enough to be sure the materials would remain stable. A scheme that would not suffer from that is to shoot the waste into space, preferably on a trajectory that would crash it into the sun. Then we would not have to worry about what would happen to it later on, but we would have to worry a lot about how to be sure that there was not some sort of accident or miscalculation in the launch that would bring the entire package back down on us.

---

1.   Cited in Dan Grossman and Seth Shulman, "A Nuclear Dump: The Experiment Begins," in Wall, *Science in Society*, p. 343.

At the present time, the solution that appears to have been chosen by all countries that now have nuclear fuel to get rid of is what is called *geologic disposal*. What this means is that it is planned to dig deep down into bedrock, perhaps using an abandoned mine shaft, to a depth that is deemed to be stable for a very long time, fill it with nuclear waste, and then seal it up, in effect, forever. This, of course, has the same problem as the first two solutions—how do we know what is going to happen in the distant future—but the consensus is that this is a more predictable and practical solution. Each country has to find a suitable site. In Canada, the plan is to drill deep into the bedrock of the Canadian Shield that is millions and millions of years old and appears to have remained stable.

In the United States, the choice is a mountain in Nevada, Yucca Mountain, the site of a former underground nuclear test site. This mountain will have many more shafts dug into it, altogether 180 kilometers of tunnels, and is projected to hold more than 60 000 tonnes of nuclear fuel waste. The U.S. nuclear reactors currently produce about 2 000 tonnes of waste per year. As might be expected, no one welcomes a nuclear fuel waste disposal site in his or her backyard, so coming to a decision about a specific location has been a difficult task everywhere. Three-fourths of the citizens of Nevada that responded to a poll in 1987 said they did not want the nuclear dump in their state. The Yucca Mountain site was chosen because it was not near settled areas and appeared to be in an extremely stable geological environment. Nevertheless, a group of scientists from the California Institute of Technology published a report in 1998 saying that they detected movement in the Yucca Mountain area ten times greater than what had been previously estimated, which would indicate that there was the possibility of earthquakes.[1]

Because nuclear energy remains an option for the Third World as it scrambles to catch up with industrialization, it is likely that the nuclear fuel waste problem will only grow greater and greater. Since even the most technologically advanced nations have found it almost insurmountably difficult to find a safe disposal method, the prospects for what could happen in small developing nations is frightening.

---

1.   William R. Mangun and Daniel H. Henning. *Managing the Environmental Crisis,* 2nd ed. (Durham, NC: Duke University Press, 1999), pp. 227-229.

Chapter 32

Abusing the Air

Another legacy of Rachel Carson's *Silent Spring* was a renewed awareness of the importance of monitoring air quality in an industrial age. In the United States, the Clean Air Act was enacted in 1970, which provided standards for air quality, limits on industrial emissions, penalties for non-compliance, and timetables for instituting remedies.

Air pollution was certainly not a new problem in the second half of the 20th century. Some of the worst air problems date back to the earliest days of urban life. People using fires to cook and keep warm will inevitably foul the air. If those people live in close proximity to each other, the fouled air will be too dense to disperse without having had some unintended effects.

London Fog

In early civilizations, and in "many Third World countries even today, wood burnt on open fires or in rooms without chimneys produces a cloud of smoke that can damage the lungs and the eyes of those who have to be around it. The invention of the chimney in Europe in the 12th century, followed by successive improvements over the next several hundred years, made a tremendous difference to the effectiveness and pleasantness of indoor heating. Early fireplaces burned wood, but as wood became scarcer the transition was made to coal.

With the burning of coal, outdoor air pollution first became a serious problem. Raw coal burns badly, releasing not only clouds of smoke, but also an acrid mixture of polluting gases, especially sulphur dioxide. In England, with a severe shortage of wood and a great abundance of coal, the switch to coal burning was adopted first, and from there we have the earliest recorded complaints about the pollution caused by the coal. As Clive Ponting reported,

> In 1257 Queen Eleanor was driven from Nottingham Castle by smoke from the numerous coal fires in the town and thirty years later a commission of enquiry was set up to investigate complaints

about smoke levels in London. In 1307 the burning of coal in London was banned but the edict was ignored.[1]

London, Ponting continued, could be recognized from the distance in the 16th and 17th centuries by the "huge pall of smoke hanging over it." In 1661, the English diarist John Evelyn wrote

> For there is under Heaven such Coughing and Snuffling to be heard, as in London churches and Assemblies of People, where the Barking and the Spitting is uncessant and most importunate.... It is this horrid Smoake which obscures our Churches, and makes our Palaces look old, which fouls our Clothes and corrupts the Waters, so as the very Rain, and refreshing Dews which fall in the several Seasons, precipitate this impure vapour, which, with its black and tenacious quality, spots and contaminates whatever is exposed to it.[2]

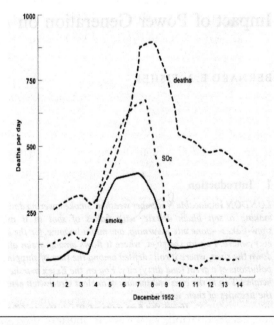

Daily air pollution levels and deaths in London

Other British cities had the same problems, but London, being the largest city, had the worst of it. The famous "London fog" that made navigating the streets impossible was a major health hazard, leading to many deaths from lung complications. Severe fogs and high death tolls continued in London through the 19th and 20th centuries, but until there was an alternative to heating by coal, not much could be done about it. A particularly bad smog, combining smoke and sulphur dioxide, occurred in December 1952, during which four

1. Clive Ponting, *A Green History of the World: The Environment and the Collapse of Great Civilizations* (New York: Penguin, 1993), p. 358.

2. Cited in Ponting, *Op. cit.,* pp. 358-59.

thousand people died, prompting governmental intervention. Britain passed its own Clean Air Act in 1956 to control fuels burnt in cities. The result was considerably less smoke in the air and more hours of sunshine in the winter. A new variety of "smokeless" coal was introduced, and then coal decreased and ultimately disappeared as a fuel in the homes in favour of electricity, gas, and oil.

Making Electricity

Coal is not used much anymore in the First World for residential heating, but that does not mean it is not used extensively. It still provides 25 percent of all the energy consumed annually in the world. Third World countries with easy access to coal and a climate with harsh winters still rely on coal for heating, making their urban air pollution problems as bad as those of European countries fifty years ago. Beijing is a particularly bad example. China has extensive coal deposits; it produces and uses about one-third of the coal consumed in the world.

Unlike some other fossil fuels, there is no foreseeable shortage of coal in the world. Its usage has been limited not by scarcity, but by the pollution it produces. Countries that have other viable alternatives will tend to favour them. Nevertheless, coal is used widely around the world for generating electricity. A coal-fired electric generator is just a modern version of the steam engines that launched the Industrial Revolution and caused so much pollution of cities and industrial areas then. But instead of having the steam engine right where the power is needed, to operate a pump or a conveyor belt, the steam turbines in modern generating stations merely spin magnets far away from where the electricity produced will be required and then is conveyed via power lines. If a generating station can be located away from populated areas, the pollution caused by the fuel used is not immediately apparent.

Electricity is made from many different energy sources: water and wind power, burning oil or gas, and from nuclear fission, but the biggest immediate polluter is the burning of coal. Most coal has a high sulphur content. When it is burned, it released great quantities of sulphur dioxide which then combines with water in the atmosphere to made sulphuric acid. This then falls to earth as acid rain and can cause acidification of the waterways and the soil, and can result in direct damage to the stone work of buildings and monuments.

Since electricity is the backbone of all advanced civilizations, it will continue to be required in ever greater amounts, both in the industrialized nations and the developing countries that are trying to become industrialized. Coal is likely to remain an important fossil fuel for the world.

Operating Cars and Trucks

Another major contributor to the pollution of the atmosphere is emission from internal combustion engines. Even when urban transportation was largely by animal power, pollution on the streets was intolerable. Especially by the 19th century, when the Industrial Revolution was in full swing and commerce in the cities was constantly growing, the streets were an unsanitary mess of horse manure and urine that made the spread of disease that much easier. Moreover the burden on the draft animals was great. By 1900, New York City had to clear away 15 000 dead horses from the streets every year. This problem had no solution—until horses disappeared from the streets altogether due to the rise of the automobile.

Unfortunately, while gasoline and diesel fuel make excellent power sources for vehicles, when consumed in internal combustion engines, they emit a range of unwanted products into the atmosphere: carbon dioxide, carbon monoxide, nitrogen oxides, various other organic compounds, and smoke. The nitrogen oxides, in particular, can decompose and form ozone, a particularly offensive pollutant at ground level. The addition of tetraethyl lead to gasoline in the first two-thirds of the 20th century led to even greater pollution in North America. Lead is still used as an additive in gasoline in some Third World countries.

Smog in Los Angeles.

Los Angeles

The worst example of air pollution in a major city caused primarily by the internal combustion engine is in Los Angeles, California. The Los Angeles area is the second largest population center in the United States (after metropolitan New York). The population of the city and its surrounding area exceed 11 million people. Not much heavy industry remains in the city; what is there has been strictly controlled since the 1970s. Nevertheless, Los Angeles has the worst air pollution in the United States, and the reason is automobiles.

Unlike New York, for example, Los Angeles developed with almost no public transportation. To get anywhere, a motor vehicle was required. Moreover, the city is laid out in a valley that tends to trap air and prevent it dispersing as it would from other cities. During periods of high pressure with low winds, the normal air circulation takes the pollutants out to sea at night, but then brings them back during the following day!

Los Angeles has the greatest density of motor vehicles in the world. There are roughly two vehicles for every three people—including children. The sprawling size of the city also means that people have farther to go to work every day. Many motorists commute 95 to 130 kilometers each way between work and home in order to live in single-family dwellings in the suburbs. Because of this serious pollution problem, the State of California and the City of Los Angeles have imposed stricter pollution controls within the city than are in place elsewhere in the United States. Even so, the city remains a pollution nightmare.

Pollution from Industry

In addition to the pollution that arises from making electricity and from driving vehicles, industries of all sorts continue to expel pollutants into the atmosphere. The familiar smokestack that marked 19th century industry with pride is now a necessary evil. Sending poisons into the air is no longer a sign of progress so much as a reason for governmental regulations to control the offending factory.

A chemical factory in Texas.

Different industries vary in the amount of pollution they cause. Metal fabrication, paper manufacture, and the chemical industry are among the worst polluters of the air, and they also have much to answer for with respect to water pollution, as well as profligate use of natural resources. Yet, they form part of the backbone of modern society. Legislation to protect the environment by regulating these industries has had mixed success.

Some of the processes used by industry produced unnecessary pollutants. These could be changed without permanent harm to the industry, though sometimes at greater expense. The simplest of these regulations merely prevented industries from dumping their wastes in the least expensive way into the water, air, and onto the ground or stipulated processes that must first be applied to minimize environmental damage. Industries that produced emissions of toxic or acrid gases, for example, were frequently required to build furnaces with very tall smokestacks so that the pollution they emitted would disperse high in the atmosphere and not settle on the surrounding community. Or, they had to install scrubbers in their exhausts to remove the worst of the offending chemicals. The chemical industry found that its very products were subject to approval and if found to be harmful were banned.

Much of this remains controversial. Agreement is hard to come by, and compliance is even harder to enforce. There have been successes in some areas, and at least progress in others. The rest of this chapter is a discussion of one industrial product that became a problem and was successfully regulated.

Chlorofluorocarbons

DDT and some of its relatives were banned because they were too dangerous. They were too effective at doing what they were created to do: kill living organisms. However, some other wonder products of the chemical industry also came to be banned even though they did their intended job quite well; they just had unexpected and unacceptable side-effects. Polychlorinated biphenals (PCBs) provides an example of this. Another product also introduced with great optimism and also very effective at what it was intended to do was the category of chemical compounds called *chlorofluorocarbons*, or *CFCs*.

CFCs were introduced with great fanfare by a flamboyant chemist named Thomas Midgely. At the April 1930 meeting of the American Chemical Society, Midgely brought a beaker of his newly synthesized compound to the podium for his talk. He dramatically leaned over the opened beaker and inhaled its vapours, then he exhaled them out through a small tube over a lit candle, which was immediately extinguished. The point of his demonstration was that his new concoction was (1) non-toxic, since he could inhale it safely, and (2) non-flammable, since it would extinguish a flame. That made it safe for consumer products. But the purpose of the product was that it could be readily cooled by compression and then would expand on being near warmth, absorbing the heat and leaving what it was near cooler. It could therefore be used as a coolant in refrigerators. In fact, the Frigidaire division of General Motors had hired Midgely to come up with just such a product. Marketed under the brand name Freon, it was the first chlorofluorocarbon and quickly replaced the cumbersome ammonia and sulphur dioxide based refrigerators that had been in use before.

It was important that Midgely demonstrate that CFCs were non-toxic. His audience of chemists knew well that any compounds containing the deadly chlorine gas could be dangerous. Chlorine is a very active element. If it is not bound tightly in a compound it will react strongly with everything around it and can be toxic. DDT is a chlorine compound as are many other pesticides. But CFCs were chemically inert because, unlike most of the pesticides, CFCs did not contain hydrogen, which tends to make weak bonds that can easily break apart. It was another triumph for modern chemistry.

A Styrofoam cup.

Soon many other uses were found for this miracle product. During the Second World War, the Dow Chemical Company began producing CFCs to make an insulating foam, with the trade name Styrofoam, leading to a doubling of CFC production by 1950. CFCs also made good propellants for all sorts of sprays, since they were liquid under pressure but quickly expanded to a gas on hitting the atmosphere and could be used to push any liquid product into a spray without interacting with it. Another closely related CFC was used as a blowing agent in flexible polyurethane foams, used in furniture, automobile seats, and carpet pads. Another made rigid foams, which rivaled fiberglass as an insulating material.

Then in the 1960s came air conditioning. This caught on quickly in businesses and then in homes. When introduced in warmer climates, it spelled an economic change for these areas as businesses and population began to flourish. The prime example is the transformation of the American Sunbelt into leading industrial centres. With air conditioning in home and business, the public soon wanted to be cool traveling as well. As vehicles tend to be poorly insulated and the connecting hoses to the air conditioning unit often leak, the typical car air conditioner requires as much CFC refrigerant as the average house. Car, bus, and truck air conditioners soon accounted for more use of CFC as a refrigerant than all others combined.

These wonder chemicals continued to find more uses. Their ability to expand when released from pressure but at the same time not interact with anything made them the perfect addition to many processes. CFC production continued to double of every five years. In 1974, total production had reached about one billion kilograms a year. Then, it all began to come apart.

Part Seven
Fouling Our Nest

The Ozone Layer

Curiously, the first investigations that led to the conclusion that CFCs were not as safe as had been assumed had nothing to do with chlorofluorocarbons. Instead, the realization that a problem might exist came out of studies of the possible effects of flight in the stratosphere. In 1970, the United States, Britain, and France were jointly considering building a fleet of supersonic transport airplanes (*SSTs*) to crisscross the Atlantic and were examining the possible implications of such a project. Several studies were published that calculated that the exhaust of SSTs, flying high in the stratosphere, would destroy significant amounts of the ozone that naturally occurs there. Though other studies at the same time came to opposing conclusions, the danger was enough that the U.S. Congress withdrew its support for the project. Ultimately the Concorde SSTs were built jointly between Britain and France only.

The *stratosphere* is a layer of very thin air that surrounds the Earth at an elevation of between 10 to 50 kilometers above the surface. Any sunlight that reaches the Earth has to travel through this layer. Back before there was life on Earth, sunlight streamed down through the atmosphere, bombarding the surface with all its radiation, including that which is below the spectrum of visible light, in the area we call *ultraviolet*. This ultraviolet light is sufficiently disruptive that it would have prevented the evolution of life on Earth, except that much of it is shielded by water. Hence, the first life forms evolved deep in the sea. These first life forms, oceanic plants, released oxygen gas, which then bubbled up to the atmosphere. When there was a sufficient layer of oxygen in the lower atmosphere, some of it drifted up to higher elevations. Oxygen normally forms a stable compound with two oxygen atoms, O_2. However another form is possible, with three oxygen atoms, O_3. This is the form we call *ozone*. Ozone can be formed in a number of ways. At ground level, ozone is a dangerous pollutant, produced from the exhausts of gasoline and diesel engines; it can also be produced by electrostatic discharges.

In the stratosphere, when ultraviolet rays strike ordinary O_2, it is sometimes broken apart into two separate oxygen atoms, which then through another process can recombine as ozone. Unlike ozone at ground level, which is a nuisance, the ozone in the stratosphere serves an essential purpose. Ozone molecules intercept and block the rays of the sun in the ultraviolet range. More precisely, it absorbs most of the ultraviolet light at the smallest wavelengths, called UV-C, and most of the ultraviolet light at the intermediate wavelengths, called UV-B. It does not absorb much of the ultraviolet light that is just below the visible spectrum, UV-A.

We would not have life on Earth as we know it without the layer of ozone that over millions of years has formed in the stratosphere. Only after there was sufficient ozone at high elevations was it even possible for life to begin to evolve on the surface of the Earth. Ozone creation and destruction is a continuous process. Both ultraviolet rays and strong elements can cause ozone either to form or to breakdown. The presence in the stratosphere of too many of the gases that can destroy the ozone layer would upset the balance that has existed for millions of years and could threaten life on Earth.

This was the concern of the scientists who worried about what the exhaust fumes from supersonic transports would do when loosed in the stratosphere. Would they come in contact with the ozone and destroy it. The worst feature of these exhausts is that the gases they contain can work as *catalysts* to destroy ozone. That is, they enter into a chemical reaction with the ozone and break it apart, but emerge in their original state where they are ready to destroy another ozone molecule. One chlorine atom, for example, can destroy as many as 100 thousand ozone molecules.

And this is where attention was suddenly drawn to chlorofluorocarbons. CFCs had been produced and used in great quantities because they would not react with anything else. But what happened to all these CFCs once they were emitted into the atmosphere? The landmark study published in 1974 that began the controversy over CFCs was by two chemists at the University of California[1] who argued that while CFCs remain inert at ground level, some of it will make its way to the stratosphere, where ultraviolet light can cause chlorine atoms to separate. Those chlorine atoms can do considerable damage to the ozone. Given the very large amounts of CFCs entering the environment every year, they calculated that there would be a destruction of in the neighbourhood of 10 percent of the ozone layer within the next century.

Thus began a scientific controversy that has continued to the present day. Other studies came to other conclusions, alarms were raised, and assurances were given. The United States issued a ban on the use of CFCs as an aerosol propellant, which represented half of all of the CFC used each year. Canada, Sweden, and Norway all followed suit. Other countries were not convinced.

Among the particular concerns was that any depletion of the ozone layer will have immediate consequences for the human species. A depletion in the amount of

---

1.   Mario   Molina   and   F.   Sherwood   Rowland,   "Stratospheric   Sink   for Chlorofluoromethanes: Chlorine Atomic-atalyzsed (*sic*) Destruction of Ozone," *Nature* 249 (June 28): 810-12.

stratospheric ozone will permit a much higher lever of ultraviolet light to reach the earth. Our skin has evolved to absorb the sun's rays optimally within a very narrow range of radiation. More than the usual amount of ultraviolet light, particularly in the UV-B range, produces a much higher risk of skin cancer. But that is not all. All living organisms, plants as well as animals, that live on the surface of the Earth have evolved to live within a fixed range of solar radiation. Any sudden change in that could wreak havoc on the food supply across the globe.

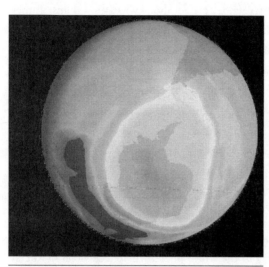

The hole in the ozone layer over Antarctica, October 1, 1998. Darker shades represent denser areas, lighter shades represent areas of lesser density. From NASA, Great Images in NASA.

The Hole in the Sky

Because of the newly discovered threat to the ozone layer, regular measurements of its density began to be made using an instrument that had been developed in 1924 to study seasonal variations in ozone. In 1981, measurements made from several stations in the Antarctic reported drastic reductions in the ozone layer above the South Pole. At first, no attention was paid to these strange measurements, because it was assumed by all that their instruments were at fault. A problem with the device used was that sometimes it just failed to give an accurate reading and instead gave a very low reading. Likewise, the next year a reading made from an orbiting satellite also recorded low levels, but the computer that logged those measurements had been programmed to ignore anything below a certain threshold, assuming it was an error. No one was expecting such a significant drop in the ozone levels. When finally it was realized that the measurement were not errors, government agencies all over the world sought to find a way to pull together and work to find a solution.

The Montreal Protocol

In September 1987, an international conference was held in Montreal to take steps to prevent further deterioration of the ozone layer. The agreement reached there was especially significant in that it was the first global treaty to protect the atmosphere from the effects of human interventions. The agreement, called the *Montreal Protocol*, set limits to the consumption of CFCs and included a target year for complete phase-out in the developed countries. Amazingly, 164 countries signed on to the agreement. Later research showed that the Montreal meeting had underestimated the rate of ozone depletion. Subsequently, tighter restrictions were put in place and effectively enforced.

Steps Toward Repairing the Damage

The Montreal Protocol has been hailed as a success of international diplomacy and vote of confidence for the methods of the United Nations. On a country-by-country basis, environmental protection agencies now regulate industrial practices and set standards with the good of the entire population in mind. Much of this has worked successfully. Some particularly harmful products, such as leaded gasoline, PCBs, CFCs, and DDT, are either banned outright or carefully controlled. Most of the regulations and restrictions apply only to the industrialized nations, but then, most of the use of these products has been in those countries—so far.

Perhaps because of the successes of these interventions, environmental groups around the world have sought to widen their mandate and come to some worldwide agreements that will work toward a healthier environment for everyone. But the jump is enormous from individual harmful products and practices to global regulations on industry and trade. This is the mission of the environmental movement. We return to this topic at the end of Part Eight.

All these actions have greatly changed the face of heavy industry in the industrialized nations, where environmental concerns have been taken seriously. The issues that remain in these countries are less a matter of problems in particular industries and more problems of quantity: too many people, too much energy consumption, too many cars, etc. These problems are less easy to regulate away, though considerable progress has been made to find better, less polluting, less wasteful ways to use electricity and to power automobiles.

However, when it comes to air pollution, there are no effective borders. One country may have stringent regulations that do effectively prevent the production of airborne pollutants, but somewhere else in the world, those same pollutants continue to be produced and will circulate around the globe. This is an area very difficult to police.

Current environmental issues: deformities caused by hormone disruptors, recycling programs, and tracking the rise in greenhouse gases at Mauna Loa in Hawaii.

PART EIGHT

Current Issues

Human civilization has reached the 21st century having scored many triumphs and suffered many defeats. We have used the resources of the Earth to accomplish technological feats that give at least some of us an amazingly comfortable and rich life. True, not everyone in the world has experienced the richness of life in the industrialized world, but there is yet hope that technology will find ways to bring health and prosperity to all. However, it is also possible that technology will put such a strain on the environment of the world that we will not be able to maintain the standards that we already have.

The environmental problems discovered in the past are mostly still with us. Some of them always will be, though we may find better ways of working around them. New concerns will always come to the forefront and demand our attention. The growing environmental movement in the world is ever alert to new perils and new challenges that must be met.

Part Eight, the final segment of this book, looks at some of these contemporary issues and discusses how we are dealing with them. These are problems at the forefront of environmental studies today. How we handle these is an indicator of our ability to cope with the ever more complex challenges that the future will bring us.

The topics here are: hormone imposters, a relatively new peril that now is of special concern in the most advanced countries; biotechnology, the leading technological hope for feeding the growing population of the world, but one with many unknown consequences; the perils of life in the technological world, both of the past and present; and the environmental movement, which has arisen to uncover problems, let the world know about them, and try to solve them. The last chapter also takes a look at what is probably the most contentious environmental issue of the day, global warming.

For Further Reading

Bailey, Ronald. *Global Warming and Other Eco-Myths: How the Environmental Movement Uses False Science to Scare Us to Death*. Roseville, CA: Prima Publishing, 2002.

Bartsch, Ulrich, and Benito Müller, with Ashbjørn Aaheim. *Fossil Fuels in a Changing Climate: Impacts of the Kyoto Protocol and Developing Country Participation*. Oxford: Oxford University Press, 2000.

Berkson, D. Lindsey. *Hormone Deception: How Everyday Foods and Products Are Disrupting Your Hormones—and How to Protect Yourself and Your Family* Chicago: Contemporary Books, 2000..

Bernards, Neal, ed. *The Environmental Crisis*. Opposing Viewpoints Series. San Diego: Greenhaven Press, 1991.

Bertell, Rosalie. *Planet Earth: The Latest Weapon of War*. Montréal: Black Rose Books, 2001.

Boehmer-Christiansen, Sonja, and Aynsley Kellow. *International Environmental Policy: Interests and the Failure of the Kyoto Process*. Cheltenham, UK: Edward Elgar, 2002.

Botkin, Daniel B. *Discordant Harmonies: A New Ecology for the Twenty-First Century*. New York: Oxford University Press, 1990.

Boulter, Michael. *Extinction: Evolution and the End of Man*. New York: Columbia University Press, 2002.

Brown, Michael, and John May. *The Greenpeace Story*. London: Dorling Kindersley, 1989.

Brown, Paige. *Climate, Biodiversity, and Forests: Issues and Opportunities Emerging from the Kyoto Protocol*. Washington: World Resources Institute, 1998.

Byrne, John, and Daniel Rich, eds. *Energy and Environment: The Policy Challenge*. Energy Policy Studies Series, Vol. 6. New Brunswick, NJ: Transaction Publishers, 1992.

Cardwell, Donald. *The Norton History of Technology*. New York: W.W. Norton, 1995.

Colborn, Theo, Dianne Dumanoski, and John Peterson Myers. *Our Stolen Future: Are We Threatening Our Fertility, Intelligence, and Survival?—A Scientific Detective Story* New York: Penguin Plume, 1997..

Court, Thijs de la. *Beyond Brundtland: Green Development in the 1990s,* trans. by Ed Bayens and Nigel Harle. New York: New Horizons, 1990.

Chase, Alston. "Harvard and the Making of the Unabomber.," *Atlantic Monthly* 285, no. 6 (June, 2000), 41-65.

Ehrlich, Paul R. *The Population Bomb.* New York: Ballantine, 1968.

Ehrlich, Paul R., and Anne H. Ehrlich, *Betrayal of Science and Reason: How Anti-Environmental Rhetoric Threatens Our Future.* Washington: Island Press, 1996.

Ehrlich, Paul R., Anne H. Ehrlich, and Gretchen C. Daily. *The Stork and the Plow: The Equity Answer to the Human Dilemma.* New York: Putnam, 1995.

Foreman, Dave. *Confessions of an Eco-Warrior.* New York: Harmony, 1991.

Fukuyama, Francis. *Our Posthuman Future: Consequences of the Biotechnology Revolution.* New York: Farrar, Strauss and Giroux, 2002.

Gordon, Anita, and David Suzuki. *It's a Matter of Survival.* Toronto: Stoddart, 1990.

Gottlieb, Robert. *Forcing the Spring: The Transformation of the American Environmental Movement.* Washington: Island Press, 1993.

Grubb, Michael, with Christiaan Vrolijk and Duncan Brack. *The Kyoto Protocol: A Guide and Assessment.* London: Royal Institute of International Affairs, 1999.

Grumbie, R. Edward. *Ghost Bears: Exploring the Biodiversity Crisis* Washington: Island Press, 1992.

Hitt, Jack, "A Gospel According to the Earth: Sown by Science, A New Eco-Faith Takes Root," *Harper's* 307, No. 1838 (July 2003), 41-55.

Hostetter, Martha, ed. *Energy Policy.* The Reference Shelf, Vol 74, No. 2. New York: H. W. Wilson, 2002.

Jevons, W. Stanley. *The Coal Question: An Inquiry Concerning the Progress of the Nation, and the Probable Exhaustion of Our Coal-Mines* London, 1865.

Jones, Laura, ed. *Global Warming: The Science and the Politics.* Vancouver: Fraser Institute, 1997.

Kandel, Robert. *Our Changing Climate.* New York: McGraw-Hill, 1992.

Kooten, G. Cornelis van, Erwin H. Bulte, and A.R.E. Sinclair, *Conserving Nature's Diversity: Insights from Biology, Ethics and Economics* Aldershot, Hampshire: Ashgate, 2000..

Kümmerer, Klaus, ed.*Pharmaceuticals in the Environment.* Berlin: Springer, 2001.

Laidlaw, Stuart, *Secret Ingredients: The Brave New World of Industrial Farming.* Toronto: McClelland & Stewart, 2003.

Lapierre, Dominique, and Javier Moro. *Five Past Midnight in Bhopal,* trans. by Kathryn Spink. New York: Warner Books, 2002.

Lee, Martha F. *Earth First!: Environmental Apocalypse.* Syracuse, NY: Syracuse University Press, 1995.

Lewontin, Richard. *The Triple Helix: Gene, Organism, and Environment.* Cambridge: Harvard University Press, 2000.

Lomborg, Bjørn.*The Skeptical Environmentalist: Measuring the Real State of the World.* Cambridge: Cambridge University Press, 1998.

Mangun, William R., and Daniel H. Henning. *Managing the Environmental Crisis,* 2nd ed. Durham, NC: Duke University Press, 1999.

Manning, Richard. *Food's Frontier: The Next Green Revolution* Berkeley: University of California Press, 2000..

Marco, Gino J., Robert M. Hollingworth, and William Durham, eds. *Silent Spring Revisited.* Washington, D.C.: American Chemical Society, 1987.

Marcus, Alan I. *Cancer from Beef: DES, Federal Food Regulation, and Consumer Confidence.* Baltimore: Johns Hopkins University Press, 1994.

Marples, David R. *Chernobyl and Nuclear Power in the USSR.* Edmonton: Canadian Institute of Ukrainian Studies, 1986.

_____. *The Social Impact of the Chernobyl Disaster.* New York: St. Martin's Press, 1988.

Marsh, George Perkins, *Man and Nature,* originally published, 1864. Reissued edited by D. Lowenthal. Cambridge: Harvard University Press, 1969.

McCormick, John. *The Global Environmental Movement. Reclaiming Paradise.* London: Belhaven, 1989, 1992.

McKibbin, Warwick J., and Peter J. Wilcoxen. *Climate Change Policy after Kyoto: Blueprint for a Realistic Approach.* Washington: Brookings Institution Press, 2002.

McKitrick, Ross, and Randall M. Wigle. "The Kyoto Protocol: Canada's Risky Rush to Judgment," *C.D. Howe Institute Commentary,* No. 169 (October 2002).

Meadows, Donella H., et al. *The Limits to Growth: A Report for the Club of Rome's Project on the Predicament of Mankind.* New York: New American Library, 1974.

Moore, Thomas Gale. *In Sickness or in Health: The Kyoto Protocol Versus Global Warming.* Hoover Institution Essays in Public Policy, No. 104 (2000).

Novotny, Patrick. *Where We Live, Work and Play: The Environmental Justice Movement and the Struggle for a New Environmentalism.* Westport, CT: Praeger, 2000.

Petroski, Henry. *To Engineer is Human: The Role of Failure in Successful Design.* New York: St. Martinís Press, 1985.

Pompe, Jeffrey J., and James R. Rinehart. *Environmental Conflict: In Search of Common Ground.* Albany, NY: State University of New York Press, 2002.

Porritt, Jonathon. *Playing Safe: Science and the Environment.* New York: Thames and Hudson, 2000.

Prestowitz, Clyde. *Rogue Nation: American Unilateralism and the Failure of Good Intentions.* New York: Basic Books, 2003.

Rees, Martin. *Our Final Hour: A Scientist's Warning: How Terror, Error, and Environmental Disaster Threaten Humankind's Future in this Century.* New York: Basic Books, 2003.

Rowell, Andrew. *Green Backlash: Global Subversion of the Environmental Movement.* London: Routledge, 1996.

Sale, Kirkpatrick. *The Green Revolution: The American Environmental Movement, 1962-1992.* New York: Hill and Wang, 1993.

Scarce, Rik. *Eco-Warriors: Understanding the Radical Environmental Movement.* Chicago: Noble, 1990.

Schell, Jonathan. *The Fate of the Earth.* New York: Alfred A. Knopf, 1982.

Shiva, Vandana. *Tomorrow's Biodiversity* New York: Thames and Hudson, 2000..

Shrivastava, Paul. *Bhopal: Anatomy of a Crisis,* 2nd ed. London: Paul Chapman, 1992.

Suzuki, David, and Holly Dressel. *From Naked Ape to Superspecies: A Personal Perspective on Humanity and the Global Eco-Crisis.* Toronto: Stoddart, 1999.

Van Kooten, G. Cornelius, Erwin H. Bulte, and A.R.E. Sinclair, eds. *Conserving Nature's Diversity: Insights from Biology, Ethics, and Economics.* Aldershot, Hampshire, England: Ashgate Publishing Limited, 2000.

Victor, David G. *The Collapse of the Kyoto Protocol and the Struggle to Slow Global Warming.* Princeton: Princeton University Press, 2001.

Weir, David. *The Bhopal Syndrome: Pesticide Manufacturing and the Third World.* Penang, Malaysia: International Organization of Consumers Unions, Regional Office for Asia and the Pacific, 1986.

Whorton, James. *Before Silent Spring: Pesticides and Public Health in Pre-DDT America.* Princeton: Princeton University Press, 1974.

Worldwatch Institute, *Vital Signs 2001: Trends That Are Shaping Our Future.* New York: W. W. Norton, 2001.

An advertisement in the *Journal of Obstetrics and Gynecology* in June 1957 urging doctors to prescribe DES for all pregnancies.

Chapter 33

Hormone Disruption

Theo Colborn was fifty years old when she decided to enroll in graduate school and work toward a Ph.D. in zoology, giving up her career at that time as a sheep farmer and also not returning to an earlier career as a pharmacist. She had been an avid amateur environmentalist, but wanted to get legitimate scientific training. In 1987, Ph.D. in hand, she got her first real scientific research job, a project to assess the environmental health of the Great Lakes. Perhaps because she was finally doing just what she wanted to do and was not trying to build a career, she saw the significance of some things that other people passed over and was willing to speak up and write about her ideas before they had been studied to death.

Theo Colborn.

In 1991, she helped organize a conference at the Wingspread Conference Center in Wisconsin to discuss the work she and others were doing. The conference produced a statement of the results of their work, called the Wingspread Consensus Statement, which set out their concerns and made recommendations for future research.

What Colborn and the others at the Wingspread conference had come to talk about was their new found evidence: chemicals that had been released into the environment were causing not just outright poisoning, as Rachel Carson had shown in 1962, but also a more subtle interference with the endocrine systems of living beings.

Five years later, she and two of her colleagues published a book that laid all these out for the public in non-specialist's language and with memorable examples. The book was called *Our Stolen Future*.[1] It did not have the revolutionary impact of *Silent Spring*, but its

---

1. Theo Colborn, Dianne Dumanoski, and John Peterson Myers, *Our Stolen Future: Are We Threatening Our Fertility, Intelligence, and Survival? A Scientific Detective Stor* (New York: Penguin Plume, 1997).

message was equally unnerving. U.S. Vice President Al Gore, who had just the year before written a foreword to the 30th anniversary edition of Rachel Carson's work also wrote a foreword to this book and called it the sequel to *Silent Spring*. The message of *Our Stolen Future* was frightening indeed.

Troubling Evidence

The book opens with a list of strange and inexplicable anomalies in animal populations from widely dispersed locations over the previous 50 years: bald eagles on the Gulf Coast of Florida that had lost all interest in mating; a mystery die-off of otters in England; mink farmers near Lake Michigan having trouble breeding their captive stock; a herring gull colony on Lake Ontario where the eggs did not hatch and the chick embryos were deformed; female gulls in the Channel Islands in California, in the Great Lakes, and in Puget Sound that shared the same nests; alligators in Lake Apopka, Florida, that had abnormally small penises; a surprising seal die-off in northern Europe and another of dolphins in the Mediterranean; and evidence of a sharp drop in human male sperm counts between 1938 and 1990. Some of these events were correlated with pesticide applications or spills, or pollution in general, but no direct link had been made that would explain the connection to these outcomes.

The link made and reported in detail in *Our Stolen Future* is through the endocrine system. All of these anomalies could be traced to some substance ingested by these creatures that disrupted the normal hormonal balance in their endocrine systems, leading to deaths, deformities, and other serious malfunctions. These substances might have been out-and-out poisons, such as DDT, or industrial chemicals that got loose in the environment, such as PCBs, or they might have been accumulations of the residues of drugs deliberately taken by people to treat certain conditions. What made the book so riveting to the public was the revelation that people inadvertently ingested all of these hormone disruptors, and there was no reason to think they were not doing damage to us as well.

Sexuality

Hormones control many of the functions of the body of all animals throughout their lives. What is most striking is the effect of a hormonal imbalance during prenatal development. The development of sexuality is certainly among the most interesting, and perhaps the most important part of the maturation process that is under the control of hormones.

Some work done by biologist Frederick vom Saal at the University of Missouri showed that female mice with higher *testosterone* levels were more aggressive than their sisters who had more normal levels of testosterone; male mice with higher than normal *estrogen* levels were more aggressive toward the newborn mice pups, while those with more normal levels made better fathers, spending nearly as much time caring for the pups as the mother.

By itself, this may seem to be no more than what we would expect different hormone levels to do, but the surprising aspect of this research was that vom Saal was able to determine that these variations in hormone levels arose from the placement of the embryos in the mother's uterus. The lab mice that vom Saal worked with tended to be born in litters of a dozen at a time. Vom Saal found that the female mice that had the higher testosterone levels—and were the more aggressive—had positions in the mother's uterus *between* two brothers,

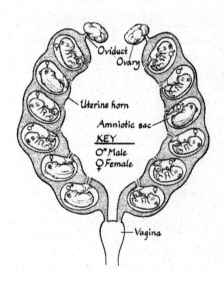

while the males born with higher estrogen levels had positions *between* two sisters. The female embryos that were between two males were bathed with an excess amount of testosterone, while the male embryos between two females were exposed to more than the normal amount of estrogen. The differences in any case were very, very small, but enough to produce noticeably different behaviour patterns in the mice after birth. Vom Saal was astounded by the amazing sensitivity of the developing fetus to miniscule differences of exposure. Hormones work in the body in extremely dilute solutions, measured in parts per trillion. The more "feminine" mouse received an exposure on the order of 100 parts per trillion of estradiol—the most potent form of estrogen—while her more aggressive sister received an exposure of 135 parts per trillion. In discussing this work, Theo Colborn and her co-authors made an analogy with a mixture of gin and tonic. Think of the estradiol as gin and the water solution it is diluted in as tonic, she says. These concentrations are comparable to 100 drops of gin versus 135 drops in one thousand railroad tank cars filled with tonic.[1] If such small differences in normal hormone balances can make noticeable personality changes in mice, what else is affected by hormonal differences in the gestation period of any animal—humans, for example?

In normal human prenatal development, there aren't the complications of siblings sharing the same womb, but there are differences in the amounts of various hormones bathing the fetus due to the mother's physical condition and what she has been exposed to. Human sexuality is ultimately determined by the 23rd pair of chromosomes in the original fertilized ovum. If both are the same, what we call *X-chromosomes*, then the fetus develops into a female. If one of them is different, the so-called *Y-chromosome*, then a male results. But how this actually happens in development is a matter of hormones. In the first six weeks of development, the fetus of a human baby is essentially the same, no matter what sex it will become. In the seventh week, if there is a Y-chromosome present, it starts a process that will cause the fetus to grow male testicles. The testicles will then secrete hormones, most importantly, testosterone, that direct the remainder of the growth pattern that distinguishes male from female. If a Y-chromosome is not present, the fetus will develop into a female.

Androgeny

Even if there is a Y-chromosome present, it may not do its job properly. The fetus may fail to get the message to develop the testicles or the testosterone that the testicles secrete may fail to produce its normal result. This can happen if something is present in the womb that interferes with these normal processes. In such cases, the male part of the anatomy does not develop and the baby that is born is, to all appearances, female. Often it is only at puberty that it is discovered that the "girl" is not developing into a normal woman, because she really is a "boy"—that is, she has the XY chromosome combination, not the XX of a normal female. Other cases are not so complete. The baby may appear to be male, but have an extremely small penis or testicles that do not descend.

DES

Another of the "wonders" of modern chemistry that was developed in the early 20th century and introduced into the market place was *diethylstilbestrol*, commonly called

---

1. *Ibid.*, p. 40.

DES. This synthetic chemical acted in the body much the same as natural estrogen. In the belief that many miscarriages were due to insufficient levels of estrogen, DES was prescribed to women who were having difficult pregnancies. Soon, doctors began prescribing DES to women with completely normal pregnancies. It was also prescribed for mothers who wished to stop nursing to suppress milk production, to ease the symptoms of menopause, and to treat everything from acne to cancer to gonorrhea. On university campuses, DES was given out by the campus clinics as a "morning after" pill to prevent conception.

The middle of the 20th century was a period of great optimism in the chemical industry and by extension in the public. So many new synthetic chemicals had been found that had miraculous effects at controlling problems: DDT and a host of other pesticides, PCBs, CFCs, the growing plastics industry, and all sorts of pharmaceuticals that cured or curtailed terrible diseases, as well as many other drugs that seemed to help nature along. One obstruction after another that got in the way of human happiness was removed with the help of science and technology—especially by the chemists. To repeat that comment by industry spokesman Dr. Robert White-Stevens (quoted in Chapter 29) that had been directed against Rachel Carson, "the modern chemist, the modern biologist and scientist, believes that man is steadily controlling nature."

The Thalidomide Scandal

Then, in 1962, the very year of the publication of *Silent Spring,* came the horrible news that another wonder drug prescribed to pregnant women frequently resulted in very serious birth defects, children born without arms and legs, for example. This was *thalidomide,* a drug routinely prescribed by doctors to expectant mothers to prevent nausea, or just as a tranquilizer. Eight thousand children were born with defects before the drug was finally removed from the market. The problem had not been anticipated because it was not thought that drugs given to the mother could cross the placenta in the womb and reach the fetus. The inescapable lesson was that a drug that has no harmful effects on an adult could be devastating to a developing fetus.

DES and Cancer

In 1971, the bad news about DES began to surface. While not the thalidomide story all over again, it nevertheless was serious. Doctors at the Massachusetts General Hospital found a link between mothers who took DES when pregnant and subsequent cancer cases in their daughters when they were between the ages of 15 and 22. They published a report of their findings in the *New England Journal of Medicine*, which was summarized in the popular press. What was particularly surprising was the length of time before the symptoms appeared in the child. The symptoms that first came to the doctors' attention were life-threatening malignancies, and it was through those diseases that the connection to DES was traced. But then, once the news of this problem hit the press, mothers who had taken DES years ago began to wonder if their own children might not have been affected in some other way. Soon it emerged that a wide range of ill effects were caused by taking DES, affecting children of both sexes and ranging from cancer to compromised immune systems and infertility.

On the one hand, the lesson of DES is that the effects of intentionally introducing a synthetic chemical into the body can upset a hormonal balance that is much more subtle that we may have realized. On the other hand, another lesson is more obvious. DES was not a hormone; it was a synthetic chemical that acted *like* a hormone. That is the real issue: the body can mistake a manufactured chemical for a hormone and react as if it is a hormone. Many manufactured chemicals find their way into our bodies, as Rachel Carson pointed out in 1962. Now it is clear that there may be all sorts of unintended effects produced by chemicals that were never intended for human consumption.

Fight Cancer—Avoid Food

All the while that medical science was uncovering a connection between pregnant mothers who took DES and later health problems with their children, DES was being fed to cattle and other animals to make them put on weight. In 1954, an animal nutritionist at Iowa State College discovered that DES would promote growth in cattle. The U.S. Food and Drug Administration approved its use, and a patent was issued for a version of DES that became the first artificial animal growth stimulant. As compared to untreated cattle, cattle taking DES quickly gained more than 10 percent in weight while consuming 200 kilograms less feed and thereby reached market 35 days sooner. With DES, cattle ranches moved from open-field grazing to confined feedlots. By the early 1960s, about 95 percent of American cattlemen fed DES to their cattle. They added it either to the cattle's feed or directly fed it into their bloodstream with implants on their necks or ears.

Even at the early stages of its agricultural use, DES was viewed as a possible carcinogen. For that reason, it was the subject of considerable discussion in scientific and governmental circles in the late 1950s and '60s. This discussion focussed on both how to protect the public from the health dangers and how not to interfere with the economic benefit of the growth stimulants. In 1958, Congress passed a law containing what was popularly called the "Delaney Cancer Clause," named after Congressman James Delaney, who chaired the House of Representatives "Select Committee to Investigate the Use of Chemicals in Food Production." The Delaney Clause outlawed the sale of food containing substances found to have induced cancer in humans or animals. In 1959, the Food and Drug Administration exercised the Delaney Clause and banned any *new* uses of DES and arsenic in cattle feed, on the grounds that both had been found to cause cancer in laboratory mice. But the FDA exempted the DES neck and ear implants on the grounds that they were not food additives and therefore not covered by the Delaney clause. And, any current uses of DES in food formulas were allowed to continue. This seemingly technical ban on new uses of DES was viewed by agri-industry as a detail to be clarified so that new uses of DES could continue to be found.

Both Iowa State College, which owned the patent, and the pharmaceutical companies that manufactured DES for animals spoke out against the ban. The Eli Lily Company, the largest manufacturer of DES cattle feed, disparaged the evidence of a cancer risk.

> The company acknowledged that in "some 200 cancer prone hybrid mice...tumors were produced in over half the mice fed stibestrol [DES]," but denied that study's validity. None of the "429 rats, 149 fowls, 13 pigs, 9 dogs, 7 goats and 1 cow," as well as assorted guinea pigs, monkeys, rabbits, and "many other strains of mice" fed DES in tests had developed cancer, and human medicine had relied on massive doses of DES for two decades without apparent mishap or tumor genesis.[1]

The National Institute on Animal Agriculture ridiculed Congress for enforcing outrageously stringent criteria on food production. Their slogan, "Fight cancer—avoid food," was intended to show in a phrase how out of touch with reality the Delaney Clause was. The dean of agriculture at Purdue University, in a widely quoted address, announced that "consumers should be eternally grateful" for agricultural chemicals. To live the good life, one had to take risks, he said. We do not outlaw "swimming pools or automobiles just because somebody might misuse them.... If we eliminated from our

---

1.　Alan I. Marcus, *Cancer from Beef: DES, Federal Food Regulation, and Consumer Confidence* (Baltimore: Johns Hopkins University Press, 1994), p. 52.

lives everything that might cause cancer in animals, our twentieth century civilization…would be impossible."[1]

In 1962, after much lobbying, Congress passed a new regulation that dealt with the applicability of the Delaney Clause to DES. A provision of this law, called the "DES Proviso," specified that the Delaney Clause would not apply so long as an additive did not harm the animal it was fed to and no residue of the additive was preseent in any edible portion of the animal after slaughter. This, in effect, re-opened the door to greater usage of DES, so long as the amounts used did not show up in the test for residues.

In the 1970s, the news of the relationship between pregnant mothers' use of DES and cancer cases among their daughters was widely discussed, but still DES-laced cattle feed and DES implants continued to be used widely in the cattle industry. It was not until 1979 that the Food and Drug Administration finally banned DES for good on the grounds of its threat to human health.[2]

Plastics

Hormones and chemicals that our bodies take to be hormones can enter our bodies in any number of ways—by medications deliberately taken, in food, and mixed in environmental pollution. These are all routes than can be monitored and regulated. We may have made many mistakes in the past in approving medications or food additives or allowing pollutants to accumulate, but now that we know better, we can work toward eliminating these risks. It's a lot harder to eliminate the risk that comes from contact with something that is all around us and that is an essential component of much of our modern civilized environment.

---

1.   *Ibid.*, p. 57.

2.   Even then, the use of the drug did not come to an end. The assumption had been that, once banned, cattlemen would faithfully comply with the law and cease using the additive. In 1980, a whistle-blower alerted the FDA that a division of Allied Chemical was still manufacturing the DES-feed. Investigations showed this was not an isolated case. Twenty-five firms were continuing to supply DES pellets for implantation. The FDA found over 400 thousand cattle with the implants. This was a very large and widespread violation of the regulations, considered by the FDA as "the biggest veterinary drug scandal in U.S. history." DES had been a financial bonanza for the cattle industry. Many cattlemen were not willing to give that up easily. *Ibid.*, pp. 154-55.

There is hardly any category of manufactured substances in the modern world more ubiquitous than plastics. Plastics are everywhere and in everything. Plastics have so many advantages that ever since they were first synthesized by the chemical industry, they have steadily grown in usages. They are impermeable, easy to clean, resist breakage, can be moulded into any shape and size, and are inexpensive. They are the ideal material out of which to make so many practical products. It would be difficult for modern civilization if

A close-up view of the structure of plastic.

we discovered that they were dangerous to our health. It's hard to imagine how we could possibly live without them. Alas, in the 1980s, evidence began to surface that plastics did pose a health risk.

At Tufts Medical School in Boston, two medical scientists, Drs. Ana Soto and Carlos Sonnenschein, had been working for some years studying cell multiplication in cancer. Their work centered on trying to locate the inhibitor that prevents cells from multiplying, and then trying to find why this inhibitor might stop working. The procedure was to take samples of breast cancer cells that had ceased to multiply, cover them with a serum that inhibited cell growth, and then slowly and precisely add very small amounts of estrogen, which would make them start to multiply again. The work required very exact and careful procedures to avoid any possibility of contamination. They took many precautions and only did the work themselves.

Contamination in a Laboratory

One day at the end of 1987, everything went haywire in their laboratory. Samples of cancer cells that they were slowly culturing—as they had done for years—suddenly started multiplying wildly. They concluded that some sort of estrogen contamination must have gotten into the lab. For four months, they sifted through every possible explanation of what could have gone wrong, including even sabotage by jealous colleagues. Finally, they reached the only remaining possibility: the contamination had come from the plastic tubes that they used to store the serum developed to inhibit cell growth. This was a complete surprise since they had been using the same kind of lab tubes for years. Yet when they tried switching to a different brand, the problem went away. Something in the lab tubes they were getting from the Corning Company was contaminating their experiments. Something that acted like estrogen must be leaching from these tubes into the serum. This seemed impossible since the plastic was supposed to be totally inert. Yet there it was.

When the Drs. Soto and Sonnenchein contacted Corning about this, they discovered that the company had recently changed the recipe for making these tubes, substituting a different resin that would make the tubes less brittle. Since the change was considered only a technical detail, the catalogue number was not changed. Moreover, Corning would not reveal the details of the resin used on the grounds that it was a trade secret.

Plastics as Hormone Disruptors

It quickly became apparent that not only were the laboratory tubes leaching a compound that acted like the hormone estrogen, but that this same resin ingredient was in a great many different plastic products used by consumers all the time. If all of these products leached even an infinitesimally small amount of a synthetic estrogen, this could add up to a significant amount being ingested by people, some of whom would have a high sensitivity to estrogen.

Further work by Soto and Sonnenschein established that the particular family of chemicals that caused the trouble, alkyphenols, were added by plastics manufacturers to polystyrene, polyvinyl chloride (PVC), contraceptive creams(!), detergents, and a range of other products. At almost the same time, as Soto and Sonnenschein were doing their investigation, another team of researchers at Stanford University was having similar trouble with their experiments. This problem also turned out to involve contamination from the plastic flasks used in their laboratories. A different chemical additive was identified as the culprit however, one that also had wide usage, in such products as bottled drinking water and the linings used in canned foods.

Surrounded by Hormone Disruptors

What makes this all so insidious is that everywhere around us are products or the residues of products that affect our endocrine systems by acting like hormones. Some of these contain chemicals that that act like hormones, *hormone mimics*, causing the body to react as though the hormone they resemble is present. Others have a similar chemical structure to natural hormones, but act very differently. These often block the natural hormones in the body from reaching their natural receptors. These chemicals, *hormone blockers*, prevent the body from responding as it should to the presence of the hormone. Together, both kinds constitute *hormone disruptors*.

When DES was first synthesized in 1938, it was discovered that it acted like estrogen in the body. Called synthetic estrogen, the name suggested that it was interchangeable with the natural product as far as the body was concerned. However, it really was a hormone mimic—a chemical that made the body react as though it had received a dose of estrogen. That, of course, is not all that it did. Since DES really was something else entirely, it also had other effects on the body. This is typical of hormone mimics. Many substances can mimic estrogen, including the pesticide DDT. One of the problems with hormone mimics is that they are effective at signaling the body that it is time to start some process, but not always effective at stopping it.

When a woman is pregnant, her body produces proteins that soak up estrogen in the blood to prevent the presence of any excess that might harm the fetus. That's the normal process, but it only works with real estrogen. Since DES was not recognized by those proteins as estrogen, it therefore remained active, continuing to flood a woman's body and that of her fetus.

An example of a hormone blocker is *vinclozolin*, a synthetic chemical developed as a fungicide for fruit. Residues of this fungicide may remain on the fruit that appears in supermarkets and be eaten by children. Vinclozolin binds with the receptor for testosterone, preventing natural testosterone from sending the signal that it should. Testosterone is the main masculine hormone, necessary for males to develop normally. Without testosterone, a male animal will not develop a normal male body, and instead may develop partial features of both sexes. Similarly, with the normal amount of testosterone in the blood system, but with vinclozolin blocking the receptors, the same anomaly may result.

A similar hormone blocker might have been the cause behind one of those troubling cases listed by Theo Colborn in *Our Stolen Future*. This was the mystery of the alligators with abnormally small penises in Lake Apopka in Florida. Their plight had been traced to a chemical spill by the Tower Chemical Company about ten years before the abnormal alligators were discovered, but even so, the reasons why that chemical should led to abnormal sexual development of the male alligators was not clear. The female alligators in the lake all had nearly twice the normal amount of estrogen in their bodies, suggesting that the spill had included an estrogen hormone mimic. However, the males had almost no testosterone. Though the detailed causes were not established, it seems likely that the chemical that mimicked estrogen also blocked testosterone, with the result that the male alligators developed abnormally and were infertile.

Coping with Hormone Disruption by Individuals

Most scientists who work on hormone disruptors and human endocrine systems conclude that not enough is known yet to establish any reliable links between hormones in the environment and their effects on human beings. The entire area is much too complicated. All sorts of natural hormones in the environment have always been part of the human experience and the human diet. Thus, it is difficult to separate what effect is due to internal processes, external natural causes, or synthetic products that have recently become part of our lives, and the majority of scientific works conclude that more research is needed.

But meanwhile, the public learns of these discoveries and governments have a responsibility to regulate the industries responsible for producing the suspect substances. One could wait forever for the scientists to agree whether there is a problem or not. Yet one of the difficulties with this particular issue is that apparently these hormone mimics and blockers are already everywhere in modern society. Almost any manufactured product that contains any synthetic chemical component is capable of emitting something that may be harmful to humans. What is the best way to cope while waiting for the definitive answers?

If some products are suspicious, it may be possible to avoid them. An article in *Scientific American* put the matter of personal responsibility simply:

> For most toxic environmental pollutants, the greatest reduction in public health risks can be achieved by reducing exposures at the personal level—by changing personal activities, habits, and lifestyles.[1]

But the environmental hazards are too complicated for an individual just to take matters into their own hands without help. By avoiding one environmental risk, a person may easily embrace another that is even greater. Thus, there is a growing literature to help sort through the labyrinths of hazards. These are admittedly often written by non-scientists,

1. W. R. Ott and J. W. Roberts, "Everyday Exposures to Toxic Pollutants," *Scientific American* (Feb. 1998): 86–91. Quoted in D. Lindsey Berkson, *Hormone Deception: How Everyday Foods and Products Are Disrupting Your Hormones—and How to Protect Yourself and Your Family* Chicago: Contemporary Books, 2000.

or at least by non-specialists, and they often come under criticism by the specialists for overstating something or even getting it entirely wrong. Yet, for ordinary citizens, this literature can help them make personal decisions based on more information.

Likely Hormone Disruptors

The first information the public needs to know is where hormone disruptors are to be found in the environment. The short answer is, of course, everywhere. For a longer answer, a list of the known candidates and what they can do could be useful. Here are some of the most notable ones:

Pesticides

Though some of the very worst offenders, like DDT, are banned, at least in the industrialized nations, many others are still in use. Their toxicity in human beings may be within acceptable limits, but their role as hormone disruptors is still unknown. We find pesticides used extensively on crops and in gardens, in insect repellents applied to the skin, in flea collars on pets, and, of course, around the home wherever pest control is necessary.

Plastics

Every year the production of over 100 thousand tonnes of plastics takes place in the world. Those still in use surround us all the time. Discarded products may sit in landfill sites where they may be incinerated with other garbage. The incinerated plastics release dioxins, which are known dangerous hormone disruptors.

Polyvinyl chloride, or *PVC*, is so common that it is impossible to enumerate all its uses. Most children's toys are now made with PVCs so that they won't break or splinter and won't have sharp edges. Much of our drinking water is delivered in PVC pipes, which won't rust and won't leach lead into our water. What they do leach is not fully known.

As with the components of the plastic tubing used by Drs. Soto and Sonnenschein, many plastics contain *plasticizers,* resins added to make them less brittle. These resins can leach into anything they come in contact with. Soto and Sonnenschein found that they had leached into the serum they were using in their experiments. They can also leach into the air. Automobiles are made with ever increasing amounts of plastic. The inside of a new car has a distinctive odor that comes from the plastics in the dashboard, the seats, and other fixtures. That odor is partly the result of the plasticizers escaping into the air and entering our lungs.

The plastic wrap used in supermarkets is particularly rich in plasticizers, and so is any coated surface that needs to be impermeable to water. Aluminum cans are now almost universally lined with a plasticizer to prevent contamination of the contents from the metal. No thought has been given to contamination from the plasticizer.

Pharmaceuticals

Another of the great triumphs of modern chemistry is the whole range of medicines that cure otherwise fatal diseases, make life tolerable for people with chronic complaints, and in general protect us from the world of parasites, fungi, bacteria, and other pathogens. Life would be very different—and life expectancy would be lower—without these miracle drugs. But, once ingested they can have effects other than those intended for the patient, and once excreted, they enter the water system and circulate around, now available to everyone. The classic case is that of birth control pills that flood women's bodies with hormones to forestall pregnancy, but which then pass through their bodies. And many pharmaceuticals are given regularly to domestic animals. A trace of these will inevitably remain in their bodies after slaughter, but in any case, the rest is excreted into public waters.

PCBs

The manufacture and sale of polychlorinated biphenals has been banned in most industrialized nations, but much of it still exists in the world and eventually finds its way into the air, water, and bodies of animals that we may eat. PCBs have been found to be carcinogenic. That may be only one of the ways in which they disrupt hormonal function in our bodies.

Detergents

Like plastics, detergents are manufactured from petroleum. They make superior cleansers both for washing clothes in the home and for extensive industrial use, all of which makes its way into our water.

Natural Hormone Disruptors

It's not just industry that has given us hormone mimics and hormone blockers. Natural evolution has come up with a few of its own. Many plants produce a hormone disruptor as a defence mechanism. An edible plant that makes the browsing animal that feeds on it sterile will gain an evolutionary advantage. Hormone disruptors can have survival value for the plants.

Plants regularly grow thorns or spines or a tough coating to discourage animals that might feed on them—or a bad taste, or even outright poisons. They can also grow fake hormones that will disrupt the normal cycles of fertility of the animals eating the plants so that next year there will not be so many. A famous case involved sheep farming in Australia in the 1940s. Though the weather had been good and the pastures green, the sheep suddenly began to have trouble reproducing. After a few years, the sheep ranchers were facing serious reductions in their flocks. After a long investigation, the problem ultimately was found in a most unsuspected place: the clover. A number of years before the problem arose, the ranchers had imported seeds of a new strain of clover from the Mediterranean area. The new clover was mixed in with the indigenous strain and grew abundantly. What the new strain also had was a natural hormone mimic in its shoots. The hormone mimic reacted in the bodies of the sheep like estrogen, giving them an enormous dose, enough to prevent conception or interfere with normal pregnancy.

There are many such plant hormone disrupters. They began to be understood in modern chemical terms in the twentieth century, but had been part of folk wisdom for centuries. The Greek physician Hippocrates wrote about the use of the weed Queen Anne's Lace as a contraceptive in the fourth century B.C.E. Another natural contraceptive mentioned in ancient literature is the pomegranate. Both of these have been found to contain hormone disruptors.

Some of these plants form a regular part of our diets. The question then arises whether we should be avoiding these foods because of their hormone disruptors. The answers are not easy to come by. A good example is *soybeans*. Soy products have formed a significant part of Oriental diets for a very long time and are becoming adopted more and more in the West. Soy is particularly rich in a form of estrogen. Some studies support greater use of soy, and some studies sound alarms. Soy is held to be a good protection against cancer, but it also may accelerate cancerous growth once the disease starts. Since it contains an estrogen mimic, it will clearly affect men and women differently. For men, soy may retard growth of the sexual organs and may accelerate growth of the prostate gland. On the other hand, it may help prevent testicular cancer. Like so many hormones and hormone disruptors, timing is everything. Any abnormal amounts that reach a developing fetus or a growing infant will have a greater impact than an imbalance later in life.

We are at the very earliest stages of learning about hormone mimics and hormone blockers, and, for that matter, we have much to learn about the ordinary effects of hormones on the endocrine system. Just as the world awoke out of a dream in the 1960s to realize that the wonder pesticides in use everywhere could be dangerous to human health, not only the health of the pests they were intended for, we are just beginning to understand what the health implications are of all of our wonder products that are now such an integral part of our lives.

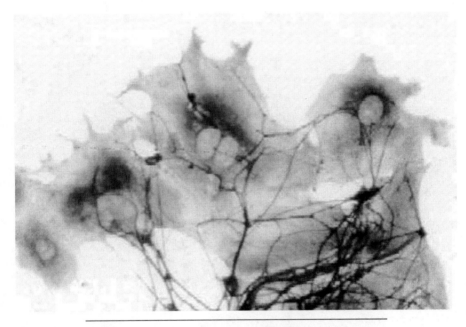

A close-up view of stem cells, the undifferentiated tissue of an organism that has the potential to grow into any part of that organism's body.

Chapter 34

Biotechnology

In a sense, biotechnology is something that human beings have engaged in since the beginnings of the Agricultural Revolution. In this wide definition, early biotechnology includes the domestication of animals and selective breeding, the selection and preservation of seeds, and the deliberate planting of crops. These are all human manipulations of the natural life cycles of plants and animals for human purposes.

A more biochemical aspect of early biotechnology was the process of fermentation of beers and wines, the making of yoghurt, and the use of yeast for both bread and beer. The early "biochemists" who learned how to do all these things, of course, had no understanding of the chemical processes, but they knew how to achieve the results they wanted.

Another biologically astute intervention practiced by early civilizations was crop rotation. Ancient farmers learned that if they planted different crops in successive seasons, they got better yields than if they planted the same ones again and again. When they planted, for example, legumes, they fixed nitrogen in the soil, which improved the grain crop the next year. The ancient Greek botanist Theophrastus wrote that planting broad beans left "magic" in the soil.

The Microscope

Biology remained at this anecdotal, descriptive level because no one could anticipate the complex hierarchies of organisms that lived inside other organisms. Scientists had to see with their own eyes the amazing variety of existence all around them. This all had to await an invention—the *microscope*.

The original microscopes were invented at the end of the 16th century, but their resolution was very poor. In the next century, a much better microscope was invented, but it was extremely hard to use. It had a single, almost spherical lens, instead of the more common arrangement of two lenses some distance apart. The only person who really mastered the single-lens microscope was the Dutchman Anton van Leeuwenhoek, who not only ground his own lenses, but also kept the techniques of grinding and of observing to himself. Nevertheless, van Leeuwenhoek did publish drawings of what he saw, and they were enough to astound his contemporaries. Among the things he discovered were amœbas, spermatozoa, and other single-celled organisms. But when van Leeuwenhoek died, serious microscopic research also died until a better microscope was invented.

A modern compound microscope.

That happened in the early 19th century. The new microscope was a return to the two-lens, compound arrangement, but with a difference. The early compound microscopes suffered from the problem of chromatic aberration—the production of colour fringes around the edge of an image that made them go out of focus. This was finally overcome by making the lenses out of more than one kind of glass, each of which corrected for the other. Once that was done, biology had its research tool and was on its way.

The first important discovery is that all complex life—whether plant or animal—is built up of arrays of cells. Second, the idea arose that these cells were not just building blocks; they were the very units of life. Moreover, cells reproduced themselves by simply dividing into two. To understand life one had to understand just what went on in the cells. With ever improving microscopes through the 19th century, all cells were seen to have a nucleus, which became the focus of research. The chemical industry helped by developing new dyes that provided much greater contrast on the microscope slides. With the help of the dyes, long stringy bodies inside the cell nucleus were identified. Because these stringy bodies absorbed the new chemical dyes very well and turned a bright colour,

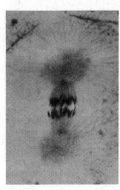

A chromosome.

they were called *chromosomes*—colour bodies. The behaviour of the chromosomes was highly suggestive: they separated and completely reproduced themselves every time the cell was about to divide. Researchers to speculated that much would be understood about heredity and life itself if they learned more about these strange little strings.

Meanwhile, following a totally different tradition of scientific observation, the Austrian monk Gregor Mendel published the results of his long, patient experiment on the garden pea plant, which pointed to the existence of units of heredity operating in pairs that were passed on unaltered from one generation to the next. Mendel called these units "factors." The microscopists who were looking for the same thing called them "genes."

The Gene

At the turn of the 20th century, scientists began combining the observational methods of Mendel, which focused on the visible characteristics of the whole organism, with the microscopic examination of changes in chromosomes. The result was that the mystery genes were found to lie somewhere along the chromosomes. But exactly how and where was still unclear.

The big break for biology was the discovery of the structure of one of the components of the chromosomes, *deoxyribose nucleic acid*, or *DNA*. This was accomplished by James Watson and Francis Crick at Cambridge University in 1953. Biology has not been the same since.

DNA

What Watson and Crick discovered was that DNA has a two-strand helical structure with a repeating sugar-phosphate backbone on each strand of the helix; between the strands were pairs of bases that held the structure together. The bases were very irregular, but they fit in pairs in only one way: whatever was on the left side determined what was on the right side. The basic outline of the structure was enough to suggest how heredity was passed on from generation to generation and how that

James Watson and Francis Crick with their model of DNA.

information made it to each cell of the body where it would direct the processes of life. The details were all to be worked out later.

The model of DNA that Watson and Crick created made it clear that a molecule of organic matter was complex enough that it could have embedded in its structure the entire set of instructions on how to make the organism: what cells to specialize into what functions, when to initiate changes in the body of the living organism, how to maintain its ongoing functions, what to do when the organism is attached by injury or disease or

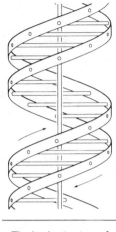

The basic structure of DNA.

toxins. Though every living thing had DNA, the DNA in any one organism was different from any other organism, even of the same species, and the DNA of different species varied widely. The DNA of an oak tree was radically different from the DNA of a gorilla, but they were both DNA.

Molecular Biology

As soon as the basic structure was known, scientists got to work trying to figure out all the details of how the DNA reproduces itself and how it sends its instructions to the cells of the body. Those who specialized in this work were called *molecular biologists*.

It took about 10 years for molecular biologists to work out the details of self-replication and the mechanisms through which the information on the DNA was turned into action in the cells. For a time, it looked as though once these details were known, that would be all there was to do. Biology would have "solved" the riddle of life—namely, how life is really only a complicated form of physics and chemistry. Their work at this point was purely a matter of trying to understand the way that nature worked.

It was extraordinarily difficult work. Genes had been identified as represented by locations on the chromosomes. With the new model of DNA, they could be seen more explicitly as sequences of the base pairs trapped inside the DNA molecule. But discovering what those sequences were, where a gene started and ended, and what any particular gene's function was turned out to be much harder. The techniques that Watson and Crick used to work out the basic structure were of little use for tracking down individual genes.

A breakthrough in research in the mid-1970s changed the character of molecular biology completely. It was discovered that in the presence of certain enzymes, a strand of DNA breaks apart at places where there is a particular sequence of the bases. These enzymes were called *cleaving enzymes.* Soon after, another set of enzymes was discovered that sewed the DNA back together. These enzymes were called *ligases.* Between the cleaving enzymes and the ligases, science now had "scissors" and "paste" tools to manipulate the DNA and then to study how it responded to certain experiments.

Recombinant DNA Technology

The new research tools also suggested new applications—ways of *changing* the DNA from what nature has evolved to something new, by cutting and pasting bits of DNA, perhaps even from different species. This opened up vast possibilities.

Insulin

Consider the case of *insulin*, a hormone that can be used to treat the serious, life-threatening disease, diabetes. Insulin is a protein hormone produced in the pancreas that the body uses to regulate blood sugar concentrations. Diabetics have lost the ability to produce insulin and must have an outside source of it. In the 1920s, insulin from cows and pigs was isolated and made available to humans with diabetes, even though it is not identical to human insulin. But supply was a major concern since the number of diabetics was on the rise. If a way of making insulin in the laboratory was found, that would be an ideal usage for recombinant DNA technology.

In 1978, Herbert Boyer and colleagues at the University of California in San Francisco created a synthetic version of human insulin using recombinant DNA technology. The DNA sequence representing the instructions on growing insulin was separated and then inserted into the bacterium E. coli. The E. coli then produced prodigious amounts of human insulin.

Boyer set up a company to manufacture and sell the products of recombinant DNA technology. His company, Genentech, began manufacturing recombinant human insulin. Now, the majority of diabetic patients are treated with recombinant DNA insulin rather than natural insulin from cattle or pigs.

Genentech manufactures a variety of synthetic hormones for the treatment of cancer, heart disease, immune system disorders, and other problems. A large industry with many companies in many countries has followed.

Cloning

This method of producing insulin is an example of the technique of *cloning*. Cloning is the process of producing a strain of DNA and then inserting that DNA into a host where it will replicate. It uses another living being, in effect, as a factory for making identical copies of some desired component of life of another species: e.g., insulin, other hormones, interferon, antibiotics, anesthetics, anticoagulants, vaccines, and any other biochemical product that is naturally produced in the bodies of the target species—usually human beings—but may not be available in sufficient quantities. In a sense it is just an extension of what the chemists had been doing for decades—producing wonder drugs and synthetic hormones—except there is a significant difference: a cloned product can be an exact copy of the natural product, not just some chemical that imitates its function. In contrast, DES acted as a synthetic estrogen, but since it was not natural human estrogen, it had other chemical properties that, it turned out, were not desirable.

Transgenics

Another industrial application of recombinant DNA is to insert genes from one species into another species altogether to make a new hybrid that has desired characteristics. One of the biggest applications of this today is genetically modified foods. Crops may be modified for a number of reasons: to grow faster or with greater nutritional value, to provide natural resistance to insects, which would make insecticides unnecessary, or to provide tolerance for herbicides so that they may then be sprayed on crops to kill weeds without killing the crop. Or, the purpose of the modification may have to do with the ultimate economic value of the crop when it finally reaches the consumer. A crop may be modified to have a more pleasing colour or texture, or just grow larger. Or it may just be altered to have a longer shelf life.

The Flavr-Savr

The Flavr-Savr Tomato.

The first food created by recombinant DNA went on sale in supermarkets in North America in 1993. It was the *Flavr-Savr* tomato, a genetically altered variety of tomato that, as its name suggests, is supposed to retain its succulent flavour while not rotting on the grocer's shelves. The idea is that the tomato will taste just like those perfectly ripe, homegrown tomatoes but be available year-round and remain hardy enough to survive getting to the supermarket and into the consumer's hands. To calm the fears of the public who were apprehensive about eating a genetically altered crop, the producers reminded everyone that even ordinary tomatoes were considered poisonous and were not eaten by people until 1820. This, they maintained, was just another scientific advance in agriculture, no different from the selective breeding that farmers have always done.

The Second Green Revolution

The Green Revolution of the mid-20th century was a humanitarian program to use the best of botanical science to find a way to make more productive crops for those parts of the world facing massive starvation. It had mixed success. It did produce much higher-yielding strains of wheat and rice and it did stave off food crises in parts of the Third World for a period of time. The downside of the Green Revolution was that it relied too much on First World agricultural technology to make it work: fertilizers, pesticides, extensive irrigation, and expensive machinery. Where it was introduced it transformed farming in unsustainable ways. It upset the social structure and violated social customs. It placed an economic burden on the countries using the technology that they could not bear.

The failures of the Green Revolution are very much tied up with the requirements of the particular crops that were developed. It was a solution that made use of the best technology of the mid-20th century. However, in the last decade of the 20th century, transgenics presented a new range of possibilities that did not necessarily have the same drawbacks as those of the mid-century.

The "Second" Green Revolution, now underway, uses the technology of transgenics to develop new crops that will grow in the climates and soils where they are needed and will be acceptable to the people who will depend on them. They will also fit in with the existing farming cultures in Third World countries and enable them to look after themselves. At least that is the goal.

The advocates of using transgenics to feed the world point out that while there are reasons for concern about the unknown dangers of bio-engineered species, there are ever more pressing reasons for concern about present practices. A bio-engineered crop *may* present some health hazards, but a pesticide-laden crop *certainly* does. Likewise, crops that are ruinous to the soil, require huge amounts of irrigation, and need expensive technology to succeed have been seen to be inappropriate. Meanwhile, the populations of Third World countries continue to expand along with their food requirements. Transgenics offers a solution. It may be the only one.

Feeding the First World, too

For that matter, a crisis may soon be reached in the First World countries. Take the United States as an example. Improvements in agricultural technology continued to raise grain yields throughout U.S. history, but at ever decreasing rates. Now arable land is no longer available for crops, and in fact, as every year goes by, less land is cultivated as suburban sprawl continues to take over productive farmland. The increases in yields in the last half-century have been largely due to increased irrigation and increased use of fertilizers. The irrigation depends on supplies of fresh water, which are diminishing. In the Midwest, the prairie farms have leaned heavily on the Ogallala Aquifer and are rapidly sucking it dry. Also, conventional cross-breeding of hybrids has produced more productive strains of crops. This too is reaching an upper limit of effectiveness. The trick here, which was the basis of the first Green Revolution, is to make more of a plant's total bulk edible. At the beginning of the 20th century, the edible percentage of the weight of a grain harvest in the United States was about 25%. With the Green Revolution, that was increased to 50%. But there may not be much room for improvement beyond this.[1]

Roundup Ready

Farming is a constant battle between crops and pests. Especially in the industrialized countries where most farming is mechanized, keeping weeds from overtaking crops is a major task. The typical approach was to spray a field with an herbicide to kill the fast-growing weeds before the crops have a chance to emerge. Once the crops appeared, the herbicides had to be curtailed lest they kill the crops too. All this changed with *Roundup Ready.*

Roundup is an herbicide, a powerful one, developed by the Monsanto Company. Spray it on anything that grows, and it will make it wither and die. Monsanto developed Roundup to compete with other herbicides and put it out on the market. It is widely available today, as a visit to any garden center can testify.

---

1.   Richard Manning, *Food's Frontier: The Next Green Revolution* (Berkeley: University of California Press, 2000), pp. 7-10.

An Advertisment for *Roundup UltraMax* and *Roundup Ready* Soybeans. There are now *Roundup Ready* versions of many common commercial crops, and ordinary *Roundup* is also sold to home gardeners.

CLEANER FIELDS, HIGHER YIELDS

Monsanto then got the idea of genetically engineering a crop that is immune to Roundup. The idea is that, instead of having to time the herbicide application to precede the emergence of the crop, it can be applied anytime. It will kill everything growing *except* the genetically engineered crop. The seeds for such crops were marketed as *Roundup Ready*.

So, the farmers could live weed-free by buying Roundup Ready seeds, waiting until the crops emerged, and then soaking the entire field with Roundup. For Monsanto, they had two products to sell the farmers: the seeds and the herbicide. The plants absorbed the herbicide without dying, but they still absorbed it and were harvested with herbicide residues. Surprisingly, Monsanto's president even bragged to farmers about the extra amount of residual herbicide that their plants could take.

> Many of you have heard of Monsanto's Roundup herbicide. It's non-persistent...biodegrading within a few weeks after application. It doesn't leach into groundwater. It's essentially non-toxic to human and other animals. And it's very effective at killing weeds—so effective, in fact, that Roundup would control soya beans as well if it should come into contact with both. At least, that was the case until Monsanto developed Roundup Ready soya beans. Roundup Ready soya beans express a novel protein which allows them to thrive, even when sprayed with enough Roundup to control competing weeds. With the spread of Roundup through genetically engineered crops, Monsanto has requested and received permission for a threefold increase in herbicide residues on genetically engineered soya beans. They can now sell soya beans contaminated with 20 parts per million compared to the earlier limit of 6 parts per million.[1]

---

1. Quoted in Vandana Shiva, *Tomorrow's Biodiversity* (New York: Thames and Hudson, 2000), p.70.

And what a success it has been! Sixty percent of all soybeans in the United States are now genetically altered. And Monsanto has Roundup Ready versions of many other crops too: canola, corn, and potatoes. It has been estimated that 70 percent of all food sold in the United States and Canada contains some genetically altered species.

Frankenstein Foods

Recombinant DNA technology has only begun to flex its muscles. Tomatoes with extra flavour and herbicide resistant crops are only the beginning. Geneticists have experimented with all the combinations they can think of, trying to come up with new varieties that have particular benefits. Once gene splicing developed a few additional techniques, it became easier to take genes from one species and insert them into totally unrelated species and see what resulted. On the one hand, it was just a step beyond selective breeding of hybrids that had been going on for millennia. On the other hand, this was something entirely new: genes not just from different species, but from different genera, sometimes from different kingdoms mixed together.

Biologists and lay people alike began to become concerned that this was going to produce monsters that were beyond our control. The new transgenics were dubbed *Frankenstein foods*.[1] One of the people who expressed concerns was Andy Kimbrell of the International Center for Technology Assessment, who said:

> We've taken flounder genes and put them into tomatoes. We've taken human genes and put them into salmon. We've taken the fluorescent genes from fireflies and put them into tobacco plants. It is very important to understand that we are crossing species boundaries at will. There is no time in history, that I'm aware of, where flounders mated with tomatoes, where humans mated with mice, where salmon mated with chickens. This is a completely new arena.[2]

---

1. A reference to the monster in Mary Shelley's 1818 book *Frankenstein, or the Modern Prometheus*. In the novel, Frankenstein is a student who creates a monster without a soul from the corpses of bodies stolen from churchyards and animates it with galvanism—i.e., electric shocks. The monster turns to evil and ultimately destroys Frankenstein—a fitting retribution for usurping the role of the Creator.

2. Andy Kimbrell, quoted in David Suzuki and Holly Dressel, *From Naked Ape to Superspecies: A Personal Perspective on Humanity and the Global Eco-Crisis*. (Toronto: Stoddart, 1999), p. 98.

Transgenic foods have raised a new issue in ethics and politics as well as science. Since the results of this technology will affect all of us, who should be making the decisions on whether such foods should be allowed to be grown, where they can be sold, and whether the public has a right to know what it is buying?

Because the companies that develop new transgenic species invest a lot of money in research, they wish to be assured of making a profit by having exclusive rights to make or sell their new product—just as the pharmaceutical companies sought protection for any new drugs they developed. Thus they applied for patents on their new creations. But these creations of their laboratories were not some new synthetic chemicals—they were new *species*. To get the exclusive right to create these species they had to be given a patent. It had never happened before that a species was patented. In 1980, the United States Supreme Court ruled that life forms could be patented. This cleared the way for biotechnology companies to invest heavily in research to produce new species.[1] In both the United States and Canada, a transgenic species was a matter for science and for agribusiness, but was not deemed to be of concern to the consuming public. There was no legal requirement that farmers or supermarkets identify produce as being genetically altered. North American agribusiness expected to extend this business-as-usual attitude to food exports as well. Europeans, however, did not react the same way as North Americans.

When ships full of Roundup Ready soybeans arrived in European ports, Greenpeace International swung into action, blocking the docks with inflatable boats to prevent the ships from tying up. If that failed, some chained themselves to the doors of the mills to prevent processing. Those and other tactics got the message across, and Europeans did respond. Some Europeans countries have banned the importation of genetically altered food altogether, others have demanded that they be labeled as such.

Why was the reaction so different in Europe? Richard Manning thinks that Europeans had seen a connection between genetically modified foods and other agricultural tampering that had unforeseen and undesirable consequences. In particular, he mentions *mad-cow disease* that infected at least 215 people and devastated the British beef industry. Mad-cow disease, bovine spongiform encephalopathy, resulted from cattle

---

1. Later that same year, the original biotechnology company, Genentech, made an initial public offering on the stock market—the first public offering of stock of any biotechnology company. The market seemed to agree that prospects were good for biotechnology; the stock was initially sold at $35 a share. Before the original day of trading was over, the price had climbed as high as $89.

being fed animal by-products mixed into their feed to raise their protein intake. What is unnatural about this is that cattle, left to their own devices, would not eat meat, and their bodies were not suited to digesting it. Hence this was tampering. Perhaps the public was particularly wary of scientists' assurances. The experts had said there was no danger in feeding these by-products to cattle, yet they were wrong. Only a few decades before scientists had said that pesticides would not harm humans. Not surprisingly, the center of European resistance to genetically modified food is in Britain.[1]

Biodiversity

In the Third World, there were other concerns. Transgenics had the potential of driving out indigenous species and diminishing the multitude of plants that poor people depend on in ways that the bio-technicians just could not understand. One of the most outspoken opponents of transgenics is the Indian physicist Vandana Shiva. She is Director of the Research Foundation on Science, Technology and Natural Resource Policy in India and has written extensively on agricultural and environmental issues. In her book *Tomorrow's Biodiversity*, she takes particular aim at the concept of crops that are designed to resist herbicides, and at Monsanto in particular:

> In biodiversity-rich regions, the spread of herbicide-resistant seeds will introduce toxic chemicals. These will destroy species as well as the livelihoods of the poorest, especially in those regions of the world where farms are small, labour is abundant, polycultures control weeds and women use the weeds for food and fodder—weeds form part of the rich biodiversity of small farms, and are a useful resource.[2]

Elsewhere she has stated that in India, 80 to 90 percent of nutrition comes from what agribusiness calls "weeds."

Speaking of weeds, another concern of Shiva's is that the miracle features of genetically modified crops can jump to closely related wild species and set off an evolutionary process that could result in what she calls *superweeds*—weeds that no herbicide will kill. Roundup Ready crops will inevitably drift into the surrounding areas and may naturally hybridize with other species that really are weeds. She says that the

---

1. Manning, *Food's Frontier*, p. 193.

2. Shiva, *Tomorrow's Biodiversity*, p. 71.

likelihood of this is much greater in the Third World, which has preserved a much greater diversity of species than the industrialized nations, which have tended to focus on only a few crops.

Another category of "miracle" crops of the biotechnology industry are those which are insect-resistant. The plants are bred to produce some substance poisonous or at least highly unpalatable to the chief pests that chew up the crops in the field. The most successful examples of this are plants, such as potatoes, cotton, and corn, developed by Monsanto, that carry a gene from *Bacillus thuringiensis* that produces a toxin, *Bt. toxin*. The plant exudes the toxin, which wards off insects, just as if the plants had been sprayed by an insecticide. Monsanto claims that this is a great advance over having to spray an entire field with pesticides. Shiva claims that this will lead to *superpests*, insects that are immune to the toxin and that will then devastate both the transgenic crop and conventional ones that it finds. Shiva claims that this has already happened in Texas with Bt. cotton where a super-bollworm developed and ruined farmers' crops.[1]

Stem Cells

The original steps of biotechnology that inserted a gene in a virus to make identical copies, or clones of a desired hormone, such as insulin or interferon, was called cloning. Since then cloning has taken a huge technological leap forward. Now, not just proteins, but whole organisms are being cloned. The advocates of this more advanced cloning point to the ability of biotechnology to solve many of the problems of shortages in the world. A particularly desirable food item—plant or animal—could be cloned in vast quantities to fight a famine or compensate for a poor harvest. Plants or animals that were in danger of becoming extinct could be cloned in sufficient numbers to take them off the endangered list. And, of course, an animal (perhaps a human) could be cloned to provide substitute organs for transplants.

1. *Ibid.*, pp. 95-101.

Dolly, the sheep.

This work is at an early stage, but moving quickly. In 1997, a sheep, named "Dolly" was cloned directly from its "mother's" cells—the first cloned mammal—causing a worldwide uproar as lay people realized how far the technology had progressed. Biologists took sides on the issue, some favouring pursuing the research further, citing its possible benefits, while others feared that we were meddling with what we did not understand.

The cells that were used to clone Dolly were what are called *stem cells.* Most of the cells in the body of an adult animal are specialized; they can only do certain things, and they only have the capacity to reproduce other cells like themselves. However, a small number of cells in the body have the ability to form into different kinds of cells as they multiply. These are stem cells.

At conception, the fertilized egg is a stem cell capable of dividing and becoming every different kind of cell that will exist in the adult body. In humans, all the cells produced in the first four days or so after conception have this capability. Later on in the embryonic stages and even in the grown adult, there are some stem cells with limited potential to grow into many different kinds of cells.

The medical potential of stem cells is enormous. It may be possible to isolate stem cells from a patient, culture them separately, and then graft them back into the patient to re-grow some degenerative organ. Since the cells are from the patient's own body, this could overcome the problem of rejection by the body of organs from a donor. There is the potential to use stem cells to regenerate brain and nerve cells, possibly heart muscle, and many other possible uses. Stem cells from aborted fetuses may have even greater potential since they retain the ability to grow into any other kind of cell.

However, if we are uneasy about creating new strains of a cereal crop by gene splicing, we are much more uncomfortable about creating life or pieces of life out of this process.

Biotechnology and Ethics

Biotechnology has made the public aware of the power of science and technology to alter the conditions of life like nothing before. The Agricultural Revolution and the Industrial Revolution changed the character of human life permanently and fundamentally. But both crept up on the world and seemed inevitable as they were happening. Biotechnology has arisen very quickly and has made scientific breakthroughs at breathtaking speed. Suddenly, the public has come to realize that the conditions of life are changing rapidly. Maybe their elected representative governments should make some decisions about where that should go. Likewise, science and technology has been faced with the realization that just continuing to do whatever is possible and interesting may have consequences they would not choose, and that their fellow citizens would not choose if they understood them. This is a new and largely unexplored area.

Chapter 35

Perils, Present and Future

There has never been a time in the history of human civilization when the choices made by people in the conduct of their lives have not entailed dangers. The earliest civilizations fought against predators, climate, and starvation. Every new technological advance brought new benefits and a more comfortable life, but also new perils to guard against. Even in the Stone Ages, improvements in making stone tools brought new dangers. Some of those tools were weapons that could be used against each other or that would entice small groups of people to attack ferocious animals that they would never have dared to attempt to kill before.

While machines can provide extra power and speed for almost any kind of task, they also can fail and cause harm on a larger scale than that risked by individuals working at the same tasks manually. The greater the power harnessed and the more exacting the standards that must be met for a technology to work, the greater the mishaps that may result. These are risks we take because the benefits outweigh the dangers. But often we only learn what those dangers are the hard way: by experiencing the disasters that come with failure, and only then do we take steps to minimize those dangers.

Present-day mechanized, industrialized, electrified, computerized, hi-tech society is more complex and powerful than anything we have known before. To be sure, we have put innumerable safeguards in place to guard against the perils that we have identified, and, as we discover new ones, we will find ways to cope with them. In the meantime, we can try to anticipate the dangers that are part of civilized life now and those that will be soon upon us, given the direction of technology.

The perils we face now and will face soon are of several different kinds: (1) the inevitable risks that accompany any technology until we understand it better, or until we take the precautions that we should have, or that just plain come with the territory and we have to accept; (2) the danger that the resources that we have come to rely upon to make our advanced civilization work will run out, or become too difficult to obtain; and (3) the risk that the environment itself will cease to be hospitable because of the strains we put upon it. We consider the first and second in this chapter. The third, the danger of making our environment unlivable, was the subject of Part Seven; however, it omitted one topic that is the most contentious of all and is a focal point for environmentalists today, namely Global Warming. That is saved for the final chapter.

Technological Mishaps

Looking back in history, we can see many disasters that occurred due to ignorance of the risks that were being run. From each of these we learned a hard lesson and then made changes appropriately to forestall reoccurrences of the same calamity. Here are three examples:

In the year 1666, when the bubonic plague had returned to London, a great fire destroyed the entire old medieval city and much of the surrounding area. A fire in a bakery that had not been properly doused started it. The embers set some firewood aflame, then the whole bakery, then other houses. In total 13 200 houses and 87 churches were destroyed. The immediate cause was the fire in the bakery, but this sort of human error is inevitable. The general conditions that made this so devastating was that all the houses were built of wood with pitch-sealed roofs, and were located close to each other. Moreover, there was no fire department whatsoever. Every church parish had to provide a supply of buckets and ladders, but these were not necessarily accessible. Lessons were learned from this about what is necessary in urban life: the London Fire Department was established soon after the fire and a new commercial venture was begun: offering fire insurance on homes. Also many new homes were rebuilt in stone or brick.[1]

A more familiar disaster is the sinking of the steamship Titanic on April 14, 1912. Here the problem was overconfidence. The Titanic was the largest and most complex ship afloat. It had a double-bottomed hull, divided into 16 watertight compartments. Four of them could be flooded without any danger to the ship. The ship was considered to be unsinkable. But this was not so. The ship struck an iceberg that scraped against the side of the ship, making the plates buckle and burst, rupturing six compartments. The captain of the Titanic had taken unnecessary risks, sailing into iceberg territory in hopes of making a speedy voyage.

The crash of the Hindenburg has already been mentioned (in Chapter 20). It was not a matter of overconfidence or negligence, but a freak accident that probably could

---

1. One irony of this is that while the fire destroyed a great deal of property, it may actually have saved a lot of lives. Not very many human lives were lost during the five-day blaze, but it killed most of the rats in London that were spreading the plague.

not have been prevented with the knowledge of the time. After the crash, airships switched to the safer gas, helium, which was not flammable, though heavier. But the public lost confidence in airships entirely.

We can look back on these disasters of the past and conclude that we now know better and will surely avoid such errors. In a sense this is true. We now know more about what precautions are necessary in an urban environment; our respect for icebergs has increased; we now have effective radar and sonar to warn ships of impending danger; and as for airships, they are a mostly curiosity of the past that we need hardly think of anymore. However, while we have learned to avoid the specific mistakes that these tragedies have shown us, it is much harder to take precautions against disasters we have not yet experienced.

Ongoing Perils of Technology

More recent accidents, involving technologies that are still very much a part of our way of life, serve as reminders that we cannot eliminate danger, especially if we want the advantages. Consider the chemical industry, which manufactures so many things on which we depend. We may find some of the products of chemical engineering unacceptable and seek to have them banned, but meanwhile huge plants exist all over the world producing materials that can be very dangerous, but are also very useful.

Bhopal

A particularly horrific accident involving chemicals occurred on December 3, 1984, at a pesticide manufacturing plant in Bhopal, India, where a technical slip-up caused the release of 40 tonnes of methyl isocyanate, a highly poisonous gas used in the production of pesticides, into the atmosphere. The casualties included 2500 dead, 100 000 injured, and enormous damage to livestock and to crops. The accident was caused by a combination of lax maintenance, severely compromised or inoperative safety and alarm systems, and a crew that did not understand the dangers of what they were working with. The factory was operated by the Union Carbide Company. Immediately after the accident, the chairman of Union Carbide flew to India to attend to the disaster. On arrival he was arrested by the Indian government and charged with negligence. An international incident resulted from this accident. The American company was accused of taking advantage of Third World India and making them do the dirty work for the First World. However, the company was partly owned by the Indian government; the products manufactured were for use in India, to control the pests that ruined Indian

The Union Carbide pesticide plant in Bhopal.

farmers' crops; and, in any case, another plant with virtually the same design and specifications was located in the United States to serve the American market.

The accident was cited as further proof that pesticides are extremely harmful to the environment. Yet in India, the alternative may have been ruined crops in a country very short of food. The difficult question that remains is, was this accident preventable? If so, who has the responsibility to see that all the proper precautions were taken? Although a subsidiary of a multinational company, the factory was under local control and management, but perhaps these managers were not competent to run the plant and should never have been allowed to do so. It could be argued the only people experienced enough to even realize that a problem existed were on the other side of the globe from Bhopal. Perhaps such plants should not be located so far from where they are properly understood. Or, maybe this accident could have happened anywhere. However, the released methyl isocyanate had particularly devastating effects in India because of poverty and crowding. Most of the deaths were among poor people living in a slum downwind of the plant. A similar accident in a First World country would probably not have affected so many people. This was an accident without a clear lesson to be learned.

Three-Mile Island

The modern world runs on electricity. Finding ways to produce enough to keep up with growing demand has been one of the biggest challenges to technological society. All of the ways of making large amounts of electricity have some environmental drawbacks. Hydroelectricity, other than that produced at natural waterfalls, requires massive dams that interfere with the local ecology. Coal-fired plants pollute the atmosphere and use up fossil fuels. Nuclear power was introduced in the 1960s as an inexpensive, clean alternative that would be able to supply unending amounts of current. It was clear from the start, however, that nuclear power was dangerous. The atomic bomb showed what could happen if a nuclear reaction got out of hand.

Nuclear power plants have elaborate fail-safe mechanisms built in with them, designed primarily to slow down the reactor or even shut it down quickly if a chain-reaction gets going faster than acceptable limits. Since overheating is the main danger, water is used in most of these safety systems as a quick and effective coolant. When nuclear power plants have had accidents that got past the safety features, the cause was usually some failure in the water system.

Though there had been minor incidents at nuclear reactors in the Western world, the public still had reasonable confidence that everything was under control until March, 1979, when a large reactor installation in Pennsylvania had a serious accident. This was at one of the reactors on Three Mile Island in the Susquehanna River. The trigger was a small valve that stuck open, causing cooling water to escape, thus exposing the fuel rods, which then began to overheat. The safety system immediately kicked in, sounding an alarm, and opening another valve to replace the necessary water.

And then occurred an event deserving of Edward R. Murrow's remark in 1952 (see Chapter 22), "The trouble with machines…is people." An operator mistook the alarm for a warning that too much water was going into the core, so within four minutes, he shut down the emergency cooling system. Then the problem escalated. The reactor needed more water; the operators made sure it got less. They were confused by the conflicting messages on their instruments. The only people who had the expertise to think this through were the designers. They were tracked down in Virginia and tried to contact the operators in the control room. But, only two (!) telephone lines went into the plant from outside, and both were busy. Finally, after some serious deterioration at the reactor, the designers figured out what was wrong, managed to get through to the control room, and instructed them to turn the pumps on.

The ultimate result of this fiasco was that 150 000 liters of radioactive wastewater were dumped into the river; there were reports of strange reactions to radiation in a wide swath around the plant; the affected reactor was shut down forever; and nuclear power went out of favour in the United States. There were a number of problems here, some of which could have been prevented, some not. There was the faulty valve that started it all. No amount of precaution is going to prevent some mechanical parts from failing from time to time. But that failure was to have been rescued by the backup cooling system, which did automatically kick in. Then there was the human error. Nothing is going to prevent miscalculations and misjudgments by operators, though better training might minimize the problem. It could be argued that the system should not have allowed for human intervention since the problem was too complicated for the technical staff in a control room some distance from the actual reactor to figure out. But another time, it might have been the mechanical system that was haywire and only the human operator who could fathom what to do. Certainly the difficulty in communicating with the designers was a serious problem. A better system could well have been designed. Having had the accident, better controls were instituted in reactors in the United States and in other countries with similar designs. It was a lesson learned at some cost, but not a major one. Probably its greatest impact was discouraging the expansion of nuclear power in the United States. For those who believe that the problems of nuclear power—both its production and the disposal of its wastes—outweigh any benefits, this was a good outcome. For those more concerned about air pollution and global warming, the greater use of coal-fired generators that has resulted has been far worse.

Chernobyl

Three Mile Island was the worst nuclear accident in the United States. But it was a minor bump in the road compared to the accident seven years later on April 25 and 26, 1986, at the nuclear power plant in Chernobyl in the Ukraine—then part of the U.S.S.R. The remoteness of the location and the Soviet policy of secrecy and cover-up make it difficult to get reliable data on the consequences of the accident. However, best estimates are: 31 people in the plant were killed immediately; 135 000 people were evacuated from a 30-kilometer radius around the plant; there were very high casualties among the clean-up workers during the years 1986 and 1990—of these, 5700 volunteer "liquidators" who ran in and out of the plant cleaning up the radioactive spill died and many others were seriously maimed. There were 125 000 deaths in the contaminated zone around the plant in the Ukraine, though not all could be attributed to the accident. Many children in the vicinity contracted thyroid cancer. (There were also reports of thyroid and other cancers among children in the region around Three Mile Island reactor after its accident.) Radioactive fallout spread as far as 3000 kilometers from Chernobyl— about the distance from Toronto to Vancouver or from Washington to Los Angeles. Protecting the environment from the still highly radioactive reactor remains problematic and enormously expensive, if successful at all.

What happened at the Chernobyl reactor was, like Three Mile Island, a problem with water, but the circumstances were different. The accident occurred in one of the reactors scheduled to be shut down for regular maintenance. Because the reactor was to be shut down anyway, the opportunity was taken to run a test of the emergency equipment. The emergency equipment ran on electricity produced from the reactor. A backup diesel generator would provide the necessary power if the reactor failed. The test was to determine whether enough power from the reactor would remain available until the Diesel engines came on line.

The normal shutdown of a reactor takes a full day. It began at 1:00 a.m. on April 25 and by the afternoon, the reactor had reached 50 percent power. It would have been further reduced to 30 percent in order to perform the test, but at that time there was an increased demand for electricity elsewhere on the grid, so it was kept at 50 percent for another nine hours before the power reduction was resumed. Then came the human error. A controller device was not reset correctly, so instead of the power easing off to the desired 30 percent, it plummeted all the way to one percent because of the water filling the core. This was too low to run the test.

Now, more human error—or, at least misjudgment: An operator removed all but six of the control rods that moderate the chain reaction to make the reactor build up power once again. This was a violation of the procedures and made the reactor unstable. The operator tried to control the water flow manually, but the power gyrated out of control. At one a.m., the instability of the reactor triggered an emergency shutdown.

Now, even more misjudgment: Since a shutdown would make the planned test impossible, the operator *disabled the shutdown* and attempted to get the reactor back to stability at low power. A few minutes later, the reactor appeared to be stable, so the operators began the test. It was, however, not stable. After one more intervention to save the test and prevent an automatic shutdown, the reactor went wildly out of control in seconds, causing all of the radioactive fuel to disintegrate. The immediate pressure build-up blew the entire top off the reactor. Two minutes later another explosion shot burning graphite and reactor fuel into the air causing fires all around the vicinity.

Here it went from bad to worse. Fire crews responded—first from Chernobyl and then reinforcements from nearby towns and even Kiev, 110 kilometers away, a total of 37 fire crews, 186 firemen, and 81 fire engines. The crews treated this as any other serious fire to be put out. They had no special clothing or equipment for a radioactive environment. The first crews went straight into the reactor to fight the blaze. They almost all died. Other crews decided to work from the roof of the next reactor, which was still operating! They suffered acute radiation sickness. The external fires were extinguished in four and one-half hours. The fires inside the reactor were not put out for nine days; they were finally smothered with sand and other materials dropped from helicopters.

Everything was botched. Not only were the rescue workers not warned about the effects of radiation, the community was not set on a special alert. The Soviet officials announced that there had been a steam discharge from the power plant. Children went to school immediately following the accident and played outdoors. There is a water reservoir next to the power plant that is also used for recreation. People were on it or out at the beach. Buses had been sent to Pripyat, the nearest town, the night after the explosion to evacuate the city, but once there the order to load the buses was not given for another 36 hours. Meanwhile the plume of radioactive fallout was spreading out across the Ukraine, Belarus, and into Europe.

Two days later, the monitoring equipment on a nuclear reactor near Stockholm, Sweden registered high levels of radiation. At first they suspected a leak in their own equipment, but when equipment in other locations in the Nordic countries also reported high radiation, it was suspected that the source was the Soviet Union. It was Western Europe that first announced that there had been a major nuclear accident. Finally Radio Moscow made an announcement that "An accident has occurred at the Chernobyl nuclear power plant—one of the atomic reactors has been damaged."[1]

---

1.   Quoted in David R. Marples, *Chernobyl and Nuclear Power in the USSR* (Edmonton: Canadian Institute of Ukrainian Studies, 1986), p. 1.

What made the Chernobyl accident so much worse than Three Mile Island? There was certainly overconfidence on the part of the operators, who, it seems, did not seek expert advice even when things continued to go wrong and persisted in overriding the safety features. Perhaps they feared the consequences of not completing the planned test on time so much that they took put normal caution aside. Had the test not been completed as scheduled, it would have to wait an entire year for the next maintenance cycle. The test itself was attendant with risks and should not have been left to the ordinary operators. There were certain design flaws in the emergency shutdown procedures that made them ineffective.

The Soviet Union was committed to nuclear power and determined to make it work. The very fact that the accident at Three Mile Island had occurred seven years before and had turned public opinion against nuclear energy made the Soviets determined to avoid another public event. There had been serious accidents with nuclear power in the Soviet Union before, but they had been completely covered up and never acknowledged. The Chernobyl accident was only admitted to when there was no other alternative.

Other Technological Risks

The tragedies at Bhopal and Chernobyl, and the major accidents such as at Three Mile Island all have individual causes that under different circumstances would not have caused these disasters. But they are indicative of a general feature of technology: the more power we can muster, the more we alter nature to do our bidding, the greater can be the failures when they happen—and it is inevitable that they will happen.

So long as we rely on vast supplies of petroleum we will have to endure occasional accidents with supertankers and a constant amount of spillage into the seas. Cars, trucks, buses, and trains will continue to have accidents on land, and airplanes will sometimes fall out of the sky. Continual attention to safety measures and design flaws will minimize but not eliminate these. The closer we are to the initial stages of any technology, the more likely it is that there will be serious accidents. The Duke University engineering professor Henry Petroski has written an interesting book, *To Engineer is Human*, in which he shows that such errors and accidents are simply part of the learning process, and indeed are inevitable. What engineers attempt to do is prevent these accidents from happening by testing for possible failures *before* the equipment is built.[1]

1.   Henry Petroski, *To Engineer is Human: The Role of Failure in Successful Design* (New York: St. Martin's Press, 1985).

Resource Depletion

One of the most hotly contested environmental issues is whether the world is running out of resources or not. Those who contend that there are alarming shortages begin from the observation that the Earth is finite and since the Industrial Revolution we have begun to use essentially irreplaceable resources at an ever-increasing pace. The supply must be decreasing. Those who say that there is no shortage point to new discoveries made all over the world that add to the known and probable reserves. They also note that the history of technology is marked by frequent changes to new kinds of resources previously unused.

The discussion of available resources harks back to Thomas Malthus' *On Population*, where the limited resource in question was arable land. Malthus projected that the population would soon outstrip the available food to feed it, because there was limited land to cultivate. A built-in assumption was that the only way to get more food was to farm more land. Critics delight in pointing out that the population is now far in excess of what Malthus saw as the upper limit, and there is still enough food to go around. That's because since 1800 there have been remarkable improvements in agricultural technology that have greatly improved the yield of crops and have made formerly infertile soil productive.

On the particular question of fossil fuels, the usual historical reference is to the work *The Coal Question* by W. Stanley Jevons, published in 1865. Jevons, from Manchester, England, was one of the pioneers of economics. His work made the convincing case that the prosperity of Britain since the Industrial Revolution was dependent on the steam engine, and clearly the steam engine relied on a prodigious supply of inexpensive coal. Just before Jevons wrote his work, the newly established Geological Survey had published a rough estimate of the coal reserves in the country. Also, Jevons had available the reports of the also newly established Mining Records Office, which gave him a figure for the tonnage of coal mined per annum. Then, in a manner reminiscent of Malthus, Jevons showed that since the rate of coal extraction was increasing three percent per year, if it continued at that rate, by 1965 Britain would need more coal every year than the entire coal reserves of the country. His point was not that this would actually happen, but that as coal become scarcer, its price would rise so high that steam engines would become prohibitively expensive to operate and the lead in manufacturing would pass to other countries, such as the United States that has greater reserves of coal.

Both sides in the resources argument cite Jevons' analysis. Supporters point out that Britain did lose its supremacy in the Industrial Revolution to the United States, just as Jevons had predicted. But on the other hand, his critics say, long before the time that Jevons had picked for the crisis, the world had moved to a new power technology with a different energy source. To the reserves of coal now one must add the reserves of everything else that can be converted to energy at will.

In the 20th century the *Limits to Growth* report to the Club of Rome in 1972 combined the viewpoint of Malthus with Jevons and added a lot of sophisticated systems analysis with the help of mainframe computers. But like Malthus, the particular predictions did not come true. Technology kept ahead of the deterioration of the environment so that the critical shortages never appeared or were not so important if and when they did.

All this is the backdrop to current debates on the demand for and the supply of resources in the world today.

Fossil Fuels

Fossil fuels include oil, coal, and natural gas. Together they account for 80 percent of global energy production. Coal is used primarily to produce electricity and in some industrial furnaces. Natural gas is used for both electricity production and for heating. Oil, in its various refined products, is used for all these purposes, plus its major use, which is to fuel transportation. If the world supply of all of these was suddenly cut off, the disruption to civilization would be unimaginable. Therefore, the issue of available reserves is of crucial importance.

Oil

To begin with oil, the most surprising aspect of the debate over oil reserves is the general agreement on all sides that the amount of conventional oil that remains in the ground is limited to an amount that would run out within the lifetimes of people living today. That is, the agreement is that *if* present usage trends continue with reliance on the same mix of fuel sources as at present, this would happen. The differences of opinion are over the "if." The viewpoint that there is no serious problem of supply can be characterized by Saudi Arabia's former oil minister, Sheik Yamani, who said, "the Stone Age came to an end not for the lack of stones, and the oil age will end, but not for a lack of oil."[1] The implication is that oil is but the fuel of choice today. In the future, we will find another alternative that is better. Also implied is that this new alternative will be available before the oil runs out. Here the argument follows the line of W. Stanley Jevons' analysis of the coal situation in Britain. We are using oil prodigiously now because it is relatively inexpensive. When oil does become scarce, its price will rise and it will become uneconomical, though not yet completely depleted. That will motivate a search for a better alternative energy source, which will be under way before any real crisis hits.

A variant of this theme is the contention that the main issue is not how much oil is in the ground, since there will be ways around that, but how fast it can be extracted. This places the constraint not on the fundamental supply but on the capability of the petroleum industry to exploit it. And then again comes the assertion that it will all work out for the best:

> Nature is generous and the human mind inventive. Scarcity is not an attribute of things but arises from the limitation of time. Technology develops in the long run; substitutes are found in the long run; episodic shifts that take the world from one technological state to another occur in the long run. If we set our sights on some distant horizon we can assume that we shall end up safely there.[2]

Coal

There is less wishful thinking with coal since the proven reserves are considerably higher than those of oil: "Coal is undoubtedly in great physical abundance."[3] "[I]t is presumed that there is sufficient coal for well beyond the next 1,500 years."[4] The problem with coal is not so much the supply, but the pollution it causes and the awkwardness of using it. Coal is bulky and not economical to transport. Hence it is mostly used in the countries where it is found, unlike oil. Coal is effective for generating

---

1. Quoted in Bjørn Lomborg, *The Skeptical Environmentalist: Measuring the Real State of the World* (Cambridge: Cambridge University Press, 1998), p. 120.

2. Ulrich Bartsch and Benito Müller, with Ashbjørn Aaheim, *Fossil Fuels in a Changing Climate: Impacts of the Kyoto Protocol and Developing Country Participation* (Oxford: Oxford University Press, 2000), p. 48.

3. *Ibid.*, p. 124.

4. Lomborg, *The Skeptical Environmentalist*, p. 127.

electricity, but it is not practical (anymore) for much else. Since coal is best used near where it is mined, a major consideration is where the supplies in the world are located. More than 50 percent of coal reserves are found in the United States, Russia, and China. The remainder is spread quite widely around the world. This contrasts with oil, which is much more concentrated in fewer places and needs transportation.

Thus, coal is often a preferred fuel whenever the price of oil skyrockets or the supply becomes problematic because of political unrest. Coal usage is rapidly rising in the developing areas of Asia, particularly China and India. It provides them with a relatively inexpensive source of energy for electricity generation. For these countries, pollution issues are secondary.

Natural Gas

Natural gas is the darling fossil fuel for both environmentalists and their critics. Compared to either coal or oil, natural gas burns cleanly, producing much less pollution. The known reserves of natural gas are greater than the reserves of oil—though nowhere near the energy equivalent of known coal deposits. If the current reserves of oil would last another 40 years, by the same measure, gas reserves would last 65 years.

The main problem with natural gas is getting it to where it is needed. As a gas, it is only practical to transport it via pipeline, which is expensive and requires both maintenance and protection. Gas usage is therefore effectively restricted to the continent on which it is found and is further restricted by the characteristics of the terrain between source and use. When national boundaries are crossed, a high degree of cooperation and common purpose among the countries involved is mandatory.

Metals and Minerals

The debate about metals and other mineral resources can be summed up fairly briefly. The viewpoint characterized by *Limits to Growth* was the following. Our civilization is utterly dependent on a variety of metals and minerals. These are non-renewable resources. Once mined, processed, and used in manufacturing, they are no longer available for use or are available in only a much more limited way than the original ores, and we are using them at an ever-increasing rate. Therefore, they will inevitably either run out or become prohibitively expensive. The other viewpoint, which might be called the "economic" view, starts from a different measure of how much there is of any resource, Instead of the abstract finite limit that is imposed by a finite world, the economic view measures the remaining supplies of all of these resources by their known reserves, meaning estimates of what has already been discovered. Whenever another discovery is made of a mineral deposit, the reserves go up. Therefore, so long as successful mining exploration continues, the world supplies of metals and minerals will continue to be restocked.

One can then compare the consumption rates, which are increasing, with the known reserves, which are increasing even faster, and conclude that supplies are growing—the very opposite of the fundamental premise of the environmentalists.

Another argument, also a quintessentially economic one, is that scarcity is reflected in price. It is a basic tenet of supply-demand economics that as materials become scarce, their price will rise. But the limiting price of commodities is the cost of extraction. More and better mining technology has in fact made minerals cheaper and has increased the known reserves. The environmentalist response to this analysis is that the cost of a natural resource is not reflected in its price. Just because a mining company is willing to sell a commodity at a price representing a markup over its exploration and extraction costs, this does not mean that it is the value of the commodity to the world,

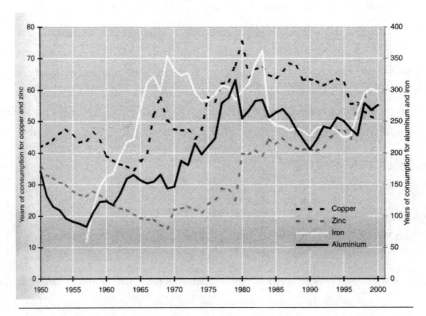

Years of consumption remaining of the four most used metals. Each data point represents the known reserves at the time, divided by the current rate of consumption. From Lomborg, *The Skeptical Environmentalist*, p. 141.

Here are the two views, side by side. First the economic viewpoint:

> All indicators seem to suggest that we are not likely to experience any significant scarcity of raw materials in the future. The prices of nearly all resources have been declining over the last century, and despite an astounding increase in production of a large number of important raw materials, they today have more years of consumption left than they did previously.[1]

Now the environmentalists' response:

> The prices of more raw materials are indeed dropping than are rising; but those who cite this statistic as evidence that everything is rosy on the material resource front fail to recognize that market prices don't capture the full social costs of resource harvesting and consumption. Put another way, market prices reflect the costs of production, marketing, and distribution, as well as taxes and profits, but don't include…undesirable side effects of production or consumption that are not borne exclusively by the producer and consumer.[2]

Fresh Water

The debate about the availability of fresh water is somewhat different from the debates over fossil fuels and mineral resources. Fresh water is a renewable resource. The debate is over whether the rate of renewal keeps up with the rate of consumption. Along with that is the debate over how much fresh water becomes unusable due to pollution. No one doubts that water is essential for life, and no one is suggesting that a substitute will be found. However, there are considerable differences of opinion over whether enough water is available where it is needed and over the advisability of using fresh water supplies as we now do.

Environmentalists point to the tremendous amounts of water used in the industrialized nations, particularly the United States, for what are arguably unworthy purposes. In Anna Gordon and David Suzuki's 1990 book *It's a Matter of Survival*, the profligate uses are enumerated:

---

1. *Ibid.*, pp. 147-148.

2. Paul R. Ehrlich and Anne H. Ehrlich, *Betrayal of Science and Reason: How Anti-Environmental Rhetoric Threatens Our Future* (Washington: Island Press, 1996), p. 98.

> North Americans are the most wasteful water users in the world. While we wash our cars and water our lawns and run our dishwashers, and keep the tap running while we brush out teeth, almost 2 billion people have access only to an inadequate supply of water that is also dangerously contaminated. Yet the United States withdraws more than twice as much water a person than the Soviet Union and more than five times as much as either China or India. Canada runs a close second: each day Canadians use more than 2000 liters of water a person for domestic, commercial, agricultural, and industrial purposes.[1]

Another usage often pointed to is the draining of the aquifers for irrigation, especially those aquifers that are essentially cut off from renewal.

> The Ogallala is being pumped out at a rate of many meters a year and is being recharged by rainfall at millimeters a year. The water in the giant aquifer accumulated over several ice ages; it's already running dry in some areas. [2]

The "economic" rebuttal to these charges does not deny the basic facts, but instead argues that with perceived scarcity will come better management. Many places in the world get by just fine with much less fresh water per capita than, say, North America. They do so by advances in agriculture that require far less water than in used by the prairie farmers who can tap the Ogallala aquifer. They forgo the compulsion to grow green lawns that require constant watering in arid climates. Cars are not washed with the same frequency nor with technology that drenches the cars in soapy water, as is done in mechanized car washes. Even changes in toilet technology can make a vast difference. Alice Outwater reported that the flush toilets in Boston in 1860 used five gallons of water per flush, compared to the more usual one gallon today. More recent water-efficient toilets use considerably less than that.[3] Another often-made point, from the economic view, is that the profligate users have had no monetary incentive to conserve water. Some municipalities charge homeowners a flat fee to be connected to the water system, instead of charge by the amount used. If using water were expensive enough, wastage would drop

1.   Anita Gordon and David Suzuki, *It's a Matter of Survival* (Toronto: Stoddart, 1990), p. 81.

2.   *Ibid.*, p. 79.

3.   Alice Outwater, *Water: A Natural History* (New York: Basic Books, 1996), p 141.

considerably. Finally, the true believers in the efficiency of the free market system advocate the establishment of water markets comparable to electricity and natural gas markets.

Deforestation

As long as human civilization has been expanding, deforestation has occurred in order to clear land for agriculture and make use of the wood for many purposes. This has already been discussed in Chapter 10. Nevertheless, it remains contentious today and is the subject of much discussion from both the environmental and the economic viewpoints.

No one denies that parts of the world have lost much of their original forests. Europe's forests in particular were devastated when its population expanded into every nook and cranny looking for more land that was arable. Perhaps 50 to 70 percent of Europe's original climax forests were lost. When Europeans moved into North America, they brought with them the same frame of mind: forests were resources to be freely used for building materials, for fireplaces, and for making charcoal, and were to be cleared for farmland whenever needed. North America has lost a smaller percentage of its forests, however, because the population density is much less. In the United States, perhaps 30 percent of the original forest area has been lost, mostly during the 19th century. The loss is much less in Canada, which has particularly dense forests and a particularly sparse population. The vast increase in farmland that occurred from 1880 to about 1920 was mostly at the expense of grasslands. In South America and other parts of the world that were subject to colonization, many forests were lost to plantations growing cash crops for export. Southern Asia and China have cleared about 50 percent of their forest land over the last 300 years, mostly to make room for intensive farming.

Altogether, perhaps 20 percent of the world's original forests have been lost due to human intervention throughout history, but because deforestation has been unevenly distributed, the losses often seem larger. But all forests are not equal. A particular concern today is the fate of the tropical rain forests that are amazingly rich in different forms of life, both plant and animal. These rain forests are particularly vulnerable targets for deforestation for several reasons. They are often located in areas where the custody of the land is not clearly defined. As a result people will come in, clear an area and use it for a while, and then move on when the land in no longer productive, just as pioneers have done everywhere throughout history. Rain forests are also especially at risk because they have extremely poor soil to begin with—all the rich life being above the ground. Moreover, the timber in tropical forests will often bring a hefty profit to the often poor nations where they are located if they decide to make a contract with the major lumber companies. In the poorest parts of the Third World, firewood is desperately needed for cooking and heating. Whole families will spend a major part of their time scavenging in the forests for wood to burn. All these have led to further deforestation.

As a peril for the present day, the issue is not what has happened to forests in the past, but what is happening now, and what the future holds. Forests in the developing countries remain under pressure, for the same reasons that forests in the developed countries have been severely compromised. There is no reason to assume that this will not continue so long as these countries desperately need what the forests can offer: quick cash, fuel for cooking, and easy to obtain farmland. In the developed countries, one of the concerns is the protection and preservation of the old climax forests, especially those with hardwood trees, hundreds of years old that may be felled for unworthy purposes. Protection here is a matter of political decision. Most of the needs of the developed countries for paper and lumber can be satisfied with soft wood, which can be grown and replenished with fast growing species on designated tree farms.

Loss of Biodiversity

Living species of plants and animals can be viewed as a natural resource. Each species has a unique configuration of its DNA that makes it different from all other species. Quite apart from the reasons one might have to regret the extinction of any species, many existing life forms can be quite useful to human beings in a direct way. Different plant species may prove useful for agriculture. They serve special nutritional functions that other foods do not. They may be more resistant to pests or to blights. Animals and plants may be sources of new medications that could save millions of lives. All of this is lost if these species are allowed to become extinct.

As with deforestation, when people moved into new regions of the world where animals lived without natural predators, many of those animals were driven to extinction, as was discussed in Chapter 26. In addition, the common practice of agriculture to plant only a very few crops and ignore all other forms of plant life has resulted in the loss of many plant species that had been indigenous in different regions.

Putting the past aside, a very contentious question concerns what is happening to the species of the world now. Much of the clamor about the issue of biodiversity today is an argument about numbers. In his book, *The Skeptical Environmentalist*, Bjørn Lomborg

cites some of the figures that are thrown about:

> We lose something in the region of 40,000 species every year, 109 a
> day. One species will be extinct before you have finished reading
> this chapter.

> This was what we were told…when Norman Myers first published
> his book *The Sinking Ark* in 1979. The message was relayed to the
> world at large in the official US environment report *Global 2000*.
> After this it became part of our shared consciousness: Former US
> vice-president Al Gore repeats the figure of 40,000 species in his
> *Earth in the Balance*, the popular science magazine *Discover* tells us
> that half the species we know today will be extinct within the next
> 100 years, and the famous Harvard biologist E. O. Wilson points out
> that we are losing between 27,000 and 100,000 species a year. Not
> to be outdone, professor Paul Ehrlich even estimated in 1981 that
> we lose some 250,000 species every year, with half of the Earth's
> species gone by the year 2000 and all gone by 2010-25.[1]

It does not require too much reading between the lines to realize that Lomborg, gives very

little credence to these numbers. His point is that the public and its political leaders take

these numbers to be well-established facts and make policy decisions based upon them.

Taken on their own, they are frightening indeed.

Before taking any action based on statistics such as these, one needs to know: (1)

what are the bases of these estimates and how reliable are they; (2) what kind of species

are we talking about—bacteria, fungi, insects, plants, mammals, etc.; and (3) to what

extent does any of this have to do with human intervention and to what extent is this the

normal course of evolution.

The estimates of the total number of species that exist and those that become extinct

have been put together by a plethora of different methods with a tremendous range of

reliability. In most cases, a very small sample is counted, and then an extrapolation is

made on the assumption that conditions are similar elsewhere. Lomborg reports that one

biologist, wishing to count the species in a rainforest, sprayed the upper foliage in one

area with an insecticide and counted the number of species that fell from the trees! There

is also a working assumption that there are many more species of very small creatures

---

1.   Lomborg, *The Skeptical Environmentalist*, p. 249.

than there are of larger creatures. On the basis of methods like these, estimates have been made that there are between 10 to 80 million different species, and the vast majority of them are insects or smaller.

As Charles Darwin taught us, extinction is a natural and frequent part of the evolution of life. Living species evolve, find a viable niche, and survive for generations, but when the environment changes, they usually die out. This occurs on a regular basis all the time, but the Earth has undergone some serious shocks in the past that have been devastating for huge numbers of species. Paleontologists have established that 65 million years ago, the many species of dinosaurs became extinct. Whatever caused their extinction must have changed the world's environments drastically enough to destroy the habitats of thousands of other species. And long before then, about 245 million years ago, there was a huge extinction of about half of all marine animals and four-legged vertebrates and two-thirds of all insects.

Fossil evidence supports these figures, and although such evidence is sketchy, it is actually no less reliable than the methods used to count living species. All these numbers are pretty vague guesstimates—the best we can do, and better than nothing, but not terribly reliable.

Proceeding along with these dubious numbers, it can be estimated that about 95 percent of all species that have ever existed are now extinct, most becoming so long before there were any human beings to affect their fates. People clearly have been responsible for extinctions, especially by over-hunting and destruction of habitat. But no matter how profligate we may have been, it is difficult to see how we could be responsible for even a tiny fraction of the alleged 40 000 extinctions per year.

A better approach would be to forget the numbers game and focus on the kinds of species that are especially important from a human perspective and consider what might be happening to them. An important area here is the many species of wild plants that grow in the Third World and that have evolved to suit those particular environments. Not only are they attuned to their particular ecological niche, they may have genetic features that could be useful to solve agricultural problems elsewhere. As discussed in Chapter 35, many of these species are seriously threatened by the extension of biotechnology into the Third World, especially where a newly introduced species can drive out the indigenous species, or comes with special herbicides and insecticides that spread beyond the fields where they were applied.

These are all perils that we face today and that may become more urgent in the near future. They are all worthy of attention. However, as can be seen, they also can all be turned into an irrational bandwagon that is ultimately counterproductive. In the next and final chapter, we will have a look at the environmental movement, that promotes awareness of many of these issues, and with that context, have a closer look at the broadest environmental issue of the day, Global Warming.

Chapter 36

The Environmental Movement

Historians of ideas often find that when looking at a subject, they are tempted to divide it into two pieces—before and after some important person or event that was a watershed. Historians of ancient philosophy speak of before and after Socrates; historians of art point to before and after linear perspective; for physics the dividing point is Newton; for biology, Darwin; for industrialization, James Watt's steam engine; for English history, the *Magna Carta*. Each person, invention, idea, or event changed the character of the subject forever in some fundamental way. For the environmental movement, that event was the publication of *Silent Spring* by Rachel Carson in 1962. Rachel Carson did not start the environmental movement, but she widened its scope considerably and brought environmental concerns before a wide audience.

Environmentalism before *Silent Spring*

There are scattered references to environmental degradation in writings throughout human history. The best known is probably Plato's comments about the deforestation of the hills around Athens in the *Critias* (see Chapter 10). Certainly environmental abuses were noted from time to time, but the general belief in the Design Argument and pre-eminence of man (see Chapter 12) was often enough to convince thinking people that the destruction they saw going on was, somehow, all for the best.

It was the Design Argument that helped to turn attention to the integrity of the environment. In the 18th century, there was renewed interest in making scientific sense of nature. The person who mobilized the most interest was the Swedish botanist Linnaeus (Carl von Linné), who set out to catalogue and classify every living species. People from all over the world—at least from all over Europe—came to his assistance, sending him samples of exotic plants and animals that they had discovered so he could put them in a sensible order. Where the Design Argument came in to this was the belief that every living thing in nature served some divine purpose in the world. Therefore, to understand and appreciate the mind of God, one should study nature with great care and respect.

In the British Isles, a new profession arose out of what had been the avocation of those who sent samples to Linnaeus: the *field naturalist*. The professional naturalist was a person who spent his working life collecting rare specimens, selling them to museums, and writing popular descriptions for an eager general audience, often beautifully illustrated by means of the new technology of lithography. The best known of these professional naturalists was, of course, Charles Darwin. Romantic poets wrote of the glorious solace of nature, and often enough, bemoaned the incursions of technology that spoiled the natural beauty. Scottish writer William Gilpin wrote

> …wherever man appears with his tools, deformity follows his steps. His spade and his plough, his hedge and his furrow, make shocking encroachments on the simplicity and elegance of landscape.[1]

The fascination with natural history led to the formation of local societies and clubs devoted to the study of nature. These clubs provided the membership out of which grew the earliest organizations with a decidedly environmentalist mandate. The Society for the Protection of Animals, later to be renamed the Society for the Prevention of Cruelty to Animals (*SPCA*), was formed in 1824, first to campaign against cruelty to domestic animals, but soon was expanded to lobby for the protection of wildlife. Later, organizations were formed for the express purpose to campaign against the killing of sea birds, especially those whose feathers were used to adorn women's hats. It is interesting that these movements got underway during the height of the optimism that accompanied Britain's leadership in the Industrial Revolution.

In the United States, when the European colonists moved in, they found a vast untouched landscape that no longer existed back home, and an indigenous population that lived in closer harmony with it. It was, perhaps, easier to see that creating a civilization in the European style meant destroying something that existed naturally and had its own integrity. If this point was missed by the early settlers, the writings of the 19th century American essayists Ralph Waldo Emerson and Henry David Thoreau made a strong case for the evils of disturbing the serenity of nature by clearing forests and planting crops.

The environmental cause was best expressed in the 19th century by George Perkins Marsh in his 1864 book, *Man and Nature*. Marsh argued that destruction and waste were

---

1. William Gilpin, *Observations on the Highlands of Scotland* Reprint (Richmond, Surrey, UK: Richmond Publishing, 1973), p. 112.

making the world unfit for human beings. In the same year, the U.S. Congress transferred the Yosemite Valley and the Mariposa Grove of Big Trees to the State of California with the proviso that "the premises shall be held for public use, resort and recreation and shall be held inalienable at all times."[1] Soon after Yellowstone National Park was established in Wyoming, the world's first national park. Others followed all over the world, including Tsavo Park in Kenya, Isle Royale in Lake Superior, and Banff in Canada. In 1892, the Sierra Club was founded by American naturalist John Muir to protect the mountainous wilderness areas on the Pacific coast.

Environmentalism at this time was primarily a matter of concern with conservation and preservation of natural settings, natural species, and their habitats. Added to this in the mid-20th century was the growing concern with feeding the world's poor, which led to the Green Revolution and to a general awareness that the resources of the world are not limitless and do need husbanding.

The *Silent Spring* Wake-up Call

Across the world, certain segments of society had begun to think about the environment and press for political action that would protect habitats and use resources wisely. But the word "environment," if known at all, did not have its present connotations. Other problems were much more pressing. Consider the plight of farmers. The late 19th century had been a time of tremendous advances in agricultural technology that enabled farmers to manage fields much more efficiently than they ever could before, and the railroad, canals, and roadways built during the same period gave them the incentive to work larger and larger fields in the confidence that they could get their produce to market. But there was a downside to these expansive farms growing row upon row of identical plants. If insects that fed on that one species of plant attacked a field, the entire crop could be destroyed in a very short time. It was particularly bad in the United States where the huge increase in farmland under cultivation was achieved by clearing forests, where the predators of many insects lived. Moreover, the new improved means of transportation to and from markets provided a conduit for insects to move from one region to another, carried along in with the harvest or on the transporting vehicles.

---

1.   Quoted in John McCormick, *The Global Environmental Movement. Reclaiming Paradise* (London: Belhaven, 1989, 1992), p. 11.

American farmers throughout the second half of the nineteenth century found themselves besieged by such unlikely sounding foes as the currant worm, the chinch bug, the codling moth, the cotton army worm, the Colorado potato beetle, the plum curculio, and most fearsome of all, the Rocky Mountain locust or Western grasshopper. The last adversary launched attacks of such fury during the middle years of the 1870s that the governor of Missouri was compelled to proclaim a day of public prayer and fasting "for the interposition of Divine Providence to relieve the calamities caused by the devastation of the Rocky Mountain locust," and the federal government had to send emergency shipments of food, clothing, and seeds to hundreds of Mississippi Valley farmers. The reports of these farmers, reluctant witnesses of the grasshopper's ravages, repeatedly described such occurrences and the appearance of locusts in "large swarms like masses of clouds," swarms that "crackle beneath the feet of persons walking over the prairies," and that "often impeded the trains on the Western railroads—the insects passing over the track or basking thereon so numerously that the oil from their crushed bodies reduced the traction so as to actually stop the train, especially on an up-grade."[1]

American farmers were desperate to find ways to rid themselves of insect infestations. Before any effective ways were found, inevitably, some farmers were hoodwinked. One swindle reported in the *American Agriculturalist* in 1882 warned readers of

...sharpers who go about the country selling packages highly recommended as a "simple, sure, cure for Potato Beetles." On the outside the parcels are labeled: "Don't open to expose to the air until ready to use," and "Directions for use inside." After the swindlers are at a safe distance, the purchaser being ready to apply the "sure cure," finds, on opening the parcel, two blocks of wood with the "direction": "Put the beetles on one block and mash them with the other."[2]

But it was not long before farmers did have an effective way to control insects: poison. In the last decades of the 19th century, American farmers began to use various

---

1. James Whorton, *Before Silent Spring: Pesticides and Public Health in Pre-DDT America* (Princeton: Princeton University Press, 1974), p. 6.

2. *American Agriculturalist* 41(1882): 100. Quoted in Whorton, *Before Silent Spring,* pp. 18-19.

preparations made with arsenic. Though arsenic was a poison known to be lethal to humans, farmers were more than glad to have a remedy that worked. There was some worry about the dangers of using arsenicals in agriculture, but the consensus was that so long as the crops were washed before eating, there was no danger to humans. Agricultural chemists assured the farmers that it would be necessary to eat "eight or ten barrels" of unwashed apples at a single sitting to do any harm. Arsenic was not the only problem. One of the most used insecticides was lead arsenate. Lead poisoning was just as much of a problem as arsenic. By the 1930s, it was becoming clear that dangerous residues built up in human tissues. Moreover, after repeated applications, a significant amount of arsenic and lead remained in the soil and some of it was being taken up by the crops themselves. Farmers needed another way to save their crops from the bugs.

When DDT was identified as a powerful insecticide in 1939, it was enthusiastically welcomed as the miracle solution. Unlike arsenic, DDT was not known to have any undesirable effect on human beings, so it was eagerly applied wherever insects were a problem: on crops, in homes, directly on the skin, in the hair to control lice, and in countless other ways.

Silent Spring came as a terrible shock to the American public when they learned that this valuable defence against the insect hordes was killing the world around them, and threatening to kill them too. Suddenly an obscure issue of toxicity that might have concerned entomologists, farmers, and a few health professionals was being talked about everywhere. Carson's book was on the *New York Times* best-seller list for 31 weeks. The affronted chemical industry responded with such vigorous denials that they painted themselves as the villains in the public eye. More than anything else, *Silent Spring* aroused a passionate interest in the environment in a wide swath of the public, giving the existing conservation and preservation groups a sudden influx of new members and prompting the establishment of many new groups of concerned citizens with a common cause. From then on, anyone raising matters of concern to the environment had a ready audience, willing to take action against the perceived enemy.

The Movement Mushrooms

Silent Spring prompted a Presidential Commission, the Environmental Protection Agency was formed, and the usage of DDT was banned. The message was clear: the concerns of ordinary citizens about the world they live in can be taken seriously. Other books soon appeared raising new environmental concerns. Paul Ehrlich's *The Population Bomb* appeared in 1968, sounding the alarm about a world population out of control. In no time the group Zero Population Growth was formed in Washington to lobby for birth control measures the world over. Earth Day was held in 1970, with demonstrations and parades on 1500 college and university campuses and 10 000 schools across the United States. *Time* magazine estimated that 20 million people took part one way or another, generating more enthusiasm for all kinds of environmental issues. Then the Club of Rome's reports began coming in, starting with *Limits to Growth* in 1972. Meanwhile memberships in the traditional conservation groups were growing rapidly and new organizations were being formed to oppose all sorts of perceived abuses. Friends of the Earth was formed to oppose nuclear power plants, and Greenpeace was formed, originally to oppose the testing of nuclear weapons.

Environmental issues became newsworthy, making front page and cover stories in the major newspapers and newsmagazines. World summits began to be held to assess environmental problems and propose solutions: The Biosphere Conference in Paris in 1968, The United Nations Conference on the Human Environment in Stockholm in 1972, The Vienna Convention for the Protection of the Ozone Layer in 1985 followed by the Montreal Protocol in 1987, the Brundtland Commission's report in the same year, the United Nations Conference on Environment and Development (the "Earth Summit") in 1992.

New political parties sprang up with environmental protection as their mandate. "Green" parties were formed in New Zealand, Tasmania in Australia, Switzerland, Belgium, in some of the former Soviet bloc countries, and in several Third World countries around the world. The most successful has been the Green Party in Germany *Die Grünen*, founded in 1980. It won seats in the *Bundestag* in 1983 and 1987, and in 1998 formed part of the coalition government with the Social Democratic Party. The more successful of these parties combined a platform of environmental concerns with the more traditional political issues of social and economic policy, defence, foreign policy, etc. Their goals have been to work with the existing political structures and find the ways to address environmental concerns through the normal channels of government.

Environmental Activism

Not all of those on the environmental bandwagon were interested in working for change through the processes of representative government. Some believed that their causes were so urgent that direct action had to be taken to prevent harm to the environment. These groups decided to pursue tactics of deliberate obstruction in order to gain publicity for their viewpoint and perhaps even to put a halt to some of what they viewed as unjust abuses. Of the new environmental groups formed during that first euphoric period after *Silent Spring*, the most overtly activist was Greenpeace.

When Greenpeace was formed, the major countries with the capability of atomic weapons had all conducted nuclear tests in remote locations in the Pacific. One of the first activities of Greenpeace was to sail yachts into the region where the tests were to be done and refuse to leave. In 1972, a yacht sailed into the area around a French test site and was only 80 kilometers away when the bomb was detonated. The next year, Greenpeace planned

The *Rainbow Warrior*.

another such interference, but were boarded by French commandos. In 1985, a Greenpeace ship, the *Rainbow Warrior*, was blown up in the harbour at Auckland, New Zealand. Greenpeace has adopted similar tactics in its campaigns against other causes—whaling, sealing, nuclear power, nuclear waste disposal, genetically modified food. Always the tactic is to obstruct some action and to do it with the greatest amount of media coverage possible. This approach has been very effective at making the public aware of their concerns and has also branded them as outlaw renegades who have no respect for the rule of law and property rights.

Though Greenpeace is the best known of the activist environmental groups, it is hardly the most radical. Greenpeace provided a model and encouragement to others who approved of the activist tactics but who were prepared to take them further. Soon more groups emerged that were far more radical: Earth First!, a group particularly concerned with forest preservation; the Sea Shepherd Conservation Society; the American Animal Liberation Front; and the People for the Ethical Treatment of Animals, to name a few. These are groups that are prepared to destroy private property through sabotage. They go way beyond civil disobedience into the realm of criminal activities. Needless to say, these groups have sown tremendous discontent within the environmental movement and prevented it from reaching universal agreement on almost any issue.

Monkeywrenching

In 1975, Edward Abbey published a *The Monkey Wrench Gang*, a novel about a group of self-styled warriors for the environment that used subversive tactics to prevent what they saw as environmentally harmful developments. The book was a novel, but it was based upon an existing group called the Eco-Raiders, who took it upon themselves to try to prevent the growth of suburban Tucson, Arizona. The Eco-Raiders had burned billboards, "decommissioned" bulldozers, and in general vandalized several development projects, causing over half a million dollars damage to private property and in so doing became local folk heroes. They were arrested in 1973. But they had become a model to be emulated by environmental extremists. Abbey's book was not about the Eco-Raiders, but inspired by them; it was a fictional story about four people who called themselves the Monkey Wrench Gang.[1] They traveled across the U.S. Southwest sabotaging machinery and planning to blow up bridges, but their goal was to demolish the Glen Canyon Dam on the Colorado River. The book was a novel, but it planted ideas.

When the Earth First! movement began, the ideals and tactics of *The Monkey Wrench Gang* were much in evidence in their newsletters and discussed at meetings. Because the tactics were clearly illegal, they were never openly advocated, nor were any occasions where such tactics were used acknowledged to be the work of Earth First!, but individuals were not discouraged from acting on their own. The connection to *The Monkey Wrench Gang* was made more explicit by a planned demonstration/prank by Earth First! at the Glen Canyon Dam. Seventy-five members of Earth First! gathered at a bridge near the dam with placards and speeches denouncing the damóand drawing off the damís security force. Meanwhile a contingent of five slipped onto the dam and unfurled a hundred meter black plastic wedge down the side of the dam, meant to look like a crack in the dam. There was no actual damage; it was all a publicity stunt, but it established the ideals of "monkeywrenching" among Earth First!ers.

Though monkeywrenching was not openly advocated, any practitioners who were caught were praised as heroes. One of the favourite tactics of monkeywrenchers was *tree spiking*. The eco-warrior would go out into a forest that was in danger of being logged with a large supply of long nails and a hammer. Any tree that was deemed to be in danger would then get a ring of nails driven into it all around at the level where it a logger would apply a chainsaw. The nails were driven in completely so they were hidden. They did little damage to the tree, but if a woodsman came at it with a chainsaw, the teeth of the

---

1. For the benefit of readers who don't understand the significance of the name, a monkey wrench is American slang for an adjustable wrench, or spanner. If a spanner or monkey wrench were (accidentally) dropped into the gear mechanisms of a large factory power train—for example by a repairman who slipped—it could disrupt and in many cases break the machinery and cause a major problem. To "throw a monkey wrench into the works" is to disrupt or disable a process deliberately and prevent its functioning.

saw would hit the nails, probably wrecking the saw and perhaps very seriously injuring the logger. This was true sabotage; an act that could get one in a lot of trouble with the law. It could not be owned up to, but it could be celebrated in song. Part of the "Ballad of the Lonesome Tree Spiker," a favourite song at Earth First! gatherings went like this:

> Well I've spiked me some redwoods and I've spiked me some pines
> And they've tried to stop me with rewards and fines
> The cops and the Freddies are hot on my trail
> But I'm a tree spiker and I'll never get nailed.[1]

The Earth First! movement preferred to think of themselves as individuals with a common purpose rather than as an organization with a membership. That made any monkeywrenching actions by individuals their own responsibility and not something the movement could be held accountable for. The more extremist the ideals and methods of an environmental group became, the more they chose to make the (often illegal) acts matters of individual choice.

Tree Huggers and Sitters

The term "tree hugger" has become a derisory epithet for anyone in the environmental movement, no matter what their cause. But there really were tree huggers, who did just that in South India starting in the 1930s. These were not individuals acting alone, but an organized protest, the Chipko Movement, led mostly by local women who were trying to protect their forests from deforestation. In the 19th century, the area had been extensively logged by the British Raj. More recently the forests were again in danger because of plans to build a hydroelectric dam that would flood the area. The Chipko women would go into the forests whenever the loggers were thought to be coming and spend the day embracing trees to save them from the ax.[2]

The campaign to save the forests has been one of the most vigorously fought by environmental groups and has prompted some of the most aggressive actions. The Earth First! movement originally focused on preventing logging in the American West. Saving trees has been a popular cause among the lone "eco-warriors." One tactic has been to

1. Quoted in Martha F. Lee, *Earth First!: Environmental Apocalypse* (Syracuse, NY: Syracuse University Press, 1995), p. 55.

2. Thijs de la Court, *Beyond Brundtland: Green Development in the 1990s,* trans. by Ed Bayens and Nigel Harle (New York: New Horizons, 1990), pp. 15-18.

The original ìtree huggers; women of the Chipko movement in Indian Himalayas

climb a tree that was in danger and refuse to come down so the loggers could not fell the tree. This was first made popular in 1998 when a young woman named Julia Hill climbed a California redwood and stayed there for two years. The fact that the timber companies have legal permits and may own the land and the trees that are to be felled is of no consequence. This has proven to be one of the more personally dangerous environmental protection missions. Two sitters have died, many others have been seriously injured. And, these protestors pit themselves against irate loggers with chainsaws. In one ugly incident, loggers chased a tree sitter further up a tree, lopping off the lower limbs along the way so that there was no way down. The sitter leapt to another tree, which was also sheared of its lower branches. Eventually the sitter passed out and fell to the ground after two days.[1]

The Unabomber

Theodore Kaczynski was a graduate of Harvard University, had a Ph.D. in mathematics from the University of Michican, and was a professor in the Department of Mathematics at the University of California at Berkeley. In 1971, he threw his career over and moved to the backwoods of Montana and built a cabin in which he lived alone. He had decided that modern civilization was all wrong and wished to return to nature, putting aside all the trappings of industrial society and living a far simpler life. In this he was not alone. The backwoods of Montana and many other regions were dotted with other hermits who had come to similar conclusions and chose to live at the margins of society.

But Kaczynski chose to do more than withdraw himself from the civilization he renounced. He also wished to do what he could to destroy it. He had even consciously chosen to do this by killing people. His method was letter bombs, and his first targets

1. Jack Hitt, "A Gospel According to the Earth: Sown by Science, A New Eco-Faith Takes Root," *Harper's* 307, No. 1838 (July 2003), 49-50.

were universities and airlines, hence he came to be known as the *Unabomber*. His reign of terror lasted from May 26, 1978, when his first bomb injured a public safety officer at Northwestern University, and ended on Aril 24, 1995, when one of his letter bombs killed the president of the California Forestry Association. He managed to remain undetected until, in 1995, he began to write letters to newspapers and magazines giving his reasons for his actions. One of his writings was a 35,000 word "manifesto" that he titled "Industrial Society and Its Future." The manifesto explained why, in Kaczynski's view, society had taken a completely wrong turn and needed to be brought forcibly back to a pre-industrial state. The manifesto opens with "The Industrial Revolution and its consequences have been a disaster for the human race." He concluded that the "system" of modern society was beyond reform and had to be destroyed. Therefore he took aim at and attacked the critical nubs of society, such as universities, where the technological skills are taught, and airlines, which transport the executives of society.

When *The Washington Post* and *The New York Times* published his manifesto, his younger brother recognized Kaczinski's writing and informed the F.B.I. of the identity of the infamous Unabomber. Kaczynski is serving out a life sentence without parole in a maximum-security prison in Colorado.[1]

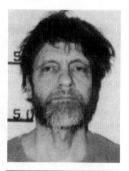

Theodore Kaczynski, the Unabomber.

Nearly everyone deplored the methods used by the Unabomber, but there was much sympathy for the views he expressed in this manifesto. Kaczynski had eloquently expressed an uneasiness shared by many people in the highly technological society of the industrialized nations. The way that Kaczynski had linked them altogether into one seamless system implied that any one aspect of modern society has an affect on any other. Therefore, it made sense for, say, environmentalists concerned with any of the usual list of problems, pollution, resources, population, biodiversity, etc. to broaden their scope to protest against some other aspect of complex social life that might be seen to be related.

---

1. Alston Chase, Harvard and the Making of the Unabomber., *Atlantic Monthly* 285, no. 6 (June, 2000), 41-65.

The Mainstream of Environmentalism

Above: Paul and Anne Ehrlich. Below: David Suzuki.

While the radical activists took environmental issues into their own hands and the "green" parties sought a political mandate, the mainstream advocates of environmental issues continued to do what they had done all along: write books, give speeches, lobby lawmakers—in general, to work through persuasion. In the United States, Paul Ehrlich and his wife Anne Ehrlich published book after book on their views of the impending population crises. Barry Commoner, another American professor, began speaking and writing against nuclear power and a variety of pollution issues concerns. Ralph Nader took on auto safety and then a variety of other consumer protection issues. In Canada, David Suzuki, a genetics professor from the University of British Columbia became a full-time science and environment spokesman for the Canadian Broadcasting Company and the host of several radio and television series. In India, Vandana Shiva began writing about the dangers of biotechnology, and the Club of Rome continued to publish study after study analyzing trends and predicting consequences of environmental and economic practices around the world.

In the early 1970s, Paul Ehrlich and Barry Commoner squared off against each other, arguing about what was the greatest threat to the environment, the growth of the population itself, or the way that the economy was growing. Though in a general way they could agree about what was bad at the present time, they proposed different solutions and saw different dangers. Ehrlich accused Commoner of being fixated on pollution, and Commoner charged Ehrlich with not being able to see past the growing population numbers.

When the Brundtland Commission published its report in 1987, calling for sustainable development across the world to relieve poverty, Third World environmentalists objected that development was the problem, not the solution. References were made to the famous rejoinder by Mahatma Gandhi to one of the British colonials when asked if Gandhi hoped to reach Britain's standard of living once India achieved independence. Gandhi is said to have replied, "It took Britain half the resources of the planet to achieve this prosperity; how many planets will a country like India require?"

Different environmental groups and individual advocates have different agendas and see different problems with different solutions as most important. There certainly are common themes on which there is broad agreement: the First World uses much too much of the world's resources and creates too much pollution; the Third World continues to be used as a handmaiden to the First World and a supplier of cheap labour and resources; some of the wonders of modern technology, particularly biotechnology, are insufficiently tested and dangerous. About these there is general agreement among environmentalists. About solutions to these problems there is not.

The Anti-Environmentalists

Almost every proposed solution to environmental problems recommends some form of slowing down or even reversing the tide of technological and economic development. It is therefore not surprising that those who see technology and development as the pinnacle of human achievement would not be inclined to jump on the environmental bandwagon. To the contrary, the tendency among the supporters of technology is to find fault with the environmentalists, to accuse them of twisting facts to suit their own purposes, and lumping them all together in with the extremists among them.

Now, countering the flood of books advocating some form of environmental intervention, is a growing list of books, magazines articles, and newspaper "op-ed" articles, claiming that the environmentalists have gotten it all wrong. A good example of a book is one publication of the Competitive Enterprise Institute. The title tells all: *Global Warming and Other Eco-Myths: How the Environmental Movement Uses False Science to Scare Us to Death.* The book is a detailed, chapter and verse rebuttal of the warnings issued on all of the major environmental issues. In the preface, the editor, Ronald Bailey, states that environmentalists, despite their claims, are not proceeding from a basis in science, but have an ideological and political agenda and misstate scientific evidence to suit their viewpoints.

> Not a single major prediction of ideological environmentalism has come true—no global famines, no cancer epidemics, and no resource depletion crisis. Environmental ideologues have been proven wrong because they fail to understand that the economic processes in which humans engage are radically different from the

ecological processes that govern other creatures. Human beings not only consume given resources but also make new resources by using their fertile minds. … Coal, tin, freshwater, forests, and so forth may all be limited, but the ideas for extending and improving their uses are not.[1]

This attack has not gone unnoticed. Environmentalists have countered with their own slurs on their critics. Paul and Anne Ehrlich published a book with the title *Betrayal of Science and Reason: How Anti-Environmental Rhetoric Threatens Our Future.* The Ehrlichs call their opponents "brownlash"—the backlash against the "green" movement. Another book is simply titled, *Green Backlash: Global Subversion of the Environmental Movement.*

It all has come to a head in the dispute over Global Warming. One interesting feature is that both sides accuse the other of being "anti-science." The "eco-freaks" are lined up against the "brownlash," but even within the environmental movement, the shades of disagreement are such that recommended actions have become muddled and no one quite agrees on what the best solutions are, even if they can agree on what the problem is. This typifies the problems faced by the environmental movement today. This case is as good a place as any to conclude this book.

Global Warming—Apocalypse Soon

In 1938, a scientist named G. S. Callendar measured the concentration of *carbon dioxide* (CO_2) in the atmosphere and compared it with measurements made in the 19th century. He found them to be significantly higher. Callendar suggested that the increased burning of fossil fuels since the beginning of the Industrial Revolution could account for the additional carbon dioxide measured. Callendar was following up an idea first expressed by the Swedish chemist Svente Arrhenius in 1896. Arrhenius had noted that CO_2 has the ability to trap the sun's rays and keep them from escaping back into the atmosphere, that is, it is a *greenhouse gas*. He calculated that a doubling of the carbon dioxide in the atmosphere could lead to a rise in the average temperature of the Earth of around five degrees Celsius.

---

1.   Ronald Bailey, *Global Warming and Other Eco-Myths: How the Environmental Movement Uses False Science to Scare Us to Death* (Roseville, CA: Prima Publishing, 2002), p. xxiii.

Greenhouse gases help to moderate the changes in the temperature of the Earth, letting the short wavelengths of the Sun's light pass inward, but preventing heat, in the form of much longer wavelengths of infrared radiation from passing out, thus keeping the surface temperatures within a narrow range. Life on Earth has evolved to exist within those temperature ranges. Greenhouse gases are essential for life, as we know it. But the concentrations have to be right. Too little greenhouse gases and the Earth would be too cold for life; too much and the climate would be too hot for any life to flourish. The range is fairly narrow of what makes life possible, and within that range different concentrations of greenhouse gases would favour different kinds of life.

Callendar published an article warning that if CO_2 concentrations were rising, the climate of the entire globe could warm up, and perhaps this was not such a good thing.[1] His article produced an immediate response from his scientific colleagues, excoriating him for being alarmist and questioning his data. Thus began the controversy over *Global Warming*, the idea that the average temperature of the Earth is slowly rising due to human activities and thus threatening the balance of nature and the viability of life.

Global warming has been controversial from the start, because if it is happening, then it is the result of the very activities that have made life comfortable and affluent in the last 250 years. This would not be welcome news to any of us who live in a modern industrialized setting.

Callendar's conjecture of a rising trend in carbon dioxide in the atmosphere has been confirmed conclusively by a the reports from careful measurements of CO_2 concentrations made since 1957 at the observatory on Mauna Loa in Hawaii, 3.5 kilometers above sea level. These observations show that while there is an annual seasonal variation in CO_2 levels, the overall trend is steadily upward.

---

1. G. S. Callendar, "The Artificial Production of Carbon Dioxide and Its Influence on Temperature," *Quarterly Journal of the Royal Meteorological Society* 64 (1938): 223-37; cited in Daniel B. Botkin, *Discordant Harmonies: A New Ecology for the Twenty-First Century* (New York: Oxford University Press, 1990), p. 175.

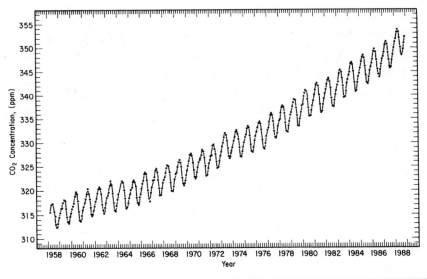

Average monthly carbon dioxide concentrations at Mauna Loa, Hawaii.

Since Callendar's first warning, scientists have discovered that several other greenhouse gases have been steadily rising, along with our standard of living. Chlorofluorocarbons, already seen to be destructive to the ozone layer, are also greenhouse gases. Though their use has been severely curtailed, a large quantity of CFCs is already in the upper atmosphere and will remain there for quite a long time. Meanwhile more is on the ground that will ultimately end up released into the atmosphere. Nitrous oxide is a compound that has the right geometrical configuration to act as a greenhouse gas. There are many ways that nitrous oxide can be formed. There is no shortage of nitrogen and oxygen in the environment; its components are the two main components of atmospheric air. The most likely cause of increased nitrous oxide in the atmosphere is application of fertilizers in agriculture.

Methane is a gas that has helped to produce the greenhouse effect from the earliest days of the history of the Earth. Methane is released into the atmosphere by a number of natural processes: bogs and marshes produce methane gas from rotting vegetable matter; so do fires in forests and on grasslands. Termites are a significant producer of methane gas, about 5 million tonnes per year. But civilization has added to the total methane produced considerably, in ways that might seem surprising. The miracle of intensive farming in the Orient is rice farming in paddies. Growing rice in fields kept flooded with a few centimeters of water made an enormous increase in yields. But this way of farming also produces a considerable excess of methane. The methane forms at the bottom of the paddy, is captured by the roots of the plants, and is passed right up into the air. Estimated methane production from rice paddies alone is 150 million tonnes per year.

Another factory for methane is in the digestive process of ruminants. This might seem to have nothing to do with human activities, except that we have completely changed the natural balance of animal life on Earth by our appetites for meat. Gordon and Suzuki explain:

> The Western world's desire for beef has doubled the cattle population in the past 40 years. [*This was written in 1990.*] There is now one cow for every four humans on the planet. Bacteria that break down the cellulose in the guts of cattle convert between 3 and 10 percent of the food the cattle eat into methane, which comes out the other end. It is estimated that the *flatulence factor* adds almost 100 million tons of methane to the atmosphere each year, conceivably enough to warm up the planet.[1]

Though most of the methane gas is absorbed by chemical reactions in the atmosphere, roughly 50 million tonnes more enter the atmosphere each year. With methane, CFCs, and carbon dioxide building up, the prospects are that the atmosphere will begin to trap more of the Earth's heat and the overall temperature will rise.

The amount of these gases in the atmosphere in the past, the present, and projected into the future is a subject of some disagreement and uncertainty, though few people dispute the general trends. What *is* controversial is the effect of these gases on global temperatures. In 1990, the Intergovernmental Panel on Climate Change (IPCC) concluded that temperatures could increase by just over one-quarter of a degree Celsius per decade if present trends are maintained. This figure became the basis of discussions and planning at the summit in Rio in 1992, and was again used as a benchmark at the negotiations in Kyoto in 1997.

The IPCC figures were based on very complex models that contain many working assumptions. The final figures settled upon and reported by the IPCC were surrounded by caveats and measures of uncertainty. Moreover, they were based upon models that themselves have been highly criticized as being too simplistic. Nevertheless, these figures were reported in a summarized form which itself suggested more certainty than was

---

1. Gordon and Suzuki, *It's a Matter of Survival*, p. 12.

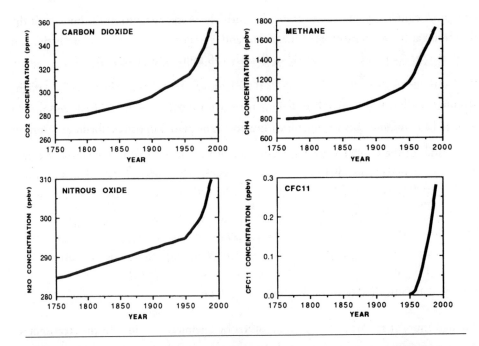

The amounts of the four main greenhouse gases in the atmosphere from the beginning of the
Industrial Revolution. Source: The Intergovernmental Panel on Climate Change Scientific
Assessment.

implied by the model; then that summary was further condensed to one or two figures
when reported to the public. An article in the May 16, 1997 issue of *Science* reported that
many of the IPCC scientists who produced the assessment said that "neither the public
nor many scientists appreciate how many if's, and's, and but's peppered the report."[1]

One of the biggest problems in predicting the effect of increased greenhouse gases is
that most of the "greenhouse effect" of trapping heat is provided not by carbon dioxide
and the other greenhouse gases, but by water vapour and clouds. The crucial interaction
is that increased CO_2 concentrations will raise the temperature of the earth a bit, causing
more evaporation, which will lead to more water vapour, which will trap even more
heat—a positive feedback loop. And then a completely different effect is possible: if there
is more CO_2 in the atmosphere, plants will grow faster, including the phytoplankton in
the ocean. Phytoplankton release a chemical (dimethyl sulfide) that might create

1.   Richard Kerr, "Greenhouse Forecasting Still Cloudy," *Science* (May 16, 1997): 1040.

additional clouds capable of reflecting solar radiation back out into space, thus lowering the temperature—a negative feedback.

Unfortunately the details of all these interactions are not known very well at all. If the actual effect of CO_2 is but slightly different from what was predicted, the resulting greenhouse effect will be greatly different. These are among the "if's, and's, and but's" that need to be considered before much confidence can be placed in any prediction.

Critics of the Global Warming prediction also point out that unpredictable natural events occur all the time that can have much greater effects than that predicted to result from small increases in global temperatures. A significant volcanic eruption, such as the one that occurred on Mount Pinatubo, can cause the very opposite effect, several years of unusually colder temperatures due to the particles in the atmosphere that block incoming solar radiation. These variables may have nothing to do with human activities.[1]

The Kyoto Protocol

In 1992, the United Nations held the Conference on Environment and Development in Rio de Janeiro, which came to be called the *Rio Earth Summit*. At this meeting the report of the IPCC was discussed, and it was proposed that to protect the environment from the effects of Global Warming, the participating countries would undertake to cut back their emissions of greenhouse gases to 1990 levels and hold them there. In total, 154 countries signed the agreement. The date for compliance was 2000. It did soon became obvious that it was easier to agree in principle than it was to make the changes necessary to reach the targets. Something more than goodwill would be required.

Another conference was held in Kyoto, Japan, in 1997, and a different scheme was proposed. The agreement reached at this meeting is referred to as the *Kyoto Protocol*. Under the protocol is each of the participating countries was assigned a target level of emissions of greenhouse gases for the years 2008-2012, based upon their 1990 recorded emissions. Unlike the Rio agreement that sought to maintain emissions at 1990 levels, the Kyoto Protocol sets out to achieve total emissions of five percent less than 1990 among the participating countries. Since the Rio accord was proving to be unachievable, setting target emissions levels five percent lower would seem to be even less realistic.

---

1. Laura Jones, ed., *Global Warming: The Science and the Politics* (Vancouver: Fraser Institute, 1997).

But the Kyoto Protocol approached the task in a different way. Each country negotiated a target based not just upon their past usage but their projected needs and their access to alternatives. Then, with the target levels set, a system of credits would allow a country that could reach its targets with room to spare to "trade off" the difference to another country in return for some compensation. A country that could not meet its emissions targets, could buy credits from another country. Meanwhile, the developing countries were excused from participation altogether. Their production of increased greenhouse gases was assumed to be inevitable as their economies develop, and it was deemed too much of a hardship for them to have to comply with any imposed targets.

This was meant to be more flexible, more achievable, and indeed environmentally better than the Rio Summit agreement. Instead, it has revealed the nearly intractable problem of getting the world to agree on how to handle any global environmental crisis. Putting aside the issue of whether there really is a global warming crisis and just accepting the IPCC projections as reliable, how does one reach a workable consensus? At Kyoto, it was done quickly, perhaps too quickly, by omitting consideration of all the hard issues. David Victor summed up the road to the agreement as follows:

> The Kyoto Protocol was negotiated in great haste, with most of the agreement assembled in just two months prior to the final negotiating session in December 1997. That compressed negotiating process gave almost no attention to how the commitments would be implemented, and thus negotiators essentially ignored the huge financial implications of the system they were creating. More than anything, negotiators from the advanced industrialized countries wanted a deal—any deal—that would give the impression that their governments were taking global warming seriously. They deferred final agreement on almost every issue that would determine the allocation of Kyoto's costs. They agreed in principle to create an emission trading system; yet the actual legal language in the Protocol does not require the creation of such a system. ... Speedy agreement in Kyoto was possible because a great veil of uncertainty put all the critical details in shadow.[1]

---

1. David G. Victor, *The Collapse of the Kyoto Protocol and the Struggle to Slow Global Warming* (Princeton: Princeton University Press, 2001), p. 26.

The Kyoto Protocol remains a complicated bit of bureaucratic wishful thinking. Some countries have signed on to the agreement, but not found a way to comply. Some countries that had favoured the agreement back in 1997 have since backed out, notably the United States. Even if the Kyoto agreement achieves binding legal status, it seems unlikely that its goals will ever be achieved.

Prime Minister Jean Chrétien ratifies the Kyoto Protocol.

In Canada, Prime Minister Jean Chrétien, having previously announced that Canada would ratify the Protocol, unveiled a new $1.3 billion plan in August, 2003, that would provide federal government subsidies to Canadians to retrofit their homes and commercial buildings to make them more energy efficient. It also will provide assistance to the Canadian ethanol industry to raise the domestic production of this gasoline substitute that emits fewer greenhouse gases. Predictably, environmentalists immediately charged that the real purpose was to win favour with prairie farmers who grow the grain that would be used to make ethanol, rather than for an environmental purpose. Greenpeace's spokesman Steven Guilebeault said, "Let's not pretend it's for climate change purposes." These measures, if all successful, would cut Canada's greenhouse gas emissions by about 20 megatonnes per year. The Kyoto formula calls for Canadian reductions of 240 megatonnes each year. Other ways of reducing greenhouse gas emissions are likely to be much more difficult, and perhaps impossible without fundamental changes in the Canadian way of life.[1]

One might ask why such an unworkable scheme was ever proposed and then given the tentative assent it achieved, all in record time. To make sense of this, it is necessary to look once again at the play of forces within the environmental movement and their impact on governments.

The Gamut of Environmentalism

Concerns about the Earth's environment take many forms, some quite specific, such as the desire to protect the whale population, and some quite general, such the worry about global pollution levels. The people behind these concerns range from ideological

---

1. Steven Chase, "PM Unveils $1.3 Billion Toward Kyoto," *The Globe and Mail* (August 13, 2003).

extremists, like the Unabomber, to mild-mannered academics, who analyze detailed changes in ecological systems and report their findings in learned journals. In between is a vast assortment of activists, broadcasters, politicians, scientists, amateur naturalists, and concerned citizens who possess different levels of technical understanding, financial resources, and political influence. Finding common ground is not easy.

It's not surprising that there is no unanimity on what the greatest threats to the environment are. What is surprising is that there is also little agreement on how facts and trends are established. To see this, one need only look at the name-calling between environmentalists and "anti-environmentalists," both of which accuse the other of being anti-scientific. If science is agreed to be the final judge of truth, there is no agreement on what science is and what criteria it should use. The anti-environmentalists accuse environmentalists of putting an ideology first and twisting facts to support it. Some environmentalists accuse the anti-environmentalists of sophistry, of sowing seeds of doubt about environmental concerns for their own nefarious purposes.

Global Warming is an illuminating example of an environmental cause that demonstrates all the problems of trying to reach a consensus on an important issue. First, is the question of whether the increase in greenhouse gases in the world today does make any appreciable difference to the global temperatures. Very few people, it seems, want to sift through all the conflicting theories, models, and data that predictions are based upon. This is normal in almost any scientific discipline, but the difference for environmental issues is that those concerned with the environment are not content to leave the matter to specialists to argue over at scientific conferences. They want answers, and they want them to be simple enough to understand. Hence the best estimates of duly constituted scientific commissions are interpreted to be incontrovertible facts instead of very tentative estimates.

Once these estimates begin to take a life of their own, the various environmental interests begin to lobby their governments to take action, based on predictions made using the estimates. Governments have to balance the interests of all their citizens, make peace with other countries, and stay within the range of what is possible. Hence world summits are held. At these summits, problems are discussed and solutions proposed. No one likes to go to all the trouble to have these meetings and come away with nothing. So some proposals are hammered together into a statement that enough countries can agree to so that progress can be said to have been made. Unfortunately, the compromise solutions may be the most unworkable of all.

There are no easy answers. The human race has achieved a phenomenal level of prosperity through technological ingenuity. All of those ingenious technological advances have come at some price to the environment. Sometimes the cost is so high that the technology is dropped and we find a better way. Often we like the results and value them more highly than the environmental cost. And often, very often, we don't know what that environmental cost is until later. The study of the environment can help us become aware of these costs, and we can then wrestle with our choices.

Index

A

Abbey, Edward 469
Abu Simbel 364
activism, environmental 468
Africa
    population growth in 275
Agricultural Revolution 77
agriculture 77–97
    and deforestation 82
    and fertilizer use 100
    and population growth 78–79, 89, 97, 111
    and social stratification 90
    and surplus food 87
    and the Nile River 91–92
    and the rise of civilization 87–97
    definition of 78
    destructive nature of 100–101, 109, 301, 359–361
    in China 94–95, 111–114
    in Egypt 91–93
    in Europe 81, 114–119
    in Mesoamerica 95
    in Sumer 89–90
    in the colonies 136–138, 141
    in the Far East 82
    in the Fertile Crescent 79–81
    in the Indus Valley 94
    in the New World 83
    transition to 83–84
air conditioning 395
air pollution 389–399
air travel, commercial 220

airplane 211–221
    Douglas DC-3 220
airships 443
Alaska 64
Alexander the Great 92
alligators 417
America
    aboriginals 65
    appropriate technology in 331
    settlement of 64
American Animal Liberation Front 469
American bison 68, 145
An Essay on the Principle of Population, As it Affects the Future Improvement of Society 310, 313
anti-environmentalists 475–476, 484
apes 54
Appropriate Technology 328–337
aquifer, Ogallala 361
Aristotle 106, 130
ARPANET 251
Arrhenius, Svente 476
arsenic 467
Asia
    population growth in 275
asteroids 45
Aswan Dam 93
Atherton, W.A. 252
atmosphere 42
atmospheric pressure 163–169, 179
atmospheric steam engines 179
Australia

aborigines 64, 67
    extinctions 300
    rabbit population 278–280
    settlement of 64
Aztecs 128

B

Babbage, Charles 248
Babylonia 91
Bacillus thuringiensis 437
Bacon, Francis 131
Bailey, Ronald 475
Ballad of the Lonesome Tree Spiker 471
balloon, hot air 212
Banaba 148
Banff 465
beavers 307, 356–358
Beijing 391
Belarus 448
Belgium 468
Bell, Alexander Graham 242–243
Bell, Charles 130
Bering Strait 64
Bhopal 443–444
bicycle, the 199–201
biodiversity 436, 458
Biosphere Conference 468
biotechnology 425–439
birds, flightless 69, 303
Bissell, G.H. 227
Black Death 13, 117, 123, 294–296
Black, Joseph 232
blast furnaces 122

bleaching of fabric 231
blimps 213
blue boxes 380
Boston 456
Botkin, Daniel 1, 25–26
Boulton, Matthew 167, 179, 224
bovine spongiform encephalopathy 435
Boyer, Herbert 429
breadwheat 80
brownlash 476
Brundtland Commission 468, 474
Bt. toxin 437
bubonic plague 117, 123, 293–296
buffalo 68, 145
Burma 146
Bushmen 60
Bushmen of the Kalahari Desert 60
Byzantine Empire 126

C

California Forestry Association 473
California Institute of Technology 387
Callendar, G. S. 476
Canada 457, 483
Canadian Broadcasting Company 474
Canadian Shield 387
canal system 180
cannibalism 5
Caravel 126–127
carbon dioxide 42, 46, 49, 476, 479
carnivores 51
Carrack 126–127
carrying capacity 27, 29, 78, 117
Carson, Rachel 340, 343–352,

463
cash crop system 137
catalysts 397
catastrophism 43–46
Cayley, George 213
cells 426
Central America 83
CFCs 394–399, 478–479
charcoal 105, 122, 172
chemical industry 223–236, 350–351, 365–366, 443
Chernobyl 384, 446–449
Chile 148
chimney 389
China 94–95, 104, 391, 457
    appropriate technology in 333–334
    development of agriculture 111–114
    social structure 116
Chipko Movement 471
chlorofluorocarbons. See CFCs
cholera 292–293
Chrétien, Jean 483
Christopher Columbus 128
chromosomes 410, 426–427
Church of Santa Maria della Salute 12
Cicero 129
Claudius Ptolemy 128
Clean Air Act
    Britain 391
    United States 389
Clean Water Act 355
Clermont, the 184
cloning 429, 437–438
Club of Rome 316, 323, 451, 468, 474
coal 168–169, 172, 259, 262, 389–391, 452–453
coal oil 226
coke 172
Colborn, Theo 407–409
colonies 135, 138–144, 174
    advantages of 135

and the spread of disease 139
    cash crop model 137
    dependence of 136
    Madeiras Islands 136
    pattern of development 138
    plantation system 137–138
    slavery in 137–139, 143
colonization by Europeans 127–129, 132
comets 45–46
Commoner, Barry 474
communications 240
Competitive Enterprise Institute 475
computer, the 248–251
Concorde 396
conservation of energy 256
Constantinople 126
contamination, by plastic 415
continental drift 37–40, 42, 47, 50
    evidence for 37–38
convicts, as labour 139–140
Cooke and Wheatstone telegraph 241
corn 83
Corning Company 415
cottage industries 158
cotton 173–174
    in Egypt 93
Crete 41
Crick, Francis 427–428, 430–433, 435–437
Cro Magnon 56
crop rotation 116
    in China 113
Cugnot steam dray 198
cuneiform 89, 101
Cuvier, Georges 44–45, 299

D

da Vinci, Leonardo 211

dams 362–364

Darby, Abraham 172

Dark Ages 111

Darwin, Charles 26, 44, 50, 299, 304, 314, 348, 464

DDT 344, 408, 467

de la Condamine, Charles 229

deforestation 66–67, 101–106, 122–123, 137, 146, 359, 457
  and agriculture 82
  by fire 66–67, 136
  for charcoal 105, 123
  in China 104
  in Ethiopia 105
  in Europe 122–123
  in Greece 105–106
  in Lebanon 105
  in North America 359
  in Sumer 101–102
  in the Madieras 136
  in the Mediterranean 105
  in the Roman Empire 106
  in Tsavo National Park 18
  of Venice 12–13
  on Easter Island 8
  on Isle Royal National Park 24

Delaney Cancer Clause 413–414

Delaney, James 413

deoxyribose nucleic acid. See DNA

DES 411–414, 417, 430

deserts 53

Design Argument 50, 129, 463

detergents 369

diabetes 429

diethylstilbestrol. See DES

dinosaurs 44, 54, 299, 460
  extinction of 46

dirigible 213

diseases 290–296
  among hunter-gatherers 290
  among native Americans 292

from domesticated animals 291–292
  from human waste 292
  from irrigation 293
  from land clearance 293
  the Black Death 294

disposal 378

DNA 427–429, 458
  recombinant 429–437

dodo, the 303

Dolly, the sheep 438

Domesday Book 156

domesticated animals 78, 81, 83, 105, 136, 145, 284

Dow Chemical Company 395

drainage
  in England 124
  in the Netherlands 124

drainage, in England 125

drainage, in the Netherlands 124

draisienne 200

Drake, Edwin L. 227

dry farming 326

Du Pont Company 235

Du Toit, Alexander 38

Duke University 449

Dunlop, John 202, 230

Dust Bowl 361

dyes, synthetic 232–233

dynamite 234

dysentery 292

E

Earth
  average temperature of 283
  formation of 37–47
  orbit of 46

Earth Day 468

Earth First! 469–471

Earth Summit 468

East India Company 160

Easter Island 5–9, 15
  decline of 8–9

deforestation of 8
  Moai 4
  settlement of 5, 7
  statues of 5, 7–8

Eckert, John P. 249

eco-freaks 476

ecology 26–28
  definition of 26
  mathematical models of 27–30

economic view 453–455

Eco-Raiders 470

ecosystems 50–54, 99
  definition of 50
  types of 52–53

Edison, Thomas Alva 244–245

Egypt 91–93
  decline of 92–93

Ehrlich, Anne 474, 476

Ehrlich, Paul 459, 467, 474, 476

electric lighting 244–245

electric power generating station 245

electricity 239–241, 252, 260–263

Electronic Numerical Integrator and Computer. See ENIAC

Emerson, Ralph Waldo 464

emmer 80

endocrine system 407–422

energy 255–264
  and agriculture 258
  and craft industries 258
  and electricity 260
  and hunter-gatherers 257
  from coal 262
  from fossil fuels 259
  from nuclear power 262–263
  from solar power 261
  from water power 261–262
  from wind power 260–261

ENIAC 249

environment movement 351–352

environmental activism 468
Environmental Protection Agency 351, 355
environmentalism 474, 483
environmentalist viewpoint 455
epidemics 13, 109–110, 114, 293
Essay on Population 309–316, 325
estrogen 409–411, 415–418, 421, 430
Ethiopia 104
Euphrates River 89, 102
Europe
    development of agriculture 114–119
    population growth in 275
    social structure 116
    soil conditions 114
European colonization 127–129, 132
    by Portugal 136
    reasons for 121, 127
    treatment of native cultures 128–129
Europeans, spread of 116–119
Evelyn, John 390
evolution 304
    theory of 50
explosives 233–234
exponential growth 272–274, 277, 304, 337
extinctions 299–307
    ancient and medieval 301
    and hunters and gatherers 300
    local 306–307
Exxon Valdez 371–372

F

famines 109–110, 285–290
Faraday, Michael 226
farming. See agriculture

feedback 314–318
Fertile Crescent 79–81, 89
fertilizers 100, 147
Fessenden, Reginald 247
feudalism 115
financial institutions, origin of 159
fire, land clearance 66–67, 136
First World 144
    definition of 142
fishing 306–307
flatulence factor 479
Flavr-Savr tomato 430
Fleming, J.A. 252
flight
    heavier-than-air 213–215, 219
    in the First World War 219
    lighter-than-air 211–213
    steam-powered 214
flightless birds 69, 302–303
food chain 51
food supply 109
    and population growth 109–110
    in China 111–114
    in Europe 114–119
    spoilage of 109
    storage of 109
    transportation of 109
fossil fuels 42, 185, 259, 262, 451–453
fossils 299
Fourth World, definition of 142
Franklin, Benjamin 239
fresh water 455–456
Friends of the Earth 383, 468
Frigidaire 394
Fulton, Robert 184
fur trade 307, 356–357

G

Gandhi, Mahatma 474

garbage 377–387
Gas Light and Coke Company 224
gas lighting 224–225
gasoline 228
gasoline engines 392–393
Gause, G.F. 29–30
GDP. See Gross Domestic Product
Genentech 429, 435
General Electric 245
General Motors
    Frigidaire Division 394
genes 427–428
Genesis 130
genetically modified foods 430–437
Gesner, Abraham 226
Gilbert, Richard 381
Gilpin, William 464
Glen Canyon Dam 470
Glen, John 386
Global Warming 46, 461, 476–484
GNP. See Gross National Product
Gondwanaland 39, 43, 47, 93
Goodyear Charles 230
Gordon, Anita 279, 377, 455, 479
Gore, Al 352
Grand Banks, the 306
Grand Canal 112
grasslands 53
Great Ouse River 125
Greece 105
Greek Fire 225
Green Party 468
Green Revolution 325–337, 431–432, 465
greenhouse effect 42, 480
Greenpeace 435, 468–469
Gross Domestic Product 189
Gross National Product 189
guano 147

guilds 158

H

habitat 300–301
  and agriculture 301
Hadza, the 66
Haeckel, Ernst 26
Hale, Matthew 131
half-life of radioactive material
  385
Hancock, Thomas 229
hazardous waste 381, 383–384
heavier-than-air flight 213–215,
  219
heavy plough 88, 115
herbivores 51
Herculaneum 41
Herodotus 106
Heyerdahl, Thor 5
High Dam 93, 364
high-pressure steam engine 180
Hill, Julia 472
Himalayan Mountains 93
Hindenburg 213, 442
HMS Beagle 44
Hoffmann, A.W. 232
Holland 124
Homestead Act 360
hominids 54
homo erectus 54–55, 61–62
homo sapiens 56
homo sapiens sapiens 57, 62, 64
honey 136
Hooker Chemicals and Plastics
  Corporation 381
hormone blockers 416–418, 421
hormone disrupters
  plant 421
hormone disruptors 408, 418–
  422
hormone mimics 416–418, 421
hormones 408–422
horse harness 116

hot-air balloon 212
Hudson's Bay Company 307
human intervention 446
human waste, diseases from 292
hunter-gatherers 59–70
  and farming 77
  Bushmen 60
  Bushmen of the Kalahari
    Desert 60
  diet of 77
  migration of 61–65, 77
  population pressure on 62–
    63
  the Hadza 66
  way of life 59–63
hunting, to extinction 67–69,
  300, 302
hydrochloric acid 231
hydroelectricity 261

I

Ice Age 63–64, 283
Inappropriate Technology 331
Incas 128
incineration 379–380
indentured servants 139
India 93–94, 146
Indus River 94
Indus Valley 93–94
  agriculture of 93
industrial pollution 393–399
Industrial Revolution 151, 171–
  190
infant mortality 109
influenza 293
insecticides. See pesticides
insulin 429, 437
intensive farming 147
interferon 429, 437
Intergovernmental Panel on Climate Change 479–482
Intermediate Technology Development Group 328

Intermediate Technology. See
  Appropriate Technology
International Business Machines
  251
International Maize and Wheat
  Institute 325
International Rice Research In-
  stitute 326
Internet, the 251–252
IPCC 479–482
Irish potato blight 287–289
iron 171, 179–180
irrigation 88–89, 100–101
  diseases from 293
Islam, rise of 122
Isle Royale National Park 23–28,
  465
  deforestation of 24
  predator/prey relationship
    25, 28

J

Jevons, W. Stanley 450, 452

K

Kaczynski, Theodore 472–473
Kenya 17
kerosene 226–227
Keynes, John Maynard 189
Kiev 448
Koko, Nigeria 383
Kyoto Protocol 481–483

L

Lake Apopka 408
Lake Beemster 124
land
  reclaimed 378
landfill 378
Langley, Samuel Pierpont 215

LANs 251
Lateen sails 127
Laurasia 39, 43
lead arsenate 467
Lebanon 105
Leblanc, Nicholas 231
Lebon, Phillipe 223
Leptis Magna 106
life expectancy 109
life forms, patents on 435
life, origin of 49–57
lighter-than-air flight 211–213
Limits to Growth 316–318,
    320–321, 451, 453, 468
Linnaeus 463–464
Little Ice Age 284–285
Local Area Networks. See LANs
Locomotive Act. See Red Flag
    Act
locomotives 180–181, 197–198
logistic curve 27–30
Lomborg, Bjørn 380, 459
London
    Great Fire 442
London fog 389–391
Los Angeles, CA 392
Lotka-Volterra equations 28–29
Love Canal 381–383
Lyell, Charles 44

M

Macintosh, Charles 229
mad-cow disease 435
Madeiras Islands 136
maize 83, 95
malaria 232, 293
Malthus, Thomas Robert 309–
    316, 325, 450
Mankind at the Turning Point
    321–323
Manning, Richard 435
manorial system 115
manure 100, 109, 113–114, 147

Maoris, the 69
Marconi, Guglielmo 246
Mariposa Grove 465
market economy 188
market prices 455
Marsh, George Perkins 464
Mauchly, John W. 249
Mauna Loa 477
Maxim, Hiram 214
Mayans, the 95
measles 291–292
meat, consumption of 144–145
mechanistic model 27
medieval economy 158–159
Mediterranean, the 105
Mendel, Gregor 426
mercury 368
Mesoamerica 83, 95
Mesopotamia 89, 91, 101–102
metabolism 256
metals 453
meteors 45–46
methane 478–479
methyl isocyanate 443
Micronesia 148
microscope, the 425
Middle Ages 156, 158, 160
Midgely, Thomas 394
migration, of hunter-gatherers
    62–63
millet 82
mineral resources 453, 455
minerals 146
    distribution of 147
minicomputer 250
Minimata 368
mining 171
Minoan civilization 41
Moa, the 69
Mobro 378
Mongol invasion 114
Mongols 126
Monkey Wrench Gang, The
    469–470
monkeys 54

monkeywrenching 469–471
Monsanto Company 432, 436–
    437
Montgolfier, Joseph and Etienne
    212
Montreal Protocol 399, 468
Moon, formation of 45
moose
    in Isle Royale National Park
        24–28
Morse code 241
Morse, Samuel 241
Mount Pinatubo 481
Mount Vesuvius 41
Muir, John 465
Müller, Paul 344
Murdoch, William 224
Murie, Adolf 24
Murrow, Edward R. 445
Myers, Norman 459
myxomatosis 278–279

N

Nader, Ralph 474
naphtha gas 225
natural gas 453
natural preserves, definition of
    17
natural selection 304, 314
Nauru 148–149
Neander Valley 56
Neanderthal man 56
Neolithic Age 62, 67
Netherlands 124, 157
networks 251
Nevada 386
New Guinea 64
New World 83
New Zealand 468
Newcomb, Simon 216
Newcomen steam engine 165–
    166, 171
Newcomen, Thomas 164, 166

Newton, Isaac 27, 163, 296
Niagara Falls 262
Niagara Falls, NY 382
Nigeria 383
Nile River 91–93
nitroglycerin 233–234
nitrous oxide 478
Noah and the Flood 131
Nobel, Alfred 234
non-renewable resources 169
noria 156
North America
      population growth in 276
Northern Elephant Seal, the 271
Not in my backyard 378
nuclear power 262–263, 445
nuclear reactor 263
nuclear tests 469
nuclear waste 384–387
      geologic disposal 387
nuclear winter 46
nylon 235

O

Occidental Chemical Corporation 382
Ocean Island 148
ocean-going vessels 126–127
Oceania
      population growth in 276
      settlement of 65
Ogallala Aquifer 361, 432, 456
oil 226–227, 451–452
      drilling for 227
oil spills 369–372
oil, drilling for 227
On Population 450
Origin of Species 299
Ottoman Turks 126
Our Stolen Future 407–408
Outwater, Alice 356–357, 359, 363, 365, 456
ozone 396–399

ozone layer 397–398

P

Paleolithic Age 62
pancreas 429
Pangaea 39, 47
passenger pigeon 304–305
PCBs 366–368, 408, 420
Pennsylvania Oil Field 227
Penny Farthing, the 200
People for the Ethical Treatment of Animals 469
Perkin, William 232–233
personal computer, the 251
pesticides 343–352, 366, 419
petroleum 147, 226–227, 259
Petroski, Henry 449
pharmaceuticals 420
phosphates 148, 369
photosynthesis 49, 51
photosynthesizers 51–52
plague 117, 123, 293–296
plantation system 136–138, 143, 174–175
plasticizers 419–420
plastics 235–236, 414, 419–420
      and the environment 236
plate tectonics 37–40
Plato 106, 463
Plexiglas 235
plough 88
      digging stick 88
      heavy 88, 115
      scratch 115
plough, scratch 115
pollution
      air 389–399
      from coal 389–391
      from gasoline engines 392–393
      from industry 393–399
      water 355–375
polychlorinated biphenals

(PCBs) 366
Polynesians 7
polyurethanes 235
polyvinyl chloride. See PVC
Pompeii 41
Ponting, Clive 1
Population Bomb, The 467
population control, by hunter-gatherers 62
population growth 99, 107, 109–111, 271–280
      and food supply 109
      in Africa 275
      in Asia 275
      in Europe 122, 275
      in North America 276
      in Oceania 276
      in South America 276
      of hunter-gatherers 63
post-windmill 157
potash 231
potassium hydroxide 231
potato blight, in Ireland 287
potatoe blight, in Ireland 288
pottery 81, 87
power
      wind and water 155–161
prairies 359–362
predator/prey relationship 25–26, 28–30, 78, 99, 271–272, 304
predator-prey relationship 271
pre-eminence of man argument 130–131
Priestly, Joseph 229
primates 54
Pripyat 448
progress, idea of 309–310
PVC 416, 419

Q

quinine 232

R

rabbits, in Australia 278–280
radio 247
Radio Moscow 448
railroad tracks 181
railroads 180–183, 197
Rainbow Warrior 469
Rainhill Competition 181
reclaimed land 378
recombinant DNA. See DNA,
    recombinant
recycling 380–381
        garbage 380
Red Flag Act 198
Renaissance 125
resource depletion 450–460
Rhodes, Cecil 149
rice 82
        paddy 479
        production of 112
Rio Earth Summit 481
road building 199, 201
Rockefeller, John D. 227
Roggeveen, Admiral 5
Roman Empire, the 106
Roundup Ready 432–433, 435–
    436
Royal College of Chemistry,
    London 232
rubber 229–230
        plantations 230
        tires 230

S

Safety Bicycle, the 200
salinisation 89, 93, 100, 102–
    103
San Andreas Fault 40–41
San. See Bushmen
Santa Maria della Salute 12
Sawyer, Grant 386
scarcity 454

schistosomiasis 293
Schumacher, E.F. 329, 331
scratch plough 115
Sea Shepherd Conservation So-
    ciety 469
Second World, definition of 142
seed drill 88, 113
semaphore 240
semiconductor 250
sewage 373–374
sewers 373
sexuality, development of 408–
    410
Sheldrick, David 17, 19, 26
Shiva, Vandana 436, 474
Siberia 64
Sierra Club 465
Silent Spring 343–352, 408,
    463, 465, 467, 469
Silliman, Jr., Benjamin 227
slash and burn 82, 122
slavery 137–139, 143, 175
        abolishment of 139
        in the ancient world 138
Small is Beautiful 329–330
smallpox 291–293
smelting 122
Smith, Adam 187
Snider-Pellegrini, Antonio 37
Society for the Prevention of
    Cruelty to Animals 464
soda 231
solar power 261
Sonnenschein, Carlos 415–416
Soto, Ana 415–416
South America 457
        population growth in 276
Soviet Union 449, 456
soybeans 82, 421
SSTs 396
Standard Oil Company 227
Standard World Model Run
    318–321
standardization of goods 175
Stanford University Linear Ac-

celerator 41
starvation 109, 114–115, 284–
    288
stationary steam engines 180
steam engine
        high pressure 180
        Newcomen 165–166, 171
        Watt-Boulton 167, 171,
            173–174, 179,
            184
steam-powered flight 214
steamships 183–185
stem cells 437–438
Stephenson, George 181
Stephenson, Robert 181
Stockholm 448, 468
stratosphere 396–397
Styrofoam 236, 395
sugar 137
Sumer 89, 91, 101–102
        decline of 103
superpests 437
superweeds 436
supply-demand economics 454
Susquehanna River 445
Suzuki, David 279, 377, 455,
    474, 479
swidden system 82, 122
Switzerland 468
synthetic dyes 231–232

T

taiga 52
Tanzania 66
Tasmania 64, 468
teak 146
tectonic plates 42, 47, 52
Teflon 235
telegraph, the 241–242
telegraphy 240
telephone, the 242–243
television 247
temperate forest 52

temperature, of the earth 283
Teotihuacan 95
testosterone 409–411, 417–418
textile industry 173, 175
thalidomide 411
theory of evolution 49
thermodynamics 255–256
    first law of 256
    second law of 256
Third World 142–149, 174
    economic dependence of
        142–149, 331,
        335–337
Thoreau, Henry David 464
Three Gorges project 363
Three Mile Island 384, 445,
    447, 449
three-field crop rotation 116
Tigris River 89, 102
timber 146
timber wolf
    in Isle Royale National Park
        24–26
Titanic 442
toilet, the 373
tool making, importance of 155
tools, stone-age 55–56, 61, 67
top carnivores 51
Torrey Canyon 370
Tower Chemical Company 417
towns, beginning of 81
transgenics 430–437
tree hugger 471
tree sitters 472
tree spiking 470
tropical rainforests 53, 457
Tsavo National Park 17–20, 465
    environmental controversy
        19–20
Tuchman, Barbara 285, 294
Tucson 470
tundra 52
two-field crop rotation 116

U

Ukraine 447–448
ultraviolet light 396–398
Unabomber 472–473, 484
undersea cables 242
uniformitarianism 43–44
uniformity 175
Union Carbide 443–444
United Nations Conference on
    Environment and Develop-
    ment 468
United Nations Conference on
    the Human Environment 468
UNIVAC 250
Ur 98, 101
uranium fuel rods 384
urbanization, early evidence of
    90
Ure, Andrew 225
Uruk 90–91

V

van Helmont, Johann Baptista
    223
van Leeuwenhoek, Anton 425
Venice 11–15
    and the plague 13
    canals of 12–14
    construction of 11–12
    cultural importance of 13
    deforestation of 11, 13
    environmental problems of
        14
    floodgates of 14
    settlement of 11
    sewage system of 14
    sinking of 14
Vermuyden, Cornelius 125
vicious circle 114, 174
Victor, David 482
Vienna Convention for the Pro-
    tection of the Ozone Laye 468

vinclozolin 417
virtuous circle 172, 174
volcanoes 40, 42, 44, 49
Volta, Alessandro 240
vom Saal, Frederick 409
von Guericke, Otto 164
von Zeppelin, Graf Ferdinand
    212
vulcanization 230

W

Wallace, Alfred Russel 304–305,
    314
waste 365
waste disposal 377–387
water pollution 355–375
water power 261
waterlogging 89, 102
waterwheels 156–157, 159, 161
Watson, James 427–428, 430–
    433, 435–437
Watt, Gregory 224
Watt, James 167, 179, 224, 232,
    315
Watt-Boulton steam engine 167,
    171, 173–174, 179, 184
    in mines 171
Wegner, Alfred 37
Wenke, Robert 68, 84
wet rice farming 112
wetlands 358
wheat 80
White-Stevens, Robert 352
wind power 260–261
windmills 124, 156–157, 161,
    260–261
Wingspread Consensus State-
    ment 407
Winzer, F.A. 224
Wireless Telegraph and Signal
    Company 246
wireless telegraphy 246
wool 173

Woolley, Leonard 101
world models 309–323
    An Essay on the Principle of
        Population, As it
        Affects the Future
        Improvement of
        Society 310, 313
    definition of 309
    Essay on Population 309–
        316
    Limits to Growth 317–318,
        320–321
    Mankind at the Turning
        Point 321–323
    Standard World Model
        Run 318–321
Wright, Wilbur and Orville
  218–219

X

Xenophon 106

Y

Yamani, Sheik 451
Yangtze River 95, 112, 116
yellow fever 293
Yellow River 82, 95, 104, 111
Yellowstone National Park 465
Yosemite Valley 465
Young, James 226
Yucca Mountain 387

Z

Zeppelin, the 212–213
Zero Population Growth 468
ziggurat 90, 98